Introduction

Welcome to the 2008 edition of our Hotels, Inns, Resorts & Spas Guide to The Americas, Caribbean, Atlantic & Pacific featuring some significant and refreshing changes. While retaining its visual impact and informed text, the new design features easier to read entries and clearer maps. Using less paper, the reduced weight also helps us to be more environmentally friendly as our worldwide distribution increases, currently stretching from Chile to China.

The Guide has been designed to help you make the right choice. Our Recommendations offer a breadth of variety and value as we understand that today's traveler often seeks out different experiences: a romantic anniversary celebration, a tranquil and informal environment in which to relax, a contemporary city base or classic gourmet sophistication.

Our collection comprises 6 Guides, representing more than 1,300 annually inspected and recommended hotels, resorts, spas and meeting venues across 67 countries. You can read about the other Guides on page 447 or see the entire collection at www.johansens.com.

This 2008 edition includes many new Recommendations as well as longtime favorites for you to try. You can be sure that our team of Inspectors select only the very best places, rejecting those that do not meet our exacting standards.

If you have a chance we would love to hear about your experience. Complete a Guest Survey Report at the back of this Guide or online. Feedback is an influencing factor, not only in maintaining standards but also in compiling nominations for our Annual Awards for Excellence.

Above all, we hope you enjoy your stay and please remember to mention "Condé Nast Johansens" when you make an enquiry or reservation.

Andrew Warren
Managing Director

Image from Grand Velas All Suites & Spa Resort, Nayarit, Mexico, p50

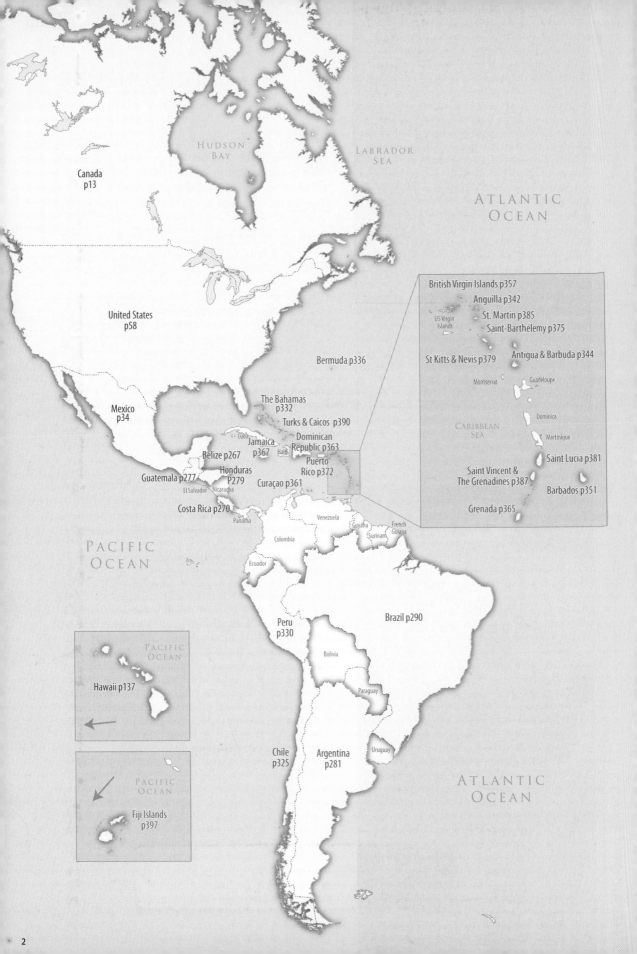

HUDSON BAY

LABRADOR SEA

Canada
p13

ATLANTIC
OCEAN

United States
p58

Bermuda p336

Mexico
p34

The Bahamas
p332

Turks & Caicos p390

Cuba
Jamaica
p367
Dominican
Republic p363
Haiti

Belize p267
Puerto
Rico p372

Honduras
P279
Guatemala p277
El Salvador
Nicaragua
Curaçao p361

Costa Rica p270
Panama

PACIFIC OCEAN

Venezuela
Guyana
French Guiana
Surinam
Colombia

Ecuador

Brazil p290

Peru
p330

Bolivia

PACIFIC OCEAN
Hawaii p137

Paraguay

PACIFIC OCEAN
Fiji Islands
p397

Chile
p325
Argentina
p281
Uruguay

ATLANTIC OCEAN

Image from Sundance Resort, Utah, U.S.A., p243

Contents

BEYOND COMPARE...

Image from Tauana, Bahia, Brazil, p294

About this Guide

To find a hotel by location:

• Use the **map** at the front of this Guide to identify the country you wish to search.

• Turn to the relevant country / state / regional section where properties are featured alphabetically by location.

• Or, turn to the title page of the state / country required where you will find a map. The location of each property is shown, with a number corresponding to the page on which the property entry is published.

To find a property by its name or the name of its nearest town look in the indexes on pages 439-446.

Once you have made your choice please contact the property directly. The majority of prices throughout the Guide refer to "room" rate, not "per person" rate. In addition, some prices are subject to state taxes. Rates are correct at the time of going to press but should always be checked with the property before you make your reservation. **When making a booking please mention that Condé Nast Johansens is your source of reference.**

We occasionally receive letters from guests who have been charged for accommodation booked in advance but later canceled. Readers should be aware that by making a reservation with a property, either by telephone, e-mail or in writing, they are entering into a legal contract. A hotelier under certain circumstances is entitled to make a charge for accommodation when guests fail to arrive, even if notice of the cancellation is given.

All Guides are available from bookstores or by calling Freephone 0800 269397 (U.K.) or 1 800 564 7518 (U.S.)

Key to Symbols

Total number of rooms

Quiet location

Access for wheelchairs to at least 1 bedroom and public rooms

24-hour room service

Meeting/conference facilities with maximum number of delegates

Children welcome, with minimum age where applicable

Dogs accommodated in rooms or kennels

Fireplaces in rooms

Cable/satellite TV in all bedrooms

CD player in bedrooms

ISDN/modem point in all bedrooms

Wireless Internet connection available in part or all rooms

At least 1 non-smoking bedroom

Air conditioning

Elevator available for guests' use

Jacuzzi/whirlpool

Gym/fitness facilties on-site

SPA   A dedicated spa offering extensive health and beauty treatments

Indoor swimming pool

Outdoor swimming pool

Tennis court on-site

Fishing on-site

Fishing can be arranged

Golf course on-site

Golf course nearby

Horse riding can be arranged

Scuba diving can be directly managed/arranged by the property

Scuba diving nearby (no direct association with property)

Water sport activities available – 2 or more water sports can be managed/arranged by the property e.g. sailing/boarding/jet-skiing

Water sport activities nearby – 2 or more water sports can take place nearby (no direct association with the property)

Located in a ski resort

Skiing nearby

Property has a helicopter landing pad

Licensed for wedding ceremonies

NR
HP   National Register of Historic Places

Image from Sorrel River Ranch Resort & Spa, Utah, U.S.A., p242

We'll give you a warm welcome,
bienvenue, willkommen, benvenuto
and recepción all over Europe.

When it comes to buying or selling hotels, commercial or residential
property in the UK and on the continent, we'll exceed your expectations.
With one of the most experienced teams in the industry, we're market
leaders in expert service and attention to detail.

+44 (0)20 7861 1086   www.knightfrank.com

Knight
Frank

Condé Nast Johansens

Condé Nast Johansens Ltd, 6-8 Old Bond Street, London W1S 4PH, U.K.
Tel: +44 207 499 9080 Fax: +44 207 152 3565
E-mail: info@johansens.com
www.johansens.com

Vice President & Publishing Director:	Lesley J. O'Malley-Keyes
PA to Publishing Director:	Jane Tucker
Hotel Inspectors:	Terri Bisignano
	Brooke Burns
	Felipe Candiota
	Mollie Christensen
	Griselda Contreras
	Tiffany Dowd
	Anna Lucia Fernandez
	Dana Halliday
	Kass Hanson
	Michael Kelly
	Kerry Kerr
	Renata Medeiros
	Cheryl Murphy
	Christiane Potts
	Roberto Prata
	Pablo Pries
	Joanne Priestley
	Arianna Rossell
	Freda Rothermel
	Sasha Travers
Production Manager:	Kevin Bradbrook
Production Editor:	Laura Kerry
Senior Designer:	Michael Tompsett
Copywriters:	Sasha Creed
	Tiffany Dowd
	Jane Tucker
Marketing & Sales Promotions Executive:	Charlie Bibby
Client Services Director:	Fiona Patrick
PA to Managing Director:	Mairead Aitken
Managing Director:	Andrew Warren

Copyright © 2007 Condé Nast Johansens Ltd.
Condé Nast Johansens Ltd. is part of The Condé Nast Publications Ltd.
ISBN 978-1-903665-36-7
Printed in England by St. Ives plc
Distributed in the U.K. and Europe by Portfolio, Greenford (bookstores).
In North America by Casemate Publishing, Pennsylvania (bookstores).

Image from Biras Creek Resort, British Virgin Islands, p360

Individuality Matters to our Partnership

We recognise that every client is individual and has particular legal requirements.

Our approach

We seek to anticipate your legal needs by understanding your business and by developing a close working relationship with you.

We aim to reduce the burden of the legal aspects of decision making, enabling you to maximize opportunities whilst limiting your business, financial and legal risks.

We structure our services with a view to saving expensive management time, thereby producing cost effective decision making.

Our expertise

Since the firm was founded over 50 years ago, we have developed an acknowledged expertise in the areas of corporate & commercial law, litigation, property, employment and franchising law. We also have a leading reputation as legal advisors in the media and hotels sectors. For personal matters, we also have a dedicated Private Client Group which provides a comprehensive and complementary range of services to the individual and their families.

We take pride in watching our clients' businesses grow and assisting them in that process wherever we can.

For more information about how we can help you or your business visit www.gdlaw.co.uk or contact Belinda Copland bcopland@gdlaw.co.uk tel: +44 (0)20 7404 0606

GOODMAN DERRICK LLP

Condé Nast Johansens Preferred Legal Partner

Awards for Excellence

The Condé Nast Johansens 2007 Americas Awards for Excellence were held at Hotel Bel-Air, Los Angeles, U.S.A. on February 5th 2007. Awards were presented to hotels throughout the Americas that represented the finest standards and best value for money in luxury independent travel. An important source of information for these awards was the feedback provided by guests who completed Condé Nast Johansens Guest Survey Reports and who voted online. Guest Survey Reports can be found on page 448.

2007 Winners appearing in this Guide:

Mexico & Central America:

Most Excellent Romantic Hideaway
• CASA NALUM – Quintana Roo, Mexico, p56

Most Excellent Hotel
• GAIA HOTEL & RESERVE – Puntarenas, Costa Rica, p276

Most Excellent Spa Hotel
• GRAND VELAS ALL SUITES & SPA RESORT
– Nayarit, Mexico, p50

Most Excellent Eco Resort
• HOTEL PUNTA ISLITA – Guanacaste, Costa Rica, p273

South America:

Most Excellent Lodge
• ISLA VICTORIA LODGE – Rio Negro, Argentina, p288

Most Excellent Spa
• KUROTEL – Rio Grande do Sul, Brazil, p315

Most Excellent Hotel
• PONTA DOS GANCHOS – Santa Catarina, Brazil, p317

Most Excellent Romantic Hideaway
• SÍTIO DO LOBO – Rio de Janeiro, Brazil, p305

Most Excellent Resort
• TXAI RESORT – Bahia, Brazil, p296

Image from Vila Naiá - Paralelo 17º, Bahia, Brazil, p295

Image from Vila Naiá - Paralelo 17º, Bahia, Brazil, p295

Awards for Excellence

Canada and the United States of America:

Most Excellent Inn
• CHÂTEAU DU SUREAU & SPA – California, U.S.A., p88

Most Excellent Small Hotel
• L'AUBERGE CARMEL – California, U.S.A., p68

Most Excellent Romantic Hideaway
• RANCHO DE SAN JUAN – New Mexico, U.S.A., p181

Most Excellent Spa Hotel
• SANCTUARY ON CAMELBACK MOUNTAIN – Arizona, U.S.A., p62

Most Excellent Ranch
• SORREL RIVER RANCH RESORT & SPA – Utah, U.S.A., p242

Most Excellent Hotel
• THE HAY-ADAMS – District of Columbia, U.S.A., p118

Most Excellent Golf Resort
• THE INN AT PALMETTO BLUFF – South Carolina, U.S.A., p226

Most Excellent Resort
• THE LODGE AT TURNING STONE – New York, U.S.A., p194

Most Excellent Lodge
• WICKANINNISH INN – British Columbia, Canada, p18

Atlantic, Caribbean and Pacific:

Most Excellent Resort
• GRACE BAY CLUB – Turks & Caicos Islands, p391

Most Excellent Hotel
• HORNED DORSET PRIMAVERA – Puerto Rico, p374

Most Excellent Spa Hotel
• PARROT CAY – Turks & Caicos Islands, p392

Most Excellent Romantic Hideaway
• ROYAL DAVUI – Fiji Islands, p403

The Americas, Atlantic, Caribbean and Pacific:

Most Excellent Service
• HOTEL BEL-AIR – California, U.S.A., p81

Most Excellent Business Partner
• SPICE ISLAND BEACH RESORT – Grenada, p366

The Perfect Combination...

Condé Nast Johansens Gift Certificates

Condé Nast Johansens Gift Certificates make a unique and much valued gift for birthdays, weddings, anniversaries, special occasions and as a corporate incentive.

Gift Certificates are available in denominations of $150, $75, £100, £50, €140, €70, and may be used as payment or part payment for your stay or a meal at any Condé Nast Johansens 2008 recommended property.

To order Gift Certificates call +44 207 152 3558 or purchase direct at www.johansens.com

Condé Nast Johansens Guides

As well as this Guide, Condé Nast Johansens also publish the following titles:

Recommended Hotels & Spas, Great Britain & Ireland 2008
Recommended Small Hotels, Inns & Restaurants, Great Britain & Ireland 2008
Recommended Hotel & Spas, Europe & The Mediterranean 2008
Luxury Spas Worldwide 2008
Recommended International Venues for Meetings & Special Events 2008

To purchase Guides please call TOLL FREE 1 800 564 7518 or visit our Bookshop at www.johansens.com

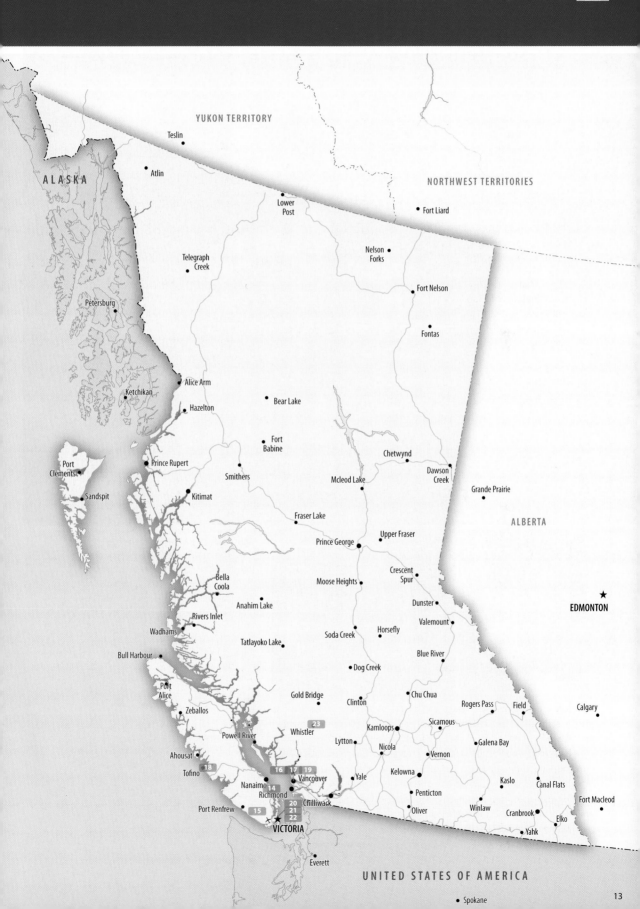

YUKON TERRITORY

ALASKA

NORTHWEST TERRITORIES

Teslin

Atlin

Lower Post

Fort Liard

Telegraph Creek

Nelson Forks

Fort Nelson

Petersburg

Fontas

Ketchikan

Alice Arm

Hazelton

Bear Lake

Port Clements

Fort Babine

Chetwynd

Prince Rupert

Smithers

Mcleod Lake

Dawson Creek

Sandspit

Kitimat

Grande Prairie

Fraser Lake

ALBERTA

Upper Fraser

Prince George

Bella Coola

Moose Heights

Crescent Spur

EDMONTON

Anahim Lake

Dunster

Rivers Inlet

Soda Creek

Horsefly

Valemount

Wadhams

Tatlayoko Lake

Blue River

Bull Harbour

Dog Creek

Port Alice

Gold Bridge

Chu Chua

Zeballos

Clinton

Rogers Pass

Field

Calgary

Sicamous

23

Kamloops

Whistler

Powell River

Lytton

Nicola

Galena Bay

Ahousat

Vernon

18

Tofino

16 **17** **19**

Kelowna

Kaslo

Nanaimo

Vancouver

Yale

Canal Flats

14

Richmond

20
21
22

Chilliwack

Penticton

Winlaw

Fort Macleod

Port Renfrew

15

Oliver

Cranbrook

Elko

VICTORIA

Yahk

Everett

UNITED STATES OF AMERICA

Spokane

13

HASTINGS HOUSE COUNTRY ESTATE

160 UPPER GANGES ROAD, SALT SPRING ISLAND, BRITISH COLUMBIA V8K 2S2
Tel: +1 250 537 2362 **Fax:** +1 250 537 5333 **U.S./Canada Toll Free:** 1 800 661 9255
Web: www.johansens.com/hastingshouse **E-mail:** info@hastingshouse.com

Our inspector loved: Relaxing on the porch of the Farm House West before enjoying a gourmet dinner at the Estate House.

Price Guide: (double occupancy, including morning hamper)
rooms C$336.30-C$410.40
suites C$450.30-C$564.30
deluxe hillside C$564.30-C$678.30

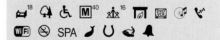

This graceful and intimate resort is set along 22 acres of rolling lawns, gardens and forests overlooking Ganges Harbour. The stately 11th-century, Sussex-style Manor House is central to the Estate and was built in 1940 from natural stone and native woods. The 18 suites are situated in 6 buildings. Each is filled with English country antiques, sumptuous fabrics and local artwork. Full English breakfast is served in the Manor House each morning. The cuisine, created by European-trained Chef Marcel Kauer, includes Salt Spring Island lamb, local seafood and the freshest produce and herbs from the Estate's gardens and orchards. His daily menus are complemented by an exceptional wine cellar offering the best of British Columbia and worldwide wines.

Attractions: Stoneridge Pottery, 2 miles; Salt Spring Island Cheese Co., 10 miles; Salt Spring Vineyard and Garry Oaks Winery, 7 miles; Sidney Marine Safarai, 500 yards
Towns/Cities: Duncan, 20 miles; Victoria, 30 miles; Vancouver, 50 miles
Airports: Victoria International Airport, 15 miles; Vancouver International Airport, 40 miles

Affiliations: Small Luxury Hotels

SOOKE HARBOUR HOUSE

1528 WHIFFEN SPIT ROAD, SOOKE, BRITISH COLUMBIA V0S 1N0
Tel: +1 250 642 3421 **Fax:** +1 250 642 6988
Web: www.johansens.com/sookeharbour **E-mail:** info@sookeharbourhouse.com

Our inspector loved: *The Blue Heron Room with its spectacular panoramic ocean views at sunset.*

Price Guide: (including breakfast and picnic lunch) rooms C$269-C$599

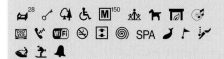

Awards/Ratings: Wine Spectator Award of Excellence 2007; DiRoNA

Attractions: Wine Cellar Tours, on-site; Fishing Charters and Whale Watching, 5-min drive; Butchart Gardens, 28 miles
Towns/Cities: Victoria, 45-min drive
Airports: Victoria International Airport, 60-min drive; Vancouver International Airport, 60-min drive

Once a migratory camping ground of the T'sou-ke First Nations on picturesque southwest Vancouver Island, Sooke Harbour House is a charming small hotel that celebrates food, art and wine. Individually decorated rooms are cozy and brimming with original West Coast artwork and brilliant sculptures, ceramic basins, unique hand-painted pillows and beautiful ocean views. The hotel is a certified organic property with flower-filled gardens containing more than 200 edible herbs, flowers and vegetables. Wine Director and Owner, Sinclair Philip, his wife Frederique and their team of chefs take great pride in their exceptional wine cellar and the produce grown in their garden that is used alongside the freshest of local ingredients to create exquisite gourmet dining. The Sea-renity Spa combines elements of stone, garden herbs and the sea for total relaxation.

PAN PACIFIC VANCOUVER

300-999 CANADA PLACE, VANCOUVER, BRITISH COLUMBIA V6C 3B5
Tel: +1 604 662 8111 **Fax:** +1 604 685 8690 **U.S./Canada Toll Free:** 1 800 937 1515
Web: www.johansens.com/panpacific **E-mail:** reservations.yvr@panpacific.com

Our inspector loved: The incredible views of the harbor, city and mountains from the rooms.

Price Guide: (room only)
rooms C$299-C$610
suites C$610-C$4,000

SPA

A grand waterfront hotel, the Pan Pacific Vancouver is one of the area's larger traditional hotels. The splendid glass lobby provides breathtaking panoramic views of the harbor, majestic mountains, Stanley Park and the city skyline. Beyond the showcase lobby, the hotel hallways and rooms have a more intimate feel. Each room is luxuriously appointed with modern hotel amenities including Frette linens, marble baths and flat-screen televisions. Watch the sea planes land in Coal Harbour from the comfort of your room. The waterfront restaurants and lounge provide award-winning selections of West Coast Cuisine, including the Five Sails Restaurant. In the summer, enjoy lunch on the patio terrace overlooking the sea. The spa will pamper you with customized treatments.

Awards/Ratings: AAA 5 Diamond; Condé Nast Traveler Gold List 2007

Attractions: Robson Street, 1 mile; Stanley Park, 1.5 miles; Vancouver Aquarium, 1.5 miles; Capilano Suspension Bridge, 5.5 miles
Towns/Cities: Burnaby, 8.5 miles; Whistler, 76 miles; Seattle, 143 miles
Airports: Vancouver International Airport, 12 miles

THE SUTTON PLACE HOTEL VANCOUVER

845 BURRARD STREET, VANCOUVER, BRITISH COLUMBIA V6Z 2K6
Tel: +1 604 682 5511 **Fax:** +1 604 682 5513 **U.S./Canada Toll Free:** 1 866 3SUTTON
Web: www.johansens.com/suttonplacebc **E-mail:** res_vancouver@suttonplace.com

Our inspector loved: The wine tastings and wine-making seminars at the hotel's new "Sutton Place Wine Merchant."

Price Guide:
rooms C$169-C$350
suites C$350-C$500

Awards/Ratings: AAA 5 Diamond 2007; Condé Nast Traveler Gold List 2007

Attractions: Robson Street, close by; Stanley Park, 1 mile; Orpheum Theater, 1 mile; Granville Island, 3 miles
Towns/Cities: Victoria, 70 miles; Whistler, 77 miles
Airports: Vancouver International Airport, 8 miles

This grand hotel brings a touch of Europe to Vancouver with its luxurious and elegant setting. Rated AAA 5 Diamonds 18 years in a row, the level of service and attention to detail is evident. In addition to comfortable and well-appointed modern guest rooms, the hotel also offers extended stays at La Grande Résidence. Fleuri Restaurant showcases exceptional French cuisine by Executive Chef Raman Anand, and chocolate lovers can indulge in chocolate fondue or exotic fruit drizzled with chocolate at the all-you-can-eat chocolate buffet. For spiritual health, try the Vida Signature Ayurvedic treatment at the Vida Wellness Spa. A favorite for entertainment industry professionals, the popular Gerard Lounge is reminiscent of an English club with leather chairs and tapestries. Sit by the cozy fireplace for cocktails and bistro fare.

WICKANINNISH INN

OSPREY LANE AT CHESTERMAN BEACH, TOFINO, BRITISH COLUMBIA V0R 2Z0
Tel: +1 250 725 3100 **Fax:** +1 250 725 3110 **U.S./Canada Toll Free:** 1 800 333 4604
Web: www.johansens.com/wickaninnish **E-mail:** info@wickinn.com

Our inspector loved: The amazing panoramic ocean views from the Pointe Restaurant.

Price Guide:
rooms C$260-C$680
suites C$380-C$1,500

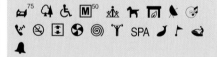

Awards/Ratings: Condé Nast Johansens Most Excellent Lodge, U.S.A. & Canada 2007; Condé Nast Traveler Gold List 2007

Attractions: Clayoquot Sound UNESCO Biosphere Reserve, on-site; Pacific Rim National Park Reserve, 10 miles
Towns/Cities: Ucluelet, 25 miles; Nanaimo, 124 miles; Victoria, 196 miles
Airports: Tofino Airport, 3 miles; Victoria International Airport, 196 miles

Affiliations: Relais & Châteaux

Located on Vancouver Island's picturesque rugged West Coast, this rustic retreat sits on nature's edge overlooking expansive Chesterman Beach. Luxurious rooms and suites are highlighted with floor-to-ceiling picture windows, cozy fireplaces, double-soaker tubs and magnificent pieces of local art. Step out onto your balcony to breathe the fresh salt air and watch the Tofino surfers or perhaps a bald eagle soaring by. Beautiful all year-round, and the home of winter storm watching, the setting will inspire you to explore the rainforest and beaches with rain slickers and boots provided for you by the inn. The West Coast Canadian gourmet cuisine at The Pointe Restaurant, with its incredible 240° views of the open Pacific Ocean, is not to be missed!

WEDGEWOOD HOTEL & SPA

845 HORNBY STREET, VANCOUVER, BRITISH COLUMBIA V6Z 1V1
Tel: +1 604 689 7777 **Fax:** +1 604 608 5348 **U.S./Canada Toll Free:** 1 800 663 0666
Web: www.johansens.com/wedgewoodbc **E-mail:** info@wedgewoodhotel.com

Our inspector loved: The Romantic Getaway package, which includes dinner at Bacchus and a relaxing treatment at the Spa at the Wedgewood.

Price Guide:
rooms C$280-C$600
suites C$380-C$1,500

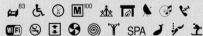

Awards/Ratings: Condé Nast Traveler Gold List 2007

Attractions: Robson Street, close by; Stanley Park, 2 miles; Vancouver Aquarium, 3 miles; Capilano Suspension Bridge and Park, 6 miles
Towns/Cities: North Vancouver, 7 miles; Burnaby, 9 miles; Victoria, 61 miles; Whistler, 76 miles
Airports: Vancouver International Airport, 9 miles; Victoria International Airport, 35 miles

Affiliations: Relais & Châteaux

This world-class boutique hotel has long been Vancouver's best kept secret. Located in chic downtown, this intimate and romantic hotel exudes elegance and charm. Beautiful personal touches by the hands-on owner, Eleni Skalbania, can be seen throughout, from the fresh flowers to the rich upholstered furniture and Murano Venetian crystal fixtures. Exceptional service levels, discreetly presented, ensure the perfect romantic getaway. The beautiful rooms have balconies, fine linens and duvets and the expansive Penthouse Suites are unrivaled with fireplaces, wet-bars, Jacuzzi tubs in luxurious spa bathrooms and scenic garden terraces - frequented by celebrities! Executive Chef Lee Parsons creates delectable French cuisine at the popular Bacchus Restaurant & Piano Lounge, with its inviting fireplace, bar and lounge.

BRENTWOOD BAY LODGE

849 VERDIER AVENUE, VICTORIA, BRITISH COLUMBIA V8M 1C5
Tel: +1 250 544 2079 **Fax:** +1 250 544 2069 **U.S./Canada Toll Free:** 1 888 544 2079
Web: www.johansens.com/brentwood **E-mail:** info@brentwoodbaylodge.com

Our inspector loved: The spa-like bathrooms with jetted tubs and massage showers.

Price Guide: (including breakfast)
oceansuites C$199-C$699

Attractions: Butchart Gardens, 2 miles; Royal B.C. Museum, 14 miles; Parliament Buildings, 14 miles; Craigdarroch Castle, 15 miles
Towns/Cities: Sidney, 8 miles; Victoria, 14 miles; Malahat, 23 miles
Airports: Victoria International Airport, 20 miles; B.C. Ferries, 90-min ferry ride from Vancouver to Victoria (Tsawwassen to Swartz Bay)

Affiliations: Small Luxury Hotels of the World; Preferred Boutique

Located on pristine Brentwood Bay, in the heart of the wine country, close to the charming city of Victoria, this boutique hotel is a 5-star luxury lodge with a contemporary flair. Each elegant oceansuite has beautiful handcrafted furnishings, fine Italian linens, spa bathrooms and romantic fireside seating areas, perfect for savoring a glass of British Columbia wine from the Lodge's very own award-winning wine cellar. Dine seaside at the acclaimed SeaGrille where you can find the freshest in west-coast cuisine. The wood-burning fireplaces, dramatic artwork, and cozy wine bar complete the romantic ambience. A variety of sports are available at the Eco-Adventure Centre located dockside at the Lodge's 50-slip marina, and don't forget to indulge in a treatment at the ocean-front Essence of Life Spa!

FAIRHOLME MANOR

638 ROCKLAND PLACE, VICTORIA, BRITISH COLUMBIA V8S 3R2
Tel: +1 250 598 3240 **Fax:** +1 250 598 3299 **U.S./Canada Toll Free:** 1 877 511 3322
Web: www.johansens.com/fairholme **E-mail:** info@fairholmemanor.com

Our inspector loved: *The delicious breakfasts with home-made maple cranberry granola.*

Price Guide: (including breakfast, excluding taxes) rooms C$125-C$325

Attractions: Royal B.C. Museum, 2 miles; Victoria Symphony 2 miles; Swartz Bay, 13 miles; Butchart Gardens, 13 miles
Towns/Cities: Victoria Inner Harbour, 1 mile
Airports: Victoria International Airport, 16 miles

This pleasantly restored Victorian mansion is nestled in a quiet area of Victoria's Rockland area, near Victoria's Inner Harbour, bordering the gardens of Government House. European in style, and extremely private, the inn showcases beautiful original artwork and Viennese antiques. Popular with honeymooners and couples, the inn's suites are spacious in size and most have a king bed, fireplace and lovely views. The Olympic Grand Suite features an elegant chandelier and private ocean-view deck. The 2-bedroom Rose Garden Suite has a kitchen and a private deck. Sumptuous breakfasts are served daily in the sunlit dining room or on the common porch overlooking the gardens. Lemon ricotta pancakes are a favorite among guests, in addition to the home-made granola and mouth-watering baked goods.

Villa Marco Polo Inn

1524 SHASTA PLACE, VICTORIA, BRITISH COLUMBIA V8S 1X9
Tel: +1 250 370 1524 **Fax:** +1 250 370 1624 **U.S./Canada Toll Free:** 1 877 601 1524
Web: www.johansens.com/villamarcopolo **E-mail:** enquire@villamarcopolo.com

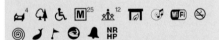

Our inspector loved: The Zanzibar Suite with its gorgeous views of the cherry blossoms and Italianate gardens from the Juliette balcony.

Price Guide: (including breakfast)
suites C$190–C$325

Attractions: Art Gallery of Greater Victoria, 0.5 miles; Royal British Columbia Museum, 1 mile; Inner Harbour, 2 miles; Butchart Gardens, 14 miles
Towns/Cities: Salt Spring Island, 28.4 miles; Vancouver, 68 miles; Tofino, 197 miles; Seattle, WA, 30-min flight
Airports: Victoria International Airport, 17.6 miles

The elegant Villa Marco Polo Inn, located in Victoria's historic Rockland quarter, is designed in the style of an Italianate Renaissance mansion. Built in 1923 as a gift to a young bride, and now a popular venue for destination weddings, the inn features 4 beautifully appointed suites, elegant interiors and an Italianate garden with reflecting pool and fountains. Suites feature double soaker tubs, fine linens, hardwood floors with Persian carpets, antiques and fine arts from the owner's family collections. Gourmet breakfasts are served in the dining room or the Italian Orangerie; special diets such as vegan, gluten-free or vegetarian meals are available upon request. In the afternoon, enjoy tea and sherry in the garden or by the fire in the wood-paneled library. En-suite spa services and activities such as whale watching, sailing, kayaking and wine country tours can be arranged.

ADARA HOTEL

4122 VILLAGE GREEN, WHISTLER, BRITISH COLUMBIA V0N 1B4
Tel: +1 604 905 4009 **Fax:** +1 604 905 4665 **U.S./Canada Toll Free:** 1 866 50 ADARA
Web: www.johansens.com/adara **E-mail:** info@adarahotel.com

Our inspector loved: *The inspirational urban lodge décor, and excellent service.*

Price Guide:
rooms C$279-C$869

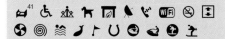

Attractions: All a short walk away: Whistler Mountain; Blackcomb Mountain; Whistler Golf Club; Zip Trekking
Towns/Cities: Squamish, 60 miles; Vancouver, 75 miles
Airports: Vancouver International Airport, 70 miles

Affiliations: Small Luxury Hotels of the World

Adara Hotel is the first boutique urban lodge-style hotel to open in the celebrated ski resort Whistler, home of the 2010 Olympic Winter Games. Small, sophisticated and rustic, this contemporary hotel is comfortable yet stylish, with each of its rooms rich in color and playful in décor. Innovative minimalist furniture and touches of faux mink throws put a playful spin on the typical lodge experience with spa-like bathrooms, luxurious beds, "floating" fireplaces and artful design details. With an outdoor summer pool and hot tub to take a dip while enjoying the spectacular mountain views, this luxury hotel will accommodate you all year round. You are steps away from the village's best restaurants and night-life.

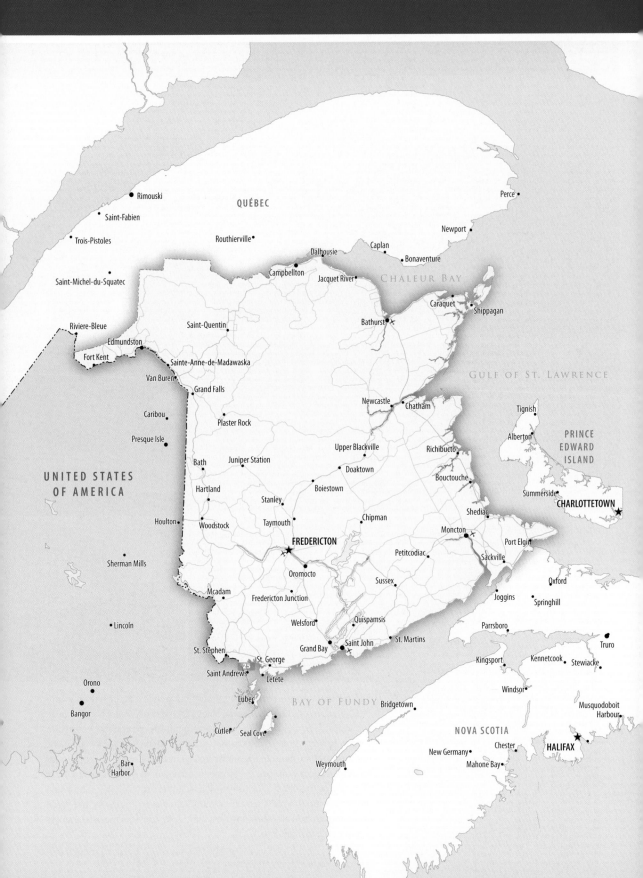

QUÉBEC

Rimouski
Saint-Fabien
Trois-Pistoles
Routhierville
Saint-Michel-du-Squatec
Riviere-Bleue
Edmundston
Fort Kent
Sainte-Anne-de-Madawaska
Van Buren
Caribou
Presque Isle
Saint-Quentin
Grand Falls
Plaster Rock

Perce
Newport
Caplan
Bonaventure
Dalhousie
Campbellton
Jacquet River
CHALEUR BAY
Bathurst
Caraquet
Shippagan

GULF OF ST. LAWRENCE

UNITED STATES
OF AMERICA

Bath
Juniper Station
Hartland
Stanley
Houlton
Woodstock
Taymouth
Sherman Mills
Mcadam
Fredericton Junction
Lincoln
Welsford
Quispamsis
St. Stephen
Grand Bay
St. George
Saint Andrews
25
Letete
Orono
Lubec
Bangor
Cutler
Seal Cove
Bar
Harbor

Newcastle
Chatham
Upper Blackville
Doaktown
Boiestown
Chipman
FREDERICTON
Oromocto
Petitcodiac
Sussex
Saint John
St. Martins

Richibucto
Bouctouche
Shediac
Moncton
Sackville
Joggins
Parrsboro
Kingsport
Kennetcook

Tignish
Alberton
PRINCE
EDWARD
ISLAND
Summerside
CHARLOTTETOWN
Port Elgin
Oxford
Springhill
Truro
Stewiacke
Windsor
Musquodoboit
Harbour
HALIFAX
Chester
NOVA SCOTIA
New Germany
Mahone Bay
Bridgetown
BAY OF FUNDY
Weymouth

KINGSBRAE ARMS

219 KING STREET, ST. ANDREWS-BY-THE-SEA, NEW BRUNSWICK E5B 1Y1
Tel: +1 506 529 1897 **Fax:** +1 506 529 1197 **U.S./Canada Toll Free:** 1 877 529 1897
Web: www.johansens.com/kingsbraearms **E-mail:** reservations@kingsbrae.com

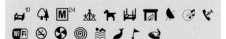

Our inspector loved: *The fine restaurant.*

Price Guide: (including full breakfast and tasting menu dinners, double occupancy)
rooms U.S.$575-U.S.$750
suites U.S.$800-U.S.$1,750
dinner only U.S.$85-U.S.$125

Awards/Ratings: Wine Spectator Award of Excellence 2000-2007

Attractions: Kingsbrae Horticultural Garden, close by; Golf and Whale Watching, 5-min drive; Franklin and Eleanor Roosevelt Campobello Park, 90-min drive
Towns/Cities: Saint John, 62 miles; Fredericton, 62 miles; Bangor, 90 miles; Charlottetown, P.E.I., 186 miles
Airports: Saint John, 62 miles; Fredericton; 62 miles; Bangor, 90 miles

Affiliations: Relais & Châteaux

This private enclave on the Atlantic has welcomed international guests since 1897, and is the only Relais & Châteaux hotel and restaurant in the Canadian Maritimes. After enjoying cocktails in the library and admiring the sea view, savor the exquisite multi-course tasting menu in the dining room. Chef Marc Latulippe works with an array of fresh seafood, game, fowl and meats enhanced by organic produce from his own garden and is a slow food advocate presenting "cuisine du terroir et de la marée," that is simple and bursting with flavor. The extensive award-winning wine list has been specifically assembled to complement the fare. Upstairs, 8 suites and 2 rooms are luxuriously appointed with marble bathrooms, deep soaking tubs and sweeping views of the gardens and sea. In-room massage services are available using hot lava rock therapies.

HUDSON BAY

NUNAVUT

MANITOBA

• Weir River

• Thompson

QUÉBEC

• Winisk

JAMES BAY

• Sachigo Lake

• Moosonee

• Chibougamau

• Balmertown

• Great Falls

• Kenora
• Vermilion Bay

• Armstrong

Hearst

• La Tuqu

• Mine Centre

Terrace Bay

• Thunder Bay

White River

Timmins

• Rouyn-Noranda

• Val-d'or

Kirkland Lake

Joliette

LAKE SUPERIOR

Sault Ste. Marie

Elliot Lake

Sudbury

North Bay

Montréal

Minneapolis

OTTAWA ★

Midland

Peterborough

Kingston

LAKE HURON

Owen Sound

Barrie

Belleville

Oshawa

Brampton
28
Toronto

LAKE ONTARIO

Kitchener

27

St. Catharines

Madison

Port Huron

Hamilton

Syracuse

London

Buffalo

Milwaukee

LAKE MICHIGAN

Detroit

Chatham

Windsor

Erie

LAKE ERIE

Chicago

Des Moines

Toledo

Davenport

Cleveland

New

UNITED STATES
OF AMERICA

RIVERBEND INN & VINEYARD

16104 NIAGARA RIVER PARKWAY, NIAGARA-ON-THE-LAKE, ONTARIO L0S 1J0
Tel: +1 905 468 8866 **Fax:** +1 905 468 8829 **U.S./Canada Toll Free:** 1 888 955 5553
Web: www.johansens.com/riverbend **E-mail:** fd@riverbendinn.ca

Our inspector loved: *Enjoying the sun on the beautiful patio overlooking the vineyard.*

Price Guide: (room only)
rooms C$160-C$325
suites C$260-C$370

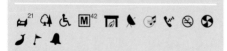

Attractions: Reif Estates Winery, 3-min drive; Shaw Festival, 3-min drive; Niagara Falls, 30-min drive
Towns/Cities: Niagara-on-the-Lake, 5-min drive; Buffalo, 45-min drive
Airports: Niagara District Airport, 6.5 miles; Welland-Port Colborne Airport, 23 miles; Buffalo Niagara International Airport, 27 miles

This historic 1860s Georgian mansion was carefully restored in 2002 by the Wiens family to create a beautiful country inn with Old World charm. Set within its own working chardonnay and merlot vineyards overlooking the Niagara River, the atmosphere is quiet and casual. Each of the classically elegant rooms and suites is decorated with rich colors, antique furnishings, fireplaces and original hardwood flooring. The 1890s salon bar, with its marble pillars and roaring fireplace, is a popular place to meet. Enjoy the creative country cuisine in the 26-seat dining room or relax in the 40-seat vineyard patio with a bottle of the estate's wine. Explore the manicured lawns and gardens, 17 acres of vineyards and take in the breathtaking views.

WINDSOR ARMS

18 ST. THOMAS STREET, TORONTO, ONTARIO M5S 3E7
Tel: +1 416 971 9666 **Fax:** +1 416 921 9121 **U.S./Canada Toll Free:** 1 877 999 2767
Web: www.johansens.com/windsorarms **E-mail:** reserve@windsorarmshotel.com

Our inspector loved: The great history and extraordinary dining room.

Price Guide: (including Continental breakfast)
rooms C$275-C$295
suites C$325-C$2,000

Originally constructed in 1927 to mirror the University of Toronto's signature Victorian buildings, the hotel underwent an extensive renovation to preserve the historical characteristics and update its facilities. The result combined in Old World charm alongside modern luxury. The 2-floor spa maintains a philosophy of "intimate privacy" designed to provide the ultimate pampering experience. The 3-story Courtyard Café serves excellent cuisine in one of Toronto's most impressive dining rooms with dramatic David Bierk paintings, huge chandeliers and a grand piano. Afternoon and high tea can be savored in the Tea Room with original 1927 fireplace.

Attractions: Exclusive Boutique Shopping, 1-min walk; Royal Ontario Museum, 5-min walk; Royal Conservatory of Music, 5-min walk
Towns/Cities: Ottawa, 250 miles
Airports: Pearson International Airport, 15 miles

Affiliations: Small Luxury Hotels of the World

HUDSON
BAY

UNGAVA
BAY

LABRADOR
SEA

JAMES
BAY

NEWFOUNDLAND
& LABRADOR

Labrador City

Baie-Comeau

Rouyn-Noranda

Val-d'Or

Jonquiere
La Baie

Matane

Gaspe

GULF OF
SAINT LAWRENCE

Rimouski

30

La Tuque

Bathurst

QUEBEC

Edmundston

North Bay

NEW
BRUNSWICK

Trois-Rivieres

CHARLOTTETOWN

Glace Bay

31

Drummondville

FREDERICTON

ONTARIO

Gatineau

32

Truro

NOVA
SCOTIA

OTTAWA

33

Montreal

Sherbrooke

Saint John

Bangor

Plattsburgh

HALIFAX

ATLANTIC
OCEAN

UNITED STATES OF AMERICA

LA PINSONNIÈRE

124 SAINT-RAPHAËL, CAP-À L'AIGLE, LA MALBAIE, QUÉBEC G5A 1X9
Tel: +1 418 665 4431 **Fax:** +1 418 665 7156 **U.S./Canada Toll Free:** 1 800 387 4431
Web: www.johansens.com/lapinsonniere **E-mail:** pinsonniere@relaischateaux.com

Our inspector loved: *The views from almost everywhere on the property.*

Price Guide: (excluding tax)
rooms C$335-C$385
suites C$435-C$485

Perched on a hill in the charming village of Cap-à-l'Aigle with stunning views of the St. Lawrence River, the 5-star La Pinsonnière blends naturally into the beauty of the Charlevoix region of Québec. Formerly the home of Senator Marc Drouin, this family-run inn offers luxurious guest rooms with spa bathrooms, fireplaces, down bedding and frette robes and slippers. The terrace is the perfect setting to enjoy a light lunch or dinner overlooking the colorful gardens, and the noteworthy restaurant offers delectable and creative cuisine prepared from many local produce. Take a tour of the multiple award-winning wine cellar with its impressive 12,000 bottles and 750 labels, and make sure you visit the art gallery, walk the nature trails, and relax on the private beach.

Attractions: Casino, 7 miles; Golf, 7 miles; Whale Watching Cruises, 20 miles; Parc des Hautes Gorges de la Riviere Malbaie, 40 miles
Towns/Cities: Québec City, 90 miles; Montréal, 250 miles
Airports: Jean Lesage International Airport, 90 miles; Trudeau Airport, Montréal, 250 miles

Affiliations: Relais & Châteaux

HÔTEL QUINTESSENCE

3004 CHEMIN DE LA CHAPELLE, MONT-TREMBLANT, QUÉBEC J8E 1E1
Tel: +1 819 425 3400 **Fax:** +1 819 425 3480 **U.S./Canada Toll Free:** 1 866 425 3400
Web: www.johansens.com/quintessence **E-mail:** info@hotelQuintessence.com

Our inspector loved: *The infinity pool overlooking the lake and mountains.*

Price Guide:
Q and Executive Suites C$299–C$649
Deluxe and Presidential Suites C$599–C$1,549

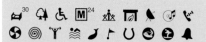

Attractions: Tremblant Resort, on-site; Golf Le Maitre, 8 miles; Mont-Tremblant National Park, 20 miles; Le Ranch Mont-Tremblant, 30 miles
Towns/Cities: Montréal, 85 miles; Ottawa,ON, 100 miles; New York City, NY, 680 miles; Boston, MA, 520 miles
Airports: Mont-Tremblant International Airport, La Macaza, 15 miles; Pierre-Elliott-Trudeau Airport, Montréal, 85 miles; Ottawa International Airport, ON, 110 miles

"The quintessential things of life" are what this boutique hotel strives to provide, allowing you to experience a lasting sense of well-being. This unique area is a year-round destination with luxuriously decorated suites featuring oversized bathrooms, wood-burning fireplaces and stunning lake views. The multitude of outdoor activities include down-hill and cross-country skiing, sledding and mountain biking, but there are also many places to relax in the 3-acre landscaped grounds with its Garden of the Five Senses, boardwalk by the lake, and lake-facing infinity pool and hot tubs. Q Restaurant and Wine Bar is a great dining experience where traditional specialties are complemented by fresh organic herbs grown in the hotel gardens. And let's not forget the 5,000 bottle capacity wine cellar located in a secluded turret with tasting rooms where connoisseurs can experience some of the world's finest wines.

HÔTEL NELLIGAN

106 RUE SAINT-PAUL OUEST, MONTRÉAL, QUÉBEC H2Y 1Z3

Tel: +1 514 788 2040 **Fax:** +1 514 788 2041 **U.S./Canada Toll Free:** 1 877 788 2040
Web: www.johansens.com/nelligan **E-mail:** info@hotelnelligan.com

Our inspector loved: The loft suites with large bathrooms and Jacuzzis.

Price Guide:
rooms C$235-C$260
suites C$300-C$1,450

   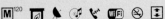

This boutique hotel mingles contemporary décor with the warmth and charm of Old Montréal. Rooms are furnished with high quality custom linens and drapery, dark wood furniture and many have fireplaces; suites are spacious with luxurious bathrooms. Passages of Emile Nelligan's most beautiful poems are transcribed on the walls, immersing guests in Québec culture. The elegant ground floor consists of an efficient check-in and full concierge service, a library with fireplace, a garden atrium serving both breakfast and afternoon tea, and a bar-salon with welcoming leather and rattan furniture. Verses Restaurant is one of Old Montréal's hippest new restaurants, where modern French cuisine is underscored by Québec's finest fresh produce. Enjoy a pre-dinner drink in Verses Bar; martinis are their specialty.

Attractions: Casino de Montréal, 1 mile; Montréal Museum of Fine Arts, 1 mile; Old Port of Montréal, 3 miles; Montréal Olympic Park, 5 miles
Towns/Cities: Mont-Tremblant, 85 miles; Ottawa, 125 miles; Québec City, 160 miles
Airports: Montréal-Pierre Elliott Trudeau International Airport, 13 miles; St. Hubert Airport, 30 miles; Montréal-Mirabel International Airport, 36 miles

Le Place d'Armes Hôtel & Suites

55 RUE SAINT-JACQUES OUEST, MONTRÉAL, QUÉBEC H2Y 3X2
Tel: +1 514 842 1887 **Fax:** +1 514 842 6469 **U.S./Canada Toll Free:** 1 888 450 1887
Web: www.johansens.com/hotelplacedarmes **E-mail:** reservation@hotelplacedarmes.com

Our inspector loved: *The beautifully designed bathrooms with their large rain showers and luxuriously deep tubs.*

Price Guide:
rooms C$230-C$285
suites C$325-C$1,200

Attractions: Old Montréal; Casino de Montréal, 1 mile; Montréal Museum of Fine Arts, 1 mile; Biodôme de Montréal, 3 miles
Towns/Cities: Mont-Tremblant, 85 miles; Ottawa, 125 miles; Québec City, 160 miles
Airports: Pierre Elliott Trudeau International Airport, 13 miles; St. Hubert Airport, 30 miles; Mirabel International Airport, 37 miles

Old Montréal's first boutique hotel combines classic urban chic with the 19th-century architecture of the 3 historic buildings that comprise Le Place d'Armes. Rooms have high ceilings, exposed brickwork and a contemporary, comfortable feel. The bathrooms are large and luxurious with rain showers and deep soaking tubs. Guests are offered several dining options: Restaurant Aix Cuisine du Terroir, devoted to the enjoyment of local Québec cooking with an elaborate seasonal menu; Suite 701, which serves great martinis and creative cuisine in a chic gourmet bar/lounge setting; and there is also a rooftop terrace offering lunch, dinner and cocktails during the summer. Rainspa, featuring Montréal's only hammam, is a must! The traditional Middle Eastern steam bath, along with many body and facial treatments, is a great experience.

Mexico

UNITED STATES OF AMERICA

Mexicali · 35
Baja California Norte
Sonara
Hermosillo
Baja California Sur
Chihuahua
Chihuahua
Coahuila
La Paz
Sinaloa
Culiacan
Durango
Nuevo Leon
39 · 38 · 36 · 37
Cabo San Lucas
Durango
Monterrey
Mazatlán
Zacatecas
Tamaulipas
Zacatecas
San Luis Potosi
Ciudad Victoria
Nayarit
Tepic · 50
Aguascalientes
Puerto Vallarta · 45 · 46
San Luis Potosi
CARIBBEAN SEA
44 Jalisco · 42
Leon
Guadalajara
Guanajuato
43
Querétaro
40
Colima
47 · 48
49
Hidalgo
Michoacán
Morelia
Zihuatanejo
Guerrero
Toluca · 41 · 53
MEXICO CITY
Puebla
Chilpancingo
Campeche
57 Yucatan
Merida
54
Cancun
55
Acapulco
Veracruz
Villahermosa
Quintana Roo
52 · 51
Oaxaca
Tabasco
Campeche
Chetumal
56
PACIFIC OCEAN
Oaxaca
Chiapas
BELIZE
GUATEMALA
HONDURAS
EL SALVADOR

RANCHO LA PUERTA

TECATE, BAJA CALIFORNIA NORTE

Tel: +1 877 440 7778 **Fax:** +1 858 764 5560 **U.S./Canada Toll Free:** 1 800 443 7565
Web: www.johansens.com/rancholapuerta **E-mail:** reservations@rancholapuerta.com

Our inspector loved: The beautiful setting that helps you to focus on your health and well-being.

Price Guide: (per person per week, minimum 2 people, including 3 meals per day, excluding tax)
rooms U.S.$2,690-U.S.$3,350
suites U.S.$3,210-U.S.$4,065

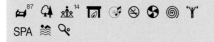

Attractions: All on-site: Hiking; Biking; Cooking Classes
Towns/Cities: San Diego, 1-hour drive; Coronado, 1-hour drive; La Jolla, 75-min drive
Airports: Tijuana International Airport, 40-min drive; San Diego International Airport, 1-hour drive

Founded in 1940, Rancho La Puerta, meaning "Ranch of the Door," is a sophisticated wellness resort named after the 2 arching oaks - the "door" to the original campsite. Privately owned, the resort creates balanced programs of mind/body/spirit for each 7 day, Saturday-to-Saturday stay. Each weekly program includes an equal mix of exercise, relaxation, meditation and massage. Beautifully set on 3,000 acres of unspoiled nature preserve at a 1,700-ft. altitude, there are 30 miles of hiking trails amidst the wilderness, which lead up to Mount Kuchumaa at 3,885 ft. Back at the ranch, the Villas Health Center offers first-class personalized treatments, and a dining room with primarily vegetarian and fresh daily menus based on what is available nearby or from the organic ranch garden. Cooking classes are available weekly at the resort's own cooking school.

ESPERANZA

KM. 7 CARRETERA TRANSPENINSULAR, PUNTA BALLENA, CABO SAN LUCAS, BAJA CALIFORNIA SUR 23410
Tel: +52 624 145 6400 **Fax:** +52 624 145 6499 **U.S./Canada Toll Free:** 1 866 311 2226
Web: www.johansens.com/esperanza **E-mail:** info@esperanzaresort.com

Our inspector loved: Watching the whales pass by while relaxing on the terrace.

Price Guide: (excluding tax and service fee)
casitas U.S.$550-U.S.$2,000
suites U.S.$1,350-U.S.$7,500
villas U.S.$1,250-U.S.$5,000

Awards/Ratings: Condé Nast Traveler Gold List 2007

Attractions: La Galeria, 2-min walk; Whale Watching, 10-min drive; Kayaking, 10-min drive
Towns/Cities: Cabo San Lucas, 2 miles; San José del Cabo, 14 miles; Todos Santos, 42 miles; La Paz, 100 miles
Airports: Los Cabos International Airport, 15 miles

Affiliations: The Leading Small Hotels of the World

Situated atop the bluffs of Punta Ballena, overlooking 2 private coves on the Sea of Cortés, this modern Cabo San Lucas resort combines Mexican culture with traditional Baja style. All ocean-front rooms have outdoor terraces, original handcrafted furnishings and beautiful local artwork. Your stay in a Luxury Suite is complete with a private butler and chef services. The regional cuisine served seaside at El Restaurante, with its expansive wine and tequila menus, is not to be missed, while small regional plates are served in the new TAPAS restaurant. Alternately, dine at the excellent Palapa Bar & Grill. After a day at the private beach, pamper yourself at the spa, or enjoy a rejuvenating hand and foot massage by the pool.

MARQUIS LOS CABOS BEACH RESORT & SPA

LOTE 74, KM. 21.5 CARRETERA TRANSPENINSULAR, FRACCIONAMIENTO CABO REAL, LOS CABOS, BAJA CALIFORNIA SUR 23400
Tel: +52 624 144 2000 **Fax:** +52 624 144 2001 **U.S./Canada Toll Free:** 1 877 238 9399
Web: www.johansens.com/marquisloscabos **E-mail:** info@marquisloscabos.com

Our inspector loved: *The stunning view of the Sea of Cortés from the lobby with its dramatic waterfall.*

Price Guide: (including breakfast)
rooms U.S.$465-U.S.$550
suites U.S.$825-U.S.$1,100

Attractions: Whale Watching and Kayaking, 1 mile; Cabo San Lucas Night-life and Restaurants, 4 miles; Sport Fishing, 5 miles; Sailing, 5 miles
Towns/Cities: Cabo San Lucas, 4 miles; San José del Cabo, 12 miles; Todos Santos, 42 miles; La Paz, 100 miles
Airports: Los Cabos International Airport, 10 miles

Affiliations: The Leading Hotels of the World

This family-owned resort, set in lush landscaping and looking out to incredible views, offers the ultimate in luxury and service. Upon entering the lobby, the stunning infinity pool appears to fall into the Sea of Cortés with its water cascading dramatically down 36 feet to a spectacular pool. Each of the resort suites has lovely ocean views from private balconies or terraces and is adorned with original oil paintings. Those of you who prefer to hear the waves while you sleep can stay in one of 28 beach-side casitas, each with private pool. Lounge on the pristine, white sand beach or relax in the resort's full-service spa, one of the largest in Latin America. There are 3 outstanding restaurants including the highly-acclaimed Canto del Mar.

Casa Del Mar Golf & Spa Resort

KM 19.5 CARRETERA TRANSPENINSULAR, SAN JOSÉ DEL CABO, BAJA CALIFORNIA SUR 23400
Tel: +52 624 145 7700 **Fax:** +52 624 144 0034 **U.S./Canada Toll Free:** 1 888 227 9621
Web: www.johansens.com/casadelmar **E-mail:** reservations@casadelmarmexico.com

Our inspector loved: *The Old World charm, and dining on the beach.*

Price Guide: (excluding 10% service charge)
deluxe rooms U.S.$395-U.S.$683
suites U.S.$435-U.S.$886

Casa Del Mar is wonderfully located on a long stretch of beach where blue skies meet turquoise ocean. The charming lobby is decorated in traditional Mexican style and the surrounding grounds are tropical lush gardens. With several pools and dining areas to choose from you can go wherever your mood takes you and find relaxation and serenity. The suites feature the classic design of old Mexican haciendas with rich dark woods and soft colors that blend effectively with hand-crafted antique furniture from the fine craftsmen of Guadalajara. Recently voted Mexico's Leading Golf Resort, transportation is provided for guests to Cabo Real Golf Course, which, with a variety of hazards, is considered the toughest front-nine in Los Cabos! A relaxing day should be spent at The Spa. Spoil yourself with a sensorial experience like no other with the Mexican Hot Stone Massage Ceremony. The Spa has 7 indoor cabins and beautiful ocean-front "on the sand palapas."

Attractions: Whale Watching, 2-min walk; Golf, 5-min drive; Sport Fishing, 5 miles; Sailing, 5 miles
Towns/Cities: Cabo San Lucas, 5 miles; San José del Cabo, 10 miles; Todos Santos, 35 miles; La Paz, 110 miles
Airports: Los Cabos International Airport, 15 miles

Affiliations: Small Luxury Hotels of the World

CASA NATALIA

BLVD. MIJARES 4, SAN JOSÉ DEL CABO, BAJA CALIFORNIA SUR 23400
Tel: +52 624 146 7100 **Fax:** +52 624 142 5110 **U.S./Canada Toll Free:** 1 888 277 3814
Web: www.johansens.com/casanatalia **E-mail:** casa.natalia@casanatalia.com

Our inspector loved: *Dining at Mi Cocina surrounded by towering palm trees.*

Price Guide: (excluding 13% tax and 15% service charge per room per night)
deluxe rooms U.S.$230-U.S.$395
spa suites U.S.$375-U.S.$545

Attractions: 17th-Century San José del Cabo Historic Town, 5-min walk; Boutique Shopping, 5-min walk; Sport Fishing, 2 miles; Whale Watching and Water Sports, 12 miles
Towns/Cities: San José del Cabo, on the doorstep; Cabo San Lucas, 20 miles; Todos Santos, 50 miles; La Paz, 186 miles
Airports: San José del Cabo International Airport, 9 miles

Affiliations: Mexico Boutique Hotels; Small Luxury Hotels

This European-style boutique hotel nestles amidst palm trees and tropical bougainvillea in the heart of historic San José del Cabo. The owners, Nathalie and Loïc Tenoux, were inspired by the natural beauty of the region and worked with a famed Mexican architect to create an environment that reflected the spectacular landscape by creating hand-plastered walls, wood-beams, tropical flowers and waterfalls. Each guest room is individually named and decorated combining local artwork, striking contemporary furnishings and earthy colors. Step out onto your own private balcony where a complimentary breakfast is served daily and relax in a hammock overlooking the courtyard, pool or neighboring tropical estuary. At night, open flame braziers light up the outdoors where you can enjoy dinner and cocktails alfresco. Owner, Loïc Tenoux, serves innovative Mexican-Euro cuisine at Mi Cocina restaurant.

HACIENDA DE SAN ANTONIO

MUNICIPIO DE COMALA, COLIMA, COLIMA 28450
Tel: +52 312 316 0300 **Fax:** +52 312 316 0301 **U.S. Toll Free:** 1 866 516 2611
Web: www.johansens.com/sanantonio **E-mail:** reservations@haciendadesanantonio.com

Our inspector loved: The Mexican flavor of all the activities that can be enjoyed within the hacienda grounds and surroundings.

Price Guide: (excluding tax and service charge)
suites U.S.$400-U.S.$1,300

Attractions: Comala Town, 16 miles; Volcano Excursion, 31 miles
Towns/Cities: Comala, 16 miles; Colima, 25 miles; Guadalajara, 162 miles
Airports: Colima Airport, 22 miles; Guadalajara International Airport, 155 miles

An architectural phoenix, Hacienda de San Antonio has withstood both volcanic eruption and revolution. Through extensive renovations in 1978 and 1988, this stately 19th-century hacienda has been restored to greatness. Interiors reflect brilliant color and craftsmanship of the indigenous people of Mexico. Of particular note are the Highland Maya textiles, primitive Colonial antiques and hand-painted frescoes and armoires. From the rooftop terrace, you can enjoy dramatic views of the surrounding mountains and volcanoes. Meander through the formal gardens, an area that also features a 105-ft. pool, outdoor dining area and amphitheater, and explore the property dotted with lakes. Do not miss the dramatic volcanic rock aqueduct that channels water around the estate. The hacienda is the centerpiece of a 5,000-acre working ranch, which produces organically raised meat, produce and coffee.

CASA VIEJA

EUGENIO SUE 45 (COLONIA POLANCO), MEXICO DISTRITO FEDERAL 11560
Tel: +52 55 52 82 0067 **Fax:** +52 55 52 81 3780
Web: www.johansens.com/casavieja **E-mail:** sales@casavieja.com

Our inspector loved: The great terraza where you can relax and enjoy a drink overlooking the city.

Price Guide:
suites U.S.$325-U.S.$950

Attractions: Chapultepec Park, 1 mile; Anthropological Museum, 1 mile; Teotihuacan Archeological Site, 30 miles
Towns/Cities: Cuernavaca, 53 miles; Puebla, 78 miles; Taxco, 94 miles
Airports: Mexico City International Airport, 9 miles

This exquisite mansion, once home to and still owned by television journalist and broadcaster Lolita Ayala, Casa Vieja has been transformed into a boutique hotel. The interior designer traveled throughout Mexico to gather furniture, textiles, paintings, statuary, chandeliers and rugs reflecting vibrant aspects of Mexican culture. Walls are vividly hand-painted by artisans, and treasures from the proprietor's personal art collection are on display for you to enjoy. The 10 suites include a 2-bedroom, 2-bathroom presidential suite, master suites with living room and 1-bedroom junior suites. There is a casual roof terrace restaurant bar, and an adjoining formal salon that serves traditional and modern cuisine by award-winning Chef Fernando Guadalupe, who is happy to prepare special requests according to your wishes.

QUINTA LAS ACACIAS

PASEO DE LA PRESA 168, GUANAJUATO, GUANAJUATO 36000
Tel: +52 473 731 1517 **Fax:** +52 473 731 1862 **U.S./Canada Toll Free:** 1 888 497 4129
Web: www.johansens.com/acacias **E-mail:** quintalasacacias@prodigy.net.mx

Our inspector loved: *The home-from-home ambience.*

Price Guide: (double occupancy)
standard rooms U.S.$240-U.S.$260
suite with Jacuzzi U.S.$305-U.S.$330

Attractions: Diego Rivera Museum, 20-min walk; Theather Juarez, 20-min walk; Mommies Musseum, 10-min drive; Valenciana Mine, 10-min drive
Towns/Cities: Leon, 45-min drive; San Miguel Allende, 90-min drive; Queretaro, 2.5-hour drive
Airports: B.J.X. International Airport (Bajio o Leon), 30-min drive

Affiliations: Mexico Boutique Hotels

Evoking the atmosphere of former times in Mexico, the striking façade of Quinta Las Acacias is a testament to the French architecture that once dominated the city of Guanajuato. The interior has retained the characteristics of the original building and is filled with wood and marble floors, period furniture and Oriental rugs. Standard suites are individually appointed with brass, wicker and wooden furnishings and the Mexican suites have Jacuzzis and are bedecked with Mexican arts and curio from the country and terraces covered in flowers and verdant plants. The balcony by the opulent European-styled Master Suite affords magnificent views across Florencio Antillon Park. Master Chef, Pedro Garcia, has combined authentic family recipes with international favorites and the result is a gourmet menu that appeals to all palates.

EL TAMARINDO BEACH & GOLF RESORT

KM 7.5 HIGHWAY 200, CARRETERA BARRA DE NAVIDAD - PUERTO VALLARTA, CIHUATLAN, JALISCO 48970

Tel: +52 315 351 5031 ext. 204 **Fax:** +52 315 351 5070
Web: www.johansens.com/eltamarindo **E-mail:** ycwtamarindo@ycwemail.com

Our inspector loved: *The privacy in each casita surrounded by nature and looking out to the Pacific Ocean.*

Price Guide:
ocean-front casitas U.S.$1,125-U.S.$1,300
garden casitas U.S.$875-U.S.$1, 095
luxurious 4-bedroom ocean-front residences
U.S.$3,600-U.S.$10,000

Attractions: Jungle Tour, 19 miles; Deep-Sea Fishing/Scuba Diving, 31 miles; Polo, 31 miles
Towns/Cities: Barra de Navidad, 6 miles; Manzanillo, 28 miles; Puerto Vallarta, 137 miles
Airports: Manzanillo Airport, 22 miles; Puerto Vallarta Airport, 137 miles

Affiliations: Mexico Boutique Hotels

Costalegre on the Mexican Pacific Coast covers 124 miles of undeveloped, unspoiled, eco-friendly resorts. Chic décor and casual elegance are what you will find at El Tamarindo. This intimate resort features 29 spacious, open casitas and 3 private 4-bedroom ocean-front residences surrounded by lush palm trees and gardens. Each accommodation has a marble bathroom, teak flooring, a private garden and plunge pool. Encompassed by 2,040 acres, the resort is located alongside 2 miles of private beach that looks out to magnificent views of the Pacific Ocean and Sierra Madre. At the end of the day choose your location for dinner: in the main restaurant, at your casita, on the private pier or on the beach! The signature 18-hole golf course by David Fleming is set against spectacular views of the Pacific, and of course a great variety of water sports are available to all.

CUIXMALA

COSTA CUIXMALA, CARRETERA MELAQUE - PUERTO VALLARTA KM 46.2, LA HUERTA, JALISCO 48893
Tel: +52 315 351 0044 **Fax:** +52 315 351 0040 **U.S. Toll Free:** 1 866 516 2611
Web: www.johansens.com/cuixmala **E-mail:** reservations@cuixmala.com

Our inspector loved: The wild animal park, and the afternoon breeze.

Price Guide:
casitas U.S.$450-U.S.$1,050
private villas U.S.$2,000-U.S.$15,000

Attractions: Chamela-Cuixmala Biosphere Reserve, on-site; Polo, 9 miles; Golf, 19 miles
Towns/Cities: Melaque, 16 miles; Manzanillo, 81 miles; Puerto Vallarta, 162 miles
Airports: Manzanillo Airport, 75 miles; Puerto Vallarta Airport, 155 miles

The 4 houses and 9 casitas of Cuixmala are set within a majestic 25,000-acre estate dotted with lagoons and bordered by 2 miles of gold sand beach. Founded by Sir James Goldsmith as a simultaneous ecological reserve and opulent private getaway, Cuixmala now offers the very best in luxury within a pristine location. Striking interior design comes together with a stunning natural setting in the form of houses and casitas set in the hillside overlooking the ocean. All accommodations exhibit a bold, innovative use of color and exquisite attention to detail and the ultra-luxurious houses feature private pools and come fully staffed. The Cuixmala Ecological Foundation features an organic farm and exotic animal park inhabited by zebras, gazelles and jaguars.

Casa Velas Hotel Boutique

PELICANOS 311, FRACC. MARINA VALLARTA, PUERTO VALLARTA, JALISCO 48354
Tel: +52 322 226 6688 **Fax:** +52 322 226 6699 **U.S./Canada Toll Free:** 1 866 529 8813.
Web: www.johansens.com/casavelas **E-mail:** reservaciones@hotelcasavelas.com

Our inspector loved: *The view of the golf course enjoyed from the swimming pool.*

Price Guide: (including all meals, snacks, and beverages, per person)
suites U.S.$320-U.S.$3,500

Attractions: El Malecon (Boardwalk), 7 miles; Canopy Tour, 15 miles; Sport Fishing, 50 miles; Las Caletas, 50 miles
Towns/Cities: Puerto Vallarta, 5 miles; Nuevo Vallarta, 7 miles; Punta de Mita, 40 miles; San Sebastian Silver Town, 70 miles
Airports: Puerto Vallarta Airport, 5 miles

Affiliations: The Leading Small Hotels of the World

This hotel is well-known for its secluded location and sense of intimacy. The traditional Mexican-style textures and colors are stunning and enhance the luxurious accommodations. The hotel is surrounded by Marina Vallarta Golf Course, and has 2 artificial turf tennis courts and a state-of-the-art gym. At the heart of the resort is SPA Casa Velas, a world-class spa and wellness retreat designed to revitalize and rejuvenate both body and soul. Personalized treatments and pampering services are enhanced by the tranquil, tropical atmosphere. A private ocean-front beach club has a comfortable lounge area and a superb restaurant, which serves Oriental specialties. For gourmet dining, enjoy the elegant Elmiliano restaurant in the main hotel.

LAS ALAMANDAS RESORT

CARRETERA BARRA DE NAVIDAD - PUERTO VALLARTA KM 83.5, COL. QUEMARO, JALISCO 48850
Tel: +52 322 285 5500 **Fax:** +52 322 285 5027 **U.S./Canada Toll Free:** 1 888 882 9616
Web: www.johansens.com/alamandas **E-mail:** info@alamandas.com

Our inspector loved: The on-site lake, river and private beaches where you can enjoy a picnic.

Price Guide: (excluding taxes and service charge)
luury rooms U.S.$360-U.S.$1,990

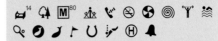

Attractions: Bird Island Tour, on-site; 4 Secluded Beaches, on-site
Towns/Cities: Perula, 6 miles; Barra de Navidad, 51 miles; Manzanillo, 68 miles; Puerto Vallarta, 74.5 miles
Airports: Manzanillo Airport, 68 miles; Puerto Vallarta Airport, 74.5 miles

Affiliations: Mexico Boutique Hotels; Preferred Boutique

A perfect paradise for those seeking beauty, romance and privacy, Las Almandas is surrounded by 1,500 acres of tropical gardens, breathtaking blue lagoons and endless white sandy beaches. Colorful décor is in a traditional Mexican style with stunning fabrics and elegant design complemented by hand-painted artifacts and Mexican folk art. Pale yellow paths with stone mosaics wind through fragrant flowers to the bedrooms, which have oversized bathrooms with private outdoor showers and spacious terraces overlooking the Pacific Ocean. The 2 excellent restaurants serve unique dishes featuring freshly-caught fish, free-range chicken and organic meats, fruits and vegetables from the hotel's orchards. Owner, Isabel Goldsmith-Patiño, has spearheaded many projects to preserve the Mexican coastline and bird lovers will appreciate the bird sanctuary within the grounds.

HOTEL LOS JUANINOS

MORELOS SUR 39, CENTRO, MORELIA, MICHOACÁN 58000

Tel: +52 443 312 00 36 **Fax:** +52 443 312 00 36

Web: www.johansens.com/juaninos **E-mail:** juaninos@hoteljuaninos.com.mx

Our inspector loved: *The contrast between the contemporary and Colonial architecture.*

Price Guide: (excluding tax)
rooms U.S.$180
suites U.S.$220-U.S.$320

Attractions: Cathedral, 0.6 miles; Convention Center, 2 miles
Towns/Cities: Patzcuaro, 31 miles
Airports: Morelia International Airport, 16 miles

Affiliations: Mexico Boutique Hotels

Once the Episcopal Palace in the capital of Michoacán state, this magnificent pink limestone building has been restored to its former grandeur. The romantic design of the hotel fuses Mexican Colonial architecture with art nouveau, neo-classical and gothic elements. This eclectic style continues inside, incorporating stately corridors, majestic staircases and elegant furniture with contemporary design features such as the high-tech elevator. Each bedroom is individually appointed with unique original doors, windows, bathroom woodwork and European-style tubs. Some of the rooms afford wonderful views of the cathedral and downtown Morelia, an attribute shared by the restaurant, La Azotea, where Mexican haute cuisine is served. The hotel bar has an extensive selection of wines and liquors but its specialty is the unusual cocktails known as "remedies".

HOTEL VIRREY DE MENDOZA

AV. MADERO PTE. 310, CENTRO HISTÓRICO, MORELIA, MICHOACÁN 58000
Tel: +52 44 33 12 06 33 **Fax:** +52 44 33 12 67 19 **U.S./Canada Toll Free:** 1 877 88 92 161
Web: www.johansens.com/hvirrey **E-mail:** hvirrey@prodigy.net.mx

Our inspector loved: *The individually decorated guest rooms, and the centuries-old castle.*

Price Guide: (including breakfast)
rooms MXN$2,100-MXN$2,700
suites MXN$2,900-MXN$4,100

Attractions: Convention Center, 0.6 miles; Historical Center, 1 mile
Towns/Cities: Patzcuaro, 33 miles
Airports: Michoacán Airport, 53 miles

Housed in a building that since 1595 has witnessed many memorable events in Mexican history, this hotel has a reputation of being one of the most beautiful in the country, dating back to its opening in 1938. Retaining the magnificence of its former Colonial atmosphere, the patio, with its exquisite features and majestic glass window, provides a stunning and singular touch. The comfortable and elegant rooms, suites and Virreynal Suite are distinctively decorated with priceless antiques. Some have balconies overlooking either the Main Square, Cathedral or Avenida Madero. The Del Virrey Restaurant serves breakfast, lunch and dinner, and offers traditional Michoacán food and international haute cuisine.

VILLA MONTAÑA HOTEL & SPA

PATZIMBA 201, VISTA BELLA, MORELIA, MICHOACÁN 58090
Tel: +52 443 314 02 31 **Fax:** +52 443 315 14 23
Web: www.johansens.com/montana **E-mail:** res@villamontana.com.mx

Our inspector loved: *The elegant spa that is simply amazing.*

Price Guide:
rooms U.S.$249-U.S.$342
suites U.S.$417-U.S.$579

Attractions: Convention Center, 6 miles; Historical Center, 8 miles; The Cathedral, 8 miles
Towns/Cities: Patzcuaro, 33 miles
Airports: Francisco J. Mujica Airport, 21 miles

Affiliations: Mexico Boutique Hotels

Nestled in the Santa Maria Hills, with stunning views over the city of Morelia, Villa Montaña offers a serene and tranquil private retreat. Each cottage-like room and suite enjoys a secluded setting amongst sub-tropical gardens interconnected by paths and patios adorned with statues and exotic plants. In the bedrooms, exquisite Colonial antiques combine with traditional Michoacán crafts; even the fireplaces are works of art. The elegant yet casual dining area serves an innovative menu of contemporary international and Mexican cuisine. The restaurant's specialty is roasted Cornish rock hen with black truffle, and there is an extensive wine list to complement every dish. Business clients will benefit from the full-service conference center and smaller meeting rooms, while the enchanting hilltop setting provides a wonderful backdrop for weddings.

GRAND VELAS ALL SUITES & SPA RESORT

AV. COCOTEROS 98 SUR, NUEVO VALLARTA, NAYARIT 63735
Tel: +52 322 226 8000 **Fax:** +52 322 297 2005 **U.S./Canada Toll Free:** +1 877 398 2784
Web: www.johansens.com/grandvelas **E-mail:** reservas@grandvelas.com

Our inspector loved: The sophisticated spa, and 3 gourmet restaurants.

Price Guide: (all inclusive)
rooms U.S.$450-U.S.$4,500
suites U.S.$960-U.S.$10,000

Artfully constructed in a crescent shape allowing every suite an ocean view, this beach-front resort is a blend of the traditional and contemporary. The décor expresses a new take on original Mexican design, utilizing indigenous materials from native villages and the Asian tropics. Hand-made carvings and engravings adorn the walls and the use of rich, natural hues creates an inviting ambience. There are a wealth of activities to choose from including water sports, golf and tennis, and the spa has an extensive range of therapies and indoor treatment area. The entertainment continues into the evening with shows by the resident magician and performances in the outdoor theater. There are no less than 5 restaurants serving snacks, international, Mexican, Italian and French cuisine.

Awards/Ratings: Condé Nast Johansens Most Excellent Spa Hotel, Mexico & Central America 2006 and 2007; Condé Nast Johansens Most Outstanding Resort 2005; AAA 5 Diamond

Attractions: Malecon Puerto Vallarta, 16 miles; Marietas Islands, 124 miles; Whale Watching, 124 miles
Towns/Cities: Puerto Vallarta, 16 miles
Airports: Puerto Vallarta Airport, 9 miles

Affiliations: The Leading Hotels of the World

CASA OAXACA

CALLE GARCÍA VIGIL 407, CENTRO, OAXACA, OAXACA 68000
Tel: +52 951 514 4173 **Fax:** +52 951516 4412
Web: www.johansens.com/oaxaca **E-mail:** reservaciones@casaoaxaca.com.mx

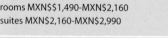

***Our inspector loved:** The individual Mexican décor in each room, and the personal service.*

Price Guide: (including breakfast, excluding 18% tax)
rooms MXN$$1,490-MXN$2,160
suites MXN$2,160-MXN$2,990

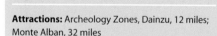

Attractions: Archeology Zones, Dainzu, 12 miles; Monte Alban, 32 miles
Towns/Cities: Noxhitlan, 53 miles
Airports: Oaxaca Airport, 9 miles

Located in the center of the beautiful ancient city of Oaxaca, declared part of the world's cultural heritage by UNESCO, Casa Oaxaca is a traditional Colonial house that perfectly combines Old World charm with the convenience of modern living. Open spiral staircases are stunning against white and earth tone walls, complemented by designer armchairs and amazing Mexican pieces of art. A picturesque garden has a heavenly "Temazcal" steam bath, where herbs, used for centuries by the indigenous Mexican people, cure and balance the body, mind and spirit. Aromatherapy massages, facials, yoga and pedicures and manicures with reflexology can be arranged. Tempting classic, seasonal Oaxacan dishes are lovingly created, by appointment only, in the superb restaurant, which has a quiet, intimate ambience. Tour guides of Oaxaca and transportation can be organized.

HOTEL LA PROVINCIA

PORFIRIO DIAZ #108 CENTRO HISTORICO, OAXACA, OAXACA 68000
Tel: +52 951 51 40999 **Fax:** +1 951 514 0990 **U.S./Canada Toll Free:** 1 800 506 28 24
Web: www.johansens.com/hotellaprovincia **E-mail:** reservaciones@hotellaprovincia.com.mx

Our inspector loved: The beautiful decoration and calm atmosphere.

Price Guide: (including breakfast)
rooms MXN$1,500-MXN$2,000
suites MXN$2,200-MXN$2,500

Attractions: Arquelogicall Zone Monte Alban, 6 miles; Nopala, 32 miles
Towns/Cities: Huatulco, 183 miles
Airports: Oaxaca Airport, 12 miles

Occupying a restored centuries-old Colonial house, Hotel La Provincia feels worlds away from the hustle and bustle of the vibrant city that surrounds it. Tiled floors, rich mahogany furniture, columns, arched doorways, open-air courtyards, and a garden add to this intimate hotel's charm, as do the complimentary cocktails served upon arrival. The hotel features 14 elegant yet comfortable guest rooms, consistent with the style of the public rooms, ornamented with artwork by contemporary Oaxacan painters. Traditional Oaxacan and international cuisine is served in the restaurant, which is decorated by hand-detailed columns and a charming fountain that fully evoke the old Colonial ambience. The rooftop terrace, open to the public, offers views of the city, as well as delicious drinks and snacks from the bar.

LA QUINTA LUNA

3 SUR 702, SAN PEDRO CHOLULA, PUEBLA 72760
Tel: +52 222 247 8915 **Fax:** +52 222 247 8916
Web: www.johansens.com/quintaluna **E-mail:** reservaciones@laquintaluna.com

Our inspector loved: *The attention to detail of the owners that is evident throughout the property.*

Price Guide: (including breakfast)
standard U.S.$165
junior suite U.S.$190
master/presidential suite U.S.$230-U.S.$320

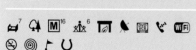

Attractions: Barroque Colonial Churches, 1 mile; Cholula's Pyramid, 10-min walk
Towns/Cities: Puebla, 7 miles; Mexico D.F., 70 miles
Airports: Puebla International Airport, 15 miles; Mexico City International Airport, 70 miles

Affiliations: Mexico Boutique Hotels

Situated in the oldest city of the American Continent, La Quinta Luna is a completely restored 17th-century mansion thanks to the family who still reside here and run the hotel. They have created a beautiful contrast between the building's classical Colonial architecture and the colorful contemporary Mexican art that adorn its walls. The luxurious rooms are housed within thick walls and tall beamed ceilings and overlook the central patio and fountain. There are 3 standard rooms, 2 junior suites, 1 master suite with a Jacuzzi and living area, and a presidential suite with terrace, Jacuzzi, living room and separate bedroom. Enjoy a romantic candle-lit dinner by the patio, or at the Restaurant where a carved stone of Colonial origin and a beam that dates back to 1736 are displayed.

CASA DE LOS SUEÑOS

LOTE 9A Y 9B, A 200 MTS DE GARRAFON, FRACC TURQUESA, ISLA MUJERES, QUINTANA ROO 77400
Tel: +52 998 877 0651 **Fax:** +52 998 877 0708 **U.S./Canada Toll Free:** 1 866 705 169
Web: www.johansens.com/lossuenos **E-mail:** ventas@casadelossuenosresort.com

Our inspector loved: The spectacular view of the Caribbean Ocean.

Price Guide: (including Continental breakfast)
rooms U.S.$350-U.S.$1,120

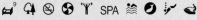

Attractions: Day Trip to Chichen Itza; Swimming With Whale Sharks (May -Sept), close by; Golf Course, 35-min drive; Tulum Archeological Site, 2.5-hour journey
Towns/Cities: Playa del Carmen, Mayan Riviera, 1-hour drive; Valladolid, 2-hour drive; Mérida, 3.5-hour drive
Airports: Cancun International Airport, 1-hour journey; Miami International Airport to Cancun International Airport, 1.5-hour flight

Approaching a hotel by boat is a romantic treat, and reaching this tiny little island off Cancun is the start of a special experience. Casa de los Sueños means "house of dreams," and it lies at the most southern point on the highest part of Isla Mujeres, providing the most breathtaking views of the ocean from every aspect of the hotel. The bedrooms are located in the main building, and have been designed to take advantage of the beautiful scenery, while the restaurant is across the street on the ocean side. A clever fusion of Mexican/Asian influenced cuisine is served here; a marriage that is evident throughout the hotel with its delightfully simple yet luxurious style. The small rustic dock is a stunning backdrop for yoga classes, and the renowned spa offers fantastic treatments. The intimacy of this hotel creates a unity with nature and the stunning blue and aqua waters are regular stages for dolphins, sea turtles and pelicans.

CEIBA DEL MAR SPA RESORT

COSTERA NORTE LTE. 1, S.M. 10, MZ. 26, PUERTO MORELOS, QUINTANA ROO 77580
Tel: +52 998 872 8060 **Fax:** +52 998 872 8061 **U.S./Canada Toll Free:** 1 877 545 6221
Web: www.johansens.com/ceibademar **E-mail:** reserve@ceibadelmar.com

Our inspector loved: The incredible terrace-topped penthouses as well as the excellent spa menu.

Price Guide: (excluding 17% tax and service charge)
rooms U.S.$390-U.S.$480
suites U.S.$440-U.S.$1,315

Attractions: Xcaret Park, 25 miles; Xelha Eco Park, 62 miles; Tulum Archeological Site, 68 miles
Towns/Cities: Cancun, 12 miles; Playa Del Carmen, 19 miles; Cozumel, 50 miles
Airports: Cancun Airport, 9 miles

Affiliations: Preferred Boutique

Set on a stretch of pristine beach along the Caribbean coast of Mexico's Yucatan Peninsula, Ceiba del Mar Spa Resort is secluded, yet only a walk away from the charming seaport town of Puerto Morelos. The 88 guest rooms include spacious master suites and terrace-topped penthouses with dazzling views of the sea, whose interiors are quietly exquisite with a soothing sensation of space and innovative touches. The vast swimming pool features a congenial swim-up bar and there are 2 restaurants. One is located on the beach with a rooftop bar and serves a variety of Mexican and international cuisine, while the palapa-topped pagoda at the end of a long wooden pier is a lovely choice for candle-lit dinners and even weddings. The Spa at Ceiba del Mar is famous for its holistic treatments and revitalizing aromatherapy with indigenous Maya elements.

CASA NALUM

SIAN KA'AN BIOSPHERE RESERVE, QUINTANA ROO
Tel: +52 19991 639 510
Web: www.johansens.com/casanalum **E-mail:** info@nalum.com

Our inspector loved: *The amazing natural setting of white sand beaches, almost exclusive to Casa Nalum guests.*

Price Guide: (per week, all inclusive, 4-night minimum stay)
house U.S.$10,500-U.S.$21,000

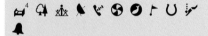

Casa Nalum is a private villa located inside the biosphere reserve of Sian Ka'an. The house combines eco-design with all the modern comforts of home and has only 4 rooms, including a master bedroom. This all-inclusive villa has a beautiful open-air common area that expands into a deck with gorgeous views of the Mexican Caribbean waters, and a scenic lagoon located behind the main house where a private boat can take you to explore ancient Mayan canals. The location offers complete peace and relaxation, and the welcoming staff includes a maid, cook, butler and gardener to accommodate your every need. Dining is a wonderful experience with its exciting fusion of Mexican and European flavors that can be experienced in the formal dining room or alfresco on one of the terraces.

Awards/Ratings: Condé Nast Johansens Most Excellent Romantic Hideaway, Mexico & Central America 2007

Attractions: Mayan Canals, close by; Fly Fishing, close by; Tulum Archeological Site, 12 miles
Towns/Cities: Tulum, 9 miles; Playa del Carmen, 50 miles; Coba, 34 miles; Cancun, 87 miles
Airports: Cancun International Airport, 75 miles

HACIENDA XCANATÚN - CASA DE PIEDRA

CALLE 20 S/N, COMISARÍA XCANATÚN, KM. 12 CARRETERA MÉRIDA - PROGRESO, MÉRIDA, YUCATÁN 97302
Tel: +52 999 941 0273 **Fax:** +52 999 941 0319 **U.S./Canada Toll Free:** 1 888 883 3633
Web: www.johansens.com/xcanatun **E-mail:** hacienda@xcanatun.com

Our inspector loved: *The tranquility of the hotel, garden and surroundings.*

Price Guide: (including breakfast)
suites U.S.$245-U.S.$345

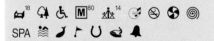

Awards/Ratings: Condé Nast Johansens Most Excellent Boutique Hotel, Mexico & Central America 2006

Attractions: Dzibilchaltun, 3 miles; Uxmal Archeological Site, 50 miles; Chichen Itza Archeological Site, 75 miles
Towns/Cities: Downtown Mérida, 8 miles; Progreso, 12 miles; Cancun, 202 miles
Airports: Mérida Airport, 16 miles; Cancun Airport, 199 miles

Affiliations: Mexico Boutique Hotels

Set in 9 acres of gardens, this former 18th-century sisal plantation offers privacy, 5-star cuisine and attentive service. All of the spacious, romantic suites feature carved cedar doors, Caribbean Colonial furnishings and original oil paintings. Each has a private veranda or balcony strung with hammocks and sky-lit marble-wrapped bathrooms fitted with a hydrotherapy tub/shower or hand-crafted stone tub filled by a waterfall. Start the day by taking breakfast on the dining terrace or in your own suite, and savor international-Caribbean cuisine and Yucatecan specialties in Casa de Piedra. Stress-reducing, detoxifying massages, body-wraps and ancient Mayan healing treatments are available in the spa. Private meetings, weddings and parties are accommodated in the family chapel with on-site planners.

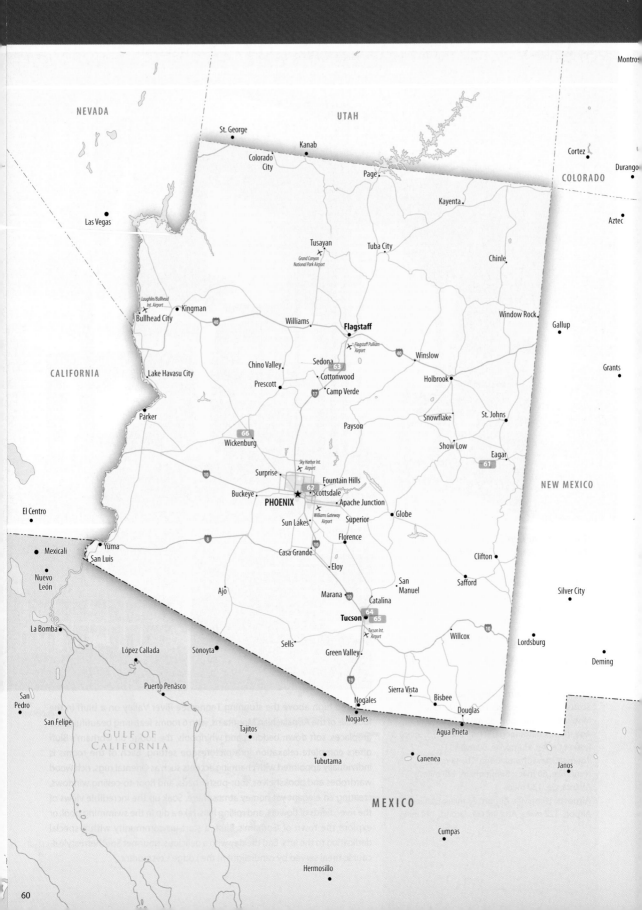

U.S.A. - ARIZONA (GREER)

HIDDEN MEADOW RANCH

620 COUNTRY ROAD 1325, GREER, ARIZONA 85927
Tel: +1 928 333 1000 **Fax:** +1 928 333 1010 **U.S./Canada Toll Free:** 1 866 333 4080
Web: www.johansens.com/hiddenmeadow **E-mail:** information@hiddenmeadow.com

Our inspector loved: *Enjoying amazing meals at the Ranch House beneath the beautiful timber framed roof and in front of a roaring fire.*

Price Guide: (all inclusive, double occupancy)
private cabin from $550

Attractions: Apache-Sitgreaves National Forest, 0.1 miles; Antique Tours, 20 miles; Historical Museum Tours, 20 miles
Towns/Cities: Greer, 5 miles; Sunrise Ski Area, 15 miles; Show Low, 30 miles; Phoenix, 225 miles
Airports: Springerville Municipal AIrport, 15 miles; Show Low Airport, 30 miles; Phoenix International Sky Harbor Airport, 225 miles

Embraced by 2 million acres of spectacular Apache-Sitgreaves National Forest and shaded by towering aspen and ponderosa pine trees, this acclaimed retreat within Arizona's White Mountains is a luxurious and peaceful getaway. The rhythms of the ranch are governed by the seasons: cool summers, falls framed by golden leaf glows, snowy, sunshine-filled winters and spring fields of purple iris. The well-appointed log cabins have cozy wood-burning fireplaces and living areas, and if you travel with your pet, there are even cabins available with attached dog runs. Enjoy decadent full mountain breakfasts, picnic lunches and 4-course gourmet dinners in the casually elegant Ranch House. Cookout breakfasts, margarita wagon rides, barbecues and campfire picnics are regularly arranged. Children enjoy participating in the specifically-designed Ranch Roundup program.

SANCTUARY ON CAMELBACK MOUNTAIN

5700 EAST MCDONALD DRIVE, SCOTTSDALE, ARIZONA 85253
Tel: +1 480 948 2100 **Fax:** +1 480 483 7314 **U.S./Canada Toll Free:** 1 800 245 2051
Web: www.johansens.com/sanctuarycamelback **E-mail:** info@sanctuaryaz.com

Our inspector loved: *The view of Camelback Mountain from the pool.*

Price Guide:
casita rooms $235-$725
casita suites $340-$855

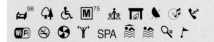

Awards/Ratings: Condé Nast Johansens Most Excellent Spa Hotel, U.S.A. & Canada 2007

Attractions: Hiking and Biking, 5-min walk; Golf, 5-min drive; Shopping, 5-min drive; Desert Lakes and Fishing, 35-min drive

Towns/Cities: Sedona, 100 miles; Tucson, 120 miles; Flagstaff, 130 miles

Airports: Phoenix International Airport, 8 miles; Scottsdale Airport, 15 miles

Affiliations: Small Luxury Hotels of the World

Perched atop Camelback Mountain, everything about the Sanctuary complements its spectacular setting. Luxuious Mountain Casitas feature modern furnishings, spacious bathrooms with oversized tubs and special touches such as silk throws. Some have wood-burning fireplaces and outdoor terraces. Chic Spa Casitas are set around the infinity-edge pool and intimate spa. Some have outdoor soaking tubs and lava-rock fireplaces. The Sanctuary Spa practices Asian-inspired treatments in 14 indoor and outdoor treatment rooms, a meditation garden, reflecting pond and Watsu pool. There is also a state-of-the-art fitness center and movement studio. The award-winning "elements" restaurant overlooks Paradise Valley and serves fine American cuisine with Asian accents. The adjoining "jade bar" has both indoor and outdoor seating with a fire bowl to warm cool desert evenings. There is an extensive wine cellar and amazing cocktails conceived by the Sanctuary's "mixologists".

SEDONA ROUGE HOTEL & SPA

2250 WEST HIGHWAY 89A, SEDONA, ARIZONA 86336
Tel: +1 928 203 4111 **Fax:** +1 928 203 9094 **U.S./Canada Toll Free:** 1 866 312 4111
Web: www.johansens.com/sedonarouge **E-mail:** info@sedonarouge.com

Our inspector loved: *Sitting on the rooftop terrace and enjoying the view of Sedona's Red Rock country.*

Price Guide:
rooms $185-$300
suites $240-$400

Awards/Ratings: Wine Spectator Award of Excellence 2007

Attractions: Indian Ruins and Vortexs, 10 miles; Out of Africa Wildlife Park, 20 miles; Verde Valley Railroad, 30 miles; The Grand Canyon, 120 miles
Towns/Cities: Flagstaff, 30 miles; Phoenix, 100 miles; Scottsdale, 110 miles; Las Vegas, 290 miles
Airports: Sedona Airport, 2 miles; Flagstaff Airport, 30 miles; Phoenix International Sky Harbor 100 miles

Surrounded by landscaped gardens, secluded courtyards and the stunning Red Rock country vistas of Arizona, this city boutique hotel has gained a reputation as a relaxing and stylish retreat with an exotic ambience. The opulent, modern décor features intricate and rich textures reminiscent of Andalucía, while cascading fountains and delicate ironwork balconies enhance the welcoming exterior. Each of the cool, attractive guest rooms has an individual and tranquil charm with fine linens, a spacious bathroom and imported furniture. The rooftop terrace enjoys a 360° panoramic view and is the perfect spot to lounge in the shade or chat over a cool drink. The Spa at Sedona Rouge offers seasonal custom treatments, yoga classes, a spa boutique, a tranquility room and gardens. Reds restaurant serves an imaginative menu of American cuisine.

ARIZONA INN

2200 EAST ELM STREET, TUCSON, ARIZONA 85719
Tel: +1 520 325 1541 Fax: +1 520 881 5830 U.S./Canada Toll Free: 1 800 933 1093
Web: www.johansens.com/arizonainn E-mail: reservations@arizonainn.com

Our inspector loved: *Relaxing in the beautiful gardens and enjoying the Arizona sun.*

Price Guide: (excluding tax)
rooms $170-$400
suites $290-$800

With more than 75 years of family ownership, this beautiful Mediterranean-style inn is situated in a residential area close to the city center. Surrounded by 14 acres of immaculate lawns, mature trees, flowerbeds, hedged private patios and water features, the inn combines modern comfort with antique charm, and is as eclectic in décor as it is cosmopolitan in service and clientele. Little has changed since opening in the 1930s when owner and Arizona Congresswoman Isabella Greenway welcomed guests such as Eleanor Roosevelt and John D. Rockefeller Jr. Today's men and women of distinction and of the entertainment world return time and again to enjoy their favorite rooms or private villas.

Attractions: Major League Baseball Spring Training, 15-min drive; Pima Air & Space Museum, 20-min drive; Sabino Canyon, 25-min drive; Arizona-Sonaran Desert Museum, 25-min drive
Towns/Cities: Tombstone, 60 miles; Phoenix, 120 miles; Bisbee, 120 miles
Airports: Tucson International Airport, 10 miles; Phoenix International Airport, 120 miles

TANQUE VERDE RANCH

14301 EAST SPEEDWAY BOULEVARD, TUCSON, ARIZONA 85748
Tel: +1 520 296 6275 **Fax:** +1 520 721 9427 **U.S./Canada Toll Free:** 1 800 234 3833
Web: www.johansens.com/tanqueverde **E-mail:** dude@tvgr.com

Our inspector loved: *Relaxing after a full day of horseback riding in the beautiful swimming pool with an amazing view of the Rincon Mountains.*

Price Guide: (including 3 meals per day and scheduled activities. Double occupancy, excluding tax and service charge.)
rooms $325-$560
suites $390-$640

Attractions: Pima Air & Space Museum, 20-min drive; Major League Baseball Spring Training, 25-min drive; Old Tucson, 35-min drive; Arizona Sonoran Desert Museum, 35-min drive
Towns/Cities: Tombstone, 60 miles; Bisbee, 120 miles; Phoenix, 135 miles
Airports: Tucson International Airport, 25 miles; Phoenix International Airport, 135 miles

The magic of the American West is waiting for you here. Established in 1868, this quality resort is recognized as the last luxurious outpost of the Old West. Located on 640 acres in the spectacular, lush desert foothills of the Rincon Mountains, surrounded by the Saguaro National Park and adjacent to Coronado National Forest, Tanque Verde offers breathtaking mountain and desert views. Rates are fully inclusive of all the scheduled ranch activities such as hiking, mountain biking, nature programs, a children's program and more. 3 sparkling pools, 2 whirlpool spas and 2 saunas provide the perfect way to relax after a long day in the saddle, while soothing massages and luxurious body treatments may be arranged on-site in La Sonora Spa.

RANCHO DE LOS CABALLEROS

1551 SOUTH VULTURE MINE ROAD, WICKENBURG, ARIZONA 85390
Tel: +1 928 684 5484 **Fax:** +1 928 684 9565 **U.S./Canada Toll Free:** 1 800 684 5030
Web: www.johansens.com/caballeros **E-mail:** home@sunc.com

Our inspector loved: The horseback trails in the high desert and "team penning", a must try horseback riding experience.

Price Guide: (including breakfast, lunch and dinner)
rooms $280-$544
suites $385-$616

This full-service ranch is enveloped in 20,000 acres of desert cactus plants and blooming flowers; the epitome of South Western allure. Inside, each of the rooms and suites of this family-owned property has been carefully decorated with handcrafted furniture and Mexican tiling and fabrics, while outside there is an abundance of activities to enjoy. Admire the awe-inspiring flora and fauna of Arizona, and the 300 species of birds in the area. At dusk, head down to the South Yucca Flats for a cookout and enjoy a barbecue over an open mesquite fire. But make sure to take time out to visit Los Caballeros Spa where the menu includes a variety of massages, nourishing body wraps and luxurious spa manicures and pedicures by the fire. Events can be organized at the 4,500ft.[2] Palo Verde conference center.

Attractions: Trap and Skeet Shooting, 5-min walk; Hot-Air Ballooning, 10-min drive; Hassayampa River Preserve, 10-min drive; Ghost Towns and Abandoned Mines, 20-min drive
Towns/Cities: Wickenburg, 5-min drive; Jerome, 30 miles; Phoenix, 50 miles; Sedona, 50 miles
Airports: Phoenix Skyharbor International Airport, 50 miles

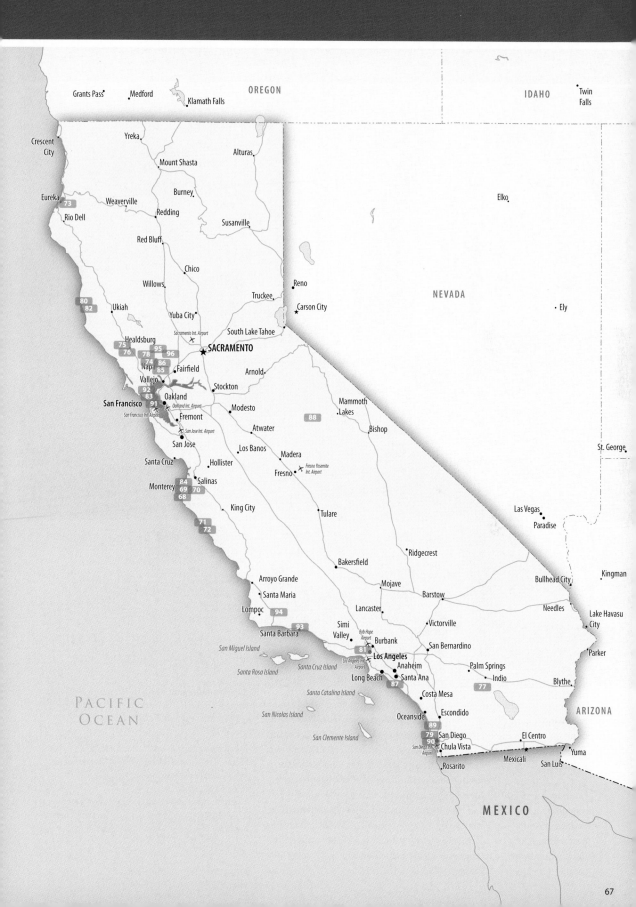

Grants Pass • • Medford
• Klamath Falls
OREGON
IDAHO • Twin Falls

Crescent City •
Yreka •
Alturas •

Mount Shasta •
Burney •
Elko •

Eureka • 73
Weaverville •
Redding •
Rio Dell •
Susanville •

Red Bluff •
Chico •

80
82
Willows •
Ukiah •
Yuba City •
Reno •
Truckee •
Carson City •

NEVADA

Healdsburg • 75 76
74 86
Napa 85
Vallejo 92
83 Oakland
91
Sacramento Int. Airport
95 96
78
SACRAMENTO
Fairfield •
Arnold •
South Lake Tahoe •
Stockton •
Ely •

Oakland Int. Airport
Modesto •
Mammoth Lakes •
Bishop •
88

San Francisco
San Francisco Int. Airport
Fremont
San Jose Int. Airport
Atwater •
St. George •

Santa Cruz •
San Jose •
Hollister •
Los Banos •
Madera •
Fresno Yosemite Int. Airport
Fresno •

Monterey 84
69 70
68
Salinas •
King City •
Tulare •
Las Vegas •
Paradise •

71
72

Bakersfield •
Ridgecrest •
Bullhead City •
Kingman •

Arroyo Grande •
Santa Maria •
Mojave •
Barstow •
Victorville •
Needles •
Lake Havasu City •

Lompoc •
94
Lancaster •
San Bernardino •
Palm Springs •
Parker •

93
Simi Valley
Bob Hope Airport
Burbank •
81
Los Angeles Int. Airport
LOS ANGELES
Anaheim •
Santa Ana •
Indio •
Blythe •

Santa Barbara
San Miguel Island
Santa Rosa Island
Santa Cruz Island
Long Beach •
87
Costa Mesa •
77
ARIZONA

Santa Catalina Island
San Nicolas Island
San Clemente Island
Oceanside •
Escondido •

89
79
90
San Diego Int. Airport
San Diego •
Chula Vista •
El Centro •
Yuma •

Rosarito •
Mexicali •
San Luis •

PACIFIC OCEAN

MEXICO

L'Auberge Carmel

MONTE VERDE AT SEVENTH, CARMEL-BY-THE-SEA, CALIFORNIA 93921
Tel: +1 831 624 8578 **Fax:** +1 831 626 1018
Web: www.johansens.com/laubergecarmel **E-mail:** reservations@laubergecarmel.com

This romantic European-style inn is the ideal getaway for the discerning gourmand. Built in 1929, the inn has undergone major renovation work, transforming the entrance, guest rooms and landscaped courtyard. Bedrooms are individually decorated and have every modern comfort with generous bathrooms and flat-screen T.V.s. Warm jewel tones and fine fabrics complement the charm of the architecture, and the floor heating is very welcoming and cozy. A truly memorable gastronomic experience awaits you: a sumptuous French country Continental breakfast is served each morning, and the 12-table restaurant, ruled by Head Chef Tim Mosblech, creates gastronomic delights that will please the most refined palate. The underground wine cellar houses a 4,500-bottle worldwide wine collection, notably from Monterey County, California and France.

Our inspector loved: *The gorgeous courtyard and private wine cellar.*

Price Guide: (including breakfast, excluding $20 service fee)
rooms $295-$595

Awards/Ratings: Condé Nast Johansens Most Excellent Small Hotel, U.S.A. & Canada 2007; Condé Nast Traveler Gold List 2006

Attractions: Carmel-by-the-Sea Shops and Restaurants, 1 mile; Hiking, 5 miles; 17-mile Scenic Drive and Pebble Beach, 10 miles; Monterey Bay Aquarium, 15 miles
Towns/Cities: Carmel Valley, 5 miles; Monterey, 15 miles; Big Sur, 40 miles; San Francisco, 110 miles
Airports: Monterey Airport, 15 miles; San José Airport, 90 miles

Affiliations: Small Luxury Hotels

TRADEWINDS CARMEL

MISSION STREET AT THIRD AVENUE, CARMEL-BY-THE-SEA, CALIFORNIA 93921
Tel: +1 831 624 2776 **Fax:** +1 831 624 0634 **U.S./Canada Toll Free:** 1 800 624 6665
Web: www.johansens.com/tradewinds **E-mail:** reservations@tradewindscarmel.com

Our inspector loved: *The beautiful Asian-style rooms and appointments as well as the peaceful Bhudda garden.*

Price Guide:
rooms $295-$550

Attractions: Carmel Beach, 1 mile; 17-mile Scenic Drive and Pebble Beach, 3 miles; Carmel-by-the-Sea Shops and Restaurants, 3-min walk; Monterey Bay Aquarium, 6 miles
Towns/Cities: Carmel Valley, 5 miles; Monterey, 6 miles; Big Sur, 27 miles;
Airports: Monterey Airport, 7 miles; San José International Airport, 90 miles

Nestled on a quiet, tree-lined residential street, this luxury boutique hotel has a Zen-like quality that guarantees a tranquil, relaxing stay. Tradewinds' guest rooms provide ultimate comfort in opulent surroundings and most have been styled with an Asian influence complemented by authentic Balinese and Chinese wooden furnishings. Inspiring views of the lush courtyard, Point Lobos and Carmel Bay can be enjoyed from bedroom balconies. King and queen rooms have stylish, custom marble bathrooms and most king rooms boast spa jets in tubs. King suites offer the utmost privacy and are situated in the View Wing, which offers spectacular vistas across the Pacific Ocean. There are many art galleries in the area, in addition to great shopping, renowned wineries and world-class restaurants.

U.S.A. - CALIFORNIA (CARMEL VALLEY)

BERNARDUS LODGE

415 CARMEL VALLEY ROAD, CARMEL VALLEY, CALIFORNIA 93924
Tel: +1 831 658 3400 **Fax:** +1 831 658 3584 **U.S./Canada Toll Free:** 1 888 648 9463
Web: www.johansens.com/bernardus **E-mail:** reservations@bernardus.com

Our inspector loved: The oversized tubs for 2!

Price Guide: (excluding 10.5% occupancy tax and a $20 per room, per night exclusive resort fee)
rooms $285-$815
1 and 2-bedroom suites $965-$1,970

Awards/Ratings: Wine Spectator Award of Excellence 2000-2007; Condé Nast Traveler Gold List 2007

Attractions: Hiking, 2 miles; Monterey Bay Aquarium, 20 miles; 17-mile Beach, 20 miles
Towns/Cities: Carmel Valley, 5 miles; Carmel-by-the-Sea, 15 miles; Big Sur, 45 miles
Airports: Monterey, 15 miles; San José, 90 miles; San Francisco, 120 miles

Affiliations: The Leading Small Hotels of the World

Nestled within verdant acres of oak trees and pines, Bernardus Lodge was designed to complement and enhance the pristine beauty of the natural landscape. Both the exterior and interior convey Carmel Valley's signature welcoming charm and blend intimacy with sophistication. The sumptuous suites are located in adobe village-style buildings along a terraced hillside. All have French doors that open out to spacious balconies with stunning mountain or garden views. Dining options include the restaurant Marinus, which boasts 1,850 wine labels with over 35,000 bottles to choose from. Unwind and enjoy a game of croquet or bocce on the lawn, or take time out to relax in the spa. All in all, the Lodge is the perfect place for those who wishing to immerse themselves in the beauty and lifestyle of California's Wine Country.

POST RANCH INN

HIGHWAY 1, P.O. BOX 219, BIG SUR, CALIFORNIA 93920
Tel: +1 831 667 2200 **Fax:** +1 831 667 2512 **U.S./Canada Toll Free:** 1 800 527 2200
Web: www.johansens.com/postranchinn **E-mail:** reservations@postranchinn.com

Our inspector loved: *The breathtaking beauty, rustic elegance and secluded peacefulness. The in-room spa treatments are heavenly.*

Price Guide: (including breakfast)
rooms $550-$2,185
suites and villas $1,785-$3,000

   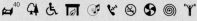

SPA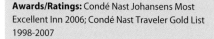

Awards/Ratings: Condé Nast Johansens Most Excellent Inn 2006; Condé Nast Traveler Gold List 1998-2007

Attractions: Hawthorne Gallery, 1 mile; Henry Miller Library, 1.5 miles; Point Sur Lighthouse, 9 miles
Towns/Cities: Carmel-by-the-Sea, 30 miles; Monterey, 35 miles
Airports: Monterey Peninsula, 35 miles; San José Intl., 106 miles; San Francisco Intl., 150 miles

Affiliations: Small Luxury Hotels of the World

Like a jewel in its setting, Post Ranch Inn sits amid the unparalleled beauty of Big Sur's rugged coastline, rolling mountains and towering redwoods. Luxurious redwood and stone accommodations provide stunning panoramas of the Pacific while stilted tree houses enjoy mountain vistas. Each room has a wood-burning fireplace, slate spa tub, organic-cotton linens, massage table and private terrace. Many rooms feature private deck hot tubs. Post Ranch Inn offers a world-class amenity package attuned to natural surroundings. Bask in the infinity pool or heated lap pool, take a guided nature walk or yoga class, or harmonize the body and soul with luxurious spa treatments. The Inn's Lexus Hybrid S.U.V.s provide guest shuttles for local sightseeing adventures. Dining is a distinct pleasure: Sierra Mar offers breathtaking views, award-winning cuisine and an extensive wine list.

VENTANA INN AND SPA

HIGHWAY 1, BIG SUR, CALIFORNIA 93920
Tel: +1 831 667 2331 **Fax:** +1 831 667 2419 **U.S./Canada Toll Free:** 1 800 628 6500
Web: www.johansens.com/ventana **E-mail:** reservations@ventanainn.com

Our inspector loved: The spacious yet cozy rooms and decks overlooking the beautiful natural grounds.

Price Guide:
rooms $500-$700
suites $700-$1,500

Awards/Ratings: Condé Nast Traveler Gold List 2007; Condé Nast Traveler Gold List 2005; Wine Spectator Award of Excellence 1992-2007

Attractions: Hiking, 1-min walk; Ventana Discovery Walk, 5-min walk; Cielo Restaurant, 10-min walk
Towns/Cities: Big Sur, 1 mile
Airports: Monterey Airport, 45 miles

Snuggly nestled on a gently sloping wooded hillside overlooking Big Sur's rugged coastline, the enchanting Ventana Inn provides unforgettable luxury, unique architecture, world-class dining and spectacular spa treatments. Newly decorated rooms are stunning with wood paneling, open fireplaces and plenty of space. Many rooms have their own balconies with sweeping vistas of the Pacific Ocean and the green and gold flowered hills of the surrounding countryside. Some rooms benefit from private decks with Jacuzzi tubs and hammocks. Each meal in the restaurant is outstandingly fresh, simple and delicious. The fantastic spa offers complimentary yoga as well as a large variety of holistic treatments, and the hotel is situated in 243 acres of meadows and hills, ideal for those who enjoy the outdoors.

THE CARTER HOUSE INNS

301 L STREET, EUREKA, CALIFORNIA 95501
Tel: +1 707 444 8062 **Fax:** +1 707 444 8067 **U.S./Canada Toll Free:** 1 800 404 1390
Web: www.johansens.com/carterhouse **E-mail:** reserve@carterhouse.com

Our inspector loved: *The menu and wine list offered at Restaurant 301; a gastronomic delight.*

Price Guide: (including breakfast, wine and hors d'oeuvres, cookies, tea, turndown service and chocolate truffles, excluding 9% tax)
rooms $190-$233
suites $304-$612

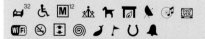

Awards/Ratings: Wine Spectator Grand Award 1998-2007

Attractions: Hiking, 5-min walk; Horseback Riding, 10-min drive; Kayaking, 5 miles; Redwood National Park, 30 miles
Towns/Cities: Redding, 145 miles; Santa Rosa, 181 miles; Napa - Sonoma, 200 miles; San Francisco, 275 miles
Airports: Arcata Airport, 15 miles

Comprised of 4 beautifully renovated buildings, Carter House Inns is the jewel of the crown that is the historic district of Eureka. The warmest of welcomes awaits you and the hospitable staff are attentive but never intrusive. Tasteful interior design incorporates sumptuous fabrics, original artwork and antique furnishings. In each one of the luxurious bedrooms, aspects of a bygone era meet contemporary in-room entertainment centers, and large windows bathe the room in natural sunlight. At Restaurant 301 dishes are created from local ingredients such as freshly caught Kumamoto oysters from Humboldt Bay and produce from the property's very own garden. In the grounds over 300 varieties of herbs, fruit and vegetables are grown and each afternoon you will be invited to collect ingredients for the evening's menu.

THE GAIGE HOUSE

13540 ARNOLD DRIVE, GLEN ELLEN, CALIFORNIA 95442
Tel: +1 707 935 0237 **Fax:** +1 707 935 6411 **U.S./Canada Toll Free:** 1 800 935 0237
Web: www.johansens.com/gaige **E-mail:** gaige@sprynet.com

Our inspector loved: The spacious new Zen Spa Suites, the Zen garden and exceptional service.

Price Guide: (breakfast $15)
rooms $175-$375
suites $395-$595

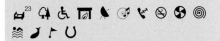

Nestled in the beautiful Sonoma Valley, Gaige House offers luxurious accommodation in a calm and peaceful environment. Most of the individually designed rooms enjoy elegant fireplaces, outside decks and designer linens. Particularly outstanding are the new spa suites with immense windows affording views over the glorious Calabazas Creek. Another exceptional feature is the Gaige Suite bathroom, which boasts an enormous 2-person shower and a wraparound deck overlooking the delightful verdant gardens. The heated pool is set in the lawn at the rear of the estate and health facilities include a spa room and whirlpool. Breakfasts are created by Chef Charles Holmes who brings his artistic flair and unique style to the dishes; consisting of 2 or 3 courses the cuisine is light yet extremely satisfying.

Attractions: Fine Dining, 5-min walk; Napa/Sonoma Wineries, 15 miles; Russian River, 25 miles
Towns/Cities: Sonoma, 10 miles; Napa, 20 miles; Calistoga, 25 miles; Healdsburg, 30 miles
Airports: Sonoma Airport, 15-min drive; San Francisco Airport, 80-min drive; Oakland Airport, 80-min drive

THE GRAPE LEAF INN

539 JOHNSON STREET, HEALDSBURG, CALIFORNIA 95448
Tel: +1 707 433 8140 **Fax:** +1 707 433 3140 **U.S./Canada Toll Free:** 1 866 732 9131
Web: www.johansens.com/grapeleaf **E-mail:** info@grapeleafinn.com

Our inspector loved: *The delicious gourmet country breakfast.*

Price Guide: (including breakfast)
rooms $225-$395
vineyard cottages $425-$790

Attractions: Healdsburg Plaza and Fine Restaurants, 1 mile; Hiking and Hot-Air Balloon Rides, 1 mile; Wineries, 5 miles
Towns/Cities: Russian River, 5 miles; Calistoga, 30 miles; Napa, 45 miles
Airports: Sonoma Airport, 10 miles; Oakland Airport, 90-min drive; San Francisco Airport, 105-min drive

The 106-year-old Grape Leaf Inn has 12 distinct beautifully appointed rooms. Many accommodations feature 2-person spa tub/showers, king beds and fireplaces; 1 room boasts a 2-person steam shower and Japanese soaking tub. A 10-acre vineyard property with 3 charmingly renovated cottages has recently been added, affording the opportunity to experience authentic vineyard living. Surrounded by 80-year-old Zinfandel vines, each cottage has its own private outdoor hot tub, and 1 even has its own 100-year-old wine cellar. After a day of relaxation or wine-hopping among the more than 120 wineries within 20 minutes of the inn, you may step behind the secret bookcase and enjoy complimentary tastings of Sonoma County wines and cheeses in the "Speakeasy" cellar before dining out.

HOTEL HEALDSBURG

25 MATHESON STREET, HEALDSBURG, CALIFORNIA 95448
Tel: +1 707 431 2800 **Fax:** +1 707 431 0414 **U.S./Canada Toll Free:** 1 800 889 7188
Web: www.johansens.com/healdsburg **E-mail:** frontoffice@hotelhealdsburg.com

Our inspector loved: The striking décor, open walkways and elegant furnishings.

Price Guide: (including breakfast)
rooms $275-$595
suites $690-$790

Awards/Ratings: Condé Nast Traveler Gold List 2006

Attractions: Historic Healdsburg Plaza, close by; Vineyards, 1 mile; The Russian River, 1 mile; Lake Sonoma, 10 miles.
Towns/Cities: Santa Rosa, 12 miles; Sebastopol, 22 miles; Calistoga, 27 miles; Sonoma, 45 miles
Airports: Sonoma Airport, 11 miles; Oakland Airport, 75 miles; San Francisco Airport, 85 miles

Situated in the picturesque Northern Sonoma Wine Country, Hotel Healdsburg captures the charm of its surroundings with its simplistic yet elegant accommodations. Each of the 55 rooms is spacious, and many feature French doors that lead onto balconies with views of the surrounding countryside, town plaza or hotel grounds. You may wish to take advantage of the many activities the Wine Country affords, including hiking, canoeing, and of course, exceptional vineyard tours! After the day's activities, return to enjoy Hotel Healdsburg's fine dining options at its signature restaurant, Dry Creek Kitchen. With indoor and outdoor seating options, the Dry Creek kitchen draws upon local flavors to present a constantly-evolving menu and comprehensive wine list.

MIRAMONTE RESORT AND SPA

45-000 INDIAN WELLS LANE, INDIAN WELLS, CALIFORNIA 92210
Tel: +1 760 341 2200 **Fax:** +1 760 568 0541 **U.S./Canada Toll Free:** 1 800 237 2926
Web: www.johansens.com/miramonte **E-mail:** info@miramonteresort.com

Our inspector loved: *The Bagno Vino (wine bath) at THE WELL spa.*

Price Guide:
rooms $159-$359
suites $379-$879

Attractions: Indian Wells Tennis Garden, 5-min drive; Palm Springs Aerial Tramway, 20-min drive; Joshua Tree National Park, 30-min drive
Towns/Cities: Orange County, 115 miles; San Diego, 122 miles; Los Angeles, 128 miles
Airports: Palm Springs International Airport, 15-min drive

Nestled at the foothills of the Santa Rosa Mountains, amidst fragrant olive and citrus groves, colorful flowers and gardens, this Mediterranean-inspired resort offers uninterrupted relaxation in a stunning desert setting. The 2-story bougainvillea-covered villas, influenced by northern Italian architecture, are luxurious and tastefully appointed in warm colors and feature marble baths, private terraces, elegant crown molding and the signature "Desert Dream Bed" laid with overstuffed comforters and 4 pillows. Ristorante Brissago serves appetizing dishes with a Mediterranean flare and The Vineyard Lounge offers cocktails and lighter options. The award-winning spa, THE WELL, reminiscent of a Tuscan village, provides a haven of innovative treatments ideal for those seeking rejuvenation and escape from the outside world.

THE KENWOOD INN AND SPA

10400 SONOMA HIGHWAY, KENWOOD, CALIFORNIA 95452
Tel: +1 707 833 1293 **Fax:** +1 707 833 1247 **U.S./Canada Toll Free:** 1 800 353 6966
Web: www.johansens.com/kenwoodinn **E-mail:** info@kenwoodinn.com

Our inspector loved: The peaceful, elegant courtyard, and spacious bathrooms. The beds are heavenly!

Price Guide: (including breakfast)
rooms $350
suites $700

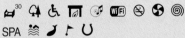

SPA

Located on a hillside in Sonoma's Valley of the Moon, overlooking 2,000 acres of vineyard, The Kenwood Inn and Spa is reminiscent of a sultry Mediterranean villa. Situated around 3 private courtyards, this lovely inn's well-appointed suites have cozy wood-burning fireplaces, plush feather beds and rich fabrics, all which enhance the romantic mood of the property. During your stay, visit the full-service spa, which encircles the impressive salt-water pool. The estate also boasts the first Caudalíe vinothérapie center in the U.S. where treatments are based on the extracts of vine and grape seeds combined with organic essential oils to restore and rejuvenate. Enjoy these therapies in the barrel bath cabin and terrace, which have stunning views of the vine-covered hills.

Attractions: Wine Tasting/Vineyards, 1 mile; Boyes Hot Springs, 5 miles; Lake Sonoma, 10 miles
Towns/Cities: Sonoma, 10 miles; Calistoga, 15 miles; Napa, 20 miles
Airports: Santa Rosa Airport, 15 miles; Oakland Airport, 55 miles; San Francisco Airport, 65 miles

ESTANCIA LA JOLLA HOTEL & SPA

9700 NORTH TORREY PINES ROAD, LA JOLLA, CALIFORNIA 92037
Tel: +1 858 550 1000 **Fax:** +1 858 550 1001 **U.S./Canada Toll Free:** 1 877 4 ESTANCIA
Web: www.johansens.com/estancialajolla **E-mail:** reservations@estancialajolla.com

Our inspector loved: Dining at Adobe el Restuarante overlooking the courtyard.

Price Guide:
rooms $250-$360
suites $520-$1,500

Attractions: Torrey Pines Glider Port, 1 mile; Torrey Pines Golf Course and State Preserve, 1 mile; Birch Aquarium, 1 mile; University of California, San Diego, 1 mile
Towns/Cities: La Jolla, 3 miles; Del Mar, 5 miles; San Diego, 12 miles; Carlsbad, 20 miles
Airports: San Diego International Airport, 12 miles; Palomar Airport, 25 miles

Set on almost 10 acres on the bluff of La Jolla, Estancia La Jolla Hotel & Spa is an adobe-style luxury hotel, spa and executive learning retreat. The well-appointed rooms include one Presidential Suite and have attractive marble baths and lovely patios or balconies with views of lush courtyards. The surrounding fragrant gardens showcase many native California plantings and are enhanced by fountains, flamenco guitar music, outdoor fireplaces and picturesque pathways. The hotel's 2 restaurants offer traditional California and Spanish fusion cuisine in the casual-chic Adobe el Restaurante and the Mustangs & Burros where you can dine alfresco or indoors while listening to live music. The Bodega Wine Bar serves some of California's finest wines. The Spa at Estancia La Jolla is a full-service spa with an array of organic treatments with 9 treatment rooms, and the state-of-the-art Learning Retreat is a certified I.A.C.C. conference center with 25,000 sq. ft. of meeting facilities.

STEVENSWOOD SPA RESORT

8211 NORTH HIGHWAY 1, LITTLE RIVER, CALIFORNIA 95456
Tel: +1 707 937 2810 **Fax:** +1 707 937 1237 **U.S./Canada Toll Free:** 1 800 421 2810
Web: www.johansens.com/stevenswood **E-mail:** stay@stevenswood.com

Our inspector loved: *The lovely property, and wonderful spa space.*

Price Guide:
rooms $149-$255

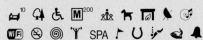

Attractions: Ocean/Bluff, 0.25 miles; Tennis and Golf, 1 mile; Wineries, 10 miles
Towns/Cities: Mendocino, 2-min walk; Fort Bragg, 5 miles
Airports: Sonoma Airport, 45 miles; Oakland Airport (OAK), 3-hour drive; San Francisco Airport (SFO), 3-hour drive

Flanked by the Pacific Ocean and a forest of redwoods, Stevenswood Spa Resort takes full advantage of its scenic Northern California location. Each of the suites features imported furnishings, Tempur-pedic mattresses covered with 1,000-thread count Egyptian cotton linens, wood-burning fireplaces, and Northern Californian art. All offer stunning views of the ocean, meadows or the resort's private botanical garden and beautifully landscaped grounds. The Restaurant at Stevenswood serves innovative Wine Country cuisine, much of its ingredients coming directly from the Stevenswood Ranch, and provides lavish gourmet breakfasts each morning. Wellness is a top priority at Stevenswood, the home of "Indigo Eco/Spa," California's first eco-spa, as well as the state-of-the-art Ocean View Fitness Room. Complimentary beach-front yoga classes are also offered.

HOTEL BEL-AIR

701 STONE CANYON ROAD, LOS ANGELES, CALIFORNIA 90077
Tel: +1 310 472 1211 **Fax:** +1 310 909 1611 **U.S./Canada Toll Free:** 1 800 648 4097
Web: www.johansens.com/belair **E-mail:** sales@hotelbelair.com

Our inspector loved: The sense of seclusion and superior service.

Price Guide:
rooms $395-$625
suites $825-$4,000

Awards/Ratings: Mobil 5 Star 2007; Condé Nast Traveler Gold List 2007; Condé Nast Johansens Most Excellent Service, The Americas, Atlantic, Caribbean & Pacific Islands 2007; Condé Nast Johansens Most Excellent Hotel 2006

Attractions: Getty Museum, 1 mile; Rodeo Drive, 5 miles; Malibu Beach, 15 miles; Universal Studios, 10 miles
Towns/Cities: Westwood, 1 mile; Brentwood, 2 miles; Century City, 2 miles; Beverly Hills, 5 miles
Airports: Los Angeles Airport, 13 miles; Burbank Airport, 19 miles

Affiliations: The Leading Hotels of the World

With its pink stucco structure, intimate courtyard areas and iron terraces, Hotel Bel-Air reflects the essence of sophistication. Enveloped by 12 acres of verdant gardens, the 91 rooms, including 39 suites, are individually appointed (some suites are customized for longstanding guests) and have private entrances from the lush gardens or fountain courtyards. Most bathrooms include double marble sinks, large showers and spacious bathtubs, some feature tiled patios, wood-burning fireplaces and Jacuzzis. A popular venue for private parties and weddings, the recently-opened Palm Room boasts a plasma monitor, pocket doors to create breakouts, 2 fireplaces and a private patio with fountain. Exquisite meals are served in the restaurant and alfresco on the terrace while the wood-paneled bar provides inviting surrounds.

THE STANFORD INN BY THE SEA

COAST HIGHWAY ONE & COMPTCHE-UKIAH ROAD, MENDOCINO, CALIFORNIA 95460
Tel: +1 707 937 5615 **Fax:** +1 707 937 0305 **U.S./Canada Toll Free:** 1 800 331 8884
Web: www.johansens.com/stanford **E-mail:** info@stanfordinn.com

Our inspector loved: *Ravens restaurant: a culinary treat even for non-vegetarians!*

Price Guide:
rooms $265-$325
suites $395-$465

Awards/Ratings: Previous Recipient of Wine Spectator Award of Excellence

Attractions: Canoeing and Kayaking on Big River; Hiking and Biking, on-site
Towns/Cities: Mendocino, 1 mile; St. Helena, 115 miles
Airports: San Francisco Airport, 150 miles; Oakland Airport, 160 miles

This relaxing retreat on the rugged California coastline rests comfortably between lush forest and the majestic Pacific Ocean. The Eden-like grounds surrounding the property are stunning and consist of flower, herb and vegetable gardens. In fact, the inn is a family home and certified organic farm, the products of which are used to create fantastic gourmet vegetarian and vegan cuisine in the highly-acclaimed Ravens restaurant. You will not be disappointed with the exquisite overnight accommodation: all of the rooms and suites boast pine and redwood paneling, a roaring log fire, king or queen four-poster or sleigh bed and are embellished with plants, antiques and works of art. Enjoy a relaxing massage, private yoga session, the spa and sauna, or more energetic pursuits in nearby Mendocino.

MILL VALLEY INN

165 THROCKMORTON AVENUE, MILL VALLEY, CALIFORNIA 94941
Tel: +1 415 389 6608 **Fax:** +1 415 389 5051 **U.S./Canada Toll Free:** 1 800 595 2100
Web: www.johansens.com/millvalleyinn **E-mail:** millvalleyinn@jdvhospitality.com

Our inspector loved: *The tranquil creek-view rooms and location so close to the town center.*

Price Guide: (including breakfast)
rooms $169–$419

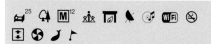

Attractions: Muir Woods National Park, 5 miles; Mount Tamalpais, 5 miles; San Francisco Bay, 15 miles

Towns/Cities: San Francisco, 15 miles; Wine Country, 45 miles

Airports: San Francisco Airport, 26 miles; Oakland Airport, 34 miles

30 minutes north of San Francisco, Mill Valley is set in a unique location at the foot of Mount Tamalpais, surrounded by redwood trees. This romantic hideaway combines the quaint charm of a historic Californian mill town with the sophisticated air of a contemporary European hotel. With a modern, Tuscan-style ambience the 25 distinctive bedrooms, including 2 cottages built along a creek, offer an eclectic style and king or queen-size beds. All reflect a respect for nature and incorporate furnishings handcrafted in Northern California. Breakfast is served on the splendid flower-filled Sun Terrace and includes fresh fruit, local pastries and espresso drinks. A wine and cheese reception is also served on the Sun Terrace during the afternoon. The Terrace Room offers space for small meetings and presentations.

OLD MONTEREY INN

500 MARTIN STREET, MONTEREY, CALIFORNIA 93940
Tel: +1 831 375 8284 **Fax:** +1 831 375 6730 **U.S./Canada Toll Free:** 1 800 350 2344
Web: www.johansens.com/oldmontereyinn **E-mail:** omi@oldmontereyinn.com

Our inspector loved: The spa suites, which boast garden views, fireplaces and a free-standing spa tub.

Price Guide: (including breakfast)
rooms $300-$380
suites $415-$480

Steeped in the history of and flavor of its surroundings, Old Monterey Inn is reminiscent of the days of pioneers and the infamous Californian Golf Rush. Much of the original stonework of the manor remains, and the interior has been lovingly restored to its former glory. The guest rooms evoke the romance of a bygone era and antiques adorn every pocket and corner of the public rooms. Breakfasts may be served in the garden, dining room or simply in bed, and tempting afternoon treats include freshly-baked cookies served with tea and coffee. Wine and hors d'oeuvres tease the palate in the evenings, while there is a splendid choice of restaurants nearby.

Attractions: Monterey Aquarium and Boardwalk, 2 miles; Pebble Beach Golf Courses, 5 miles; 17-mile Scenic Drive, 5 miles; Wineries, 5 miles
Towns/Cities: Carmel-by-the-Sea, 5 miles; Big Sur, 30 miles; Santa Cruz, 45 miles
Airports: Monterey Peninsula Airport, 15-min drive

1801 First Inn

1801 FIRST STREET, NAPA, CALIFORNIA 94559
Tel: +1 707 224 3739 **Fax:** +1 707 224 3932 **U.S./Canada Toll Free:** 1 800 518 0146
Web: www.johansens.com/1801inn **E-mail:** info@1801first.com

Our inspector loved: *The beautiful guest rooms and sun-drenched dining room.*

Price Guide: (excluding tax)
rooms $325-$525

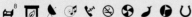

Attractions: Copia, 1 mile; Wine Tasting and Touring, 1 mile; Napa Boutiques and Restaurants, 1 mile; Ballooning, 10 miles.
Towns/Cities: Sonoma, 15 miles; Calistoga, 15 miles; Russian River, 30 miles; San Francisco, 60 miles
Airports: Oakland Airport, 65 miles; Sacramento Airport, 70 miles; San Francisco Airport, 75 miles

Built in 1903 by architect William Corlett, 1801 First Inn is an elegant boutique bed and breakfast property in the heart of downtown Napa. Stylish décor with natural colors will relax you immediately. With only 5 spacious suites, 2 cozy cottages and the Carriage House, your comfortable guest room offers a luxurious bed with sateen linens, bath with large soaking tub or Jacuzzi, plush bathrobes and romantic fireplace. After a restful night's sleep, treat yourself to a gourmet 3-course breakfast prepared by the inn's private chef! In the evening, wine, and often tastings from local wineries, and hors d'oeuvres are perfect ways to indulge before dinner. An invigorating morning massage or a late night therapy with candles, music and wine - all given in the privacy of your guest room - will complete your stay.

MILLIKEN CREEK INN & SPA

1815 SILVERADO TRAIL, NAPA, CALIFORNIA 94558
Tel: +1 707 255 1197 **Fax:** +1 707 255 3112 **U.S./Canada Toll Free:** 1 800 809 2986
Web: www.johansens.com/milliken **E-mail:** info@millikencreekinn.com

On the banks of the Napa River, this intimate and elegant inn is nothing short of magical. The estate has a lively history dating back to 1857 when the main building served as a stagecoach stop during the days of the California Gold Rush. One of its most notable attributes is the attention to detail. Drawing from exotic Indian and Thai influences, the décor of the rooms enhances the placid beauty of the property. Everything from the gentle music and dimmed lighting that welcomes you to your room, to the linens, towels and French spa, has been impeccably chosen. This a special destination with special touches such as Magic Hour, a wine and gourmet cheese reception with local vintners pouring their favorite selections, complimentary breakfast served wherever you wish within the property, and an exclusive luxury spa.

Our inspector loved: *The luxurious rooms with patios overlooking the peaceful garden and Napa River.*

Price Guide: (including breakfast)
rooms $325-$800

SPA

Awards/Ratings: Previous Recipient of Wine Spectator Award of Excellence

Attractions: Napa River and Wine Train, 1 mile; Vineyards and Wine Tasting, 1 mile; Napa Fine Dining, 1 mile; Fishing, Golfing, Hiking, 5 miles
Towns/Cities: Yountville, 9 miles; Sonoma, 15 miles; St. Helena, 17 miles; Calistoga, 27 miles
Airports: Sonoma Airport, 48 miles; Oakland Airport, 51 miles; San Francisco Airport, 58 miles

THE ISLAND HOTEL NEWPORT BEACH

690 NEWPORT CENTER DRIVE, NEWPORT BEACH, CALIFORNIA 92660
Tel: +1 949 759 0808 **Fax:** +1 949 759 0568 **U.S./Canada Toll Free:** 1 888 321 4752
Web: www.johansens.com/newportbeach **E-mail:** reservations@theislandhotel.com

Our inspector loved: *The casual elegance, and great location*

Price Guide: (excluding taxes)
rooms from $405
suites from $615

Awards/Ratings: AAA 5 Diamond

Attractions: Shopping at Fashion Island, 2-min walk; Newport Harbor, 2 miles; Irvine Barclay Theater, 5 miles; Orange County Performing Arts Center, 7 miles
Towns/Cities: Corona Del Mar, 2 miles; Laguna Beach, 9 miles; Anaheim, 19 miles; Los Angeles, 44 miles
Airports: John Wayne Airport, 6 miles; Los Angeles Airport, 45 miles

Affiliations: The Leading Hotels of the World

Overlooking the nearby islands of Balboa, Lido and Catalina, The Island Hotel is a luxurious coastal gem with an aura of relaxation. The accommodations come in warm, neutral tones and feature balconies or furnished patios offering views of the Pacific and Newport Harbor. Original art, marble bathrooms, custom-designed mattresses, Italian linens, goose down and curtains designed to block out the light, are standard fittings throughout. For those desiring more space, the 1 or 2-bedroom Pacific Suites offer spacious living and dining areas. Food is taken seriously at Palm Terrace, the hotel's restaurant headed by acclaimed Executive Chef Bill Bracken. The innovative American cuisine is served in a tropical and elegant ambience or on the terrace, overlooking the pool and lush gardens.

CHÂTEAU DU SUREAU & SPA

48688 VICTORIA LANE, OAKHURST, CALIFORNIA 93644
Tel: +1 559 683 6860 **Fax:** +1 559 683 0800
Web: www.johansens.com/chateausureau **E-mail:** chateau@chateausureau.com

Our inspector loved: *The great full-service spa.*

Price Guide:
rooms $375-$575
suites $2,800

SPA

Awards/Ratings: Mobil 5 Star; AAA 5 Diamond; Condé Nast Johansens Most Excellent Inn, U.S.A. & Canada 2007

Attractions: Bass Lake, 10 miles; Sierra National Forest, 30 miles; Yosemite National Park, 45 miles
Towns/Cities: Merced, 65 miles; Fresno, 55 miles
Airports: Fresno Airport, 55 miles

Affiliations: Relais & Châteaux

Situated in a nature lover's paradise, with a backdrop of Yosemite National Park, this romantic haven will immediately make you feel relaxed in its warm and luxurious ambience. There are only 12 guest rooms and each is immaculately designed and appointed to incorporate a sense of traditional luxury and style while providing every modern convenience. The carefully chosen soft furnishings complement beautiful antique pieces and encourage you to indulge in lazy days spent reading and enjoying the comfort of indoors. Over the kitchen door hangs a quotation from Oscar Wilde, "I have the simplest of tastes, I only want the best," and this is reflected in Erna's Elderberry House restaurant where a French country estate atmosphere has been created. 2 and 3-day cooking courses can be arranged.

THE INN AT RANCHO SANTA FE

5951 LINEA DEL CIELO, RANCHO SANTA FE, CALIFORNIA 92067
Tel: +1 858 756 1131 **Fax:** +1 858 759 1604 **U.S./Canada Toll Free:** 1 800 843 4661
Web: www.johansens.com/ranchosantafe **E-mail:** reservations@theinnatrsf.com

Our inspector loved: The romantic setting among California's golden foothills.

Price Guide:
rooms $295-$420
suites $610-$1,350

Attractions: Del Mar Racetrack, 3 miles; Old Town San Diego, 20 miles; San Diego Zoo and Seaworld, 25 miles; Temecula Wine Country and Ballooning, 45-min drive
Towns/Cities: Del Mar, 6 miles; La Jolla, 15 miles; San Diego, 20 miles; San Clemente, 40 miles
Airports: Palomar Airport, 10 miles; Montgomery Field Airport, 15 miles; San Diego International Airport, 20 miles

This romantic inn is set amidst 23 acres of beautifully landscaped grounds in the center of the exclusive upscale residential community of Rancho Santa Fe. Designed in 1924 by Lillian Rice, one of the first female architects in California, the inn is a unique example of Spanish Colonial revival style. The beautifully newly renovated guest rooms, including 14 suites and several individual Spanish-tiled cottages with up to 3 bedrooms, are dotted around the gardens, surrounding the original main building. Many rooms offer private outdoor patios and the romance of wood-burning fireplaces. The Dining Room serves Rancho cuisine that celebrates the history and harvest of Southern California in a romantic courtyard setting, while the new poolside restaurant, Innfusion, is where East meets West. Unique amenities include a croquet lawn, and box seats and turf club passes are available during the thoroughbred racing season.

TOWER23 HOTEL

4551 OCEAN BLVD., SAN DIEGO, CALIFORNIA 92109
Tel: +1 858 270 2323 **Fax:** +1 858 274 2333 **U.S./Canada Toll Free:** 1 866 TOWER23
Web: www.johansens.com/tower23 **E-mail:** Reserve23@t23hotel.com

Our inspector loved: *Enjoying the ocean breeze and view from the restaurant.*

Price Guide:
spirit pads $179-$389
sky pads $199-$409
surf pads $259-$469

Tower23 Hotel has a beautiful beach hotel atmosphere in both architecture and design. Its 44 sleek, modernist rooms are divided into 3 types: Spirit, Sky, and Surf Pads and 2 distinctive suite categories: Sanctuary and Sweet. Each features a signature Serenity bed, step-in rain shower, plush bathrobes by Boca Terry, Egyptian cotton bath towels and customized bar and nutrition centers. The fresh design schemes include private balconies or patios, high-end amenities and teak furnishings. Massage and spa services are available en suite. In the evenings, the Tower Deck is the ultimate place to watch spectacular sunsets while lounging on a teak chaise. The indoor/outdoor ocean-front restaurant, JRDN Surf:Sky:Spirit, features California fresh cuisine in a hip, contemporary environment.

Attractions: Beach Cruising and Bike Trails, 1-min walk; Surfing and Fishing, 1-min walk; Jet Skiing and Windsurfing, 10-min walk; Golf, 15-min drive
Towns/Cities: La Jolla, 3 miles; Coronado, 10 miles; Del Mar, 10 miles; San Clemente, 55 miles
Airports: San Diego International Airport, 10 miles; Palomar Airport, 30 miles

THE UNION STREET INN

2229 UNION STREET, SAN FRANCISCO, CALIFORNIA 94123
Tel: +1 415 346 0424 **Fax:** +1 415 922 8046
Web: www.johansens.com/unionstreetsf **E-mail:** innkeeper@unionstreetinn.com

Our inspector loved: *The delicious daily baked home-made cakes and cookies in the parlor.*

Price Guide: (including breakfast)
rooms $189-$289

Attractions: Union Street Shopping; Golden Gate Bridge, 2 miles; Fisherman's Wharf, 20-min walk; Alcatraz Tour, 30-min walk
Towns/Cities: Napa/Sonoma, 37 miles; Monterey/Big Sur, 84 miles; Russian River, 60 miles
Airports: San Francisco International Airport, 15 miles; Oakland Airport, 21 miles

Imagine taking afternoon tea in an English cottage garden, surrounded by a wealth of colors from magnificent potted plants and aromas of roses, lavender, sage and rosemary while only being a short stroll from the most fashionable shopping and dining district of San Francisco. This becomes possible while staying here. The owners of this elegant Edwardian home pride themselves on offering guests the ultimate hospitality experience and place enormous emphasis on their home-away-from-home, relaxing ambience. All of the bedrooms are individually decorated with antique furniture, rich fabrics and exquisite artwork. The Carriage House is extremely quiet and private with a bubbling Jacuzzi in the center of the room, ideal for a honeymooning couple.

INN ABOVE TIDE

30 EL PORTAL, SAUSALITO, CALIFORNIA 94965
Tel: +1 415 332 9535 **Fax:** +1 415 332 6714 **U.S./Canada Toll Free:** 1 800 893 8433
Web: www.johansens.com/innabovetide **E-mail:** stay@innabovetide.com

Our inspector loved: *The stunning views of San Francisco Bay.*

Price Guide:
rooms $285-$975

Attractions: Coastal Bike Trails, on the doorstep; Golden Gate Bridge, 5 miles; Golden Gate National Recreation Area, 5 miles; Golden Gate Park, 10-min walk
Towns/Cities: Downtown San Francisco, 10 miles; Napa, 20 miles; Sonoma, 20 miles; Healdsburg 50 miles
Airports: San Francisco Airport, 30 miles; Oakland Airport, 35 miles

There can be few more spectacular settings than this relaxing retreat situated on the waters of San Francisco Bay. The inn claims, "There are hundreds of hotels around San Francisco Bay. There is, however, only one on it." Each room and suite is carefully and luxuriously designed with private decks on the bay where waves lap just below your feet. Many of the bedrooms have fireplaces, which in winter provide wonderful coziness while watching the otters play in the waters outside. Generous breakfasts can be served in your room, private deck or in the drawing room; during sunset, enjoy cheese and wine while taking in the panoramic City skyline and Bay or water views. The concierge will happily arrange dinner reservations and spa treatments.

HARBOR VIEW INN

28 WEST CABRILLO BOULEVARD, SANTA BARBARA, CALIFORNIA 93101
Tel: +1 805 963 0780 **Fax:** +1 805 963 7967 **U.S./Canada Toll Free:** 1 800 755 0222
Web: www.johansens.com/harborview **E-mail:** sylvie@harborviewinnsb.com

Our inspector loved: The stunning ocean-view suites with beautiful mosaic bathrooms.

Price Guide:
rooms $175-$425
suites $255-$795

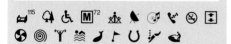

Attractions: Stearns Wharf, 2-min walk; Santa Barbara Shopping and Dining, 1 mile
Towns/Cities: Santa Barbara, 1 mile; San Luis Obispo, 90 miles
Airports: Santa Barbara Airport, 11 miles; Los Angeles Airport, 95 miles

This ocean-front hotel lies across the white sands of West Beach and the historic Stearn's Wharf, just a short stroll from Santa Barbara's downtown boutiques and attractions. Casually elegant and inviting, the spacious and well-appointed rooms and 13 luxury suites all have a private patio or balcony. Eladio's Restaurant & Bar serves California comfort food and looks out to gorgeous panoramic views. The heated fountain patio is an ideal place to relax, enjoy a great meal and people watch. Cocktails are also served and there is a bar with an extensive list of regional and international wines. The Harbor View Inn's impressive location is ideal for those of you interested in water sports such as kayaking and surfing.

THE SANTA YNEZ INN

3627 SAGUNTO STREET, SANTA YNEZ, CALIFORNIA 93460-0628

Tel: +1 805 688 5588 **Fax:** +1 805 686 4294 **U.S./Canada Toll Free:** 1 800 643 5774
Web: www.johansens.com/santaynez **E-mail:** info@santaynezinn.com

Our inspector loved: The wonderful European spa tubs.

Price Guide:
rooms $295-$405
junior suites $495

SPA

This charming property exudes the grace of a bygone era. The 14 rooms and junior suites are individually appointed with antiques, frette linens, whirlpool marble baths and private balconies or patios affording panoramic vistas of the Santa Ynez Valley. Gourmet treats, served in the elegant parlor area, are complemented by fine wines from the well-stocked cellar, while flower essence energy massages and sage and warm stone treatments can be enjoyed in the spa area. Relax in the heated whirlpool or enjoy the sundeck before indulging in a wine tasting tour at one of the many nearby wineries. Outdoor activities include glider rides above the valley, golf at Rancho San Marcos, horseback riding in Rancho Oso's superb mountain setting, hiking and eagle watching.

Attractions: Wine Tasting, 5 miles; Horseback Riding, 5 miles; Museums and Missions, 5 miles; Golf, 10 miles
Towns/Cities: Solvang, 3 miles; Santa Barbara, 30 miles; Santa Maria, 30 miles
Airports: Santa Barbara Airport, 45 miles

LEDSON HOTEL & HARMONY LOUNGE

480 FIRST STREET EAST, SONOMA, CALIFORNIA 95476
Tel: +1 707 996 9779 **Fax:** +1 707 996 9776
Web: www.johansens.com/ledsonhotel **E-mail:** info@ledsonhotel.com

Our inspector loved: *The charming, majestic rooms, and wonderful ambience of Sonoma Plaza.*

Price Guide: (including Continental breakfast) rooms $350-$395

Attractions: Napa and Sonoma Wineries, 1 mile; Fine Dining, 1 mile; Ledson Winery and Vineyards, 13 miles; Russian River Activities, 25 miles
Towns/Cities: Napa, 10 miles; Russian River, 25 miles; Calistoga, 35 miles
Airports: Sonoma Airport, 10 miles; San Francisco Airport, 45 miles; Oakland Airport, 50 miles

Blending into the rustic background of Sonoma stands this charming Old World-style hotel, conceived by Sonoma farmer and winemaker Steve Ledson. Situated on the historic Sonoma Plaza, the property is elegant, romantic and offers 6 bedrooms on the upper floor. Each has its own tasteful design and features intricately designed wood flooring, fine linens and crystal fixtures in the bathrooms. The impressive décor continues throughout the hotel: the Harmony Lounge spans the ground floor and incorporates cool marble and warm hand-carved wood. You are invited to enjoy handcrafted, world-class wines and cocktails at the bar and mouth-watering light fare that is accompanied by an extensive list of wines. Inside the stylish bar and lounge bask in the glow of the fireplace, while outside, take in the sunset at a sidewalk table.

MEADOWOOD NAPA VALLEY

900 MEADOWOOD LANE, ST. HELENA, CALIFORNIA 94574
Tel: +1 707 963 3646 **Fax:** +1 707 963 3532 **U.S./Canada Toll Free:** 1 800 458 8080
Web: www.johansens.com/meadowood **E-mail:** reservations@meadowood.com

Our inspector loved: *The quiet and serene environment, and well-appointed fitness center.*

Price Guide:
rooms $500-$920
suites $875-$6,775

Meadowood is an elegant private estate nestled in over 250 acres in the beautiful Napa Valley. It is a center for social, cultural and viticultural life, and as soon as you leave the highway, there is an overwhelming sense of tranquility and relaxation. The grounds are perfect for both relaxing weekend retreats and extravagant country parties, and the clubhouse commands a magnificent position overlooking the lawns. Most guests rooms have their own private decks from which to enjoy the surroundings, and you can choose where to take breakfast, whether in your room, on the deck or even as a picnic to take out into the countryside. The Restaurant, and the more informal Grill, serve a careful balance of fresh flavors with tempting colors and aromas.

Attractions: Hiking, within the grounds; Wineries, 2 miles; World-Class Restaurants, 2 miles; Art Galleries and Antique Shopping, 2 miles
Towns/Cities: St. Helena, 2 miles; Rutherford, 5 miles; Oakville, 10 miles; Yountville, 15 miles
Airports: San Francisco Airport, 105-min drive; Oakland Airport, 105-min drive; Sacramento Airport, 105-min drive

Affiliations: Relais & Châteaux

Colorado

SOUTH DAKOTA

Casper

WYOMING

Wheatland

Alliance

NEBRASKA

Rawlins

Green
River

Kimball

Ogallala

Laramie

CHEYENNE ★

Vernal

Julesburg

Craig

Steamboat
Springs 105

Fort Collins

Greeley

Sterling

Holyoke

Meeker

Hot Sulphur Springs

Boulder
98

Brighton

Fort Morgan

Wray

UTAH

Rifle

108
109

Denver Int. Airport

Vail

Golden 100
101 DENVER

Glenwood Springs

Littleton

102

Grand Junction

Aspen

Leadville

Castle Rock

Burlington

Colby

Moab

Delta 99

Montrose 104

Gunnison

Salida

103 Colorado Springs

City of Colorado Springs Airport

Cheyenne Wells

KANSAS

Cañon City

Eads

Telluride 107
106

Pueblo

Lamar

La Junta Las Animas

Cortez

Pagosa Springs

Alamosa

Walsenburg

Ulysses

Durango

Trinidad

Springfield

RIZONA

Aztec

Raton

OKLAHOMA Guymon

Taos

NEW MEXICO

Gallup

TEXAS

Amarillo

★
SANTA FE

Hugo

97

THE BRADLEY BOULDER INN

2040 16TH STREET, BOULDER, COLORADO 80302
Tel: +1 303 545 5200 **Fax:** +1 303 440 6740 **U.S./Canada Toll Free:** 1 800 858 5811
Web: www.johansens.com/bradleyboulderinn **E-mail:** reservations@thebradleyboulder.com

Our inspector loved: The Great Room with its polished wooden floor, crackling fire and stunning original artwork.

Price Guide: (including breakfast)
rooms $160-$200

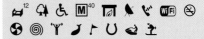

Attractions: Pearl Street Mall, 1-min walk; Art Galleries, 3-min walk; Hiking and Mountain Biking, 5-min drive; University of Colorado, 5-min drive
Towns/Cities: Denver, 30 miles
Airports: Denver, 45 miles

Set in a residential and picturesque neighborhood of downtown Boulder, The Bradley Boulder Inn is a lovely retreat for a romantic getaway or short business stay. Each of the comfortable and stylish rooms has a Jacuzzi tub, a mountain view from a balcony, luxury fine linens, Aveda bath amenities, flat-screen T.V. and selection of movies on D.V.D. A sumptuous breakfast is provided each morning in the dining room, and in the evenings you can gather around the artwork in the magnificent Great Room while complimentary wine and cheese is served. The stunning art collection is provided by some of Boulder's top galleries, shown in changing rotation throughout the year. Before exploring the area, why not enjoy home-made cookies and bottled water, a treat for guests on the go.

SMITH FORK RANCH

45362 NEEDLEROCK ROAD, CRAWFORD, COLORADO 81415
Tel: +1 970 921 3454 **Fax:** +1 970 921 3475
Web: www.johansens.com/smithfork **E-mail:** info@smithforkranch.com

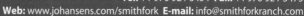

Our inspector loved: *The private and lovely wilderness location with fly fishing at the door, friendly horses to ride, gourmet food and wine, and a dedicated staff giving attention to details throughout.*

Price Guide: (per person, including activities and meals)
$425-$510

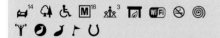

Attractions: Rock Formations and Smith Fork of the Gunnison River, 1-min walk; Black Canyon of the Gunnison, 20 miles; Aspen, 113 miles; Telluride Ski and Recreation, 125 miles
Towns/Cities: Grand Junction, 77 miles; Aspen, 113 miles; Telluride, 125 miles
Airports: Montrose Airport, 60 miles; Grand Junction Airport, 77 miles; Aspen Airport, 113 miles

Halfway between Aspen and Telluride lies Smith Fork Ranch, one of North America's most secluded mountain retreats. Guests come here to enjoy the tranquility and charm of rustic life without sacrificing luxury and comfort. Smith Fork Ranch blends the old with the new: many of the ranch's buildings retain their original 19th-century form and character but have been refurbished to offer modern comforts and luxury. Cozy, individual guest cabins offer privacy along with a taste of the rustic life without the drawbacks of roughing-it! Daytime activities include trail rides led by experienced guides, fishing and hiking through Colorado's scenic mountain trails. Gourmet cuisine at Smith Fork Ranch features local ingredients such as game meats, poultry and trout combined with Western Colorado's best produce and fruits and an exceptional wine list. For a truly unforgettable and unique experience, enjoy a romantic sunset dinner ride during your stay.

CASTLE MARNE BED & BREAKFAST INN

1572 RACE STREET, DENVER, COLORADO 80206
Tel: +1 303 331 0621 **Fax:** +1 303 331 0623 **U.S./Canada Toll Free:** 1 800 926 2763
Web: www.johansens.com/castlemarne **E-mail:** info@castlemarne.com

Our inspector loved: The surprise of the tree-top level private decks with hot tubs that adjoin several of the rooms.

Price Guide:
rooms $105-$235
suite $260

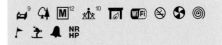

This Victorian home, now an elegant bed and breakfast inn, maintains many vestiges of the castle's past such as hand-rubbed woods, family heirlooms and ornate fireplaces. Following a careful restoration, original features dominate the interior, which is enhanced by Rococo gilt mirrors and fine antiques. The individually decorated bedrooms are stylish and display nuances of the period. Special private 6-course candle-lit dinners can be arranged and the daily delicious breakfasts and afternoon teas are delightful. House specialties include stuffed tomato with egg and spinach purée topped with parmesan and Jack cheeses, and the home-baked cakes and scones at teatime are to die for! The comfortable parlor is ideal for relaxing and reading a book beside the beautifully carved fireplace.

Attractions: Denver Botanic Gardens, 0.5 miles; Cherry Creek Shopping District, 1.5 miles; 16th Street Mall, 1.5 miles; Colorado Convention Center, 1.5 miles
Towns/Cities: Boulder, 25 miles; Colorado Springs, 60 miles
Airports: Denver International Airport, 12 miles

U.S.A. - COLORADO (DENVER)

HOTEL MONACO

1717 CHAMPA STREET AT 17TH, DENVER, COLORADO 80202
Tel: +1 303 296 1717 **Fax:** +1 303 296 1818 **U.S./Canada Toll Free:** 1 800 397 5380
Web: www.johansens.com/monaco **E-mail:** reservations@monaco-denver.com

Our inspector loved: The programs and amenities specially designed to pamper women business travelers.

Price Guide:
rooms $200-$350
suites $300-$1,000

Attractions: Center for the Performing Arts, 5-min walk; Lower Downtown, 5-min walk; Convention Center, 5-min walk; Coors Field, 10-min walk
Towns/Cities: Boulder, 28 miles; Colorado Springs, 60 miles
Airports: Denver International Airport, 23 miles

Situated in the midst of downtown Denver's attractions and sights, those of you seeking a sophisticated getaway will find that the Hotel Monaco embodies the perfect blend of modernity and elegance. Each room boasts a bold and colorful décor that creates a stylish yet inviting atmosphere, and the variety of themed suites offer more luxurious options tailored to individual tastes and preferences. Panzano offers a dining experience not to be missed! Serving an Italian-inspired menu, dishes include home-made pastas and pizzas, fresh seafood, and seasonal vegetables. Within walking distance of Denver Colorado's Convention Center, the 16th Street Mall, and a variety of shops, museums and restaurants. The hotel's convenient location enables you to fully enjoy all of the activities and sights Denver has to offer.

TAHARAA MOUNTAIN LODGE

3110 SO. ST. VRAIN, ESTES PARK, COLORADO 80517
Tel: +1 970 577 0098 **Fax:** +1 970 577 0819 **U.S./Canada Toll Free:** 1 800 597 0098
Web: www.johansens.com/taharaa **E-mail:** info@taharaa.com

Our inspector loved: The uplifting location with great views, and the many fun and challenging mountain activities just minutes away.

Price Guide: (including breakfast)
rooms $163.05-$190.23
suites $195.66-$358.71

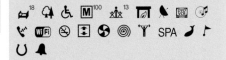

Custom-built in 1997 out of log and stone on a high plateau in the Rocky Mountains, this luxurious hotel was created with comfort and enjoyment in mind and maximizes the impact of the mountains surrounding it. The hotel has stunning large windows, crackling fires and striking wood and stone work throughout. Each bedroom has its own unique theme and benefits from a fireplace and private deck. Breakfast is served in the Dining Room or on the adjacent deck where you can relax in the fresh, clean air surrounded by pine trees. The lodge is the perfect location for wildlife watching, fishing, biking, golf, horse riding, climbing, river rafting, hiking and a host of other exciting outdoor adventures. There is also an excellent solarium and outdoor spa with scenic views.

Attractions: Rocky Mountain National Park, 4 miles; Shopping, 4 miles; Art Galleries, 4 miles; Kayaking, 4 miles
Towns/Cities: Estes Park, 4 miles; Boulder, 35 miles
Airports: Denver Airport, 80 miles

THE CLIFF HOUSE AT PIKES PEAK

306 CAÑON AVENUE, MANITOU SPRINGS, COLORADO 80829
Tel: +1 719 685 3000 **Fax:** +1 719 685 3913 **U.S./Canada Toll Free:** 1 888 212 7000
Web: www.johansens.com/thecliffhouse **E-mail:** info@thecliffhouse.com

Our inspector loved: The gourmet dining experience with fine wine and dinner selections graciously recommended by the knowledgeable staff.

Price Guide: (including breakfast)
rooms $145–$189
suites $199–$475

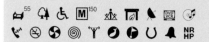

Awards/Ratings: Wine Spectator Award of Excellence 2004-2007

Attractions: Garden of the Gods, 1 mile; Cliff Dwellings, 1 mile; Pikes Peak, 8 miles; Air Force Academy, 10 miles
Towns/Cities: Colorado Springs, 3 miles; Denver, 60 miles
Airports: Colorado Springs Airport, 8 miles; Denver Airport, 70 miles

Built in 1874 as a boarding house, The Cliff House is Colorado's second oldest operating hotel and was originally a key stop on the stagecoach trail. In the last couple of years it has been the subject of a $10-million refurbishment program and is now a hotel full of character that pays tribute to its heritage,while offering the very latest in modern comforts and luxury. Each room and suite is individually designed, and the wonderful "Celebrity" suites pay homage to their previous inhabitants that includes Clark Gable, Teddy Roosevelt, Henry Ford and Buffalo Bill Cody. The hotel has gained wide renown for its gourmet dining and outstanding friendly service, and is a very romantic getaway. The menu is based on Colorado ingredients and traditional French cuisine, enhanced by modern international twists.

ELK MOUNTAIN RESORT

97 ELK WALK, MONTROSE, COLORADO 81401
Tel: +1 970 252 4900 **Fax:** +1 970 252 4913 **U.S./Canada Toll Free:** 1 877 355 9255
Web: www.johansens.com/elkmountain **E-mail:** reservations@elkmountainresort.com

Our inspector loved: *The total privacy of the mountain setting with an attentive staff offering varied and challenging activities, especially the Valhalla Shooting club.*

Price Guide:
deluxe lodge rooms $325
3-bedroom cottages $1,800

Awards/Ratings: Condé Nast Johansens Most Excellent Resort 2006

Attractions: National Forest, 1 mile; Skiing, 65 miles; Shopping, 65 miles
Towns/Cities: Montrose, 15 miles; Telluride, 65 miles
Airports: Montrose Airport, 15 miles; Tellluride Airport, 65 miles

Affiliations: Preferred Boutique

Part of the P.U.R.E. International portfolio, Elk Mountain Resort is simultaneously many things: a hidden romantic getaway, a gourmand's treasure, a spa retreat and a nature lover's paradise. The architecture blends into the natural surrounding environment, and the rustic exteriors of rough hewn log buildings conceal plush interiors. Whether you choose the main building or an independent cottage, all of the accommodations are impeccably appointed and furnished. Each fixture, piece of furniture, painting and linen has been carefully chosen; a philosophy that also extends to the staff. The service at the resort possesses an integrity that provides you with an exceptional experience. Dinner at the Tarragon restaurant is to be savored, as are selections from the impressive wine list. Elk Mountain Resort is a membership club and corporate retreat, and special booking conditions apply.

VISTA VERDE GUEST RANCH

P.O. BOX 770465, STEAMBOAT SPRINGS, COLORADO 80477
Tel: +1 970 879 3858 **Fax:** +1 970 879 6814 **U.S./Canada Toll Free:** 1 800 526 7433
Web: www.johansens.com/vistaverderanch **E-mail:** reservations@vistaverde.com

Our inspector loved: *Fine dining in the rustic lodge followed by songs around a crackling outdoor fire topped off with a soak in a private hot tub under the starlit mountain sky.*

Price Guide: (per person, including activities and meals)
cabins $350-$500

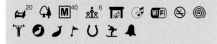

Attractions: Ranch Activities, 1-min walk; Mountain Sports, 1-min walk; Skiing, 25 miles; Shopping, 25 miles
Towns/Cities: Steamboat Springs, 25 miles
Airports: Hayden Airport, 45 miles; Denver Airport, 175 miles

Nestled deep in the Rocky Mountains, Vista Verde is a truly unique ranch experience for all seasons. This 500-acre property provides accommodation in secluded, spacious log cabins or deluxe lodge rooms. In summer the crisp air and clear skies invite you to rise early, enjoy a hearty breakfast and try your hand at fishing, hot-air ballooning, hiking, white-water rafting and kayaking among many other activities on offer. Gourmet dinners are served in the main lodge; on some evenings there is an informal cookout. In fall, the rivers run lower, the elk move back in and the aspens prepare for a magical color extravaganza. A winter ranch experience is a must! You can sleigh ride, cross-country and downhill ski, dog sled, ice climb and horse ride.

FAIRMONT HERITAGE PLACE FRANZ KLAMMER LODGE

567 MOUNTAIN VILLAGE BOULEVARD, TELLURIDE, COLORADO 81435
Tel: +1 970 728 4239 **Fax:** +1 970 728 0788 **U.S./Canada Toll Free:** 1 888 728 0355
Web: www.johansens.com/fairmont **E-mail:** franzklammer@fairmont.com

Our inspector loved: *The spectacular view from the Himmel Spa Suite while awaiting an Aromatherapy Altitude Massage.*

Price Guide: (complimentary transportation from Telluride and Montrose Airports available) 2 and 3-bedroom luxury suites $350-$2,200

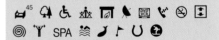

Set in the idyllic pedestrian enclave of Mountain Village, accessible from Telluride by car or complimentary Gondola, the 2 and 3-bedroom luxury residences of the Fairmont Heritage Place Franz Klammer Lodge offer stunning views of Colorado's magnificent San Juan Mountains. The Lodge, which features convenient access to skiing with slopeside ski valet, is decorated with stone, earthy tones, and high, open-beamed ceilings, creating a distinctively alpine atmosphere. Each residence includes a living room with a large, natural gas-stone fireplace, a gourmet kitchen with granite countertops, high, exposed beam or vaulted ceilings, spacious master bathrooms with jetted tubs, and a private balcony. The Lodge boasts a private spa, gameroom, fitness center, outdoor heated swimming pool, and hot tubs.

Attractions: Skiing, 3-min walk; Golf, 5-min walk; Hiking, 5-min walk; Shopping, 15-min gondola ride
Towns/Cities: Telluride, 15-min gondola ride or drive; Montrose, 67 miles
Airports: Telluride Airport (TEX), 15-min drive; Montrose Airport (MTJ), 67 miles; Denver Airport (DEN), 355 miles

THE HOTEL TELLURIDE

199 NORTH CORNET STREET, TELLURIDE, COLORADO 81435
Tel: +1 970 369 1188 **Fax:** +1 970 369 1292 **U.S./Canada Toll Free:** 1 866 468 3501
Web: www.johansens.com/telluride **E-mail:** reservations@thehoteltelluride.com

Our inspector loved: *The wonderful walk-to-everything location, and the helpful staff.*

Price Guide: (including breakfast and complimentary shuttle to town center is available)
rooms $119-$529
suites $269-$999

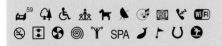

Awards/Ratings: Condé Nast Traveler Gold List 2005

Attractions: Shopping, 3-min walk; Hiking, 5-min walk; Skiing, 5-min walk; Lizardhead Wilderness Area, 15-min drive
Towns/Cities: Ridgway, 35 miles; Montrose, 62 miles
Airports: Telluride Airport, 15-min drive; Montrose Airport, 65 miles; Grand Junction Airport, 125 miles

The sense of understated luxury and alpine ambience at The Hotel Telluride is apparent from the moment you step into its impressive lobby, with its 2-story atrium, vaulted ceiling, massive stone fireplace, iron and antler chandelier, and 360° views of the magnificent San Juan Mountains. The air of mountain rusticity combined with European Old World elegance permeates through the entire hotel, and is reinforced by its heavy stone floors, warm wool rugs and leather furnishings. The luxuriously appointed guest rooms and suites include balconies offering breathtaking mountain views, custom furnishings and The Hotel Telluride's Incredible Beds, a welcome sight after a long day on the slopes. Wake up each morning to a hearty, complimentary breakfast buffet at the Bistro, which also serves drinks, tavern-style appetizers and light dinners.

The Tivoli Lodge at Vail

386 HANSON RANCH ROAD, VAIL, COLORADO 81657
Tel: +1 970 476 5615 **Fax:** +1 970 476 6601 **U.S./Canada Toll Free:** 1 800 451 4756
Web: www.johansens.com/tivoli **E-mail:** reservations@tivolilodge.com

Our inspector loved: *The thoughtful attention to artistic detail evident throughout this Vail landmark.*

Price Guide: (including breakfast)
rooms $179-$699
suites $699-$1,599

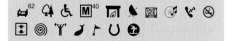

Attractions: Shopping, 3-min walk; Art Galleries, 3-min walk
Towns/Cities: Denver, 60 miles
Airports: Eagle Airport, 30 miles; Denver Airport, 100 miles

The family-owned Tivoli Lodge has earned a well-deserved reputation for providing friendly, caring and personal service. Its European-style architecture blends into the surrounding natural environment with unobstructed views of Vail Mountain and is within steps of Vail's Vista Bahn and Riva Bahn ski lifts. The luxurious and airy lobby looks out to stunning mountain views and is reminiscent of a living room with over-sized chairs, leather sofas, floor-to-ceiling stone fireplace and small wine bar. Wake up to magnificent panoramic views of the mountains in the Peter Seibert Suite or choose to rest in a spacious guest room with mountain or village views. All rooms are appointed with the finest linens and facilities, while mountain view rooms have large soaking bathtubs and separate walk-in showers.

VAIL MOUNTAIN LODGE & SPA

352 EAST MEADOW DRIVE, VAIL, COLORADO 81657

Tel: +1 970 476 0700 **Fax:** +1 970 476 6451 **U.S./Canada Toll Free:** 1 866 476 0700
Web: www.johansens.com/vailmountain **E-mail:** reservations@vailmountainlodge.com

Our inspector loved: The state-of-the-art athletic club and spa, especially soaking in the hot tub at sunset near the rushing waters of Gore Creek.

Price Guide: (including breakfast)
rooms $149-$815
condos $425-$2,600

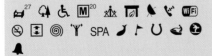

Awards/Ratings: DiRoNA

Attractions: Skiing, 3-min walk; Shopping, 3-min walk; Art Galleries, 3-min walk
Towns/Cities: Beaver Creek, 9 miles; Denver, 90 miles
Airports: Eagle Airport, 30 miles; Denver Airport, 115 miles

Beautifully situated on Gore Creek, Vail Mountain Lodge & Spa captures the charm of rustic camps of yesterday's Yellowstone. Its spacious rooms offer a comfortable and relaxing atmosphere after a long day on the slopes or at the popular Athletic Club. Terra Bistro is a local favorite, whose menu highlights seasonal ingredients influenced by Southwest, Mediterranean and Asian cultures. The Bistro also offers one of the most extensive wine lists in the area. The on-site Vail Athletic Club is an 18,000 sq. ft. gym with state-of-the-art equipment including Vail's only full-size indoor climbing wall and a wide variety of classes. The Spa at Vail Mountain Lodge practices holistic treatments as well as massages and facials designed to be therapeutic rather than superficial.

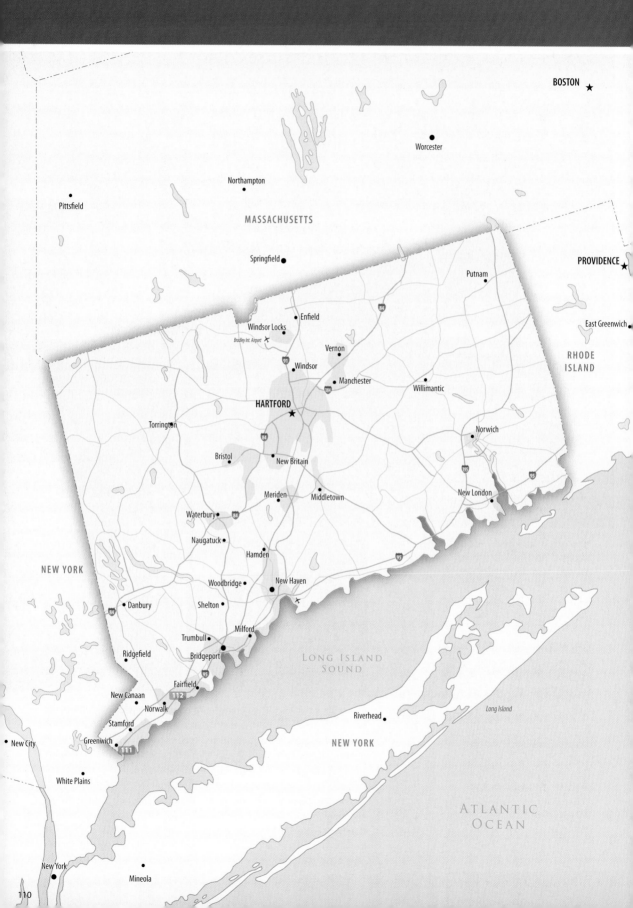

Connecticut

BOSTON ★

Worcester

Northampton

Pittsfield

MASSACHUSETTS

Springfield

Putnam

PROVIDENCE ★

Windsor Locks
Enfield

Bradley Int. Airport

Vernon

East Greenwich

RHODE ISLAND

Windsor

Manchester

Willimantic

HARTFORD ★

Torrington

Norwich

Bristol

New Britain

Meriden

Middletown

New London

Waterbury

Naugatuck

Hamden

NEW YORK

Woodbridge

New Haven

Danbury

Shelton

Milford

Trumbull

Ridgefield

Bridgeport

LONG ISLAND SOUND

Fairfield

112

New Canaan

Norwalk

Riverhead

Long Island

Stamford

NEW YORK

New City

Greenwich

111

White Plains

New York

ATLANTIC OCEAN

Mineola

DELAMAR GREENWICH HARBOR

500 STEAMBOAT ROAD, GREENWICH, CONNECTICUT 06830
Tel: +1 203 661 9800 **Fax:** +1 203 661 2513 **U.S./Canada Toll Free:** 1 866 335 2627
Web: www.johansens.com/delamar **E-mail:** info@thedelamar.com

Our inspector loved: *The luxurious treatments at the new Spa Delamar.*

Price Guide:
rooms $369-$469
suites $600-$1,600

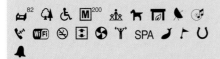

Attractions: Bruce Museum, 5-min walk; Todd's Point Beach, 10-min drive; Audubon Center, 15-min drive; Greenwich Polo Club, 8 miles
Towns/Cities: Old Greenwich, 5 miles; Stamford, 6 miles; White Plains, 14 miles; Manhattan, NY, 36 miles
Airports: White Plains Airport, 20-min drive; LaGuardia Airport, 45-min drive; J.F.K. Airport, 55-min drive

Affiliations: Small Luxury Hotels of the World

Situated in a spectacular waterfront location on Greenwich Harbor, this luxury hotel is built in the style of a beautiful Tuscan villa, with an authentic terracotta-tiled roof and soft yellow stucco walls. Inside, quality fabrics, subtle colors and distinctive Mediterranean furnishings abound, and the walls are adorned with original paintings and artworks, many of which come from a renowned private collection in Greenwich. Guest rooms are elegant with Italian linens, down duvets and spacious bathrooms with coral marble vanities and deep cast-iron tubs with all the amenities for a business traveler or luxury weekend away. Culinary delights and fine wines can be sampled at the waterfront L'Escale Restaurant & Bar, which serves inventive Provençal cuisine. The hotel has its own private dock, which berths yachts up to 160 feet.

THE INN AT NATIONAL HALL

2 POST ROAD WEST, WESTPORT, CONNECTICUT 06880

Tel: +1 203 221 1351 **Fax:** +1 203 221 0276 **U.S./Canada Toll Free:** 1 800 628 4255
Web: www.johansens.com/nationalhall **E-mail:** info@innatnationalhall.com

Our inspector loved: The opulent and elegant décor.

Price Guide: (including breakfast)
rooms $325-$380
suites $545-$850

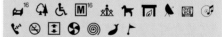

This Italianate-style red brick building is idyllically set along a picturesque waterfront and is within a short stroll of fashionable Westport's shops, restaurants and galleries. Beautiful cherry woodwork and an eclectic mix of antiques and luscious fabrics combine to create the inspiring atmosphere of Old World opulence and sophistication. Each bedroom and suite is decorated to the highest possible standard of comfort and is filled with four-poster beds, hand-stencilled walls, lavish furnishings and meticulous attention to detail. Most rooms have scenic views over the Saugatuck River. Relax in the large yet cozy common room by the fireplace, or explore the surrounding neighborhood. During the summer, Westport comes alive with theater and musical productions held at the summer playhouse and outdoor riverside pavilion.

Attractions: Westport Country Playhouse, 5-min drive; Sherwood Island State Park, 10-min drive; Bruce Museum Greenwich, 15-min drive
Towns/Cities: Stamford, 14 miles; Greenwich, 19 miles; New York City, NY, 50 miles; Hartford, 50 miles
Airports: Westchester County Airport, 40-min drive; J.F.K./L.G.A. Airport, 1-hour drive; Hartford Airport, 1-hour drive

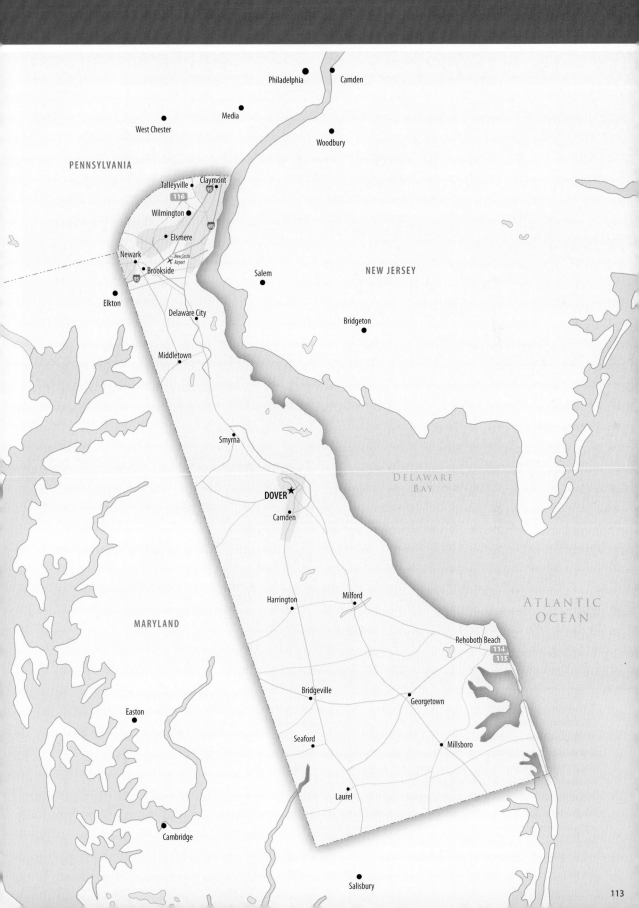

Philadelphia

Camden

Media

West Chester

Woodbury

PENNSYLVANIA

Talleyville
Claymont
116
Wilmington
495
Elsmere

Newark
New Castle
Airport
Brookside
95

NEW JERSEY

Salem

Elkton

Delaware City

Bridgeton

Middletown

Smyrna

DELAWARE
BAY

DOVER ★

Camden

Harrington

Milford

ATLANTIC
OCEAN

MARYLAND

Rehoboth Beach
114
115

Bridgeville

Georgetown

Easton

Seaford

Millsboro

Laurel

Cambridge

Salisbury

THE BELLMOOR

SIX CHRISTIAN STREET, REHOBOTH BEACH, DELAWARE 19971
Tel: +1 302 227 5800 **Fax:** +1 302 227 0323 **U.S./Canada Toll Free:** 1 800 425 2355
Web: www.johansens.com/thebellmoor **E-mail:** info@thebellmoor.com

Our inspector loved: The lovely rooms, tranquil garden area and full-service spa.

Price Guide: (including breakfast)
rooms $125-$345
suites $195-$645

Attractions: Rehoboth Beach/Boardwalk, 0.5 miles
Towns/Cities: Dover, 45 miles; Wilmington, 85 miles
Airports: B.W.I. Airport, 110 miles; Philadelphia Airport, 110 miles

This warm and residential inn combines old-fashioned hospitality with first-class accommodations in the perfect seaside setting. The comfortable guest rooms range from garden and deluxe rooms to the generously sized Bellmoor Club Suites, accessible only by private elevator key. After a long day at the beach, cozy up next to the in-room fireplace, soak in the Ultra Masseur hydrotherapy tub or enjoy a drink from the wet bar. The Bellmoor Club Library serves snacks and drinks and is a wonderful place to read a book nestled by the fire. Start your day with the complimentary country breakfast, and in the afternoon enjoy cookies and tea in the beautiful garden setting. The full-service Spa at The Bellmoor offers over 40 different services.

BOARDWALK PLAZA HOTEL

OLIVE AVENUE & THE BOARDWALK, REHOBOTH BEACH, DELAWARE 19971
Tel: +1 302 227 7169 **Fax:** +1 302 227 0561 **U.S./Canada Toll Free:** 1 800 332 3224
Web: www.johansens.com/boardwalkplaza **E-mail:** reservations@boardwalkplaza.com

Our inspector loved: The smiling, attentive staff, and the prime beach-front location.

Price Guide:
rooms $119-$479
suites $139-$529

Attractions: Rehoboth Beach and Boardwalk; Boutiques, Restaurants, Antiquing and Shopping, 5-min walk; Over 100 Outlet Stores, 5-min drive

Towns/Cities: Dewey Beach, 5-min drive; Historic Lewes, 10-min drive

Airports: Wilmington Airport, 90 miles; Philadelphia International Airport, 112 miles; Ronald Reagan Washington National Airport, 127 miles

Built in 1990, this Victorian-styled hotel, set in a premier resort town, will make you feel as if you have stepped into the past. The lively resident parrots welcome you to the lobby of this friendly hotel where the owners' collection of antiques and fine period reproductions enhances the recreated Victorian era elegance in each room. Soak in the spa pool after a jog on the beach or enjoy traditional afternoon tea in the elegant dining room. Victoria's Restaurant has beautiful views of the Atlantic from every table where you can sample an array of tasty dishes made with the freshest ingredients for breakfast, lunch and dinner. For drinks and lighter fare relax in the adjacent Plaza Pub. Enjoy the ultimate in pampering and inquire about the adults-only concierge floor, which offers upgraded amenities and access to the private rooftop sundeck and hot tub.

Inn at Montchanin Village

ROUTE 100 & KIRK ROAD, MONTCHANIN, WILMINGTON, DELAWARE 19710
Tel: +1 302 888 2133 **Fax:** +1 302 888 0389 **U.S./Canada Toll Free:** 1 800 269 2473
Web: www.johansens.com/montchanin **E-mail:** inn@montchanin.com

Our inspector loved: The beautiful gardens and first-class restaurant.

Price Guide: (excluding 8% tax)
rooms $185-$235
suites $279-$399

Attractions: Winterthur Museum, 1 mile; Hagley Museum, 2 miles; Longwood Gardens, 12 miles; Brandywine River Museum, 12 miles
Towns/Cities: Wilmington, 4 miles; Philadelphia, 28 miles; Washington D.C., 110 miles; New York City, 115 miles
Airports: Philadelphia Airport, 23 miles; Baltimore/Washington Airport, 80 miles; Newark/New Jersey Airport, 110 miles

Affiliations: Small Luxury Hotels of the World

Montchanin is a historical and charming 19th-century hamlet in the Brandywine Valley. This lovingly restored, family-run hotel retains a whimsical atmosphere of Colonial splendor that is quiet and romantic. Each of the immaculately decorated rooms is brimming with beautiful antiques and period reproductions, yet provide you with all the conveniences of a modern hotel. The spacious and exquisite bedrooms are individually decorated with an emphasis on luxury and comfort with beautiful frette linens and lovely fresh flowers. Most rooms have immaculately landscaped private courtyards and several have cozy fireplaces. The overall attention to detail creates a gracious and restful ambience. Krazy Kat's Restaurant, once the blacksmith's shop, has a fun and eclectic décor, and serves the most mouth-watering international cuisine.

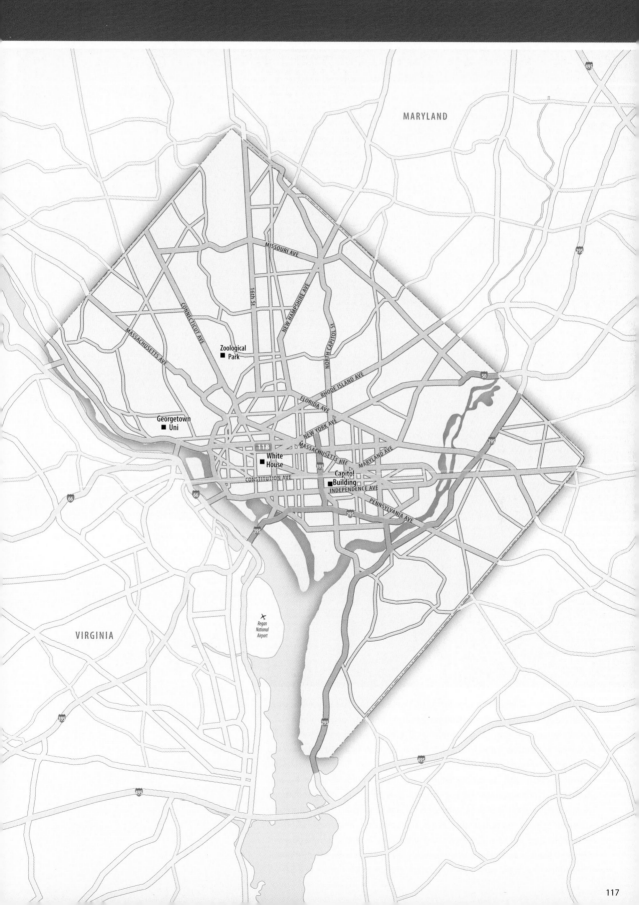

MARYLAND

MISSOURI AVE

16th St

NEW HAMPSHIRE AVE

NORTH CAPITOL ST

CONNECTICUT AVE

MASSACHUSETTS AVE

Zoological
■ Park

RHODE ISLAND AVE

FLORIDA AVE

Georgetown
■ Uni

NEW YORK AVE

118

MASSACHUSETTS AVE

MARYLAND AVE

White
■ House

D

395

Capitol
Building

CONSTITUTION AVE

INDEPENDENCE AVE

66

66

PENNSYLVANIA AVE

295

395

VIRGINIA

✈
Regan
National
Airport

395

495

50

295

295

495

495

THE HAY-ADAMS

SIXTEENTH & H. STREETS N.W., WASHINGTON D.C., DISTRICT OF COLUMBIA 20006
Tel: +1 202 638 6600 **Fax:** +1 202 638 2716 **U.S./Canada Toll Free:** 1 800 424 5054
Web: www.johansens.com/hayadams **E-mail:** info@hayadams.com

Our inspector loved: *The uninterrupted view of The White House.*

Price Guide:
rooms $425-$925
suites $1,300-$6,000

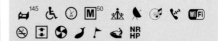

Awards/Ratings: Condé Nast Johansens Most Excellent Hotel, U.S.A. & Canada 2007; Condé Nast Johansens Most Excellent Service 2006

Attractions: The White House, 0.1 miles; Smithsonian Museum, 0.3 miles; National Monuments, 0.3 miles; The Mint, 0.3 miles
Airports: Reagan National Airport, 3 miles; Dulles International Airport, 26 miles

Affiliations: The Leading Hotels of the World

Located across Lafayette Square from The White House, The Hay-Adams has retained its popularity and importance in the social life of Washington. Its Italian Renaissance architecture reflects the elegance of the interior with traditional furnishings and eye-catching antiques complemented by neutral tones and contemporary furniture. Upon entering, you will be amazed by the opulent lobby with its ornate ceiling, mahogany-colored paneling and European color schemes. Each bedroom is individually designed to an exceptionally high standard with plush sofas, canopied beds, uniquely detailed ceilings and remarkable views. The Lafayette restaurant is flooded with light and features Chippendale-style chairs and crystal chandeliers. Superb cuisine is served here together with an impressive selection of wines. For a light meal or delicious midnight snack, retreat to Off the Record bar.

ALABAMA

GEORGIA

Brewton

Albany

Dothan

Savannah

Crestview

Milton
Pensacola

De Funiak Springs

Cairo

Nashville

Marianna

Valdosta

Brunswick

Panama City

Quincy

TALLAHASSEE

Perry

Live Oak

Jacksonville
Int. Airport

Fernandina Beach

Lake City

Jacksonville

Starke

Green
Cove Sprs.

St. Augustine

Gainseville

Palatka

ATLANTIC
OCEAN

Ocala

GULF OF MEXICO

Inverness

De Land

Daytona Beach

Tavares

Sanford

Brooksville

Orlando

Titusville

Dade City

Orlando Int. Airport

Clearwater

Tampa Int. Airport

Tampa

Kissimmee

Cocoa Beach

St. Petersburg

Bartow

Bradenton

Sarasota

Sebring

Vero Beach

Arcadia

Fort Pierce

Punta Gorda

Stuart

Ft. Myers

Southwest Florida
Int. Airport

W. Palm Beach

Naples

Palm Beach
Int. Airport

Fort Lauderdale

Fort Lauderdale-Hollywood
Int. Airport

THE BAHAMAS

Miami Int. Airport

Miami

Key Largo

Key West

119

GROVE ISLE HOTEL & SPA

FOUR GROVE ISLE DRIVE, COCONUT GROVE, FLORIDA 33133
Tel: +1 305 858 8300 **Fax:** +1 305 858 5908 **U.S./Canada Toll Free:** 1 800 884 7683
Web: www.johansens.com/groveisle **E-mail:** reservations@groveisle.com

Our inspector loved: The spectacular views while dining by the water.

Price Guide:
rooms $259-$689
suites $429-$859

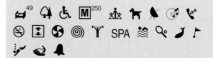

This private 20-acre gated island sanctuary offers a peaceful and secure respite. Lush gardens, views of Biscayne Bay, original artwork and guests sipping martinis by the pool as yachts dock at the marina below, create the ambience of a private luxury residence. Accommodations feature Italian marble bathrooms, iron four-poster beds, and balconies with views of the bay and shoreline of Miami. BALEENmiami, the fine dining restaurant, serves Euro-Asian fare that can also be enjoyed "Dining on the Rocks" in a tropical ocean-front setting. Alternately, choose the Palapa Bar for lighter poolside bites, island-style cuisine on the open-air loggia or an evening meal in the comfort of your very own room. The 6000 sq. ft. SpaTerre offers exotic Balinese spa treatments and Thai body rituals with a private couple's Zen steam room, outdoor yoga deck, Watsu pool and full-service salon.

Attractions: Patrick McEnroe Tennis Center, on-site; Vizcaya Museum and Gardens, 0.8 miles; CocoWalk, 1.5 miles; South Beach, 5 miles
Towns/Cities: Miami, 5 miles
Airports: Miami International Airport, 10 miles

FISHER ISLAND HOTEL & RESORT

ONE FISHER ISLAND DRIVE, FISHER ISLAND, FLORIDA 33109
Tel: +1 305 535 6000 **Fax:** +1 305 535 6003 **U.S./Canada Toll Free:** 1 800 537 3708
Web: www.johansens.com/fisherisland **E-mail:** hotel@fisherislandclub.com

Our inspector loved: *Spending an afternoon at the private Beach Club.*

Price Guide: (including welcome drink of champagne or Fisher Island mimosa, full access to recreational amenities and golf cart for island transportation)
rooms $600-$1,100
suites $750-$2,000

Attractions: The Links at Fisher Island, 5-min drive; Miami Beach, 7-min drive; Miami Design District, 10-min drive
Towns/Cities: Miami, 11 miles; Coral Gables, 12 miles; Coconut Grove, 13 miles; Hollywood, 22 miles
Airports: Miami International Airport, 20-min drive

Affiliations: The Leading Hotels of the World

Originally built in the 1920s, this luxury resort hotel was once the Vanderbilt's impressive winter estate. Beautifully restored accommodations now include the Vanderbilt-era Cottages, luxurious 1-bedroom Villa Suites with private patios and hot tubs, and the Seaside Villas overlooking the Atlantic Ocean, adjacent to the private Beach Club. The Garwood Lounge, located inside the Vanderbilt mansion, is the perfect setting for cocktails at the piano bar before dinner at one of the several casual or fine dining restaurants. Complimentary golf carts are available to all guests who may wish to enjoy the on-site par 35 championship 9-hole golf course, and tennis is played at the Grand Slam tennis center. Spa Internazionale, with Fitness Center and Salon di Bellezza, offers world-class treatments in a tropical setting.

JUPITER BEACH RESORT & SPA

5 NORTH A1A, JUPITER, FLORIDA 33477-5190
Tel: +1 561 746 2511 **Fax:** +1 561 744 1741 **U.S./Canada Toll Free:** 1 800 228 8810
Web: www.johansens.com/jupiterbeachresort **E-mail:** reservations@jupiterbeachresort.com

Our inspector loved: The spacious rooms, and incredible ocean views.

Price Guide: (room only)
rooms $199-$399
suites $269-$1,500

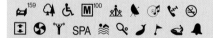

Attractions: Jupiter Inlet Lighthouse, 2 miles; Abacoa Golf Club, 5 miles; The Gardens Mall, 8 miles; Kravis Center, 18 miles
Towns/Cities: West Palm Beach, 12 miles
Airports: Palm Beach International Airport, 21 miles; Fort Lauderdale International Airport, 68 miles; Miami International Airport, 89 miles

Jupiter Beach Resort & Spa is a boutique beach hotel located on the northern tip of Palm Beach County on the Atlantic Ocean. The intimate nature of this elegant Caribbean-style resort offers more of a private club feel than a hotel. The luxurious guest rooms are spacious with island-style décor and rich dark tropical woods. The Penthouse Suites have breathtaking views of the ocean and are beautifully decorated with designer furnishings. Visit the spa and indulge in an island wrap or sugar massage after a day on the expansive private beach, and afterwards, enjoy a relaxing cup of tea or a warm Belgian chocolate shot at the Spa's Tea Bar. There are 3 on-site restaurants including the elegant Sinclairs Ocean Grill, the resort's signature Palm Beach restaurant, the Sandbar, which serves casual fare at the beach or by the pool, and Sinclairs Lounge, which provides weekend entertainment.

Ocean Key Resort & Spa

ZERO DUVAL STREET, KEY WEST, FLORIDA 33040
Tel: +1 305 296 7701 **Fax:** +1 305 292 7685 **U.S./Canada Toll Free:** 1 800 328 9815
Web: www.johansens.com/oceankey **E-mail:** contactus@oceankey.com

Our inspector loved: Dining with a view at Hot Tin Roof.

Price Guide:
rooms $279-$749
suites $359-$1,729

Attractions: Key West Aquarium, 0.1 miles; Mel Fisher Maritime Heritage, 0.2 miles; Mallory Square, 1-min walk; Duvall Street, 1-min walk
Towns/Cities: Miami, 150 miles
Airports: Key West International Airport, 3 miles; Miami International Airport, 155 miles

Overlooking the Gulf of Mexico, adjacent to the famous Mallory Square, Ocean Key Resort & Spa radiates the tropical feel of Key West. All of the island-style suites are appointed with bold and colorful fabrics, hand-painted furniture and unique local artwork. The ocean-front Hot Tin Roof serves a creative and gourmet menu of Latin, Caribbean and South Florida flavors prepared by Executive Chef Miguel Blasini who is celebrated for his delectable "conch-fusion" cuisine. For more casual fare, you can choose to dine by the pool, at the Sunset Pier, or in the comfort of your very own room. Spa Terre is a relaxing retreat and specializes in exotic Balinese spa treatments and Thai body rituals. Flowers and spices are used to enhance each spa experience.

SIMONTON COURT HISTORIC INN & COTTAGES

320 SIMONTON STREET, KEY WEST, FLORIDA 33040
Tel: +1 305 294 6386 **Fax:** +1 305 293 8446 **U.S./Canada Toll Free:** 1 800 944 2687
Web: www.johansens.com/simontoncourt **E-mail:** simontoncourt@aol.com

Our inspector loved: The tropical gardens.

Price Guide: (room only)
rooms $145-$399
cottages $279-$429

Attractions: Mel Fisher Maritime, 0.5 miles; Key West Aquarium, 0.5 miles; Ernest Hemingway Home, 0.5 miles; Duval Street Boutiques and Fashionable Pubs, 5-min walk
Towns/Cities: Miami, 150 miles
Airports: Miami International Airport, 155 yards; Key West International Airport, 3.8 miles

In 2 acres of lush tropical gardens, this elegant collection of cottages, manor house and town house is truly idyllic for rest and relaxation. Formerly a cigar factory, vast tropical palms shade the 4 swimming pools, and gentle sea breezes caress the verandas, while a series of pretty brick paths connect the various buildings by twinkling night-lights. Stay in one of the 6 enchanting and beautifully restored factory workers' cottages that boast the very latest in luxurious amenities yet still retain the period charm of their 1880 origins. The suites and guest bedrooms in the main house are breathtakingly appointed and many have private sun-decks or porches, king-size beds and Jacuzzis.

SUNSET KEY GUEST COTTAGES

245 FRONT STREET, KEY WEST, FLORIDA 33040
Tel: +1 305 292 5300 **Fax:** +1 305 292 5395 **U.S./Canada Toll Free:** 1 888 477 7SUN
Web: www.johansens.com/sunsetkey **E-mail:** rebecca.hysell@westinkeywestresort.com

Our inspector loved: *The privacy of this tropical island so close to the festivities of Key West.*

Price Guide:
1-bedroom cottage $664-$1,305
2-bedroom cottage $753-$2,080
3-bedroom cottage $1,132-$2,481

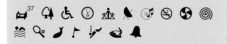

Awards/Ratings: Condé Nast Traveler Gold List 2003-2007

Attractions: Mallory Square, 1 mile; Duval Street, 1 mile; Mel Fisher Maritime, 1 mile; Ernest Hemingway's Home, 2 miles
Towns/Cities: Miami, 150 miles
Airports: Key West International Airport, 4 miles; Miami International Airport, 96 miles

Sunset Key is a 27-acre luxury island with a resort and a residential community located just 500 yards from historic "Old Town" Key West. Sunset Key Guest Cottages are accessible only by launch, which runs 24 hours a day from The Westin Key West Resort & Marina. This car-free island makes for the most tranquil vacation with its spectacular views of the Gulf of Mexico, fresh ocean air and colorful tropical blooms. Each of the luxurious 1, 2 and 3-bedroom cottages is nestled around tropical foliage and has either an ocean or garden view, wraparound veranda with Adirondack chairs, living room, dining area and a pre-stocked kitchen. Breakfast baskets are served to each cottage porch each morning, while meals are served in Latitudes Beach Cafe, an upscale yet casual dining experience in an alfresco beach-front setting. For a more intimate dinner you can request the Private Chef Service to prepare you dinner in your very own cottage.

CASA TUA

1700 JAMES AVENUE, MIAMI BEACH, FLORIDA 33139
Tel: +1 305 673 0973 **Fax:** +1 305 673 0974
Web: www.johansens.com/casatua **E-mail:** info@casatualifestyle.com

Our inspector loved: *The stylishness of this boutique hotel with its eye-catching European antiques and original art.*

Price Guide: (including breakfast)
rooms $750-$1,050

Attractions: South Beach, 5-min walk; Lincoln Road, 2-min walk; Art Deco Historic District, 2-min walk; Bass Museum of Art, 2-min walk
Towns/Cities: Miami, 11 miles; Key Biscayne, 15 miles; North Miami Beach, 17 miles; Hollywood, 21 miles
Airports: Miami International Airport, 12 miles

This stylish boutique hotel, set in the heart of the art-deco district of Miami's South Beach, will make you feel like you're staying in a private luxury home. Mediterranean Revival in style, Casa Tua hides behind wrought-iron gates and neatly trimmed hedges, just 2 blocks from the beach. 5 sophisticated guest suites are individually decorated with soft cashmere throws, crisp white Italian linens, original artwork and impressive antiques. Once a private club, attentive personalized service is their forte. Casa Tua's own casual-chic restaurant serves classic Italian and Mediterranean food. Enjoy Chef Sergio Sigala's specialty risotto while dining by candlelight in the garden or at the popular Chef's table. The exclusive Club on the second floor is a private members' bar with free access for the duration of your stay.

HOTEL VICTOR

1144 OCEAN DRIVE, MIAMI BEACH, FLORIDA 33139
Tel: +1 305 428 1234 **Fax:** +1 305 421 6281
Web: www.johansens.com/hotelvictor **E-mail:** treynolds@hotelvictorsouthbeach.com

Our inspector loved: *The new menu at VIX restaurant.*

Price Guide:
rooms $325-$695
suites $999-$10,000

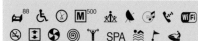

Attractions: Versace Mansion, 1-min walk; South Beach, 1-min walk; Bass Museum of Art, 1 mile; Lincoln Road, 5 miles
Towns/Cities: Miami, 8 miles; Fort Lauderdale, 32 miles; West Palm Beach, 75 miles
Airports: Miami International Airport, 11 miles

Hotel Victor is the epitome of glamour and style. The vibe is hip yet elegant, and all vibrant guest rooms have custom furniture, designer fabrics and views of the ocean or South Beach. Open bathrooms feature oversized soaking tubs, rain showers, 350-count Fili d'Oro Egyptian cotton linens, L.C.D. T.V.s and indulgent Big Bars. Enjoy unadulterated opulence at the Penthouse, which occupies the entire eighth floor and has a private entrance, gourmet kitchen, infinity-edge tub and outdoor entertainment areas with hot tubs and incredible 360° views. Dining at VIX is a provocative experience: displaying a rare jellyfish tank and original artwork, the restaurant offers an exciting spiced and culturally inspired cuisine. Visit Spa V's Cool Down Room and signature Turkish-style hammam for the ultimate pampering!

THE SETAI HOTEL & RESORT

2001 COLLINS AVENUE, MIAMI BEACH, FLORIDA 33139
Tel: +1 305 520 6000 **Fax:** +1 305 520 6600
Web: www.johansens.com/setai **E-mail:** setai@ghmamericas.com

Our inspector loved: The serenity of the hotel just steps from the buzz of South Beach.

Price Guide:
studio suites $625-$1,200
tower suites $1,500-$9,000
penthouse $30,000

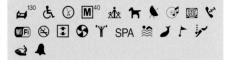

The Setai is a magnificently renovated art deco landmark that has quickly become one of the crown jewels of South Beach. Invoking Asian traditions of simplicity and elegance, the hotel's ambience is one of serenity and style. The ideal setting for a small wedding, this stunning ocean-front resort hotel, adjoined by a 40-story residential tower, offers strikingly elegant rooms set above an oasis of tropical gardens, shimmering pools and sundecks leading to the gorgeous white sand beach. Dining is unparalleled at The Grill or at The Restaurant, which serves exceptional Asian cuisine. The Pool & Beach Bar provides excellent Mediterranean-style fare. The Bar and Courtyard is the perfect place to start your evening or end your night in the buzzing South Beach. Visit the Spa at The Setai to restore your mind, body and soul.

Awards/Ratings: Condé Nast Traveler Gold List 2007; Wine Spectator Award of Excellence 2006 and 2007

Attractions: South Beach, 1-min walk; Art Deco Historic District, 3-min walk; The Bass Museum of Art, 3-min walk; Lincoln Road, 10-min walk
Towns/Cities: Downtown Miami, 10 miles; Hollywood, 22 miles; Fort Lauderdale, 30 miles; West Palm Beach, 73 miles
Airports: Miami International Airport, 12 miles; Fort Lauderdale International Airport, 29 miles

LaPlaya Beach & Golf Resort

9891 GULF SHORE DRIVE, NAPLES, FLORIDA 34108
Tel: +1 239 597 3123 **Fax:** +1 239 597 8283 **U.S./Canada Toll Free:** 1 800 237 6883
Web: www.johansens.com/laplaya **E-mail:** sales@laplayaresort.com

Our inspector loved: *The huge private balconies overlooking the beach and bay.*

Price Guide:
rooms $199-$799
suites $805-$2,600

Attractions: Waterside Shops, 5 miles; Historic Fifth Avenue Shopping, 9 miles; Miromar Outlets, 20 miles
Towns/Cities: Naples, on-site; Fort Myers, 25 miles
Airports: Southwest Florida International Airport, 27 miles; Miami International Airport, 125 miles

This is the place for sun worshippers and all who like the attractions of year-round sub-tropical weather, warm turquoise waters and sugar-white sandy beaches. The resort is situated on Vanderbilt Beach and revolves around a magnificent meandering pool complex. The interior is equally stunning. French doors attractively span the width of the first floor, and the elegant main lobby is adorned with crystal chandeliers and plush cane and wicker furnishings. Bedrooms are oversized and luxuriously appointed and decorated in fresh greens and warm yellows with bamboo-patterned bedcovers, four-poster beds, balconies and superb ocean views. An evening in Baleen, the resort's signature restaurant, begins indoors and ends on the long shoreline terrace. Adjacent to the fitness center is a fully-equipped spa decorated in 1920s décor.

U.S.A. - FLORIDA (SANTA ROSA BEACH)

WaterColor Inn and Resort

34 GOLDENROD CIRCLE, SANTA ROSA BEACH, FLORIDA 32459
Tel: +1 850 534 5000 **Fax:** +1 850 534 5001 **U.S./Canada Toll Free:** 1 866 426 2656
Web: www.johansens.com/watercolor **E-mail:** info@watercolorreservations.com

Our inspector loved: *The powder-white sand beach and clear gulf water.*

Price Guide:
rooms $365-$480
suites $525-$730
vacation homes $410-$1,750

WaterColor nestles between the shores of Florida's Emerald Coast and the banks of a 220-acre dune lake. Embraced by wind-sculptured oak groves, palmettos and sea grasses, the inn is surrounded by a maze of pathways and parks that meander from the Gulf of Mexico to the lake. With the intimacy and hospitality of a traditional Southern grand hotel the inn has magnificent David Rockwell-designed architecture and spacious guest rooms with king-size beds and sofa sleepers, walk-in showers and beach views from private balconies. There are also 150 beautifully appointed, fully-equipped vacation homes, with 1-6 bedrooms. The casual Fish Out of Water restaurant takes an imaginative approach to traditional cuisine, while the BaitHouse and The Beach Club, with its pool deck and grill, are great alternatives.

Attractions: Factory Outlet Shopping, 8 miles
Towns/Cities: Destin, 8 miles; Panama City, 36 miles; Pensacola, 75 miles
Airports: Okaloosa Regional Airport, 24 miles; Panama City-Bay County International Airport, 36 miles; Pensacola Regional Airport, 75 miles

Affiliations: Preferred Hotels & Resorts

Don CeSar Beach Resort

3400 GULF BOULEVARD, ST. PETE BEACH, FLORIDA 33706
Tel: +1 727 360 1881 **Fax:** +1 727 367 6952 **U.S./Canada Toll Free:** 1 800 282 1116
Web: www.johansens.com/doncesar **E-mail:** doncesarinfo@loewshotels.com

Our inspector loved: The old fashioned ice-cream parlor, and the beautiful beach.

Price Guide:
rooms $204-$569
suites $324-$3,000

Attractions: St. Petersburg Pier, 11 miles; Florida Aquarium, 32 miles; Busch Gardens, 38 miles; Cypress Gardens, 81 miles
Towns/Cities: St. Petersburg, 10 miles; Tampa, 30 miles
Airports: St. Petersburg/Clearwater International Airport, 19 miles; Tampa International Airport, 28 miles

Affiliations: Loews Hotels

Affectionately referred to as a grand dame of sunny Florida and widely known as the Pink Palace, Don CeSar sprawls long and high on the edge of a sugar-white beach. This internationally renowned Mediterranean-style castle was built in 1928 and is accented by Moorish bell towers and imperial turrets. The hotel provides a casually elegant ambience and luxurious accommodation with an interior filled with English carpets, Italian crystal chandeliers, French candelabras, fountains, polished mahogany and vibrant upholsteries. The beautifully decorated European-styled guest rooms, 40 spacious suites and 2 penthouses boast panoramic gulf views. Dining is a delight with a choice of restaurants ranging from the Maritana Grille, which serves creative New American cuisine, to the poolside Beachcomber Grill with its salads and burgers.

TENNESSEE

NORTH CAROLINA

Charlotte

Hendersonville

Cleveland

Greenville

Camden

Chattanooga

COLUMBIA

Toccoa

Dalton

Abbeville

Calhoun

Summerville

Gainesville

Ft. Payne

Canton

Elberton

SOUTH CAROLINA

Rome

Athens

Aiken

Cedartown

Monroe

Augusta

Barnwell

ATLANTA

Thomson

Douglasville

Hartsfield-Jackson Atlanta Int. Airport

Covington

Walterboro

Carrollton

Fayetteville

Eatonton

Waynesboro

Talladega

Griffin

Milledgeville

La Grange

Swainsboro

Opelika

Thomaston

Macon

Statesboro

Dublin

Savannah Int. Airport

Colombus

Fort Valley

Lyons

Savannah

MONTGOMERY

Eastman

Hinesville

Americus

Cordele

Jesup

ALABAMA

Fitzgerald

Dawson

Douglas

Brunswick

Albany

Tifton

Waycross

ATLANTIC OCEAN

Nashville

Blakely

Camilla

Adel

Andalusia

Dothan

Cairo

Valdosta

Fernandina Beach

Bainbridge

Thomasville

Marianna

Jacksonville

TALLAHASSEE

FLORIDA

Panama City

Gainseville

BARNSLEY GARDENS RESORT

597 BARNSLEY GARDENS ROAD, ADAIRSVILLE, GEORGIA 30103
Tel: +1 770 773 7480 **Fax:** +1 770 877 9155 **U.S./Canada Toll Free:** 1 877 773 2447
Web: www.johansens.com/barnsleygardens **E-mail:** bgr_reservations@barnsleyresort.com

Our inspector loved: The quaint village, unique and comfortable cottages, and abundance of activities on-site.

Price Guide:
rooms $299
suites $375-$1,675

Attractions: Orvis Wing-Shooting and Fly-Fishing Schools, 100 yards; Jim Fazio-designed 18-hole Golf Course and Historic Ruins and Gardens, 5-min walk; SpringBank Plantation Quail Hunting Preserve, 5-min drive

Towns/Cities: Atlanta, 61 miles; Chattanooga, TN, 68 miles; Birmingham, AL, 137 miles; Nashville, TN, 199 miles

Airports: Chattanooga Airport, 65 miles; Atlanta Hartsfield Jackson Airport, 75 miles

Affiliations: Preferred Boutique

37 charming cottages built to resemble a 19th-century English-style village, are nestled in 1,300 acres of lush gardens and historic land at the foothills of the beautiful Blue Ridge Mountains. All the gabled, fretted and shingled cottages edge tree-lined walkways and are decorated with warmth and comfort in mind. Each suite and room is individually decorated. Many suites feature antiques and fine furnishings, fireplaces, king or queen-size sleigh or poster beds and bathrooms with cast-iron ball and claw foot tubs. Dominated by the ruins of the Italian-style manor's historic mansion, the original ornamental gardens have been stunningly restored and feature more than 150 types of roses. There is a choice of 3 excellent dining areas: Southern cuisine at the Rice House, the Woodlands Grill steakhouse or German beer and sausages in the Beer Garden.

GREYFIELD INN

CUMBERLAND ISLAND, GEORGIA

Tel: +1 904 261 6408 **Fax:** +1 904 321 0666 **U.S./Canada Toll Free:** 1 866 410 8052
Web: www.johansens.com/greyfieldinn **E-mail:** seashore@greyfieldinn.com

Our inspector loved: The unbelieveable trip back in time. This is the most intriguing, restful vacation spot in America.

Price Guide: (including round-trip ferry service, 3 meals per day, guided wilderness outing and use of bicycles, kayaks and fishing equipment)
rooms $395-$525
suites $525-$595

Awards/Ratings: Condé Nast Travler Gold List 2005

Attractions: 17-mile Long Protected National Seashore, close by; Wildlife and Bird Watching, close by; Fernandina Beach, Amelia Island, 10 miles

Towns/Cities: Fernandina Beach, Amelia Island, 10 miles; Savannah, 120 miles; Hilton Head, 150 miles

Airports: Jacksonville Airport, 30-min drive; Savannah Airport, 120 miles

Affiliations: Classic Inns of the South

Cumberland Island is the largest and most southern of Georgia's 120-mile long coastal archipelago. Steel baron Thomas Carnegie and his wife built Greyfield as a wedding gift for their daughter Margaret Ricketson in 1901. In 1962 the home was converted into an inn by her daughter Lucy Ferguson, whose descendants now oversee the daily operations. Furnished with original furnishings that date from the turn-of-the-century, added luxuries and contemporary amenities are found throughout. Relax in the Baronial living room, in the cozy bar, well-stocked library, on the shady veranda or in the exquisite bedrooms with fabulous views. This is the only overnight accommodation on an island the size of Manhattan and is reached by ferry or small private plane. Surrounded by 17 miles of protected national seashore of pristine beaches and ancient oaks, there is an abundance of wildlife here including deer, wild horses, bobcats, boar, alligators and 230 species of birds.

THE JAMES MADISON INN

260 WEST WASHINGTON STREET, MADISON, GEORGIA 30650
Tel: +1 706 342 7040 **Fax:** +1 706 342 8100
Web: www.johansens.com/jamesmadison **E-mail:** reservations@jamesmadisoninn.com

Our inspector loved: This inn that is like no other. Take a carriage ride to see the antebellum home that your luxurious room is named after!

Price Guide: (including upscale Continental breakfast)
king rooms $250-$275
suites $325-$350

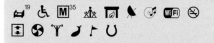

Attractions: Shopping, Dining, Galleries and City Park in Historic Downtown Madison, 5-min walk
Towns/Cities: Lake Oconee, 25 miles; Atlanta, 65 miles; Augusta, 80 miles
Airports: Hartsfield Jackson International Airport, Atlanta, 65 miles; Greenville - Spartanburg Airport, 120 miles

This landmark in the historic town of Madison, Georgia, is a "gem of the Antebellum Trail." Combining the splendor and charm of the pre-war South with modern comfort, James Madison has been designed to complement the architecture of the town and comprises 17 luxury guest rooms and 2 suites. Each room has been named after one of Madison's historic houses and features a painting of its namesake above the mantle of the fireplace. The in-room library, filled with works by local authors and artists, furthers the sense of local pride apparent in this elegant hotel. Rooms are individually appointed with custom-designed furniture, 600 thread-count linens on sumptuous king-sized beds, soft-lighting and neutral hues. They also include a furnished porch, flat-screen television, wireless Internet and an oversized walk-in black and white tile shower in every bathroom.

135

THE GASTONIAN

220 EAST GASTON STREET, SAVANNAH, GEORGIA 31401
Tel: +1 912 232 2869 **Fax:** +1 912 232 0710 **U.S./Canada Toll Free:** 1 800 322 6603
Web: www.johansens.com/gastonian **E-mail:** innkeeper@gastonian.com

Our inspector loved: *The perfect location for exploring Savannah! Rooms are comfortable, and the service and food are of the highest quality.*

Price Guide: (including breakfast)
rooms $215-$415

In the heart of Savannah's beautiful Historic District exists a landmark to Southern grandeur: The Gastonian. Built in 1868, the dual mansions reflect an elegant private residential atmosphere that are synonymous with gracious hospitality. Quiet and romantic, the hotel features a formal side garden with tiered fountain as well as a secluded walled garden with goldfish pool. Each luxurious guest room includes a working fireplace and private bath, whirlpool or claw-foot soaking tub, and as an honored guest of The Gastonian, the incredible gourmet breakfast can be delivered to your bedroom on a silver tray. Reflect on the pleasures of the day over afternoon tea or wine with hors d'oeuvres, and each evening, enjoy home-made desserts, coffee and cordials in the candle-lit ambience of the front parlor.

Attractions: Colonial Park Cemetery, 5-min walk; The Telfair Museum of Art, 10-min walk; Tybee Island, 20-min drive
Towns/Cities: Hilton Head, 45-min drive; Beaufort, 50-min drive; Charleston, 120 miles
Airports: Savannah Airport, 20-min drive; Hilton Head Airport, 40-min drive; Charleston Airport, 120 miles

NIIHAU

Puuwai

Kahaino

KAULAKAHI
CHANNEL

KAUAI

Princeville

Kekaha

Kapaa

Kalaheo

Lihue · Lihue Airport

KAUAI CHANNEL

OAHU

Wahiawa

Pearl City

Ewa Beach

Kaneohe

Honolulu Int. Airport

HONOLULU

KAIWI CHANNEL

MOLOKAI

Kalaupapa

Kaunakakai

PACIFIC
OCEAN

LANAI

Lanai City

Wailuku

Lahaina

Kahului Airport

Kahului

Makawao

Kihei

Pukalani

KAHOOLAWE

140 Hana

MAUI

ALENUIHAHA CHANNEL

Hawi

Waimea (Kamuela)

Kalaoa

Kailua-Kona

Holualoa

138 Honomu

Captain Cook

Hilo
Hilo Int. Airport
139

HAWAII

Montain View

Pahala

Naalehu

THE PALMS CLIFF HOUSE

28-3514 MAMALAHOA HIGHWAY 19, P.O. BOX 189, HONOMU, HAWAII 96728-0189
Tel: +1 808 963 6076 **Fax:** +1 808 963 6316 **U.S./Canada Toll Free:** 1 866 963 6076
Web: www.johansens.com/palmscliff **E-mail:** information@palmscliffhouse.com

Our inspector loved: *The magnificent views, and splendid detail.*

Price Guide:
suites $175-$375

SPA

Attractions: Akaka Falls, 4 miles; Beaches, 7 miles; Lyman Mission Home and Museum, 15 miles; Hawaii Volcanoes National Park, 45 miles
Towns/Cities: Hilo, 14 miles; Kona, 175 miles
Airports: Hilo Airport, 13 miles; Kona Airport, 150 miles

Perched at the cliff's edge, 100 feet above the ocean, The Palms Cliff House enviably stands within acres of its own tranquil estate. Celebrated in song and in hula, the inn has quickly become one of Hawaii's most gracious locations since opening in 2001. Find yourself captivated by the stunning setting where each of the 8 suites is carefully decorated in a unique tropical style. The views of the ocean below are truly spectacular, with whales and Spinner dolphins taking their regular morning frolic in the waters of Pohakumanu Bay as tropical birds fill the sky. The Grande Suites have 2-person sunken Jacuzzis, large seated marble showers and gas fireplaces. The full gourmet breakfasts are exquisite; fresh produce from the fruit and nut orchards bring the tropics to your table.

SHIPMAN HOUSE

131 KA'IULANI STREET, HILO, HAWAII 96720
Tel: +1 808 934 8002 **Fax:** +1 808 934 8002 **U.S./Canada Toll Free:** 1 800 627 8447
Web: www.johansens.com/shipman **E-mail:** innkeeper@hilo-hawaii.com

Our inspector loved: The inn's family history, its location in downtown Hilo and Hawaii's volcanoes and waterfalls.

Price Guide:
rooms $244-$255

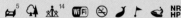

Attractions: Lyman Mission House and Museum, 5-min walk; Akaka Falls, 15 miles; Hawaii Volcanoes National Park, 30 miles; Mauna Kea Visitors Center, 33 miles
Towns/Cities: Hilo, 5-min walk; Volcano, 30 miles; Kona, 100 miles
Airports: Hilo Airport, 5 miles; Kona Airport, 100 miles

Built in 1899 and one of the few remaining Victorian mansions on Hawaii, Shipman House has been owned by the same family for over 100 years. Perched on a ridge overlooking a deep canyon, the house is surrounded by 5.5 acres of tropical gardens with streams, waterfalls and exotic stands of palm and bamboo. The bedrooms have a distinct air of Hawaiian charm, and are carefully decorated with traditional custom quilts and fabrics. Names such as "Auntie Carrie's Room" and "Flossie's" are a gentle reminder that this really is the family home where Barbara Ann Andersen played as a child. All bathrooms have large bath tubs and delicate cotton kimonos. Breakfast is served on the lanai and comprises of local ingredients such as home-made macadamia nut granola, fruit breads and muffins.

U.S.A. - HAWAII (MAUI)

HOTEL HANA-MAUI AND HONUA SPA

5031 HANA HIGHWAY, HANA, MAUI, HAWAII 96713
Tel: +1 808 248 8211 **Fax:** +1 808 248 7202 **U.S./Canada Toll Free:** 1 800 321 HANA
Web: www.johansens.com/hanamaui **E-mail:** reservations@hotelhanamaui.com

Our inspector loved: *The natural, spacious grandeur of the resort.*

Price Guide: (room only)
rooms $475-$4,500

Awards/Ratings: Condé Nast Johansens Most Excellent Spa Hotel 2006

Attractions: Hana Cultural Center, 2-min walk; Wai'anapanapa State Park, 1 mile; Hana Bay, 1 mile; Hana Town Center, 1 mile
Towns/Cities: Hana, 3 miles; Kahului, 57 miles
Airports: Hana Airport, 3 miles; Kahului Airport, 57 miles

Affiliations: Small Luxury Hotels of the World

If splendid seclusion is your desire, Hotel Hana-Maui is your destination. This plantation-style resort reflects hospitality as pervasive as the surrounding dramatic vistas. The storied town of Hana is separated from the rest of civilization by a 2-hour drive. The winding road is breathtaking, with cascading waterfalls, bountiful fruit trees and banks of wild ginger. Luxury accommodations include bungalow-style Bay Cottage Suites with patios and Sea Ranch Cottages with dramatic ocean and mountain views. All have large tiled baths with private pocket gardens. Small touches such as welcome baskets in each room and furniture made from recycled wood give a casually elegant ambience. Enjoy Honua Spa where an extensive treatment menu emphasizes traditional healing and native plants. Cultural workshops include the art of lei making and hula dancing!

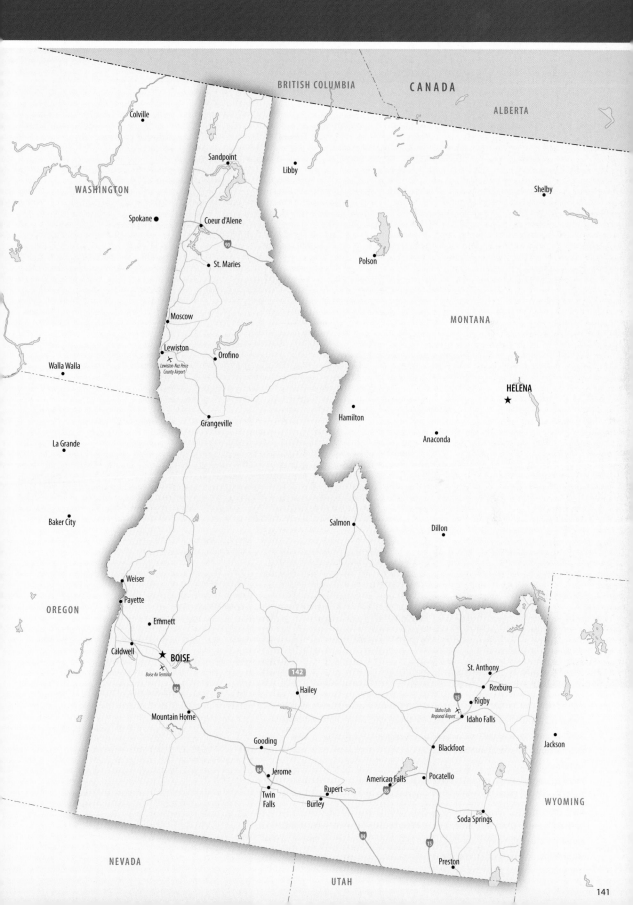

KNOB HILL INN

960 NORTH MAIN STREET, P.O. BOX 800, KETCHUM, IDAHO 83340
Tel: +1 208 726 8010 **Fax:** +1 208 726 2712 **U.S./Canada Toll Free:** 1 800 526 8010
Web: www.johansens.com/knobhillinn **E-mail:** khi@knobhillinn.com

Our inspector loved: *The breathtaking mountain views.*

Price Guide:
rooms $250-$325
suites $400-$500

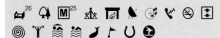

Attractions: Sun Valley Resort, 1 mile; Big Wood River, 1 mile; Bald Mountain, 1 mile; Sun Valley Championship 18-hole Golf Course, 1.5 miles
Towns/Cities: Ketchum, on-site; Elkhorn, 5 miles
Airports: Hailey Airport, 12 miles

Affiliations: Relais & Châteaux

Knob Hill Inn is an Austrian-style inn set in the heart of Hemingway country, Ketchum. Centrally located and ideal for those who enjoy both winter skiing and summer-type activities, the inn is in America's first destination ski resort overlooking the world-famous Bald Mountain, the majestic Sawtooths and the Boulder Mountain ranges. Most of the charming rooms have dressing rooms, marble bathrooms with oversized tub and separate shower. Each room has glass doors that open out to breathtaking views of the mountain peaks. Each morning, you are treated to a buffet of fresh pastries, breads and muffins with daily entrées made to order. Fine dining in the restaurant has a distinctive moutain flair created by Chef de Cuisine Laurent Loubot, who oversees a fine wine list to complement the dishes.

Sioux City

IOWA

Broken Bow

Clarinda

Lexington

York
★
LINCOLN

NEBRASKA

Maryville

McCook

Falls City

MISSOURI

St. Francis

Norton

Smith Center

Marysville

Hiawatha

Troy

Concordia

Atchison

Kansas City Int. Airport

Burlington

Colby

Osborne

Leavenworth

Oakley

Hill City

Junction City

Manhattan

Kansas City

Kansas City

Sharon Springs

Hays

Salina

Abilene

TOPEKA
★

Lawrence

Olathe

Harrisonville

Leoti

Ness City

Great Bend

McPherson

Council Grove

Ottawa

Emporia

Syracuse

Garden City

Kinsley

Hutchinson

Newton

Fort Scott

Nevada

Ulysses

Dodge City

Wichita

El Dorado

Iola

Pratt

Wichita Mid-Continent Airport

Howard

Columbus

Elkhart

Liberal

Meade

Coldwater

Wellington

Winfield

Independence

Neosho

Guymon

Bartlesville

Perryton

Woodward

Enid

Tulsa

OKLAHOMA

TEXAS

★
OKLAHOMA CITY

Amarillo

Wichita Falls

Durant

THE ELDRIDGE

701 MASSACHUSETTS, LAWRENCE, KANSAS 66044
Tel: +1 785 749 5011 **Fax:** +1 785 749 4512 **U.S./Canada Toll Free:** 1 800 527 0909
Web: www.johansens.com/eldridge **E-mail:** info@eldridgehotel.com

Our inspector loved: *The history: preserved with integrity and care.*

Price Guide:
suites $149-$295

Awards/Ratings: Wine Spectator Award of Excellence 2007

The Eldridge was originally built as temporary quarters for families of the New England Emigrant Aid Society who came to Kansas from Massachusetts and other areas in the mid 1800s. Over the years it became the Free State Hotel, then the Hotel Eldridge. Restored to its original grandeur, it is now a 48-room luxury boutique hotel that combines history with hospitality. The original furnishings have been updated with black leather chairs and hardwood furnishings alongside black and white photographs for a contemporary feel. Suites are spacious with beautiful furnishings, cozy living areas and modern amenities, while the Honeymoon Suite is perfect for a weekend getaway or romantic escape. TEN serves casual and hearty fare as well as a sumptuous Sunday brunch. The Jayhawker Bar, popular for its jazz nights, has an extensive wine list.

Attractions: Booth Family Hall of Athletics, 2 miles; University of Kansas, 2 miles; Lied Center for Performing Arts, 3 miles; Clinton Lake, 10 miles
Towns/Cities: Kansas City, 40 miles
Airports: Kansas City International, 45 miles

LITTLE ROCK ★

Batesville

ARKANSAS

Camden

Louisville

Texarkana

Greenville

El Dorado

Bastrop
Lake Providence

Minden
Ruston
Monroe
Tallulah
Vicksburg

JACKSON ★

Shreveport

MISSISSIPPI

Winnsboro

Waynesboro

Carthage
Mansfield
Winnfield

Natchitoches
Jena

Natchez

Hattiesburg

Alexandria
Marksville

Leesville
Greensburg

Jasper
Bunkie

New
Roads
Baton Rouge
Metropolitan
Airport
Covington
Biloxi

De Ridder
Ville Platte
Bay St. Louis

TEXAS
Opelousas
BATON ROUGE

Crowley
Lafayette
Plaquemine
Lhuis Armstrong
New Orleans
Int. Airport
146

Jennings
St. Martinville
Donaldsonville
147

Beaumont
Orange
Abbeville
New Iberia
New
Orleans
148

Franklin
Thibodaux

Houma
Pointe a la Hache

Galveston

GULF OF MEXICO

HOTEL MAISON DE VILLE

727 RUE TOULOUSE, NEW ORLEANS, LOUISIANA 70130
Tel: +1 504 561 5858 **Fax:** +1 504 528 9939 **U.S./Canada Toll Free:** 1 800 634 1600
Web: www.johansens.com/maisondeville **E-mail:** info@hotelmaisondeville.com

Our inspector loved: *The rich history of the hotel and the welcoming staff.*

Price Guide: (including breakfast)
rooms $179-$259
suites $239-$399
cottages $599-$699

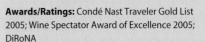

Awards/Ratings: Condé Nast Traveler Gold List 2005; Wine Spectator Award of Excellence 2005; DiRoNA

Attractions: Jackson Square, .03 miles; Royal Street Antique District, .05 miles; French Market, .65 miles; NOLA Museum of Art, 2.75 miles
Airports: New Orleans International Airport, 11.78 miles

This wonderfully preserved and charming building oozes character that perfectly reflects the period when New Orleans was a French colony and America still a British colony. Surrounding the pretty ensconced courtyards, bedrooms are located in the main building and within the Audubon Cottages, named after the naturalist John James Audubon who created many of his masterpieces here. Each bedroom has its own unique charm and style and in both the main house and the cottages the utmost care has been taken to restore everything to historical accuracy. High elegant ceilings, original paintings, antiques and individual décor are featured throughout, and the twice-daily housekeeping service ensures an unflinching attention to detail. The Bistro Restaurant enjoys a wide reputation for its innovative cuisine and unpretentious atmosphere.

THE LAFAYETTE HOTEL

600 ST. CHARLES AVENUE, NEW ORLEANS, LOUISIANA 70130
Tel: +1 504 524 4441 **Fax:** +1 504 962 5537 **U.S./Canada Toll Free:** 1 800 272 4583
Web: www.johansens.com/lafayette **E-mail:** reservations@neworleansfinehotels.com

Our inspector loved: *The decadent feather-topped beds.*

Price Guide:
rooms $159-$499
suites $229-$799

NR
HP

Attractions: French Quarter, 0.23 miles; Gallier Hall, 0.2 miles; Warehouse Arts District, 0.25 miles; Historic St. Charles Avenue, close by
Airports: New Orleans Airport, 15.25 miles

This stately and refined hotel lies on the St. Charles streetcar line in the center of the city and possesses the ambience of a historic gentleman's club. Luxurious carpets, Old World furnishings and elegant drapes are trademarks of the building's heritage, lovingly restored to their former glory, and the original French doors and wrought-iron balconies are now as beautiful as they were in their heyday. Each bedroom and suite is individually decorated in designer fabrics and filled with thoughtful touches such as French-milled soaps and thick Terry bathrobes in the exquisite marble bathrooms; suites feature wet bars, refrigerators and some have whirlpool baths. The hotel has now opened Anatole restaurant, where you can enjoy an upscale dining experience of contemporary Creole cuisine and prime steaks.

THE ST. JAMES HOTEL

330 MAGAZINE STREET, NEW ORLEANS, LOUISIANA 70130
Tel: +1 504 304 4000 **Fax:** +1 504 304 4444 **U.S./Canada Toll Free:** 1 800 272 4583
Web: www.johansens.com/stjamesno **E-mail:** reservations@neworleansfinehotels.com

Our inspector loved: The secluded plunge pool, and dining at Cuvee.

Price Guide:
rooms $149-$350
suites $179-$500

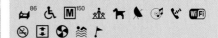

Attractions: French Quarter, 0.2 miles; Harrah's Casino, 0.6 miles; Riverwalk Attractions, 0.6 miles; D-Day Museum, 1 mile
Airports: New Orleans International Airport, 12 miles

Charm and elegance are the hallmarks of this downtown boutique hotel located in the Banks Arcade, a 19th-century landmark once the center of the Caribbean sugar and coffee trade. The hotel is just a few blocks from where it first opened its doors to guests in the mid-1800s, and offers spacious, comfortable rooms with a host of original features and 2 pretty courtyards. The attractive New Orleans' Creole-Caribbean influence in each of the guest rooms celebrates the area's connection with exquisite West Indies style. All offer special touches such as marble bathrooms and goosedown feather beds. The highly acclaimed informal Cuvee restaurant specializes in innovative Nouveau Orleans gourmet cuisine. For outdoor relaxation there is a lounging pool in a lush courtyard setting surrounded by rooftop terraces.

Montmagny

QUÉBEC

St-Georges

Lac-Mégantic

St. Johnsbury

NEW
HAMPSHIRE

CONCORD ★

Edmundston
Madawaska
Van Buren
Grand Falls
(Grand Sault)
Caribou
Perth-Andover
Presque Isle

CANADA

FREDERICTON ★

Woodstock
Houlton

NEW BRUNSWICK

Saint-John

Millinocket

Saint-
Stephen
Calais

150

Lincoln

Machias

Dover-Foxcroft

Bangor
Int. Airport Bangor

Ellsworth

Skowhegan
Pittsfield

Bar Harbor

Belfast

Farmington

Waterville

Rumford

95

AUGUSTA ★

Rockland

Norway

Lewiston

Bath

Brunswick

495

Portland
152
Portland Int.
Jetport

ATLANTIC
OCEAN

Saco

Laconia

Sandford

95 151

Kennebunk

York Village

Dover

THE LODGE AT MOOSEHEAD LAKE

368 LILY BAY ROAD, P.O. BOX 1167, GREENVILLE, MAINE 04441
Tel: +1 207 695 4400 **Fax:** +1 207 695 2281 **U.S./Canada Toll Free:** 1 800 825 6977
Web: www.johansens.com/lodgeatmooseheadlake **E-mail:** innkeeper@lodgeatmooseheadlake.com

Our inspector loved: The unique lake view location, and charming hosts.

Price Guide:
rooms $225-$385
suites $350-$680

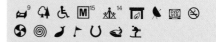

Attractions: Moose Sightings, 1 mile; Moosehead Lake, 1 mile; Lily Bay State Park, 12 miles; Mount Kineo, 20 miles
Towns/Cities: Bar Harbor, 126 miles; Québec City, Canada, 159 miles; Kennebunkport, 184 miles; Manchester, NH, 248 miles
Airports: Bangor Airport, 89 miles; Portland Airport, 158 miles; Boston Logan International Airport, MA, 259 miles

Perched gracefully atop a rise on 7.5 acres with beautifully landscaped gardens overlooking the broad waters of Moosehead Lake, this award-winning inn offers spectacular lake views, a peaceful atmosphere and warm hospitality. Built in 1917, this stately Colonial property is an ultra-private hideaway that combines elegance and comfort with an interior filled with unique imports, rich custom-designer fabrics and bespoke furnishings. You will especially enjoy the ever-changing vista across Moosehead Lake that is both stunning by day and magical by moonlight. Savor your favorite cocktail at the Sistah's Pub before heading to the Lakeview Dining Room, an enchanting setting where the service is impeccable.

THE WHITE BARN INN

37 BEACH AVENUE, KENNEBUNKPORT, MAINE 04043
Tel: +1 207 967 2321 **Fax:** +1 207 967 1100
Web: www.johansens.com/whitebarninn **E-mail:** innkeeper@thewhitebarninn.com

Our inspector loved: The Hinckley Talaria available for private charter.

Price Guide:
rooms $395-$460
suites $699-$750
waterfront cottages $799-$860

SPA

Awards/Ratings: AAA 5 Diamond Award; Mobil 5 Star

Attractions: Beaches, 0.25 mile; President Bush's Former Summer Home (Walker's Point), 2 miles; Ogunquit Play House, 14 miles; Portland Headlight, 32 miles

Towns/Cities: Portland, 30 miles; Portsmouth, NH, 32 miles; Boston, MA, 87 miles; New York City, NY, 295 miles

Airports: Portland Intl. Jetport, 27 miles; Manchester, NH, 79 miles; Boston, MA, 85 miles

Affiliations: Relais & Châteaux

Since welcoming its first travelers in the 1800s, The White Barn Inn has earned an envious reputation for its wonderfully relaxing atmosphere, charm, luxury, attentive service and superb cuisine. The interior is beautifully decorated and furnished, and guest rooms are the epitome of luxury and comfort. Each has every amenity from flatscreen plasma T.V.s to voice-mail and fresh flowers. Some have a fireplace, steam shower, whirlpool bath and private deck looking out to the manicured grounds. There are also fully-equipped waterfront cottages close by with a private marina clubhouse alongside the inn's 44-ft. Hinkley Talaria jet cruiser, which can be chartered for coastal tours. Enjoy the outdoor heated pool, canoeing, cycling and full-service spa with treatment suites, skin services, Kohler soak tub and Swiss shower.

PORTLAND HARBOR HOTEL

468 FORE STREET, PORTLAND, MAINE 04101
Tel: +1 207 775 9090 **Fax:** +1 207 775 9990 **U.S./Canada Toll Free:** 1 888 798 9090
Web: www.johansens.com/portlandharbor **E-mail:** resmgr@harthotels.com

Our inspector loved: The downtown location, close to the harbor, quaint shops and cobbled streets.

Price Guide:
rooms $189-$309
suites $289-$389

Attractions: Portland Observatory, 1 mile; Portland Head Light, 4 miles; Two Lights State Park, 7 miles; Freeport/L.L. Bean, 15 miles
Towns/Cities: Augusta, 35 miles; North Conway, NH, 45 miles; Portsmouth, NH, 50 miles; Boston, MA, 110 miles
Airports: Portland, 4 miles; Manchester, NH, 80 miles; Boston Logan Airport, MA, 110 miles

Experience Old World charm and exceptional service in the heart of the Old Port, just 1 block from the Portland waterfront. Enjoy views of the city skyline or the hotel's lush garden from the well-appointed guest rooms. Each room is distinctive with custom-made his and her armoires and luxury bathrooms include granite surround and an enclosed shower or soaking tub. Pampering touches include high-thread count bed linens, feather pillows and comforters, and plush towels and robes. Within easy walking distance from the hotel, the lovingly restored shops and restaurants reflect the charm of the Victorian Old Port district, and Portland's vibrant waterfront is a must-see, with cobblestone streets, historic landmarks and full-service marinas on both sides of the harbor. Reflect on the day's experiences over a candle-lit dinner at the award-winning Eve's restaurant overlooking the garden.

Scranton

New York

Newark

Clearfield

PENNSYLVANIA

Allentown

★ TRENTON

Indiana

Huntingdon

★ HARRISBURG

Philadelphia

Mt. Holly

Carlisle

West Chester

NEW JERSEY

York

Wilmington

Gettysburg

Elkton

Bridgeton

Somerset

Westminster

Bel Air

★ DOVER

Hagerstown

Towson

Cumberland

154

Martinsburg

Frederick

Baltimore

DELAWARE

Keyser

Ellicott City

Baltimore-Washington
Int. Airport

Rockville

Easton

Leesburg

WASHINGTON, DC

★ ANNAPOLIS, ML

Washington-Dulles
Int. Airport

Reagan
National
Airport

Cambridge

Salisbury

Front Royal

La Plata

WEST
VIRGINIA

Elkins

Culpeper

CHESAPEAKE BAY

Charlottesville

VIRGINIA

★ RICHMOND

Williamsburg

Covington

ATLANTIC
OCEAN

Bedford

SAVAGE RIVER LODGE

1600 MT. AETNA ROAD, FROSTBURG, MARYLAND 21532
Tel: +1 301 689 3200 **Fax:** +1 301 689 2746
Web: www.johansens.com/savageriver **E-mail:** info@savageriverlodge.com

Our inspector loved: *The privacy of the luxurious cabins, the excellent cuisine and the extensive list of outdoor activities to choose from.*

Price Guide: (including Continental breakfast)
cabins $185-$220

A rustic lodge, log cabins, porches with rocking chairs, gourmet dining, excellent service, mountain-side location encircled by 700 acres of forest teeming with grouse, wild turkey, white tailed deer, beaver and black bear - if that is what you want from a vacation then this is it! Nestling in 42 acres, 18 cabins are scattered along a tree-lined road and provide every solace from overstuffed furniture to down comforters on queen-size beds and oversized soaking tubs. There are telephones but no televisions. The lodge itself is for relaxing with friends or a place in which to curl up by the fire or window with a book. Dining is a casual experience where the Wine Enthusiast award-winning wine list offers a great array of choice and an open view into the kitchen enhances the informality. Continental breakfast is delivered to cabins in a picnic basket.

Awards/Ratings: Wine Spectator Award of Excellence 2006

Towns/Cities: Frostburg, 5 miles
Airports: Cumberland Airport, 25 miles

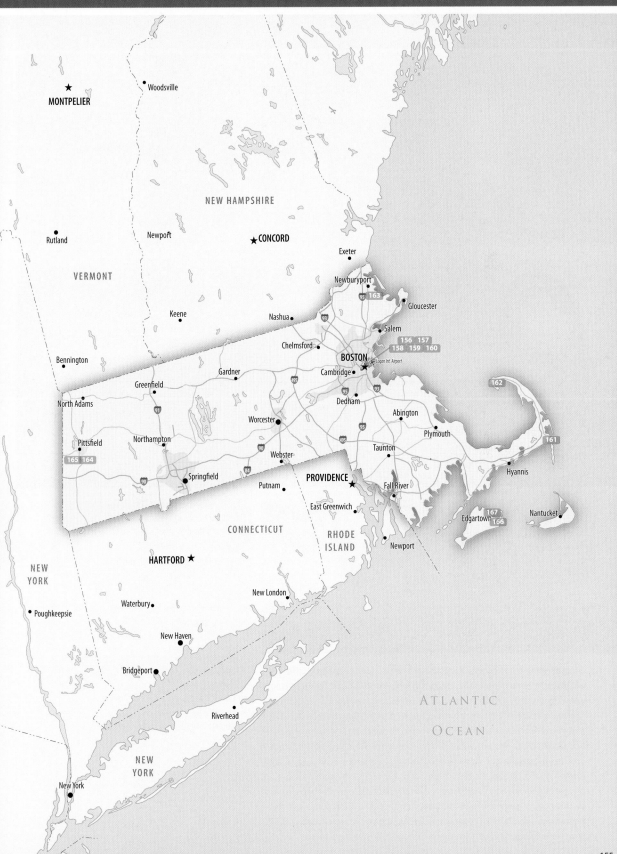
MONTPELIER ★

Woodsville

NEW HAMPSHIRE

Rutland

Newport

★ CONCORD

Exeter

VERMONT

Newburyport

95 163

Gloucester

Keene

Nashua

Salem

Bennington

Chelmsford

156 157

158 159 160

Greenfield

Gardner

93

BOSTON ★

Logan Int. Airport

Cambridge

162

North Adams

495

95

Dedham

Abington

Pittsfield

Northampton

Worcester

Plymouth

165 164

90

Webster

Taunton

161

84

495

95

Hyannis

91

Springfield

Putnam

PROVIDENCE ★

Fall River

Edgartown

167 166

Nantucket

East Greenwich

CONNECTICUT

RHODE ISLAND

Newport

HARTFORD ★

NEW YORK

New London

Waterbury

Poughkeepsie

New Haven

ATLANTIC

Bridgeport

OCEAN

Riverhead

NEW YORK

New York

155

THE CHARLES STREET INN

94 CHARLES STREET, BOSTON, MASSACHUSETTS 02114
Tel: +1 617 314 8900 **Fax:** +1 617 371 0009 **U.S./Canada Toll Free:** 1 877 772 8900
Web: www.johansens.com/charlesstreetinn **E-mail:** info@charlesstreetinn.com

Our inspector loved: *The sumptuous full breakfast, including gourmet quiche and the freshest berry bowl, served each morning.*

Price Guide: (including breakfast)
rooms $225-$525

Attractions: Beacon Hill, 1-min walk; State House, 5-min walk; Boston Common, 5-min walk; Public Garden, 5-min walk
Towns/Cities: Cambridge, 3 miles; Brookline, 4 miles; Newton, 9 miles
Airports: Boston Logan International Airport, 3 miles

This charming European-style luxury inn is conveniently situated in the heart of Boston's Beacon Hill. The elegant brownstone façade features small, decorative windows and 2 beautiful overhanging bedroom bow windows. Originally built in 1860 as a model home, the inn has been extensively renovated to preserve and enhance its original style alongside the best in 21st-century facilities and amenities. Guest rooms are are named after famous Boston writers or artists and are decorated in exquisite Victorian style with romantic king or queen-size four-poster or canopy beds, authentic period pieces, original working 1860 fireplaces and Turkish carpets. Each room has a deluxe private bathroom with air-jet whirlpool tub, a kitchenette with sub-zero refrigerator, free WiFi connection, 2-line phone with voice mail, H.D.T.V., fax, safe, minibar and coffee-maker. A laptop is also available to use.

FIFTEEN BEACON

15 BEACON STREET, BOSTON, MASSACHUSETTS 2108
Tel: +1 617 670 1500 **Fax:** +1 617 670 2525 **U.S./Canada Toll Free:** 1 877 XVBEACON
Web: www.johansens.com/xvbeacon **E-mail:** hotel@xvbeacon.com

Our inspector loved: *The complimentary in-town chauffeur-driven Lexus Sedan service available to all guests.*

Price Guide:
rooms $295-$700
suites $995-$1,400
2-bedroom suite (1,375 sq. ft.) $1,900-$2,500

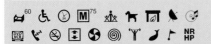

Awards/Ratings: Condé Nast Traveler Gold List 2007; Wine Spectator Award of Excellence 2007; DiRoNA 2007

Attractions: Boston Common, 2-min walk; State House, 2-min walk; Beacon Hill, 2-min walk; Quincy Market/Faneuil Hall, 5-min walk
Towns/Cities: Cambridge, 3 miles; Providence, RI, 51 miles; Cape Cod, 65 miles; Portland, ME, 108 miles
Airports: Boston Logan Intl. Airport, 5 miles

Affiliations: Preferred Boutique

Stylish and modern, Fifteen Beacon is a popular luxury boutique hotel in the heart of Boston with all the comforts and intimacy of a private residence. Situated in a 1903 Beaux Arts Building, this stylish landmark property is modernist in design with only 7 guest rooms per floor and no two are alike. Each luxury guest room and suite is richly decorated and has cozy working gas fireplaces, poster beds with custom-designed 300 count Italian linens and marble baths with rainforest showers. Several suites have lovely views of historic Beacon Street. Ideal for both business and pleasure, take advantage of the hotel's complimentary, in-town chauffeur-driven Lexus Sedan service to explore all that Boston has to offer. Fifteen Beacon's new modern steakhouse with exceptional wine cellar is not to be missed!

HOTEL COMMONWEALTH

500 COMMONWEALTH AVENUE, BOSTON, MASSACHUSETTS 02215
Tel: +1 617 933 5000 **Fax:** +1 617 266 6888 **U.S./Canada Toll Free:** 1 866 784 4000
Web: www.johansens.com/commonwealth **E-mail:** reservations@hotelcommonwealth.com

Our inspector loved: Alfresco dining at Eastern Standard restaurant followed by cocktails and live music at the ultra-cool Foundation Lounge.

Price Guide:
rooms $245-$465
suites $285-$485

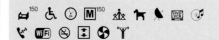

Located on historic Commonwealth Avenue, in the heart of Boston, this luxury hotel beautifully blends classic style with modern edge. A warm welcome awaits you as you take the beautiful staircase leading up to the striking lobby with its rich colors, grand floral designs and eclectic furnishings. Each of the generously sized bedrooms is elegantly decorated and has all modern conveniences. Dinner at the award-winning Great Bay restaurant is a treat offering a fresh approach to locally caught seafood. If you enjoy people watching, Eastern Standard, with its casual American cuisine, is the place to be. After hours, sit back in the plush seating at the Foundation Lounge for music, creative cocktails and Zensai appetizers. There is also a gallery of shops and a delectable chocolate boutique to satisfy your sweet tooth.

Attractions: Fenway Park, 0.5 mile; Boston University, 1 mile; Newbury Street, 1 mile; Longwood Medical Area, 2 miles
Towns/Cities: Brookline, 10-min walk; Cambridge, 10-min drive
Airports: Boston Logan International Airport, 6 miles

Affiliations: Small Luxury Hotels of the World

THE LENOX

61 EXETER STREET AT BOYLSTON, BOSTON, MASSACHUSETTS 02116
Tel: +1 617 536 5300 **Fax:** +1 617 267 1237 **U.S./Canada Toll Free:** 1 800 225 7676
Web: www.johansens.com/lenox **E-mail:** info@lenoxhotel.com

Our inspector loved: *The warm and intimate feel of this family-run hotel.*

Price Guide:
rooms $455-$675
suites from $995

Attractions: Copley Square, 1-min walk; Newbury Street, 2-min walk; Financial District, 10-min walk; Fenway Park, 15-min walk
Towns/Cities: Cape Cod,1.5-hour drive; Nantucket, 2.5-hour drive; Martha's Vineyard, 2.5-hour drive
Airports: Boston Logan International Airport, 20-min drive

Since 1900, this family-owned hotel has been synonymous with grace, style and luxury. Sympathetic modernization has taken place over the past century and today it is the epitome of personal attention and understated elegance, and has the intimacy of a boutique-style establishment. All guest rooms and suites blend Old World charm with 21st-century amenities, crystal lamps, rich dark wood furniture, high ceilings adorned with brass chandeliers and exceptionally comfortable beds. 12 suites offer wood-burning fireplaces and many have spectacular views of Back Bay and the Charles River. Azure offers fine contemporary American cuisine, while Sólás, an authentic Irish pub, serves hearty meals. The sophisticated City-Bar is a popular gathering spot.

THE LIBERTY HOTEL

215 CHARLES STREET, BOSTON, MASSACHUSETTS 02114
Tel: +1 617 224 4000 **Fax:** +1 617 399 4259 **U.S./Canada Toll Free:** 1 866 507 5245
Web: www.johansens.com/liberty **E-mail:** sales@libertyhotel.com

Our inspector loved: The historic architecture with its grand 90-foot central rotunda.

Price Guide:
rooms $299-$550
escape suites from $1,200
presidential suite $5,500

Once the storied Charles Street Jail, this hotel offers you the unique experience of staying in a newly renovated historic landmark in the heart of Boston's famed Beacon Hill. The striking granite edifice welcomes you into the building's grand interior, which is linked by catwalks below a breathtaking 90-foot central rotunda and cupola built in 1851. The actual jail cells have been preserved within the hotel lobby bar and feature striking oversized windows. Rooms are sophisticated in décor with rich mahogany woods, touches of stainless steel and high-tech conveniences. You will find some of Boston's best Charles River views from the hotel suites. Start with drinks in the chic lobby Jail Bar before dining at one of the hotel's 2 world-class restaurants.

Attractions: Beacon Hill, 2-min walk; Charles River and Esplanade, 3-min walk; Freedom Trail, 5-min walk; State House, 5-min drive
Towns/Cities: Cambridge, 3 miles; Brookline, 5 miles; Gloucester, 37 miles; Cape Cod, 67 miles
Airports: Boston Logan International Airport, 3.5 miles

Affiliations: The Leading Hotels of the World

THE CROWNE POINTE HISTORIC INN & SPA

82 BRADFORD STREET, PROVINCETOWN, MASSACHUSETTS 02657
Tel: +1 508 487 6767 **Fax:** +1 508 487 5554 **U.S./Canada Toll Free:** 1 877 276 9631
Web: www.johansens.com/crownepointe **E-mail:** welcome@crownepointe.com

Our inspector loved: *The relaxing atmosphere at the Shui Spa.*

Price Guide:
rooms $100-$469

🛏️⁴⁰ 🚴¹⁶ 📺 🔔 🎵 📞 🌐 ◎ SPA
〰️ 🎵 ♪ 🧲 🍽️

Awards/Ratings: Wine Spectator Award of Excellence 2006

Attractions: Provincetown's Museums, Galleries, Shopping and Night-life, close by; Dune Tours, close by; Whale Watching, 5-min drive; National Seashore, 10-min drive
Towns/Cities: Chatham, 30-min drive; Hyannis, 45-min drive
Airports: Hyannis Cape Cod Airport, 45-min drive; Boston Logan International Airport, 100 miles

Located at the tip of Cape Cod, The Crowne Pointe is a beautifully renovated 19th-century mansion with additional historic carriage houses. Each spacious guest room is decorated in Victorian elegance and luxury with classic colors, antiques, graceful moldings and hardwood floors. Room amenities include oversized bath towels, 250 thread count linens, down comforters, pima cotton bathrobes, and a "Heavenly Bed" premium mattress. Savor gourmet hand-made chocolates, and in the afternoon, the innkeepers invite all to gather for the free wine and cheese social. The Bistro and hotel bar create exquisite gourmet cuisine and offer carefully selected labels from the inn's very own wine cellar. The Asian-inspired Shui Spa, is a serene haven with its own meditation garden. This modern facility has an extensive menu of treatments and is surrounded by a 4,000 gallon Koi pond.

U.S.A. - MASSACHUSETTS (CAPE COD)

WEQUASSETT RESORT AND GOLF CLUB

ON PLEASANT BAY, CHATHAM, MASSACHUSETTS 02633
Tel: +1 508 432 5400 **Fax:** +1 508 430 3131 **U.S./Canada Toll Free:** 1 800 225 7125
Web: www.johansens.com/wequassett **E-mail:** info@wequassett.com

Our inspector loved: The location on Cape Cod with its beautiful views of Pleasant Bay and the Atlantic.

Price Guide: (excluding tax)
rooms $170-$870
suites $560-$1,365

Awards/Ratings: Condé Nast Traveler Gold List 2006 and 2007

Attractions: Cape Cod National Golf Club, 5 miles; Chatham Railroad Museum, 5 miles; Nauset Beach, 9 miles

Towns/Cities: Orleans, 9 miles; Brewster, 10 miles; Hyannis, 18 miles; Provincetown, 35 miles

Airports: Chatham Municipal Airport, 4 miles; Boston Logan International Airport, 90 miles

Affiliations: Preferred Hotels & Resorts

Combining old fashioned elegance with modern-day comforts, this historic Cape Cod resort sits high atop a rise with magnificent views of Pleasant Bay and the Atlantic Ocean. The secluded grounds overlook the salt marshes and woodlands and invite you to explore through meandering pathways filled with beautiful, seasonal flowers. Cozy weathered cottages and suites are comfortable and charming; all have private decks, patios or balconies. There are 4 distinct dining options: LiBAYtion, a beach-front bar offering cocktails and light fare looking out to the best water views from a fashionable pergola; the Outer Bar and Grille for sophisticated yet casual dining; and the relaxed lounge-style Thoreau's. Exceptional cuisine is served in Twenty-Eight Atlantic, decorated in an eclectic fashion with Shaker décor, nautical etchings and exquisite chandeliers.

THE INN AT CASTLE HILL

280 ARGILLA ROAD, IPSWICH, MASSACHUSETTS 01938
Tel: +1 978 412 2555 **Fax:** +1 978 412 2556
Web: www.johansens.com/castlehill **E-mail:** theinn@ttor.org

Our inspector loved: *The beautiful hand-painted walls found throughout the property.*

Price Guide: (including afternoon tea)
rooms $140-$385

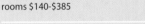

Attractions: Crane Beach, 5-min drive; Castle Hill at the Crane Estate, 5-min drive; Agassiz Rock, 8 miles; Peabody Essex Museum, 17 miles
Towns/Cities: Cape Ann, 8 miles; Newburyport, 14 miles; Salem, 15 miles; Rockport, 15 miles
Airports: Boston Logan International Airport, 31 miles

This elegantly restored sanctuary is quietly nestled at the foot of Castle Hill in the heart of the Crane Estate. The warm and serene atmosphere perfectly complements the glorious countryside of Boston's North Shore. The rooms at the inn are individually appointed and many feature impressive views over the salt marshes, sand dunes and Atlantic Ocean. There is no need for televisions or radios here. Start your day with a hearty breakfast then a leisurely picnic lunch. Later in the day sit on a rocking chair to savor afternoon tea or a glass of wine on the wraparound veranda. Crane Estate is a designated conservation area containing historical buildings, a wildlife refuge and rare maritime forest. All proceeds from the inn contribute to the conservation efforts of the area.

BLANTYRE

16 BLANTYRE ROAD, P.O. BOX 995, LENOX, MASSACHUSETTS 01240
Tel: +1 413 637 3556 **Fax:** +1 413 637 4282
Web: www.johansens.com/blantyre **E-mail:** welcome@blantyre.com

Our inspector loved: The warm welcome.

Price Guide: (excluding service charge and tax)
rooms $525-$775
suites $575-$1,650

Awards/Ratings: Mobil 5 Star; Wine Spectator Award of Excellence 2005 ; Condé Nast Traveler Gold List 2007

Attractions: Tanglewood, 10-min drive; Norman Rockwell Museum, 15-min drive; Hancock Shaker Village, 30-min drive; Massachusetts Museum of Contemporary Art, 45-min drive

Towns/Cities: Lee, 3 miles; Stockbridge, 6 miles; North Adams, 29 miles

Airports: Albany Intl., 58 miles; Hartford, CT/Bradley Intl., 66 miles; Boston Logan, 131 miles

Affiliations: Relais & Châteaux

Blantyre is an exquisite 1902 family-owned manor house hotel located in the picturesque Berkshires. The beautiful décor is highlighted with striking leaded glass windows and richly burnished woods. The impeccably designed guest rooms and suites feature romantic four-poster beds, exceptional furnishings with luxurious fabrics and spacious marble bathrooms with relaxing soaking tubs. Period pieces and treasured heirlooms are a focal point of the main floor's Baronial Main Hall, while inviting plush chairs and fresh flowers are welcoming in the sun-lit Music Room. Fine French cuisine is served in the elegant dining room; the inn boasts an impressive wine collection of more than 1,600 vintages. Magnificent picnic baskets are perfect for a summer's day lunch on the grounds or an afternoon of music at nearby Tanglewood. Ice skating, snow shoeing and cross-country skiing are available in the winter season with refreshments served in the Warming Hut.

CRANWELL RESORT, SPA & GOLF CLUB

55 LEE ROAD, ROUTE 20, LENOX, MASSACHUSETTS 01240
Tel: +1 413 637 1364 **Fax:** +1 413 637 4364 **U.S./Canada Toll Free:** 1 800 272 6935
Web: www.johansens.com/cranwell **E-mail:** info@cranwell.com

Our inspector loved: The Spa Break package that includes Swedish massage and spa lunch.

Price Guide:
rooms $245-$395
suites $295-$1,120

Awards/Ratings: Wine Spectator Award of Excellence 2001-2007

Attractions: Shakespeare & Company, 2 miles; Tanglewood, 4 miles; Norman Rockwell Museum, 9 miles; Jiminy Peak Mountain Resort, 21 miles
Towns/Cities: Stockbridge, 6 miles; Great Barrington, 15 miles; Williamstown, 30 miles
Airports: Albany International Airport, 58 miles; Hartford, CT, and Bradley International Airport, 66 miles; Boston Logan International Airport, 131 miles

In the heart of the Berkshires, surrounded by 380 acres, this Gilded Age mansion offers exceptional accommodation, fine dining, modern amenities and unforgettable service. Cranwell has been carefully renovated to preserve its original 19th-century grandeur and features beautifully decorated bedrooms. The hotel's 3 restaurants serve a variety of cuisine, and views of the picturesque golf course can be enjoyed from Sloane's Tavern. For the romantic, an intimate candle-lit meal may be taken in the Wyndhurst Restaurant or in the Music Room. For those in need of some pampering, visit the 35,000 sq. ft. spa where there are 16 treatment rooms with over 50 services available. With a mountain backdrop, the panoramic 18-hole championship golf course, with G.P.S. equipped golf carts and a driving range, provides a real challenge. Spacious rooms for conferences and weddings are available in this memorable, delightful setting.

The Charlotte Inn

27 SOUTH SUMMER STREET, EDGARTOWN, MASSACHUSETTS 02539
Tel: +1 508 627 4151 **Fax:** +1 508 627 4652
Web: www.johansens.com/charlotte **E-mail:** charlotteinn@aol.com

Our inspector loved: The magnificent Carriage House with its antiques and super outlook over the courtyard.

Price Guide:
rooms $295-$695
suites $550-$895

Attractions: Edgartown, 2-min walk; Vineyard Golf Club, 2 miles
Towns/Cities: Edgartown, 2-min walk
Airports: Hyannis Cape Cod Airport, 30 miles; Boston Logan International Airport, 120 miles

Affiliations: Relais & Châteaux

Ideally situated, just a short walk from the vibrant and historic Edgartown, this delightful inn is nestled amongst chestnut and linden trees. Originally built for a wealthy merchant in 1864, this grand house has recently been restored to recreate the ambience of a bygone era. 19th-century oil paintings line the walls and antiques including grandfather clocks remain. Each of the individually designed Victorian-style bedrooms has traditional mahogany furniture, leather-bound books, silver dressing table sets, goose-down bedding and European draperies. The inn's restaurant serves some of the finest New England cuisine in the area at its romantic candle-lit dining room or on a summer night, on the ivy-clad terrace. The attentive yet unobtrusive service will encourage you to return year after year.

WINNETU OCEANSIDE RESORT AT SOUTH BEACH

31 DUNES ROAD, EDGARTOWN, MASSACHUSETTS 02539
Tel: +1 508 310 1733 **Fax:** +1 508 310 7900 **U.S./Canada Toll Free:** 1 866 335 1133
Web: www.johansens.com/winnetu **E-mail:** reservations@winnetu.com

Our inspector loved: The great water-view location, and life-size chess set.

Price Guide: (room only)
suites $195-$2,400
weekly: homes $1,500-$9,300

Attractions: Bike Path, at the door; Canoe/Kayaking Tours, at the door; Whale Watching Trip to Cape Cod, at the door; South Beach, 250 yards
Towns/Cities: Cape Cod, 7 miles; Edgartown, 10-min drive; Nantucket, 70-min boat ride
Airports: Martha's Vineyard Airport, 4 miles; Hyannis, Cape Cod, Airport, 10 miles; Boston Logan International Airport, 70 miles

Overlooking South Beach in Edgartown, Winnetu Oceanside Resort is set on 11 acres that blend into the natural beauty of Martha's Vineyard. This welcoming resort features suites with outdoor decks or patios, private town houses and single-family homes available for rent. The delicious fine dining, with spectacular ocean views, places an emphasis on locally caught seafood and locally farmed produce and is served at the resort's Lure restaurant. The Lure Kid's Club offers a special family dining option. Lighter fare is served at the Poolside Grill, as well as at the General Store. The Activities & Fitness Center provides a range of strength-training and stretching classes, yoga, and therapeutic massage, and also has a 1,200-ft. studio, Paramount circuit training, free weights, and cardio equipment. Life-size lawn chess, a Teen Program, and free Children's Day Program (in-season) are also available. In the evening, enjoy a sunset water taxi cruise to Edgartown.

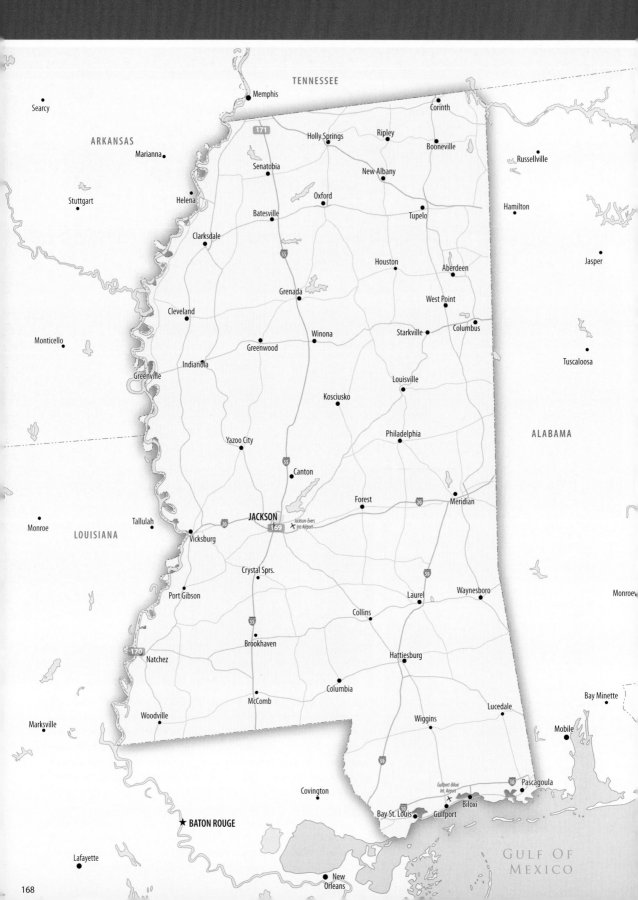

FAIRVIEW INN & RESTAURANT

734 FAIRVIEW STREET, JACKSON, MISSISSIPPI 39202
Tel: +1 601 948 3429 **Fax:** +1 601 948 1203 **U.S./Canada Toll Free:** 1 888 948 1908
Web: www.johansens.com/fairviewinn **E-mail:** fairview@fairviewinn.com

Our inspector loved: *The charming residential ambience.*

Price Guide: (including breakfast)
rooms $139-$199
suites $179-$304

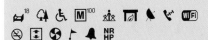

Attractions: Mississippi Museum of Art, 0.1 miles; Eudora Welty Home, 0.3 miles; Old Capitol Museum, 0.3 miles; Natural Science Museum, 2.2 miles
Towns/Cities: Madison, 13 miles; Vicksburg, 49 miles; Natchez, 117 miles
Airports: Jackson Airport, 6.5 miles

Proprietors Peter and Tamar Sharp invite you to experience their unique 18-room bed and breakfast. This 1908 Colonial revival mansion is one of the few architecturally designed homes of its period left standing and exudes the rich history of Jackson. Located in the Belhaven historic neighborhood, adjacent to Millsaps and Belhaven Colleges, The Fairview Inn offers the charm, ambience and hospitality of a small bed and breakfast with the full-service amenities of a luxury hotel. Perfect for leisure or business travelers alike, the tranquil setting is complete with over an acre of pristine gardens. The guest rooms and suites are all uniquely decorated and provide modern conveniences, and Sophia's Restaurant serves dinner from Tuesday evenings through to Saturday and Sunday brunches.

MONMOUTH PLANTATION

36 MELROSE AVENUE, NATCHEZ, MISSISSIPPI 39120
Tel: +1 601 442 5852 **Fax:** +1 601 446 7762 **U.S./Canada Toll Free:** 1 800 828 4531
Web: www.johansens.com/monmouthplantation **E-mail:** luxury@monmouthplantation.com

Our inspector loved: *The experience of staying in such a magnificently restored plantation.*

Price Guide: (including breakfast)
rooms $195-$240
suites $265-$390

Awards/Ratings: Condé Nast Traveler Gold List 2006

Attractions: Golf Course, 1.5 miles; Antique Shopping District, 1.5 miles; Antebellum Home Tours, 5 miles; Seasonal Festivals, 5-min drive
Towns/Cities: Natchez, 5-min walk; Vicksburg, 66 miles; Jackson, 122 miles; New Orleans, LA, 175 miles
Airports: Baton Rouge, LA, 85 miles; Jackson, 122 miles; New Orleans, LA, 175 miles

Affiliations: Small Luxury Hotels of the World

This is truly one of the grand old ladies of the South. Lovingly restored to her original 1818 glory by owners Ron and Lani Riches, Monmouth Plantation offers complete luxury alongside great Southern hospitality. Many distinguished guests have visited this magnificent estate of 26 immaculate acres with rose gardens, ponds and walking trails, and each of the well-appointed rooms and suites has its own personality and charm. Every modern comfort has been considered without compromising the building's architecture, resulting in a perfect blend of comfort and Southern splendor. A 5-course dinner is served by candlelight each evening, and the chef plans daily menus to incorporate traditional favorites and regional ingredients.

Bonne Terre Country Inn

4715 CHURCH ROAD WEST, NESBIT, MISSISSIPPI 38651
Tel: +1 662 781 5100 **Fax:** +1 662 781 5466
Web: www.johansens.com/bonneterre **E-mail:** info@bonneterre.com

Our inspector loved: The relaxing ambience and friendly service.

Price Guide: (including breakfast)
rooms $160-$250
suites $250

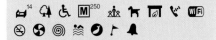

Attractions: Graceland, 10 miles; Beale Street, 20 miles; Memphis Zoo, 22 miles; Brooks Museum of Art, 22 miles
Towns/Cities: Memphis, TN, 22 miles; Tunica, 28 miles; Oxford, 66 miles; Tupelo, 101 miles
Airports: Memphis International Airport, 15 miles

In a quiet, romantic location surrounded by 120 wooded acres of Mississippi highlands, this elegant inn is the perfect retreat from the stresses of daily life. The décor is simply impeccable, and the tastefully, individually decorated guest rooms have sumptuous beds and are filled with fine art and French and English antiques. Fresh flowers and whirlpool tubs complete the feeling of utter luxury and relaxation. The 4 downstairs guest rooms have access to a quaint Southern porch, while the balconies of the rooms upstairs have stunning views of the magnificent grounds. Start your day with a full country breakfast served on the indoor veranda of the Café, and in the evenings, enjoy innovative gourmet cuisine complemented by fine wines in the sophisticated, intimate restaurant.

BIG CEDAR LODGE

612 DEVIL'S POOL ROAD, RIDGEDALE, MISSOURI 65739

Tel: +1 417 335 2777 **Fax:** +1 417 335 2340 **U.S./Canada Toll Free:** 1 800 BCLODGE
Web: www.johansens.com/bigcedar **E-mail:** bigcedar@big-cedar.com

Our inspector loved: *The refreshing and invigorating natural beauty.*

Price Guide:
rooms $129-$383
suites $179-$2,039

Attractions: Table Rock Lake, on-site
Towns/Cities: Branson, 10 miles
Airports: Springfield Branson National Airport, 50 miles

Surrounded by nature trails and 800 acres of wooded Ozark hillsides, with a ridge-side view of Table Rock Lake, this breathtaking wilderness resort is a true rustic retreat. Some interiors feature vaulted wooden ceilings, handcrafted furniture and sumptuous fabrics, and the accommodations are extremely flexible. The Private Log Cabins and Knotty Pine Cottages nestle within leafy cedar glades, and rooms are decorated in an Adirondack style with an atmosphere of coziness and comfort. Cuisine at Big Cedar Lodge celebrates the diverse and rich gastronomic traditions of the area and with 4 restaurants available to you - a variety of dishes are there for the sampling! Activities include boating, canoeing, carriage rides, spa services and Kids' Club.

EDMONTON ★

Prince Albert

Red Deer

Saskatoon

CANADA

BRITISH
COLUMBIA

ALBERTA

elson

Calgary

Brooks

SASKATCHEWAN

Elkford

Swift Current

Moose Jaw

REGINA ★

Cranbrook

Medicine Hat

Weyburn

Lethbridge

Assiniboia

Sandpoint

Libby

Glacier Park
Int. Airport

Cut Bank

Estevan

St. Maries

Kalispell

Shelby

Havre

Glasgow

Wolf Point

Williston

Conrad

Polson

Great Falls
Int. Airport

Great Falls

Sidney

Missoula
Int. Airport

Missoula

Lewistown

Glendive

NORTH
DAKOTA

Grangeville

Hamilton

Dear Lodge

HELENA ★

Dickinson

Anaconda

Salmon

Butte

Dillon

Bozeman

Livingston

Billings Logan
Int. Airport

Billings

Miles City

Hardin

IDAHO

Cody

Belle Fourche

OISE

Buffalo

Gillette

St. Anthony

Hailey

Rapid City

Idaho Falls

Thermopolis

Newcastle

SOUTH
DAKOTA

Gooding

Jackson

WYOMING

Lander

Douglas

Preston

NEVADA

Kemmerer

Rawlins

Torrington

NEBRASKA

Brigham City

UTAH

Green
River

SALT LAKE CITY ★

Tooele

CHEYENNE
★

Kimball

THE BIG EZ LODGE

7000 BEAVER CREEK ROAD, BIG SKY, MONTANA 59716
Tel: +1 406 995 7000 **Fax:** +1 406 995 7007 **U.S./Canada Toll Free:** 1 877 244 3299
Web: www.johansens.com/bigez **E-mail:** jharrison@bigezlodge.com

Our inspector loved: The Lonestar Suite's triple head steam shower.

Price Guide:
rooms $535-$785
suites $1,680-$1,870

Attractions: Fly Fishing, 5-min walk; Hiking, 5-min walk; Yellowstone National Park, 60-min drive; Skiing, 60-min drive
Towns/Cities: Big Sky, 5-min drive; Bozeman, 60-min drive
Airports: Bozeman Airport, 60-min drive

With Yellowstone Park as a backdrop, The Big EZ Lodge is a stunning retreat that blends modern luxury with Western rustic charm. The Montana Range, visible from the front of the hotel, instantly creates a sense of peace and well-being, and the impressive architecture of the hotel is evidence of the style and attention to detail apparent throughout. Large public rooms are decked with antlers and furs to evoke a sense of oasis in the wilderness and vast wooden beams and roaring log fires are combined with leather and animal skin to create a stylish yet warm ambience. The dining room takes great pride in its varying cuisine that features organic herbs from the hotel's own gardens and wild game is a house specialty.

TRIPLE CREEK RANCH

5551 WEST FORK ROAD, DARBY, MONTANA 59829
Tel: +1 406 821 4600 **Fax:** +1 406 821 4666 **U.S./Canada Toll Free:** 1 800 654 2943
Web: www.johansens.com/triplecreek **E-mail:** info@triplecreekranch.com

Our inspector loved: *Waking up to elk in the front of my cottage!*

Price Guide: (including all meals, cocktails and house wines, double occupancy)
rooms $650-$2,495

Awards/Ratings: Condé Nast Johansens Most Excellent Ranch 2006; Wine Spectator Award of Excellence 2006 and 2007

Attractions: Fly Fishing, 2-min walk; Cross Country Skiing, 3-min walk; Hiking, 3-min walk
Towns/Cities: Darby, 12 miles; Hamilton, 40 miles; Missoula, 75 miles; Salmon, ID, 75 miles
Airports: Missoula, 75 miles; Bozeman, 215 miles; Kalispell, 220 miles

Affiliations: Relais & Châteaux

Named for the 3 creeks that border the property, Triple Creek is a spectacular ranch-style hideaway deep in the Montana Mountains. Surrounded by some of the most beautiful wilderness, the snow-covered peaks are awe-inspiring in winter, while the babbling creeks turn magnificent in springtime. Alpine and cross-country skiing are popular activities during the colder months, and in springtime fly fishing on the Bitterroot River is a delight. Accommodation is available in a series of traditional log cabins throughout the grounds, each carefully designed and decorated to take advantage of the environment. Dining in the candle-lit dining room is a particular treat; the rooftop lounge offers a more informal menu with views over the West Fork of the Bitterroot River.

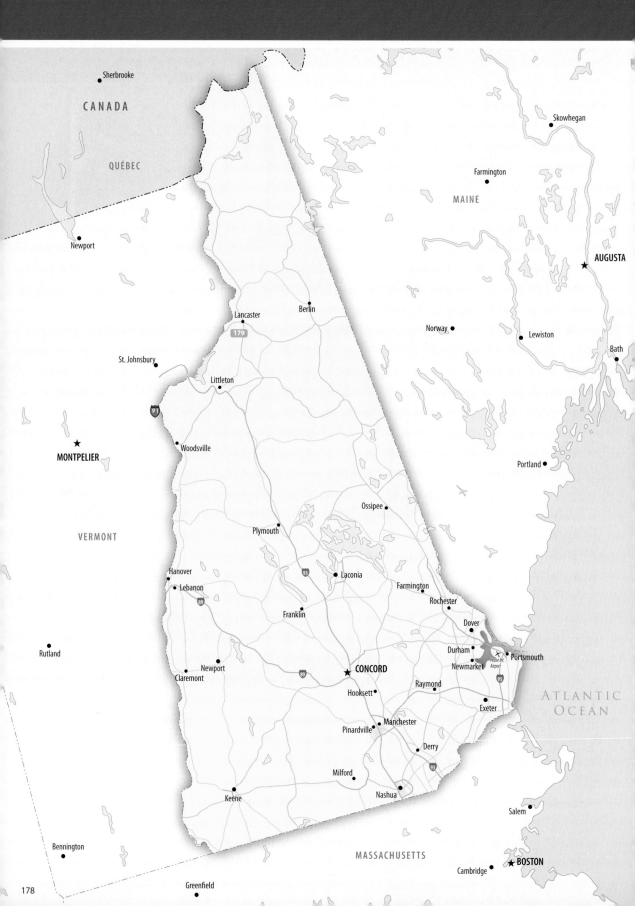

Sherbrooke

CANADA

QUÉBEC

Newport

MAINE

Skowhegan

Farmington

Berlin

Lancaster

179

Norway

Lewiston

St. Johnsbury

Littleton

Bath

91

Woodsville

MONTPELIER

AUGUSTA

Portland

VERMONT

Ossipee

Plymouth

Hanover

Lebanon

93

Laconia

Farmington

Rochester

89

Franklin

Dover

Durham

Rutland

Newport

89

CONCORD

Hooksett

Raymond

Newmarket

Pease Int. Airport

Portsmouth

95

Claremont

Manchester

Exeter

ATLANTIC OCEAN

Pinardville

Derry

Milford

93

Keene

Nashua

Salem

Bennington

MASSACHUSETTS

Cambridge

BOSTON

Greenfield

MOUNTAIN VIEW GRAND RESORT & SPA

MOUNTAIN VIEW ROAD, WHITEFIELD, NEW HAMPSHIRE 03598
Tel: +1 603 837 2100 **Fax:** +1 603 837 8720 **U.S./Canada Toll Free:** 1 866 484 3843
Web: www.johansens.com/mountainview **E-mail:** info@mountainviewgrand.com

*Our inspector loved: The panoramic view
from the hot tub located in the spa's tower.*

Price Guide: (room only)
rooms $109-$319
suites $399-$689

Attractions: Santa's Village, 8 miles; Cannon
Mountain Tram, 20 miles; Storyland, 30 miles;
N. Conway Outlet Shopping, 40 miles
Towns/Cities: Manchester, 100 miles; Portland,
ME, 100 miles; Boston, MA, 150 miles; Montréal,
QC, 170 miles
Airports: Mount Washington Regional Airport,
4 miles; Manchester-Boston Regional Airport,
100 miles; Boston Logan International Airport,
150 miles

This magnificent resort's legendary charm is matched only by its stunning location within 1,700 acres, in the heart of the White Mountains. Its tradition of hospitality dates back to 1865 and provides intimate guest areas such as the lobby with baby grand piano, the Dodge Parlor and Eisenhower Library, named in honor of the former presidential visitor. Spacious rooms and suites display custom-made mahogany furnishings, and the Main Dining Room offers a sophisticated atmosphere. The Tavern is more casual, and alfresco dining can be enjoyed along with poolside selections from The Club House. Perched high within the Colonial Revival observation tower is the comprehensive Mountain View Grand Spa. Other activities include golf on the resort's 100-year-old course, snowshoeing and sleigh rides.

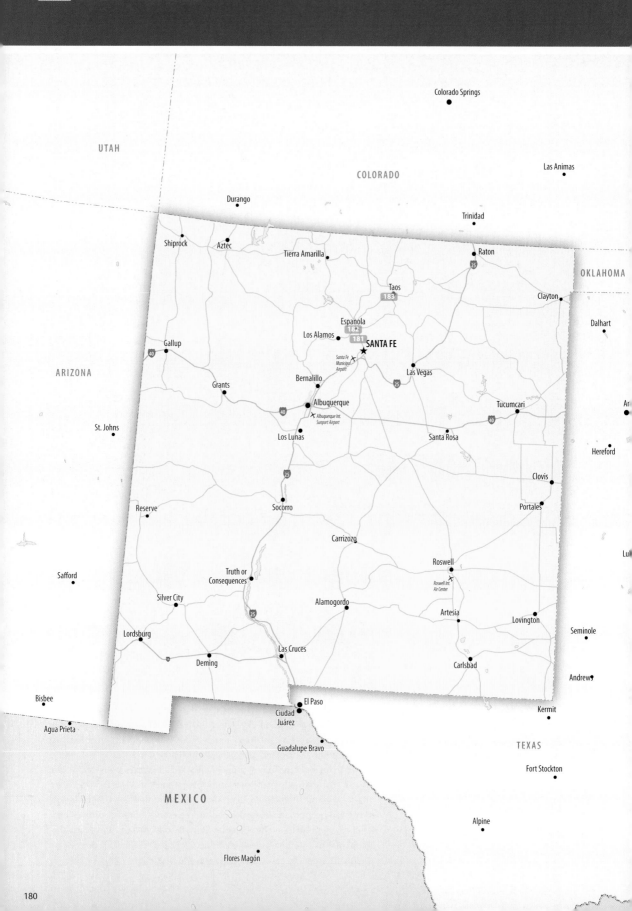

UTAH

COLORADO

Colorado Springs

Las Animas

Durango

Trinidad

Shiprock
Aztec
Tierra Amarilla
Raton

OKLAHOMA

Taos
183
Clayton

Espanola
182
Dalhart

Los Alamos
181
SANTA FE

Gallup
40
Santa Fe Municipal Airport
Las Vegas

Bernalillo
25

ARIZONA

Grants
Albuquerque
Tucumcari

40
40

Ar

Albuquerque Int. Sunport Airport

St. Johns
Los Lunas
Santa Rosa

Hereford

Clovis

25

Reserve
Socorro
Portales

Carrizozo

Lu

Safford

Roswell

Truth or Consequences

Roswell Int. Air Center

Silver City
Alamogordo
Artesia
Lovington

25
Seminole

Lordsburg
Carlsbad

Deming
Las Cruces
Andrews

Bisbee
El Paso

Agua Prieta
Ciudad Juárez

Kermit

TEXAS

MEXICO
Guadalupe Bravo

Fort Stockton

Alpine

Flores Magón

RANCHO DE SAN JUAN

P.O. BOX 4140, HIGHWAY 285, ESPAÑOLA, NEW MEXICO 87533
Tel: +1 505 753 6818 **Fax:** +1 505 753 6818
Web: www.johansens.com/ranchosanjuan **E-mail:** ranchosj@cybermesa.com

Our inspector loved: *The stunning high desert beauty and the exquisite gourmet dining.*

Price Guide: (excluding tax)
rooms $275-$385
suites $475-$675

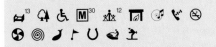

Awards/Ratings: Condé Nast Johansens Most Excellent Romantic Hideaway, U.S.A. & Canada 2007; Wine Spectator Award of Excellence 2007; Condé Nast Traveler Gold List 2006

Attractions: Hot Springs, 3 miles; Ojo Caliente River Valley, 12 miles; Georgia O'Keefe Museum/Home, 38 miles; Art Museums, 38 miles
Towns/Cities: Santa Fe, 38 miles, Taos, 48 miles
Airports: Santa Fe Airport, 38 miles; Albuquerque Airport, 100 miles

Affiliations: Relais & Châteaux

Amidst 225 acres of astonishing natural beauty, Rancho de San Juan is a Spanish hacienda with wildflower-filled courtyards. Public rooms are adorned with the owners' private art and antique collections, and bedrooms feature kiva fireplaces and private terraces overlooking glorious views. Each accommodation is decorated with eclectic furnishings, Egyptian cotton sheets, frette bath towels and Aveda toileteries. Dining is a gourmet delight served on custom-designed porcelain alongside family sterling silver. The weekly changing à la carte menu uses traditional Norteño ingredients to create classic meals combined with worldwide flavors. A diverse range of seasonal activities can be organized nearby, including white-water rafting and hiking trails. Alternately, enjoy a massage in the privacy of your own room or terrace.

THE BISHOP'S LODGE RESORT & SPA

1297 BISHOP'S LODGE ROAD, SANTA FE, NEW MEXICO 87501
Tel: +1 505 983 6377 **Fax:** 1 505 989 0832 **U.S./Canada Toll Free:** 1 800 732 2240
Web: www.johansens.com/bishopslodge **E-mail:** reservations@bishopslodge.com

Our inspector loved: *The outdoor spa treatments in this luscious oasis setting just minutes from downtown Santa Fe.*

Price Guide: (room only)
rooms $159-$499
suites $399-$999

Built in 1851 for Jean Baptiste, first Bishop of Santa Fe, this tranquil retreat encompasses lush gardens and lawns among 450 acres of desert serenity, rolling foothills and a valley just beside the Sante Fe National Forest. At an altitude of 7,300 ft. the resort enjoys crystal clear days and crisp cool nights, with snowfalls in the lofty Sierra Mountains in excess of 100 inches. An intriguing variety of opulent accommodation is located in 11 Spanish Colonial-style lodges. All have lovely kiva fireplaces and private patios from which to savor the panoramic views. Treatments at the spa, horseback riding and hiking trails leading to the canyons and foothills of Sangre de Cristos or to the campground of Mesa Vista, can all be arranged. There is also a skeet and a trap shooting range.

Attractions: Art Galleries, 5-min drive; World-Class Restaurants, 5-min drive; Santa Fe Opera, 5-min drive; Georgia O'Keefe Museum, 10-min drive
Towns/Cities: Santa Fe, 5-min drive; Albuquerque, 60 miles
Airports: Santa Fe Airport, 7 miles; Albuquerque Airport, 60 miles

El Monte Sagrado Living Resort & Spa

317 KIT CARSON ROAD, TAOS, NEW MEXICO 87571
Tel: +1 505 758 3502 **Fax:** +1 505 737 2985 **U.S./Canada Toll Free:** 1 800 828 TAOS
Web: www.johansens.com/elmontesagrado **E-mail:** info@elmontesagrado.com

Our inspector loved: *The magical ambience, and the art, culture, fine dining and excitement of Taos just minutes away.*

Price Guide:
rooms U.S.$199-U.S.$349
suites U.S.$299-U.S.$699

Awards/Ratings: Condé Nast Traveler Gold List 2006; Wine Spectator Award of Excellence 2005

Attractions: Art Galleries, 5-min walk; Shopping, 5-min walk; Hiking, 20-min drive; Skiing, 25-min drive
Towns/Cities: Santa Fe, 58 miles
Airports: Santa Fe, 68 miles; Albuquerque, 130 miles

Affiliations: Kessler Collection; The Leading Hotels of the World

Tucked away in the shadow of the Sangre de Cristo Mountains, Taos has long been considered a place of artistic and spiritual inspiration. The Sacred Circle is an area set aside for quiet events or contemplation and forms the heart of this unusual compound. It sets the theme of celebrating, embracing and respecting nature and local traditions. The Biolarium is a holistically designed structure, and the Spa offers specialized treatments and therapies. Choose to stay in one of the uniquely designed and furnished Treasure of Taos casitas, constructed by local craftsman and artists, or in a Native American Suite featuring kiva-style fireplaces, stone tiles and stained-wood furnishings. Alternately, the lavishly appointed Global Suites offer total immersion in international art and culture. The eclectic and diverse dining options include the Anaconda Bar that often provides live entertainment and displays a 1,100 gallon salt-water aquarium and a giant anaconda sculpture.

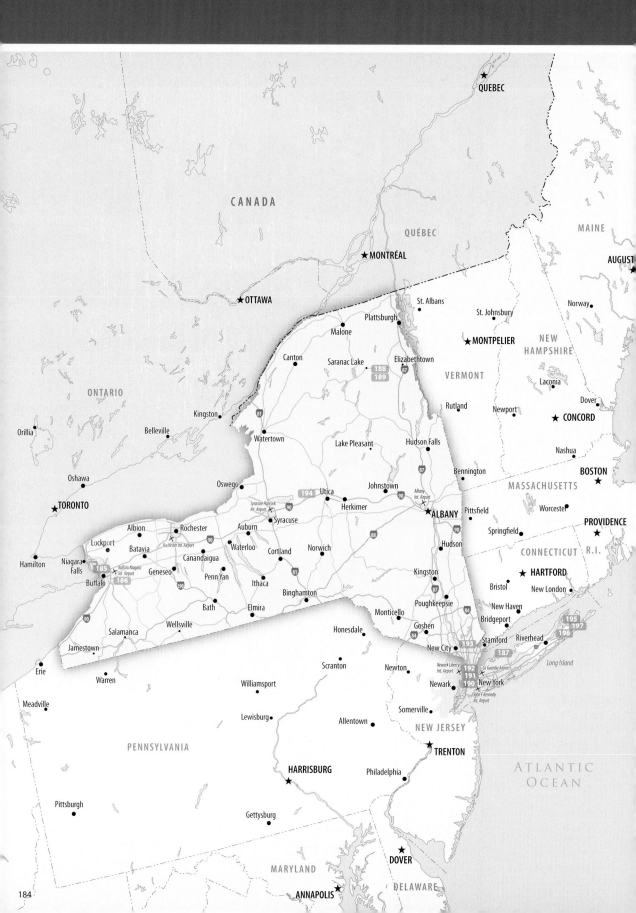

QUEBEC

CANADA

QUÉBEC

★ MONTRÉAL

★ OTTAWA

MAINE

★ AUGUST

Norway

St. Albans

St. Johnsbury

Plattsburgh

Malone

★ MONTPELIER

NEW HAMPSHIRE

Canton

Saranac Lake

Elizabethtown

188
189

VERMONT

Laconia

Dover

ONTARIO

Kingston

Rutland

Newport

★ CONCORD

Orillia

Belleville

Watertown

Lake Pleasant

Hudson Falls

Nashua

Oshawa

Oswego

Utica

Johnstown

Bennington

BOSTON

★ TORONTO

Syracuse Hancock
Int. Airport

194

Herkimer

Albany
Int. Airport

MASSACHUSETTS

Worcester

Albion

Rochester

Syracuse

Auburn

90

★ ALBANY

Pittsfield

PROVIDENCE

Hamilton

Lockport

Batavia

Rochester Int. Airport

Waterloo

Cortland

Norwich

88

Springfield

CONNECTICUT

R.I.

Niagara
Falls

185

Buffalo Niagara
Int. Airport

Canandaigua

Geneseo

Penn Yan

81

Hudson

Kingston

★ HARTFORD

Erie

Buffalo

186

390

Ithaca

Binghamton

87

Poughkeepsie

Bristol

New London

Salamanca

Bath

Elmira

Monticello

84

New Haven

Jamestown

Wellsville

Goshen

Bridgeport

195
197

Warren

Honesdale

84

New City

193

Stamford

Riverhead

196

Meadville

Scranton

Newton

192
191
190

187

Long Island

Williamsport

Newark Liberty
Int. Airport

La Guardia Airport

Pittsburgh

Lewisburg

Allentown

Somerville

Newark

★ New York

John F Kennedy
Int. Airport

PENNSYLVANIA

NEW JERSEY

ATLANTIC
OCEAN

HARRISBURG

Philadelphia

★ TRENTON

Gettysburg

MARYLAND

★ DOVER

DELAWARE

ANNAPOLIS

THE MANSION ON DELAWARE AVENUE

414 DELAWARE AVENUE, BUFFALO, NEW YORK 14202
Tel: +1 716 886 3300 **Fax:** +1 716 883 3923
Web: www.johansens.com/mansionondelaware **E-mail:** info@mansionondelaware.com

Our inspector loved: *This architectural treasure in the heart of downtown; a culturally rich neighborhood.*

Price Guide:
rooms $179-$319
suites $425

Attractions: Allentown Art and Theater District, on-site; Niagara Falls, 25-min drive
Towns/Cities: Buffalo, on-site; Niagara-on-the-Lake, 32 miles; Toronto, 96 miles
Airports: Buffalo Airport, 9 miles; Toronto Airport, ON, 96 miles

The Mansion on Delaware Avenue is without doubt, a Buffalo landmark with international status. Dating back to 1869 when it was built as a private residence, it has earned a colorful history yet stood vacant for 25 years until 2001. A 3-year, multi-million dollar restoration elevated the hotel to sought-after status with high-style design, butler service and grand luxury, and offers highly-acclaimed culinary quality, design and personal service. Upon entering through the Second Empire mahogany doors, you will be greeted by a butler who will show you to a fully prepared whirlpool bath with complimentary bath salts. Butlers will mix the perfect beverage, press your attire and organize free downtown transportation or helipad access. The exquisitely decorated guest rooms, including 3 parlor suites, are impeccably appointed with every modern amenity and first-class level of comfort.

THE ROYCROFT INN

40 SOUTH GROVE STREET, EAST AURORA, NEW YORK 14052
Tel: +1 716 652 5552 **Fax:** +1 716 655 5345 **U.S./Canada Toll Free:** 1 877 652 5552
Web: www.johansens.com/roycroftinn **E-mail:** info@roycroftinn.com

Our inspector loved: The beautiful woodwork and Mission-style; a home-away-from-home.

Price Guide:
rooms $130-$195
suites $145-$275

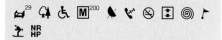

Attractions: The National Historic Landmark of Roycroft Campus, on-site; Buffalo Bills Stadium, 15-min drive; Darwin D. Martin Complex, 30-min drive; Niagara Falls, 1-hour drive

Towns/Cities: Buffalo, 25 miles; Niagara-on-the-Lake 1-hour drive; Syracuse, 150 miles; Toronto, ON, 2-hour drive

Airports: Buffalo Airport, 25 miles; Rochester Airport, 100 miles; Syracuse Airport, 150 miles

The Roycroft Inn is in every sense an American national landmark. It was founded over a hundred years ago by the philosopher and writer Elbert Hubbard to provide congenial accommodation for devotees of the local Arts and Crafts movement. The décor and furniture are either original or authentic reproduction examples of the celebrated movement to which the inn is a shrine. Bedrooms conform to the original structure, while enhancing and conserving the historic character of the entire building; all are furnished in traditional Roycroft style and feature modems, televisions and video equipment. The restaurant is open for lunches, dinners and Sunday brunches, and in the summer alfresco dining can be enjoyed. Private facilities are available for meetings and parties for up to 200 people.

OHEKA CASTLE HOTEL & ESTATE

135 WEST GATE DRIVE, HUNTINGTON, NEW YORK 11743
Tel: +1 631 659 1400 **Fax:** +1 631 592 5991
Web: www.johansens.com/oheka **E-mail:** reservations@oheka.com

Our inspector loved: *This fairy-tale castle so close to New York City.*

Price Guide:
rooms $295-$525
suites $525-975

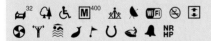

Attractions: Old Bethpage Restoration, 12-min drive; Belmont Race Track, 30-min drive; Long Island Vineyards, 1-hour drive
Towns/Cities: Huntington, 11 miles
Airports: J.F.K. Airport, 40-min drive

Affiliations: Small Luxury Hotels of the World

OHEKA Castle is a magnificent French-style château set amidst 23 acres of formal gardens with pebble-paths, statues and fountains. This historic estate was named after Otto Hermann Kahn, the wealthy philanthropist who built it as a summer home in 1919 during the golden age of American history. The castle and estate, converted to a hotel following $30 million of restoration, is lavishly decorated and boasts 32 guest rooms, an elegant, elongated indoor swimming pool, and a grand library sumptuously furnished with Oriental rugs, authentic portraits, a regal fireplace and grand piano. The guest rooms are equally impressive, individually appointed in rich, luxurious tones with exquisite details such as French-print wallpaper, chandeliers and claw-footed bathtubs. For a special treat, order a spa treatment from the hotel's extensive in-room menu.

MIRROR LAKE INN RESORT & SPA

77 MIRROR LAKE DRIVE, LAKE PLACID, NEW YORK
Tel: +1 518 523 2544 **Fax:** +1 518 523 2871
Web: www.johansens.com/mirrorlake **E-mail:** info@mirrorlakeinn.com

Our inspector loved: *The wonderful location overlooking Mirror Lake.*

Price Guide:
rooms $245-$1,300

Attractions: Lake Placid Olympic Venues, 10-min drive; Adirondack Museum, 1-hour drive
Towns/Cities: Lake Placid, 5-min walk
Airports: Adirondack Airport, 17 miles; Plattsburgh Airport, 45 miles

Affiliations: Small Luxury Hotels of the World

This traditional luxury resort, one of Lake Placid's finest, enjoys a unique prime position overlooking beautiful Mirror Lake and the Adirondack Mountain high peaks. Cozy, Old World charm is what you feel when you enter the mahogany-paneled lobby where you'll find a warm fire and afternoon tea. The beautifully appointed guest rooms range from luxurious Placid suites, to lake and mountain view rooms, to the new Colonial House ultimate suites. Service is always friendly and unobtrusive. In summer, enjoy boating, canoeing, swimming at the private beach, hiking, golf and tennis. In winter, take the family skiing at Whiteface Mountain, ice skate on the private rink, snowshoe, cross-country ski, or take a bobsled ride. After your adventures, enjoy one of many rejuvenating spa treatments in the full-service spa. Savor the world-class cuisine at The View Restaurant, and an inventive fusion of international specialties at Taste Bistro and Bar.

THE WHITEFACE LODGE

7 WHITEFACE INN LANE, LAKE PLACID, NEW YORK 12946
Tel: +1 518 523 0500 **Fax:** +1 518 523 0559 **U.S./Canada Toll Free:** 1 800 903 4045
Web: www.johansens.com/whiteface **E-mail:** info@thewhitefacelodge.com

Our inspector loved: *This true Adirondack lodge with activities unique to the area.*

Price Guide:
suites $300-$5,000

Attractions: Lake Placid Village, 1 mile; Olympic Ski Jump, 3 miles; Whiteface Mountain, 12 miles
Towns/Cities: Burlington, VT, 90 miles; Albany, 135 miles; Montréal, QC, 175 miles; New York City, 285 miles
Airports: Saranac Lake Airport, 20-min drive; Burlington Airport, Albany, 2-hour drive; Montréal Airport, QC, 2.5-hour drive

Affiliations: The Leading Hotels of the World

This all-suite resort blends rustic elegance with contemporary luxury and exceptional service. Classic American cuisine, prepared from fresh, local organic ingredients and native North American fish and game, is served in the fine dining restaurant, Steak and Stinger. Gourmands and aspiring chefs will enjoy the exhibition kitchen. The Canoe Club boasts a private beach and offers traditional camp activities such as canoeing, kayaking and horseshoeing. Other on-site facilities are in abundance and include an ice skating rink, 10-pin bowling alley and surround-sound theater. Winter sport facilities are not available on-site but are sure to be found in nearby Lake Placid. The Spa at Whiteface Lodge offers an array of treatments and featres B. Kamins and Red flower products.

HÔTEL PLAZA ATHÉNÉE

37 EAST 64TH STREET, NEW YORK CITY, NEW YORK 10065
Tel: +1 212 734 9100 **Fax:** +1 212 772 0958 **U.S./Canada Toll Free:** 1 800 447 8800
Web: www.johansens.com/athenee **E-mail:** res@plaza-athenee.com

Our inspector loved: The impeccable attention to detail and service.

Price Guide: (room only, excluding tax)
rooms $695
suites $1,470

Awards/Ratings: DiRoNa 2007; Condé Nast Traveler Gold List 2007

Attractions: Central Park, 0.5 miles; Museum of Modern Art, 0.5 miles; Children's Zoo, 0.5 miles; Madison Avenue Shopping, 0.5 miles
Airports: J.F.K. Airport, 13 miles; Newark Airport, 13 miles

Affiliations: The Leading Hotels of the World

Conveniently and fashionably situated on the East Side of Manhattan, Hôtel Plaza Athénée is nestled amidst a line of town houses on a quiet tree-lined street. Rooms feature Asian silks and soothing earth tones, and offer complimentary services such as 24-hour concierge, business center facilities, tea and coffee at 5.30-7pm, use of the fitness center and Internet access in the bar. Some suites have a sweeping view over the rooftops of Manhattan from a private balcony and atrium terrace. Modern American cuisine is served in Arabelle, a romantic gold-domed room with lovely murano glass. Enjoy an after-dinner drink in the exotic Bar Seine, where a fusion of Moroccan, African, European and Asian art are complemented by animal print fabrics and leather flooring.

THE INN AT IRVING PLACE

56 IRVING PLACE, NEW YORK, NEW YORK CITY 10003
Tel: +1 212 533 4600 **Fax:** +1 212 533 4611 **U.S./Canada Toll Free:** 1 800 685 1447
Web: www.johansens.com/irving **E-mail:** innatirving@aol.com

Our inspector loved: *High tea in Lady Mendl's Tea Salon.*

Price Guide:
rooms $445-$645

 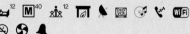

Awards/Ratings: Condé Nast Johansens Most Excellent Inn 2005

Attractions: Union Square and Gramercy Park, 2-min walk; New York Univeristy, 10-min walk; Empire State Building, 15-min walk; Times Square and Broadway, 20-min walk
Airports: La Guardia International Airport, 30-min drive; J.F.K. International Airport, 50-min drive

Affiliations: Small Luxury Hotels of the World

The Inn at Irving Place is an impressive venue to visit and a peaceful respite from the bustling city. Built in 1834, in the heart of New York's historic Gramercy Park, this unique hotel is surrounded by tree-lined streets and landmark architecture, and has been carefully renovated to reflect the timeless elegance of a bygone era. Luxurious furnishings and beautiful antiques adorn the 12 immaculate bedrooms and residences, which are reminiscent of Edith Wharton's New York. A delicious breakfast can be served in your bed or in the famous Lady Mendl's Tea Salon, renowned for its idyllic setting and fine teas. Your hosts will be happy to recommend one of the many excellent restaurants nearby, and for health enthusiasts, there is a fitness club a few minutes away.

JUMEIRAH ESSEX HOUSE

160 CENTRAL PARK SOUTH, NEW YORK CITY, NEW YORK 10019
Tel: +1 212 247 0300 **Fax:** +1 212 315 1839 **U.S./Canada Toll Free:** 1 888 645 5697
Web: www.johansens.com/essexhouse **E-mail:** JEHinfo@jumeirah.com

Our inspector loved: The stunning artwork throughout the hotel, much of it reflecting the natural beauty of Central Park.

Price Guide:
rooms $450-$750

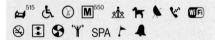

Attractions: Central Park, 0.5 miles; Broadway, 0.5 miles; 5th Avenue, 0.5 miles; MOMA, 0.5 miles
Airports: LaGuardia Airport, 7 miles; J.F.K. International Airport, 18 miles; Newark Airport, 18 miles

Stylish interiors, the latest in modern technology, a fully-equipped gym and spa, a restaurant and lounge offering fine dining, great shopping, entertainment, and nightlife only steps away, Jumeirah Essex House is everything the discerning traveler could wish for in a city hotel. This art deco-inspired hotel, recently benefiting from $70 million of refurbishments, is sleek and stylish with luxurious and well-equipped rooms featuring every desirable amenity. Towering high above Central Park, with views of midtown Manhattan and just a few blocks from Broadway, the hotel is ideally located for those wishing to take advantage of all that the Big Apple has to offer, as well as those seeking a relaxing break from the hustle and bustle of the city.

CASTLE ON THE HUDSON

400 BENEDICT AVENUE, TARRYTOWN, NEW YORK 10591
Tel: +1 914 631 1980 **Fax:** +1 914 631 4612 **U.S./Canada Toll Free:** 1 800 616 4487
Web: www.johansens.com/hudson **E-mail:** info@castleonthehudson.com

Our inspector loved: *Dining at the hotel, an exceptional experience that should not be missed!*

Price Guide:
rooms $330-$430
suites $500-$800

Attractions: Antiquing, 5-min drive; Lyndhurst Castle, 7-min drive; Kykuit (Rockefeller Family Mansion), 10-min drive; The Westchester (Shopping), 10-min drive
Towns/Cities: New York City, 31 miles
Airports: LaGuardia Airport, 28 miles; J.F.K. Airport, 36 miles; Newark Airport, 42 miles

Affiliations: Small Luxury Hotels of the World

This elegant medieval-style castle was built during the turn of the 20th century by New York writer, businessman and socialite, Howard Carroll, in order to flaunt his wealth. Following his death, the castle was converted into an opulent hotel offering traditional, warm hospitality and impeccable service. Each of the individually appointed bedrooms and bathrooms has been lavished with rich fabrics, ornate artworks, antiques and beautiful wooden furniture. The magnificent Tower Suites are the ultimate in style with four-poster beds, wood-burning fireplaces, marble bathrooms, turret alcoves and panoramic vistas over the hillside, Hudson River and Manhattan. Dining at the hotel is sublime: there are 3 different rooms, each with their own unique ambience in which to enjoy the creative gourmet dishes. The spectacular outdoor terrace is perfect for romantic alfresco meals and cocktails.

THE LODGE AT TURNING STONE

5218 PATRICK ROAD, VERONA, NEW YORK 13478
Tel: +1 315 361 8525 **Fax:** +1 315 361 8686 **U.S./Canada Toll Free:** 1 877 784 8375
Web: www.johansens.com/turningstone **E-mail:** info@turningstone.com

Our inspector loved: The American-Indian influence apparent throughout Skana, the Spa at Turning Stone.

Price Guide:
rooms $295-$595
suites $3,000-$3,500

Awards/Ratings: Condé Nast Johansens Most Excellent Resort, U.S.A. & Canada 2007

Attractions: International Boxing Hall of Fame, 10 miles; Fort Stanwix National Monument, 12 miles; National Baseball Hall of Fame, 61 miles; Finger Lakes Wine Country, 90 miles
Towns/Cities: Syracuse, 35 miles; New York City, 260 miles; Philadelphia, PA, 293 miles; Washington, D.C., 409 miles
Airports: U.C.A. Oneida County Airport, 16 miles; Syracuse Hancock International Airport, 35 miles; Albany International Airport, 111 miles

This luxury boutique hotel surrounds its guests with sophistication and comfort, and provides personal, intuitive service. Personal butler service is available upon request, delivering advanced service and anticipating guests' every need. At the Lodge's heart is the magnificent Great Room with its open fire, luxury seating, superb décor and interesting artwork. This is an ideal spot in which to relax and enjoy stunning views before enjoying a memorable gourmet dinner in the elegant Wildflowers restaurant, where traditional Continental dishes are prepared to exact preferences. Suites are lavishly furnished and appointed with every modern amenity and comfort with wonderful balcony views over 2 of the country's finest and most challenging 18-hole championship golf courses. Expansive and intimately indulgent, the Presidential Suite is an opulent retreat with 3 bedrooms, mini-spa, kitchen and deluxe media center.

THE BAKER HOUSE 1650

181 MAIN STREET, EAST HAMPTON, NEW YORK 11937
Tel: +1 631 324 4081 **Fax:** +1 631 329 5931
Web: www.johansens.com/bakerhouse **E-mail:** info@bakerhouse1650.com

Our inspector loved: *The delicious gourmet breakfast, and the fantastic pool.*

Price Guide: (including breakfast, excluding tax)
rooms $250-$845

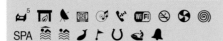

SPA

Attractions: Shops and Restaurants, 5-min walk; Ocean Beach, 15-min walk
Towns/Cities: South Hampton, 10 miles; New York City, 100 miles
Airports: J.F.K. Airport, 94 miles; LaGuardia Airport, 97 miles

The charming Baker House 1650 exudes elegance and will delight those of you in search of an exclusive hideaway with a romantic ambience. Featuring wood craftwork derived from medieval English architecture and a Colonial revival staircase, the wood-burning fireplaces and William Morris wallpaper contrast with the flat-screen T.V.s and state-of-the-art cable and D.V.D. players. Surrounded by flowering perennials and shrubs, delicately scented herbs and English gardens, the outdoor terraces are perfect for alfresco dining, and the outdoor infinity-edge pool, with teak chaises for sunbathing, is utterly relaxing. The Baker Spa, with lap pool, steam shower and sauna, is the ideal retreat. In the summer, you will receive coveted East Hampton Village beach parking passes, as well as beach towels, umbrellas and chairs.

THE MILL HOUSE INN

31 NORTH MAIN STREET, EAST HAMPTON, NEW YORK 11937
Tel: +1 631 324 9766 **Fax:** +1 631 324 9793
Web: www.johansens.com/millhouse **E-mail:** innkeeper@millhouseinn.com

Our inspector loved: The Mill House breakfast that is simply remarkable!

Price Guide: (including breakfast)
rooms $225-$695
suites $450-$1,095

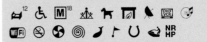

Attractions: Ocean Beach, 1 mile; World-Class Shops and Restaurants, 5-min walk; Galleries and Theaters, 10-min walk; Wineries, 15-min drive
Towns/Cities: South Hampton, 12 miles; Newport, RI, 80 miles; New York City, 105 miles; Boston, 130 miles
Airports: MacArthur I.S.P. Airport, 52 miles; J.F.K. Airport, 94 miles; LaGuardia, 96 miles

The Mill House Inn is in the heart of the village surrounded by spectacular beaches, pristine bays and picturesque country roads. Warm, inviting interiors create a relaxed ambience that is friendly and welcoming while the attention to detail, combined with old-fashioned hospitality, makes each visit truly memorable. Rooms are individually decorated with fine quality linens, lofty featherbeds, gas fireplaces and whirlpool tubs. The spacious suites have 6-foot serenity air baths, double marble showers and private decks where you can enjoy beautiful sunsets and starry skies. Views of the historic Old Hook Windmill are seen from the front porch. Wake up to imaginative breakfasts with dishes such as crawfish and Andouille omelette or 5-cheese frittata each morning, and set off to the eastern end of Long Island, which is a fisherman's playground, a vintner's paradise and an artist's inspiration.

1708 HOUSE

126 MAIN STREET, SOUTHAMPTON, NEW YORK 11968
Tel: +1 631 287 1708 **Fax:** +1 631 287 3593
Web: www.johansens.com/1708house **E-mail:** 1708house@hamptons.com

Our inspector loved: *The charming wine cellar where you can have a drink, relax or play games.*

Price Guide: (including breakfast)
rooms $150-$375
suites $175-$425
cottages $295-$625

NR
HP

Attractions: Shops and Restaurants, on the doorstep; Beaches, 1-3 miles; Wineries, 1-6 miles
Towns/Cities: Sag Harbor, 11 miles; East Hampton, 18 miles; Montauk, 35 miles; New York City, 100 miles
Airports: McArthur Islip Airport, 40 miles; LaGuardia Airport, 95 miles; J.F.K. Airport, 95 miles

This stylish, historic and charming boutique hotel exudes a quiet, romantic atmosphere that is complemented by personalized and unobtrusive service. At every turn you are reminded of the historical significance of this hotel. The cellar dates back to 1648 and has oak beams and stone walls with an original brick fireplace. Guest rooms have wooden panels and exposed beams and are beautifully decorated with luxurious antique beds, antique furnishings and sumptuous fabrics. There are also 3 cottages on the property; 2 are fitted with a kitchen and living room. The reading room is perfect for quiet reflection or the more formal parlor is ideal for meeting up with friends and family. Breakfast is served in the dining room overlooking the patio and garden, which boasts the finest Limoges china.

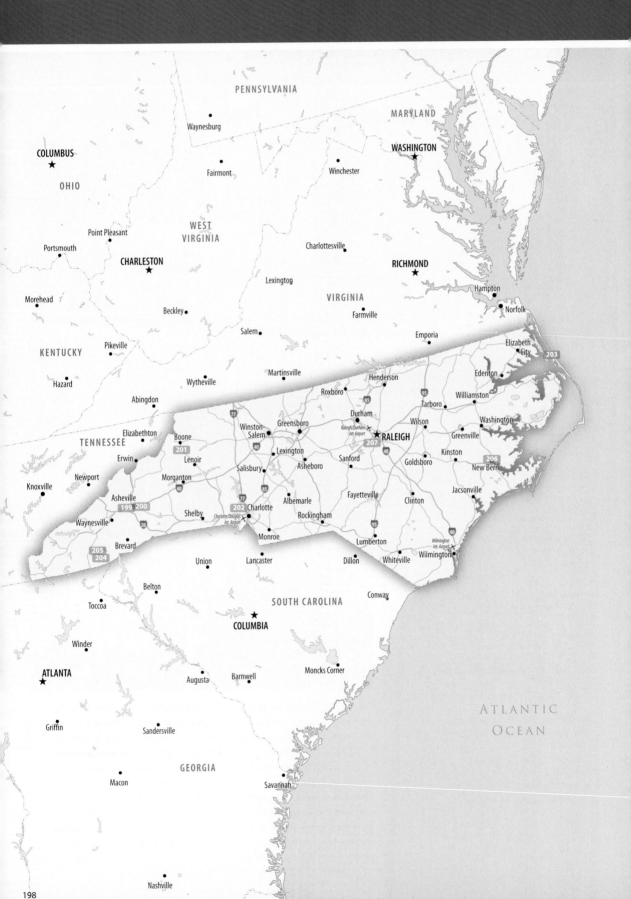

PENNSYLVANIA

MARYLAND

Waynesburg

WASHINGTON ★

COLUMBUS ★

OHIO

Fairmont

Winchester

WEST VIRGINIA

Point Pleasant

Portsmouth

Charlottesville

RICHMOND ★

Morehead

CHARLESTON ★

Lexington

VIRGINIA

Hampton

Beckley

Salem

Farmville

Norfolk

KENTUCKY

Pikeville

Emporia

Elizabeth City

203

Hazard

Wytheville

Martinsville

Henderson

Edenton

Abingdon

Roxboro

85

Tarboro

Williamston

77

Durham

Wilson

Washington

Elizabethton

Boone

Winston-Salem

Greensboro

Raleigh/Durham Int. Airport

207

RALEIGH ★

Greenville

TENNESSEE

201

Lenoir

40

Lexington

Sanford

40

Goldsboro

Kinston

206

New Bern

Erwin

Morganton

Salisbury

Asheboro

Newport

40

85

Jacsonville

Knoxville

Asheville

199 200

Shelby

77

202

Charlotte

Albemarle

Fayetteville

Clinton

Waynesville

26

Charlotte/Douglas Int. Airport

Rockingham

95

Brevard

Monroe

Lumberton

Wilmington Int. Airport

40

205
204

Union

Lancaster

Dillon

Whiteville

Wilmington

Belton

Conway

Toccoa

SOUTH CAROLINA

Winder

COLUMBIA ★

ATLANTA ★

Augusta

Barnwell

Moncks Corner

ATLANTIC OCEAN

Griffin

Sandersville

GEORGIA

Macon

Savannah

Nashville

HAYWOOD PARK HOTEL

ONE BATTERY PARK AVENUE, ASHEVILLE, NORTH CAROLINA 28801
Tel: +1 828 252 2522 **Fax:** +1 828 253 0481 **U.S./Canada Toll Free:** 1 800 228 2522
Web: www.johansens.com/haywoodpark **E-mail:** hotelsales@haywoodpark.com

Our inspector loved: The spacious rooms, breakfast on a silver tray and access to all of the activity in downtown Asheville right outside the front door!

Price Guide: (room only)
rooms from $220
suites from $475

Attractions: Biltmore House, 5 miles
Towns/Cities: Hendersonville, 30 miles
Airports: Asheville Airport, 15-min drive

For a truly all-encompassing getaway, visit this great hotel in the heart of Asheville, known as the Paris of the South for its art deco architecture and abundance of museums, shopping options, and restaurants. The hotel's expansive atrium offers enough shopping, dining, and galleries to keep you busy for days! When you're ready to explore your surroundings a bit further, Asheville's historic atmosphere and variety of attractions and tours provide endless entertainment, and the surrounding Blue Ridge Mountains facilitate a variety of outdoor activities. At the end of an action-packed day, you may return to the hotel to enjoy the flavors of The Flying Frog Café, which offers diverse menu options including French, German, and Indian cuisines.

INN ON BILTMORE ESTATE

ONE ANTLER HILL ROAD, ASHEVILLE, NORTH CAROLINA 28803
Tel: +1 828 225 1600 **Fax:** +1 828 225 1629 **U.S./Canada Toll Free:** 1 800 858 4130
Web: www.johansens.com/biltmore **E-mail:** innsales@biltmore.com

Our inspector loved: *The magnificent view, great food and wine, and the elegance of the inn.*

Price Guide:
rooms $289-$499
suites $700-$2,000

Awards/Ratings: Condé Nast Traveler Gold List 2005, 2006 and 2007

Attractions: Biltmore Estate, 10-min complimentary shuttle ride; Downtown Asheville, 15-min drive
Towns/Cities: Charlotte, 2-hour drive; Atlanta, GA, 3.5-hour drive; Raleigh, 4-hour drive
Airports: Asheville Regional Airport, 16 miles

Set within 8,000 acres of Biltmore Estate, enveloped by rolling hills, vineyards and views of the Blue Ridge Mountains, this is an elegant retreat amidst quiet, beautiful surroundings. In the vast lobby, with its marble floor and elegant seating, peaceful jazz plays as guests sip complimentary coffee in front of the stone fireplace, admiring the views from the huge windows. The Dining Room offers creative regional interpretations of Continental cuisine, and afternoon tea in the library is a distinguished affair with a delightful array of finger sandwiches, chocolate pastries, fruit tarts, jams and clotted cream. Biltmore House has countless treasures and there are acres of landscaped gardens to explore. Biltmore Estate Winery offers award-winning wines and production tours, alternately, indulge yourself with an in-room massage.

GIDEON RIDGE INN

202 GIDEON RIDGE ROAD, BLOWING ROCK, NORTH CAROLINA 28605
Tel: +1 828 295 3644 **Fax:** +1 828 295 4586 **U.S./Canada Toll Free:** 1 888 889 4036
Web: www.johansens.com/gideonridge **E-mail:** innkeeper@gideonridge.com

Our inspector loved: *The complete serenity, comfortable rooms, great food and access to so many activities. The view of the mountains is breathtaking.*

Price Guide: (including breakfast)
rooms $150-$325

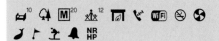

Attractions: Blowing Rock, 5-min walk; Blue Ridge Parkway, 5-min drive
Towns/Cities: Linville, 23 miles; Abington, VA, 60 miles
Airports: Charlotte/Douglas International Airport, 92 miles; Asheville Regional Airport, 100 miles

Built in 1939 as a secluded residence for a Boston family, Gideon Ridge Inn stands amidst some of the most breathtaking North Carolina scenery, with sweeping views of the Blue Ridge Mountains. Owned and operated by the same family since 1984, today it is a welcoming and individual inn that prides itself on its personal levels of service and keen attention to detail. Each of the sunny bedrooms and suites is carefully furnished with antique pieces and welcoming décor; 9 have private fireplaces and 6 open out to delightful terraces or gardens. Cuisine is a real delight and pre-dinner chats with Chef Michael Foreman explain the menu and preparations undertaken to create each meal. Advice on which wine from the restaurant's French and Californian list best complements your meal is also offered.

BALLANTYNE RESORT

10000 BALLANTYNE COMMONS PARKWAY, CHARLOTTE, NORTH CAROLINA 28277
Tel: +1 704 248 4000 **Fax:** +1 704 248 4005 **U.S./Canada Toll Free:** 1 866 248 4824
Web: www.johansens.com/ballantyneresort **E-mail:** info@ballantyneresort.com

Our inspector loved: The great food, golf, spa, and the most elegant rooms in Charlotte!

Price Guide:
rooms $225-$425
suites $500-$2,400

Awards/Ratings: Condé Nast Johansens Most Excellent Spa Hotel 2005

Attractions: Dana Rader Golf School, 1-min walk; Carowinds, 13-min drive; U.S. National Whitewater Center, 20-min drive; Downtown Charlotte, 18 miles

Towns/Cities: Asheville, 120 miles; Chapel Hill, 120 miles; Charleston, 3-hour drive; Atlanta, 4-hour drive

Airports: Charlotte Douglas Airport, 20-min drive

Ballantyne Resort, a member of The Luxury Collection by Starwood Hotels and Resorts, offers the affluent traveler luxurious rooms, golf, a spa, tennis, Dana Rader Golf School, meeting and event facilities, dining, shopping and the Lodge at Ballantyne, all in the beautiful 2,000-acre Ballantyne community. The Spa at Ballantyne practices an array of soothing and revitalizing treatments, and the health facility features Cybex equipment. Golf lovers will enjoy the par 71 course designed to challenge players of all levels. Professional tennis and golf instruction is available for individuals and groups. Gallery Restaurant, with its distinguished art collection, defines Charlotte's upscale dining with its contemporary take on American fare. The Lodge offers the ultimate venue for a private group retreat, ideal for a corporate meeting or social event. A helipad on property provides a convenient transportation option for guests.

THE SANDERLING RESORT & SPA

1461 DUCK ROAD, DUCK, NORTH CAROLINA 27949
Tel: +1 252 261 4111 **Fax:** +1 252 261 1638 **U.S./Canada Toll Free:** 1 800 701 4111
Web: www.johansens.com/sanderling **E-mail:** reservations@thesanderling.com

Our inspector loved: *The spacious rooms with spectacular views, and the excellent food at Left Bank.*

Price Guide:
rooms $256-$414
suites $330-$1,045

Attractions: Pine Isle Audobon Sanctuary, 5-min walk; Nags Head Woods, 30-min drive; Wright Brothers Memorial and Visitors Center, 20 miles; North Carolina Aquarium, 20 miles
Towns/Cities: Kitty Hawk, 20 miles; Nags Head, 30 miles
Airports: Norfolk Virginia Airport, 75 miles

The Outer Banks' only true resort, The Sanderling touches the shores of both the Atlantic Ocean and Currituck Sound. Miles of unspoiled beaches provide serenity, which, like the ocean waves, ensure your inevitable return. Relax at The Sanderling Spa with its beautiful backdrop of the tranquil waters of Currituck Sound making the experience complete. The luxurious lodging reflects classic Outer Banks architecture: each of the 3 distinctive 2-story inns is decorated with a rare collection of fine wildlife art and sculptures, and each building offers private porches, most with ocean or sound views. 4 ocean-side cottages and 1 ocean-front cottage are also available. Dine casually among nautical artefacts in a restored 1899 U.S. Lifesaving Station or play the epicure in the formal dining room, where spectacular views of Currituck Sound complement the fine cuisine.

Inn at Half Mile Farm

P.O. BOX 2769, 214 HALF MILE DRIVE, HIGHLANDS, NORTH CAROLINA 28741
Tel: +1 828 526 8170 **Fax:** +1 828 526 2625 **U.S./Canada Toll Free:** 1 800 946 6822
Web: www.johansens.com/halfmilefarm **E-mail:** mail@halfmilefarm.com

Our inspector loved: The serenity of the mountains, walking around the beautiful grounds of the inn and sitting by the pond.

Price Guide: (including breakfast)
rooms $220-$950

Attractions: Fly Fishing, 1 mile; White-Water Rafting, 4 miles
Towns/Cities: Cashiers, 10 miles; Asheville, 70 miles
Airports: Asheville International Airport, 70 miles

Tucked away on the outskirts of town, this lovely rambling inn is a paradise for nature lovers and those who hanker for the great outdoor life. There's hiking, fly-fishing, lake canoeing, white-water rafting and just about every mountain activity. Originally a mid-19th-century farmhouse, the inn is surrounded by beautiful grounds, which feature a lake, pool and an abundance of wild flowers and greenery. Sit and watch the sun rise and set over the mountain peaks while enjoying an early morning coffee or a glass of complimentary wine and hors d'oeuvres in the evening. Tennessee fieldstone fireplaces, pine floors and local wood decorations are particularly attractive features of the 4 guest rooms in the main house and those that surround a colorful courtyard and fountain.

OLD EDWARDS INN AND SPA

445 MAIN STREET, HIGHLANDS, NORTH CAROLINA 28741
Tel: +1 828 526 8008 **Fax:** +1 828 526 8301 **U.S./Canada Toll Free:** 1 866 526 8008
Web: www.johansens.com/oldedwards **E-mail:** info@oldedwardsinn.com

Our inspector loved: The first-class accommodations, unbelievable spa, magnificent dining and picturesque setting.

Price Guide:
rooms $255-$315
suites $275-$995
cottages $1,800-$2,400

Awards/Ratings: Wine Spectator Award of Excellence 2005-2007

Attractions: Shopping, close by; Hiking, 1 mile; Fly-Fishing, 1 mile
Towns/Cities: Cashiers, 10 miles; Hendersonville, 35 miles; Asheville, 70 miles
Airports: Asheville International Airport, 70 miles

Affiliations: Preferred Boutique

This is the ultimate luxurious getaway in the heart of the Blue Ridge Mountains. Highlands is a delightful and welcoming community and Old Edwards Inn forms an integral part of the town. Wide plasma T.V.s and elegant Frette linens set the scene for the bedrooms, while all the bathrooms have under-floor heating, rain-dancing showers and Bulgari amenities. Madison's Restaurant and Wine Garden serves Elevated Southern cuisine with a stunning backdrop of the wine garden. The spa features some of the most exotic and contemporary treatments and has heated limestone flooring and fine antique pieces throughout. The "Farm", located nearby, is a superb venue for meetings and social events, and remains in-keeping with the style of the inn. An Executive Conference, Fitness Center and outdoor heated mineral pool are also available.

THE AERIE BED & BREAKFAST

509 POLLOCK STREET, NEW BERN, NORTH CAROLINA 28562
Tel: +1 252 636 5553 **Fax:** +1 252 514 2157 **U.S./Canada Toll Free:** 1 800 849 5553
Web: www.johansens.com/aerieinn **E-mail:** info@aeriebedandbreakfast.com

Our inspector loved: The wonderful hospitality; expect to come away with some new friends!

Price Guide: (including breakfast)
rooms $145-$190
suites $139-$159

This delightful Victorian villa, circa 1880, is the favorite year-round spot for travelers to enjoy eastern North Carolina who understand that "North Carolina Begins Here." An inviting welcome pervades the inn, and the parlor, with its period furniture and cozy fireplace, has guests chatting eagerly over cheese and wine during the evening. Each of the bedrooms has its own distinct style, and has been carefully named, for instance, the popular "Magnolia Room," with corner whirlpool bath, is so-called for the large magnolia tree located outside. The décor is very much in-keeping with the heritage of the building, while a warmth and modern-day comfort is evident throughout. The inn serves an excellent gourmet breakfast, and the early evening appetizers are rapidly becoming legendary.

Attractions: Trolly Tours, Horse and Carriage Tours, Sailing, close by; Tryon Palace, 2-min walk; Birthplace of Pepsi Cola, 2-min walk; Waterfront, 2-min walk
Towns/Cities: Wilmington, 90 miles
Airports: Craven Regional Airport, 3 miles; Raleigh-Durham Airport, 1.5-hour drive

THE SIENA HOTEL

1505 E. FRANKLIN STREET, CHAPEL HILL, NORTH CAROLINA 27514
Tel: +1 919 929 4000 **Fax:** +1 919 968 8527 **U.S./Canada Toll Free:** 1 800 223 7379
Web: www.johansens.com/siena **E-mail:** info@sienahotel.com

Our inspector loved: Feeling as if you are in Italy.

Price Guide:
rooms $185–$285
suites $230–$350

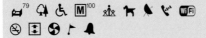

Attractions: Finley Golf Course, 2 miles; Governors Club Golf Course, 2 miles; Duke University, 13 miles
Towns/Cities: Historic Chapel Hill, 3 miles
Airports: Raleigh-Durham International Airport, 16 miles

Named after a beautiful Italian town in Tuscany, The Siena Hotel embodies the spirit of Italy in the heart of North Carolina. A personalized check-in service is surpassed only by the sight and aroma of roses grown in the gardens. The décor is luxurious, with grand European antiques, rich textured fabrics, majestic columns, warm colors and soft lighting, and the hallways and rooms are a picture of grandeur reflected by the beautiful artwork together with the hotel's overall ambience and excellent service. Each of the guest rooms and suites is individually appointed with rich fabrics and elaborate artwork; they have magnificent marble bathrooms, the latest technology and lovely additional touches such as a nightly turndown service, soft bathrobes and European toiletries. Exceptional Italian cuisine is enjoyed in Il Palio, and live entertainment is held in the bar.

THE HEATHMAN HOTEL

1001 S.W. BROADWAY, PORTLAND, OREGON 97205
Tel: +1 503 241 4100 **Fax:** +1 503 790 7110 **U.S./Canada Toll Free:** 1 800 551 0011
Web: www.johansens.com/heathman **E-mail:** reservations@heathmanhotel.com

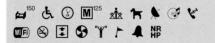

Our inspector loved: The amazing art collection throughout the property.

Price Guide:
rooms $199-$299
suites $299-$2,500

Awards/Ratings: Condé Nast Traveler Gold List 2005

Attractions: Pearl District, 0.5 miles; Portland Art Museum, 2-min walk; Pioneer Court House Square Shopping, 5-min walk
Towns/Cities: Portland; Beaverton, 7 miles; Newport, 25 miles; Hood River, 60 miles
Airports: Portland International Airport, 13 miles

Successfully evoking Old World atmosphere with a modern twist, The Heathman is full of intimate charm even with its 150 rooms. This is partly due to the warm décor of the Lobby and Tea Court Lounge, and the absence of a check-in desk. Boasting the first ever "Art of Sleep Bed Menu," each guest has the opportunity to choose from 3 mattress types: Tempur Pedic, European Pillow Top or European Feather Bed. And the special treatment continues as each guest is assigned a "personal concierge" who provides a seamless, personal service achieving a sense of intimacy you might expect at a smaller hotel. The beautiful Mezzanine holds curated art exhibits and looks down over the art deco Lobby and Lounge where jazz artists play most nights.

THE BENSON HOTEL

309 SOUTHWEST BROADWAY, PORTLAND, OREGON 97205
Tel: +1 503 228 2000 **Fax:** +1 503 471 3920 **U.S./Canada Toll Free:** 1 888 523 6766
Web: www.johansens.com/benson **E-mail:** reservations@bensonhotel.com

Our inspector loved: *The wine cellar of the London Grill and the Old World charm of the lobby with the majestic Circassian walnut columns.*

Price Guide:
rooms $139-$239
suites $214-$1,199

Awards/Ratings: Wine Spectator Award of Excellence 2006

Attractions: Pearl District, 2-min walk; Portland Center Performing Arts, 4-min walk; Pioneer Place Mall, 4-min walk; Portland Art Museum, 4-min walk
Towns/Cities: Portland, on the doorstep
Airports: Portland, 9 miles

This prestigious, grand hotel is ideally situated for shopping, sightseeing, theater-going and absorbing the culture and atmosphere of Portland's vibrant downtown. High ceilings, spacious rooms, elegant furnishings, huge chandeliers and highly polished woodwork lend a special quality to this hotel's modern luxury and classic setting. Some suites feature a grand piano, an open fireplace, French doors and Jacuzzi. The Penthouse Suites on the exclusive 14th floor, have superb views of downtown and beyond. Elegant décor and soft lighting create an intimate dining ambience in the London Grill where Executive Chef Xavier Bauser and his team produce cuisine featuring traditional favorites and bold, innovative creations. The London Grill serves one of the most extensive wine lists in the Northwest with more than 6,000 bottles.

THE CAMPBELL HOUSE

252 PEARL STREET, EUGENE, OREGON 97401
Tel: +1 541 343 1119 **Fax:** +1 541 343 2258 **U.S./Canada Toll Free:** 1 800 264 2519
Web: www.johansens.com/campbell **E-mail:** campbellhouse@campbellhouse.com

Our inspector loved: The Eva Suite and charming rooms with a warm, cozy atmosphere.

Price Guide:
rooms $159-$189
suites $239-$459

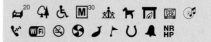

Awards/Ratings: Mobil 5 Star

Attractions: Art Galleries and Shopping, 2-min walk; Hiking and Biking Trails, 5-min walk; University of Oregon, 15-min walk
Towns/Cities: Colberg, 15 miles; Eugene, 20 miles
Airports: Coburg Airport, 15 miles; Eugene Airport, 20 miles

Surrounded by an acre of landscaped gardens and overlooking the city of Eugene, this elegant Victorian inn was originally built in 1892. The property has undergone extensive renovations thanks to owner Myra Plant who personally decorated each of the guest rooms. Bedrooms represent themes such as an English hunting lodge, French vineyard and country manor, and luxury rooms possess special amenities such as a claw-foot tub or Jacuzzi. The complimentary breakfast includes mouth-watering, freshly baked delicacies, and an evening prefix menu is prepared by Chef Carley Bronec who masterfully orchestrates the blending of locally grown, freshly harvested produce into wonderful sauces and perfectly prepared entrées. The dining room and Library are available as meeting venues while the gardens, with its rock grotto, fish pond and gazebo, create the perfect setting for an outdoor wedding ceremony.

Orillia

Belleville

Watertown

Lake Pleasant

Hudson Falls

Oshawa

Oswego

Johnstown

CANADA

★ TORONTO

Albion

Rochester

Syracuse

★ ALBANY

Hamilton

Niagara
Falls

ONTARIO

Buffalo

Norwich

NEW YORK

Kingston

Poughkeepsie

Binghamton

Monticello

Wellsville

Honesdale

Salamanca

Scranton

220

84

Newton

Paterson

Erie

90

Bradford

Warren

216

Wilkes Barre

Stroudsburg

New York

Erie Int./
Tom Ridge Field
Airport

Williamsport

85

NEW
JERSEY

New
Brunswick

Meadville

Lock Haven

Bloomsburg

Lehigh Valley
Int. Airport

Easton

Franklin

Lewisburg

81

Clarion

80

Sunbury

Pottsville

78

Allentown

TRENTON

79

Clearfield

Bellefonte

Doylestown

218

Warren

Lebanon

Reading

Philadelphia

New
Castle

Lewistown

Norristown

219

Kittanning

Huntingdon

HARRISBURG ★

217

76

Philadelphia
Int. Airport

Indiana

Harrisburg
Int. Airport

Lancaster

Wilmington

Beaver

76

Hollidaysburg

Carlisle

OHIO

Pittsburgh
Int. Airport

99

York

Elkton

Bridgeton

Pittsburgh

Greensburg

Somerset

Chambersburg

Gettysburg

83

Washington

76

81

St. Clairsville

Waynesburg

Uniontown

70

Westminster

MARYLAND

Baltimore

★ DOVER

79

Cumberland

Martinsburg

Rockville

★ ANNAPOLIS

DELAWARE

Morgantown

Winchester

★ WASHINGTON

WEST
VIRGINIA

VIRGINIA

Charlottesville

★ CHARLESTON

RICHMOND ★

Lexington

Hampton

GLENDORN

1000 GLENDORN DRIVE, BRADFORD, PENNSYLVANIA 16701
Tel: +1 814 362 6511 **Fax:** +1 814 368 9923 **U.S./Canada Toll Free:** 1 800 843 8568
Web: www.johansens.com/glendorn **E-mail:** glendorn@relaischateaux.com

Our inspector loved: *The world-class service.*

Price Guide:
rooms $495-$795

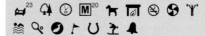

Attractions: Orvis Endorsed Fishing Guide and Fly Fishing Instruction, close by; Cross-Country Skiing and Snow Shoeing; close by; Hiking, close by; Niagara Falls, 90-min drive
Towns/Cities: Toronto, 90-min drive
Airports: Bradford Airport, 15 miles; Buffalo Airport, 40 miles

Affiliations: Relais & Châteaux

Built in 1929 the Glendorn in northwestern Pennsylvania is the ideal outdoor destination. The redwood Big House sits on a 1,280-acre estate with fly fishing, skeet shooting, hiking, and cross-country skiing. Glistening lakes and Allegheny forest surround the gated property. In the Big House guests in the afternoons and evenings can sit by the great stone hearth fireplace and sip warm cider or choose to relax in one of the 12 rustic cabins, each of which has at least one fireplace. Accommodation options also include 2 master suites and 2 luxury guest rooms in the lodge. The dining room, with cathedral ceiling and redwood beams, serves a multi-course dinner and outstanding wine list each evening by a roaring fire. In the summer months, breakfast and lunch are taken on the porch overlooking Fuller Brook and the heated pool.

THE HOTEL HERSHEY

100 HOTEL ROAD, HERSHEY, PENNSYLVANIA 17033
Tel: +1 717 533 2171 **Fax:** +1 717 534 3165 **U.S./Canada Toll Free:** 1 800 HERSHEY
Web: www.johansens.com/hershey **E-mail:** info@hersheyPA.com

Our inspector loved: *The rich history of this hotel, and the unique offerings at The Chocolate Spa.*

Price Guide:
rooms $289-$409
suites $305-$1,800

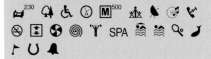

Awards/Ratings: Wine Spectator Award of Excellence 2007

Attractions: Hersheypark, 2 miles; Downtown Hershey, 3 miles; Hershey Country Club, 3 miles
Towns/Cities: Gettysburg, 1-hour drive; Washington D.C. and Baltimore, MD, 90-min drive; Philadelphia, 2-hour drive; New York City, NY, 3-hour drive
Airports: Harrisburg Intl. Airport, 15-min drive; Baltimore Washington Intl. Airport, 102 miles; Philadelphia Intl. Airport, 111 miles

Celebrating its 75th anniversary in 2008, The Hotel Hershey was described by world traveler Lowell Thomas as "a palace that out-palaces the palaces of the Maharajahs of India." Dramatically situated on a hilltop overlooking the town of Hershey, this grand hotel is an award-winning national landmark known for its elegance, exemplary service and luxurious accommodations. Displays of wonderful old photographs line the corridors, and each guest room is adorned with an original piece of artwork. Indulgence awaits you at The Chocolate Spa whose signature chocolate and Cuban themed treatments will leave you revitalized and ready for a delicious gourmet meal at the Circular Dining Room. More casual fare is served at The Fountain Café. Chocolate pastries and specialty coffees are available in The Cocoa Beanery, while cocktails and chocolate martinis are served by the open fire in the Iberian Lounge.

THE INN AT BOWMAN'S HILL

518 LURGAN ROAD, NEW HOPE, PENNSYLVANIA 18938
Tel: +1 215 862 8090 **Fax:** +1 215 862 9362
Web: www.johansens.com/bowmanshill **E-mail:** info@theinnatbowmanshill.com

Our inspector loved: *The exceptional ambience through all seasons!*

Price Guide: (including breakfast)
rooms $325-$435
suites $475-$595

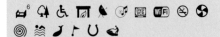

Attractions: Bucks County Playhouse, 3 miles; James A. Michener Art Museum, 3 miles; Wine Tasting and Touring, 3 miles; Washington Crossing State Park, 4 miles
Towns/Cities: Princeton, NJ, 35-min drive; Philadelphia, 45-min drive; New York City, NY, 2-hour drive; Washington D.C., 3-hour drive
Airports: Trenton Mercer Airport, NJ, Private and Commercial Jet Service, 15-min drive; Philadelphia International Airport, 1-hour drive; Newark Liberty International Airport, NJ, 1-hour drive

The charming and eclectic riverside town of New Hope is a vibrant tourist destination with a rich and diverse history. Independent and non-conformist, the rich cultural heritage of New Hope is today alive and well in theater, cabaret, piano bars, art and antiques. Close to New York and Philadelphia, yet a world apart, you can also enjoy unique dining experiences and local wine tastings. The Inn at Bowman's Hill is an intimate retreat nestled within a 5-acre manicured and gated estate just 2 miles from the town center. Private, luxurious, romantic and memorable! Indulge your senses in a 2-person heated whirlpool; relax on a king-size featherbed; enjoy an in-suite massage or simply warm your body and soul by your very own fireplace. Multi-course gourmet breakfast with daily à la carte choices is served in the fireside dining room or in bed. Celebrate, relax, connect and remember!

RITTENHOUSE 1715, A BOUTIQUE HOTEL

1715 RITTENHOUSE SQUARE, PHILADELPHIA, PENNSYLVANIA 19103
Tel: +1 215 546 6500 **Fax:** +1 215 546 8787 **U.S./Canada Toll Free:** 1 877 791 6500
Web: www.johansens.com/rittenhouse **E-mail:** reservations@rittenhouse1715.com

Our inspector loved: *The evening wine receptions held in the drawing room.*

Price Guide: (room only)
rooms from $240
suites from $459

Attractions: Philadelphia Museum of Art, 1 mile; The Kimmel Center, 5-min walk
Towns/Cities: Westchester, 45-min drive; Lancaster, 1.5-hour drive
Airports: Philadelphia Airport, 30-min drive

Rittenhouse 1715 is a traditional 19th-century carriage house in the fashionable Rittenhouse Square district of downtown Philadelphia that has been restored and combined with the neighboring 18th-century Georgian town houses to make it one of Philadelphia's most exclusive and luxurious boutique hotels. An intimate, comfortable retreat that exudes style, sophistication and charm, the hotel is adorned with fine furnishings, exquisite artwork and upholds a careful attention to detail. All guest rooms feature marble bathrooms, plush robes, triple sheeting with fine European linens, 37" plasma T.V.s and nightly turndown service. A lovely complimentary Continental breakfast is served in the Parisian-style café, and an evening wine reception is held in the drawing room each day.

SKYTOP LODGE

ONE SKYTOP, SKYTOP, PENNSYLVANIA 18357
Tel: +1 570 595 7401 **Fax:** +1 570 595 7285 **U.S./Canada Toll Free:** 1 800 345 7759
Web: www.johansens.com/skytop **E-mail:** reservations@skytop.com

Our inspector loved: The porch with rocking chairs overlooking the mountains!

Price Guide: (double occupancy, including breakfast, lunch and dinner, excluding taxes and gratuities)
rooms $230-$675
suites $575-$1,000

Inspired by nature and enveloped in 5,500 acres of pristine forest, this is an awe-inspiring holiday retreat with year-round activities as well as plenty of quiet places to relax and take in the views. Accommodations are variable and range from spacious standard rooms to stream-side cottages ideal for families. Savor the delicious tastes of American cuisine in the historical main lodge, or outstanding Continental dishes and fine wines at the lake view restaurant. A variety of activities can be arranged: during winter, sledding and skiing is superb and there is also a huge weather protected skating rink nearby. In the summer months the lake offers boating, canoeing and other water sports. The forests have many nature trails to explore, and there is a spa and health club.

Attractions: The Pocono Mountains Tourist Region
Towns/Cities: Canadensis, 3 miles
Airports: Allentown-Bethlehem-Easton Airport, 40 miles; Wilkes-Barre-Scranton Airport, 45 miles

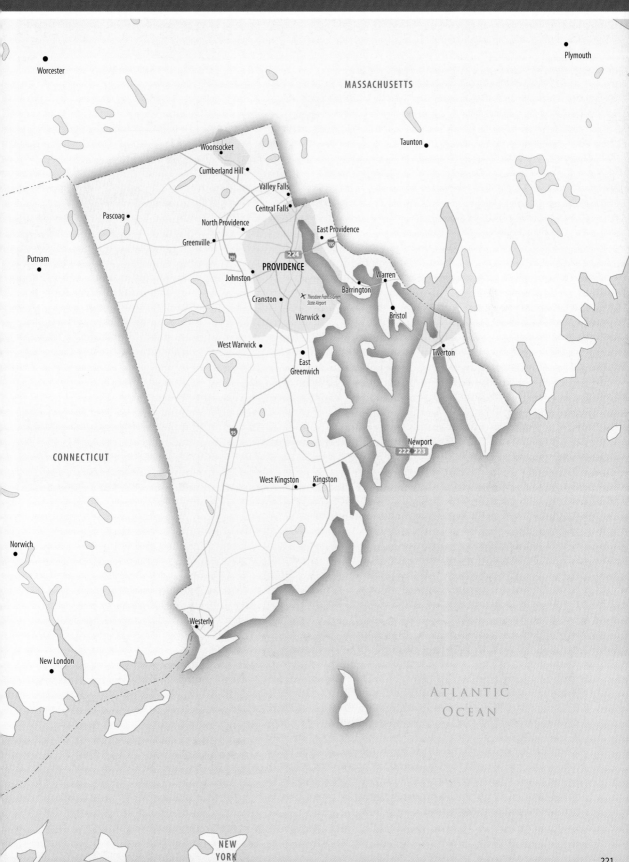

Worcester

MASSACHUSETTS

Plymouth

Taunton

Woonsocket

Cumberland Hill

Valley Falls

Central Falls

Pascoag

North Providence

East Providence

Greenville

224

Putnam

295

PROVIDENCE

Johnston

Warren

Cranston

Theodore Francis Green
State Airport

Barrington

Bristol

Warwick

West Warwick

Tiverton

East
Greenwich

CONNECTICUT

95

Newport

222 223

West Kingston

Kingston

Norwich

Westerly

New London

ATLANTIC
OCEAN

NEW
YORK

CHANLER AT CLIFF WALK

117 MEMORIAL BOULEVARD, NEWPORT, RHODE ISLAND 02840
Tel: +1 401 847 1300 **Fax:** +1 401 847 3620 **U.S./Canada Toll Free:** 1 866 793 5664
Web: www.johansens.com/chanler **E-mail:** reservations@thechanler.com

Our inspector loved: *The Butlered Bath with rose petals, bath salts, candles and Spiced Pear Champagne!*

Price Guide: (excluding tax)
rooms from $395
suites from $695

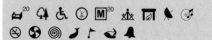

Located at the start of Newport's famous Cliff Walk, through majestic iron gates and along beautifully landscaped gardens with fountains, The Chanler is the epitome of romance. The sense of history is awe-inspiring: the authentic furniture, stunning antiques and a rich opulence is reminiscent of a bygone era. Rooms are separated into Manor Rooms, Estate Rooms and Signature Rooms, each designed to reflect a different period or theme. From your private patio, watch the waves roll in before heading outdoors to Terazza to enjoy romantic Tuscan dishes and fine wines on the terrace with breathtaking views. The acclaimed Spiced Pear restaurant serves gourmet New England seafood where you can participate in the popular Chef's Table.

Attractions: Cliff Walk, 0.5 miles; Beach, 0.5 miles; Newport Mansions, 1 mile; Downtown, 1 mile
Towns/Cities: Providence, 38 miles; Middletown, 38 miles; Boston, MA, 75 miles;
Airports: Quonset (F.B.O.) Airport, 17 miles; T.F. Green Airport, 28 miles; Boston Logan International Airport, MA, 75 miles

La Farge Perry House

24 KAY STREET, NEWPORT, RHODE ISLAND 02840
Tel: +1 401 847 2223 **Fax:** +1 401 847 1967 **U.S./Canada Toll Free:** 1 877 736 1100
Web: www.johansens.com/lafargeperry **E-mail:** innkeeper@lafargeperry.com

Our inspector loved: The home-made macaroons that are served daily.

Price Guide: (including breakfast)
rooms $175-$395
suites $295-$525

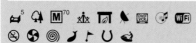

Attractions: International Tennis Hall of Fame, 1 mile; Newport Mansions, 2 miles; Cliff Walk, 2 miles; Newport Harbor, 2 miles
Towns/Cities: Fall River, 20 miles; Providence, 40 miles; Boston, MA, 70 miles
Airports: T. F. Green State Airport, 26 miles; Boston Logan International Airport, MA, 78 miles; Hartford Airport, 89 miles

This quaint Victorian-style inn, named after the renowned painter and stained-glass artist, John La Farge, and his wife Margaret Perry La Farge, is set in a quiet residential neighborhood of Newport. The luxury rooms are designed to immerse you in history, each room evoking the personality of one of Newport's most famous figures. Beautiful fresh flowers cut from the inn's vibrant gardens and personalized stationery add to the warm nature of this beautiful little inn. The innkeeper, a former restaurant chef, will tempt your palate with sumptuous breakfasts in the grand dining room each morning followed by her signature chocolate chip macaroons and tea in the afternoon, so popular with guests that she will send you home with the secret recipe!

HOTEL PROVIDENCE

311 WESTMINSTER STREET, PROVIDENCE, RHODE ISLAND 02903
Tel: +1 401 861 8000 **Fax:** +1 401 861 8002 **U.S./Canada Toll Free:** 1 800 861 8990
Web: www.johansens.com/providence **E-mail:** info@thehotelprovidence.com

Our inspector loved: *The owners' private collection of rare antiques.*

Price Guide:
rooms $199-$349
suites $429-$829

This landmark property, centrally located in the heart of Providence, has been lovingly transformed from twin brick buildings and a contemporary Liner Building to create an elegant and historical hotel. A grand stairway and Egyptian revival grandfather clock, dating back to the 1890s, are just two of the many impressive turn-of-the-century antiques found throughout. All bedrooms and suites are decorated in strong colors of burgundy, garnet, olive green and gold with plush beds, tiger maple armoires desks and contemporary amenities. Original paintings and exquisite antiques adorn the lavish suites. The highly-acclaimed L'Epicureo restaurant serves impeccable Italian cuisine and an impressive wine collection within a Renaissance-inspired décor. The piano bar lounge is surrounded by Austrian crystal chandeliers and oil paintings encased in gold leaf frames.

Attractions: Providence Performing Arts Center, 0.2 miles; Johnson and Wales University, 1 mile; Rhode Island School of Design, 1 mile; Brown University, 1 mile
Towns/Cities: Newport, 30 miles; Boston, 45 miles; New York City, 3-hour drive
Airports: T.F. Green Airport, 10 miles; Boston Logan International Airport, 55 miles

Affiliations: Small Luxury Hotels of the World

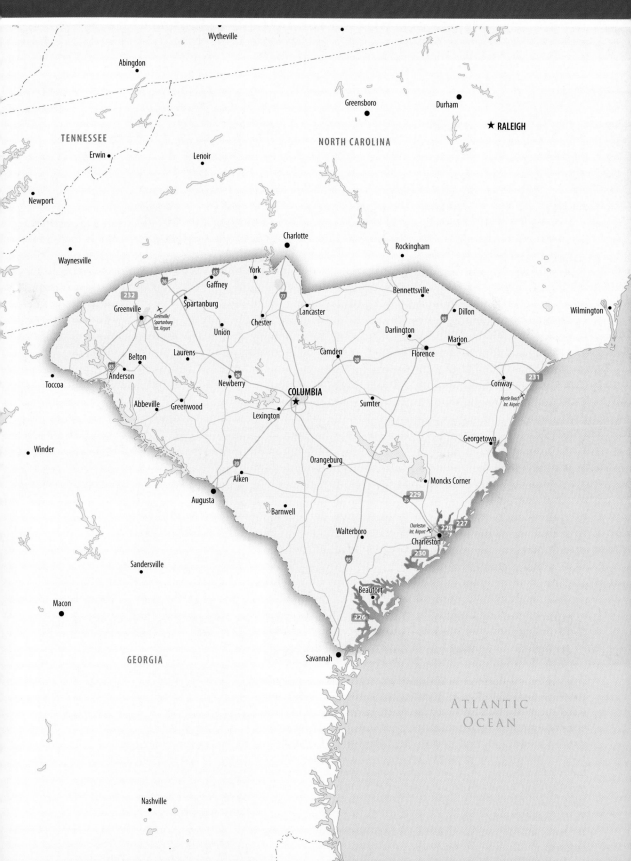

THE INN AT PALMETTO BLUFF

476 MOUNT PELIA ROAD, BLUFFTON, SOUTH CAROLINA 29910
Tel: +1 843 706 6500 **Fax:** +1 843 706 6550 **U.S./Canada Toll Free:** 1 866 706 6565
Web: www.johansens.com/palmettobluff **E-mail:** reservations@palmettobluffresort.com

Our inspector loved: *The spacious cottages with spectacular views of the water.*

Price Guide:
rooms $450-$950

Awards/Ratings: Condé Nast Johansens Most Excellent Golf Resort, U.S.A. & Canada 2007

Attractions: May River Golf Course, 5-min walk; Daufuskie Island History Tours, 30-min drive; Historic Savannah, 45 miles
Towns/Cities: Hilton Head, 30 miles; Savannah, 45 miles; Charleston, 120 miles
Airports: Hilton Head Airport, 30-min drive; Savannah Airport, 45-min drive; Charleston Airport, 100 miles

Affiliations: The Leading Small Hotels of the World

Capturing the essence of Southern hospitality in South Carolina's Lowcountry, The Inn at Palmetto Bluff is one of the region's premier golf resorts. This graceful and romantic 50-room cottage inn offers a private and spacious hideaway feel perfect for a relaxing escape or golf break. Each well-appointed room has beautiful water views, vaulted ceilings, pine floors and luxury linens. You can choose from the exceptional fine dining at the River House Dining Room, with its signature South Carolina Lowcountry dishes, the more casual May River Grille, or Buffalo's. After a day of golf at the 18-hole Jack Nicklaus Signature May River Golf Club, why not relax in the full-service Spa at Palmetto Bluff, set beside serene waterways, lush gardens and moss-laden oak trees. The Inn is an idyllic location for weddings, corporate retreats and family getaways.

THE BOARDWALK INN AT WILD DUNES RESORT

5757 PALM BOULEVARD, ISLE OF PALMS, SOUTH CAROLINA 29451
Tel: +1 843 886 6000 **Fax:** +1 843 886 2916 **U.S./Canada Toll Free:** 1 877 221 0901
Web: www.johansens.com/boardwalk **E-mail:** reservations@wilddunes.com

Our inspector loved: *The spectacular view of the ocean, and the comfort of the rooms.*

Price Guide:
rooms $120-$450
suites $150-$875

Attractions: Fort Sumter, 10 miles; South Carolina Aquarium, 10 miles; Historic Downtown Charleston, 15 miles
Towns/Cities: Charleston, 15 miles; Pawleys Island, 90 miles; Savannah, 120 miles
Airports: Charleston International Airport, 25 miles; Myrtle Beach Airport, 100 miles

In the heart of Wild Dunes Resort, just steps from the beach, The Boardwalk Inn is a wonderful combination of elegant Charleston architecture and informal island style. Each guest room and suite is spacious and comfortable with rich, colorful fabrics that complement the light, airy atmosphere. Sea Island Grill is famous for its outstanding, fresh seafood and prime meats, while pasta dishes and Low Country specials are served at Edgar's on the Links. Alternately, snacks, pizzas and groceries can be bought at Dunes Deli and Pizzeria. Outdoor facilities include 2 award-winning golf courses, tennis, water sports, and a beautifully landscaped tropical pool complex as well as a fitness center; personalized recreational programs can be organized. The miles of unspoiled beaches and preserved natural habitats surrounding the resort should not be missed!

CHARLESTON HARBOR RESORT & MARINA

20 PATRIOTS POINT ROAD, CHARLESTON, SOUTH CAROLINA 29464
Tel: +1 843 856 0028 **Fax:** +1 843 856 8333 **U.S./Canada Toll Free:** 1 888 856 0028
Web: www.johansens.com/charlestonharbor **E-mail:** reservations@charlestonharborresort.com

Our inspector loved: The beautifully decorated rooms and wonderful views of the harbor and Charleston from the balconies.

Price Guide:
rooms $129-$300
suites $225-$995

Offering an uncommon blend of unique Low Country culture, exciting downtown revelry and resort-style pampering, Charleston Harbor includes a full-service marina and stunning championship golf course that meanders along the Atlantic coast. With 459 slips, the marina ranks as South Carolina's largest pleasure boat refuge with concierge service extended to all marina guests. In return, the marina launches sailboat charters, romantic dinner cruises and fishing trips for land-based guests. Most rooms and suites have private balconies or Juliette terraces with views of the water, city skyline or historic Fort Sumter. The Grille restaurant has an international focus, and drinks are served at the beachfront Tiki Bar or the Reel Bar, decorated with antique fishing reels from the 1920s. The harbor-side pool and private beach are ideal settings for oyster roasts and island-style theme parties.

Attractions: Patriots Point Golf Course and U.S.S. Yorktown, 0.5 miles; Fort Sumter, 1 mile; Beaches, 8 miles; South Carolina Aquarium, 10 miles
Towns/Cities: Pawleys Island, 90 miles; Savannah, 100 miles
Airports: Charleston International Airport, 12 miles; Myrtle Beach Airport, 100 miles

WOODLANDS RESORT & INN

125 PARSONS ROAD, SUMMERVILLE, SOUTH CAROLINA 29483
Tel: +1 843 875 2600 **Fax:** +1 843 875 2603 **U.S./Canada Toll Free:** 1 800 774 9999
Web: www.johansens.com/woodlandssc **E-mail:** reservations@woodlandsinn.com

Our inspector loved: *The outstanding cuisine.*

Price Guide:
rooms $325-$375
suites $390-$750
cottage $850

Awards/Ratings: AAA 5 Diamond 2007; Mobil 5-Star 2007; Wine Spectator Best of Award of Excellence 2007; DiRoNA 2007

Attractions: Cypress Gardens, 15-min drive; South Carolina Aquarium, 30-min drive
Towns/Cities: Charleston, 25-min drive; Mount Pleasant, 30-min drive; Kiawah Island, 45-min drive; Savannah, 2-hour drive
Airports: Charleston International Airport, 20-min drive; Columbia Metropolitan Airport, 90-min drive

Affiliations: Relais & Châteaux

This restored 1906 mansion stands in 42 acres with a Day Spa, event center, 2 English red clay tennis courts, heated swimming pool, croquet lawn and Wedding Garden. Upon entering through the inn's columned veranda and grand doorway, you will be greeted by helpful staff and impressed by the luxurious furnishings, which reflect an English, East Indian and Jamaican influence. The top-floor guest rooms are whimsical and inviting, and a cozy guest cottage is a short stroll away at the end of a shaded path. All guest rooms have Bose C.D. players, monogrammed robes, fresh roses and Aveda products. Afternoon tea or cocktails can be enjoyed in the airy parlors, and in the evenings gather for dinner and savor the international and regional delicacies of the glamorous Dining Room's New American cuisine.

THE SANCTUARY AT KIAWAH ISLAND GOLF RESORT

ONE SANCTUARY BEACH DRIVE, KIAWAH ISLAND, SOUTH CAROLINA 29455
Tel: +1 843 768 6000 **Fax:** +1 843 768 5150 **U.S./Canada Toll Free:** 1 877 683 1234
Web: www.johansens.com/sanctuary **E-mail:** reservations@thesanctuary.com

Our inspector loved: The comfort of the rooms, and wonderful view of the ocean.

Price Guide:
rooms $299-$4,500

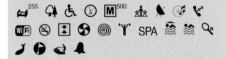

The shores of Kiawah Island are home to this luxurious ocean-front hideaway where the custom-made furniture and luxurious fabrics add to the unflinching attention to detail in this grand yet inviting resort. The Ocean Room restaurant seats 110 and the private wine room and spacious ocean view terrace add a sense of grandeur. Casual dining can be enjoyed in the Jasmine Porch, and drinks taken at the martini bar and grand lobby bar. Enjoy a round of golf at the 5 championship courses including Pete Dye's Ocean Course, host of the 2007 Senior PGA and 2012 PGA Championships, or play tennis on the 23 clay or 5 hard courts before relaxing in one of the 12 treatment rooms in the garden-themed spa.

Awards/Ratings: AAA 5 Diamond; Condé Nast Johansens Most Excellent Golf Resort 2006; Condé Nast Traveler Gold List 2007; Wine Spectator Best Award of Exellence 2007

Attractions: Charleston Museum, 25 miles; Charles Towne Landing, 25 miles; Fort Sumter, 25 miles; Cypress Gardens, 50 miles
Towns/Cities: Charleston, 45-min drive; Hilton Head, 70 miles; Savannah, 80 miles
Airports: Private Executive Airport, 15-min drive; Charleston International Airport, 45-min drive

Affiliations: Preferred Hotels & Resorts

MARINA INN AT GRANDE DUNES

8121 AMALFI PLACE, MYRTLE BEACH, SOUTH CAROLINA 29572
Tel: +1 843 913 1333 **Fax:** +1 843 913 1334 **U.S./Canada Toll Free:** 1 877 913 1333
Web: www.johansens.com/marinainn **E-mail:** paul.brown@grande-dunes.com

Our inspector loved: *The European-style service, excellent food, and beautiful views of the Waterway.*

Price Guide:
rooms $155-$310
suites $255-$425

Attractions: Resort Transportation to Beach Cabana, on-site; Carolina Opry, on-site; Broadway at the Beach, 5 miles; Coastal Grand Mall, 8 miles
Towns/Cities: Myrtle Beach, 5-min drive; Charleston, 2-hour drive
Airports: Myrtle Beach International Airport, 10 miles

Affiliations: Small Luxury Hotels of the World

Located in a 2,200-acre privately planned community set against the Atlantic Ocean, this is an ideal destination for the active, discerning traveler with a taste for luxury. The Marina Inn is the perfect place to relax while taking in the beauty of coastal South Carolina. Each suite has at least one private balcony overlooking the Intracoastal Waterway or the adjacent marina. Surrounded by several world-class golf courses, shopping centers and other attractions, there is truly something for everyone. The dining options are equally tailored to suit a diversity of tastes: options range from the sophisticated and elegant modern American cuisine served in the featured restaurant, WaterScapes, to the more casual Poolside Grill, where you can enjoy an open-air lunch without taking time away from the sun!

THE INN AT CRESCENT MOUNTAIN VINEYARDS

10 ROAD OF VINES, TRAVELERS REST, SOUTH CAROLINA 29210
Tel: +1 864 836 8463 **Fax:** +1 864 836 4820 **U.S./Canada Toll Free:** 1 877 836 8463
Web: www.johansens.com/crescentmountain **E-mail:** frontdesk@cliffscommunities.com

Our inspector loved: The views of the vineyards from the windows.

Price Guide: (including breakfast)
rooms $260-$310

Attractions: Table Rock State Park, 15 miles; The Greenville Museum of Art and Tryon Fine Arts Center, 20 miles; Lake Keowee, 25 miles; Blue Ridge Parkway, 45 miles
Towns/Cities: Greenville, 20 miles; Hendersonville, NC, 30 miles; Asheville, NC, 45 miles
Airports: Greenville/Spartanburg International Airport, 25 miles; Charlotte Douglas Airport, 110 miles

Framed by lush vineyards at the foothills of the Blue Ridge Mountains, The Inn at Crescent Mountain Vineyards (formerly La Bastide) is an intimate country inn and restaurant. Relax in a hand-made bed within your individually decorated room, or cozy up by the fire and sip a glass of wine in the living room lounge. Alternately, take a leisurely stroll through the vineyards. For those wishing to explore the area, the inn's central location affords easy access to Greenville and the Lakes Region of South Carolina as well as the historic towns of Hendersonville and Asheville, North Carolina. The restaurant emphasizes upscale farm to table cuisine from the inn's very own organic farm and the highest quality natural meats and seafood.

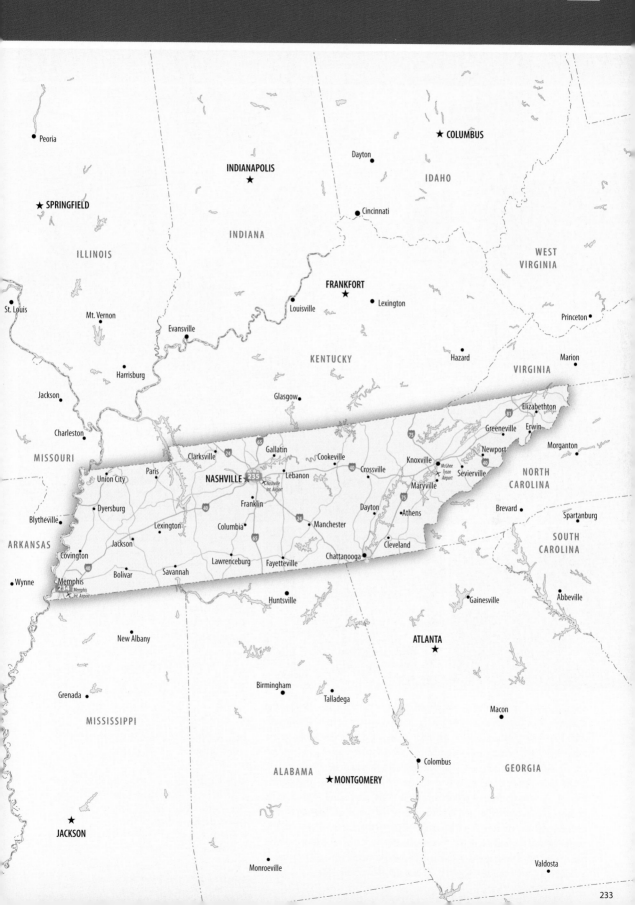

★ COLUMBUS

• Peoria

• Dayton

INDIANAPOLIS
★

IDAHO

★ SPRINGFIELD

• Cincinnati

INDIANA

WEST
VIRGINIA

ILLINOIS

• St. Louis

FRANKFORT
★

• Mt. Vernon

• Louisville

• Lexington

• Princeton

• Evansville

KENTUCKY

VIRGINIA

• Harrisburg

• Hazard

• Marion

• Jackson

• Glasgow

MISSOURI

• Charleston

Elizabethton
81

Greeneville • Erwin

Clarksville
24

Gallatin

Cookeville

Knoxville

75

Newport

Morganton

• Paris

Union City

NASHVILLE ★ 235

Lebanon

40
Crossville

McGhee
Tyson
Airport

Sevierville

40

NORTH
CAROLINA

• Dyersburg

Nashville
Int. Airport

Franklin

Maryville

• Blytheville

Lexington

Columbia

24
Manchester

Dayton

75
• Athens

• Brevard

• Spartanburg

ARKANSAS

40

Jackson

65

Cleveland

SOUTH
CAROLINA

• Covington

40

Bolivar

Savannah

Lawrenceburg

Fayetteville

Chattanooga

• Wynne

Memphis
234
Memphis
Int. Airport

• Huntsville

• Gainesville

• Abbeville

• New Albany

ATLANTA
★

• Grenada

MISSISSIPPI

• Birmingham

• Talladega

• Macon

• Columbus

GEORGIA

ALABAMA
★ MONTGOMERY

★
JACKSON

• Monroeville

• Valdosta

Madison Hotel Memphis

79 MADISON AVENUE, MEMPHIS, TENNESSEE 38103
Tel: +1 901 333 1200 **Fax:** +1 901 333 1210 **U.S./Canada Toll Free:** 1 866 446 3674
Web: www.johansens.com/madisonhotelmemphis **E-mail:** madison@madisonhotelmemphis.com

Our inspector loved: The quiet elegance of this beautiful boutique hotel right in the heart of vibrant Downtown Memphis.

Price Guide: (excluding taxes)
rooms from $280
suites from $350
presidential suite $1,350

Awards/Ratings: Condé Nast Traveler Gold List 2006 and 2007

Attractions: Beale Sreet, 10-min walk; Mississippi River, 10-min walk; Memphis Botanical Gardens, 20-min drive; Graceland,10 miles
Towns/Cities: Nashville, 195 miles
Airports: Memphis International Airport, 10 miles; Nashville Airport, 195 miles

Affiliations: Small Luxury Hotels of the World

The Madison Hotel is a tribute to the musical history of Memphis - home of the Blues and Rock and Roll - and a reflection of its sophisticated hospitality and style. After browsing the shops, seeing the sights, hopping on a trolley or hitting the nightlife, the Madison's luxurious embrace is a mere stroll away. The unique and artistic lobby welcomes you to this tastefully decorated retreat whose vibrant colors and carefully designed interior will excite the senses. Make reservations for high tea, a treat no guest should miss! Your every need is anticipated thanks to the excellent concierge service, efficient business center and rooftop garden with spectacular views of the Mississippi River and Downtown Memphis. The contemporary and well-equipped rooms include Italian linens and your own wet bar. At the end of the day enjoy a swim in the heated indoor lap pool and dinner at Grill 83, a dinner choice enjoyed by guests and Memphians alike.

THE HERMITAGE HOTEL

231 SIXTH AVENUE NORTH, NASHVILLE, TENNESSEE 37219
Tel: +1 615 244 3121 **Fax:** +1 615 254 6909 **U.S./Canada Toll Free:** 1 888 888 9414
Web: www.johansens.com/hermitagetn **E-mail:** info@thehermitagehotel.com

Our inspector loved: The exquisite décor and furnishings.

Price Guide:
rooms $249-$439
suites $800-$2,200

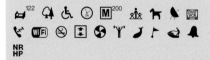

NR
HP

Awards/Ratings: AAA 5 Diamond; Mobil 5 Star

Attractions: Broadway, 5-min walk; Schermerhorn Symphony Center, 5-min walk; Tennessee Performing Arts Center, 5-min walk; Country Music Hall of Fame, 5-min walk
Towns/Cities: Knoxville, 180 miles; Memphis, 197 miles
Airports: Nashville International Airport, 10 miles; Knoxville Airport, 180 miles

Affiliations: Preferred Hotels & Resorts

Situated in the heart of Nashville, The Hermitage is a picture of elegant grandeur. This historic hotel opened in 1910 and was recently renovated to feature paneled walls, ornate vaulted ceilings and polished floors in its public spaces. Luxurious refinement pervades its guest rooms, many of which offer views of the Nashville skyline, and special touches such as afternoon tea and evening cocktails are served in the grand lobby. Complimentary newspapers are delivered to your room in the morning, and a Pampering Pet Program and special Family Offerings lend this opulent hotel a feeling of personal warmth. Fine dining is offered in the Capitol Grille, which uses only the freshest local ingredients and serves 3 meals a day. The distinguished, rich wood-paneled Oak Bar serves drinks.

The Mansion at Judges' Hill

1900 RIO GRANDE, AUSTIN, TEXAS 78705
Tel: +1 512 495 1800 **Fax:** +1 512 691 4461 **U.S./Canada Toll Free:** 1 800 311 1619
Web: www.johansens.com/judgeshill **E-mail:** lisa@judgeshill.com

Our inspector loved: *Taking breakfast on the beautiful balcony outside the Celebrity Suite.*

Price Guide: (room only)
rooms $139-$395
suites $169-$395

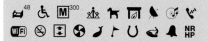

Attractions: 6th Street, 1 mile; Convention Center, 2 miles; University of Texas, 5-min walk; State Capitol, 10-min walk
Towns/Cities: Georgetown, 35 miles; San Antonio, 60 miles
Airports: Austin Bergstrom International Airport, 12 miles

This restored 19th-century mansion offers a serene and refined atmosphere reminiscent of a bygone era. Although situated deep within the heart of Austin, the mansion is set in a secluded location away from day-to-day noise and distraction. The classically-styled bedrooms feature splashes of bright colors and unique touches of style with bathrooms decorated in mosaic tile and marble flooring. Local game and vegetables and seafood flown in from the Gulf of Mexico combine to make East and West Coast specialties on the modern American menu that is prepared with a classic French influence. Chef will also prepare personally chosen menus for weddings, meetings and conferences for up to 300 in the elegantly appointed ballroom and conference center. Professional staff will help organize events and exclusive use of the property can be arranged. 1900 bar is the perfect place for a cocktail after a full day in Austin.

THE INN ON LAKE GRANBURY

205 WEST DOYLE STREET, GRANBURY, TEXAS 76048
Tel: +1 817 573 0046 **Fax:** +1 817 573 0047 **U.S./Canada Toll Free:** 1 877 573 0046
Web: www.johansens.com/lakegranbury **E-mail:** info@innonlakegranbury.com

Our inspector loved: *The calming lake views from the beautifully landscaped pool area.*

Price Guide: (including breakfast)
rooms $185-$295
suites $325-$375

Attractions: Granbury Opera House, 5-min walk; Granbury Live Entertainment, 5-min walk; Barking Rocks Winery, 5 miles; Fossil Rim Wildlife Park, 20 miles
Towns/Cities: Forth Worth, 35 miles; Dallas, 80 miles
Airports: Dallas Fort Worth Airport, 75 miles

This private oasis, on approximately 2 acres of landscaped gardens and scenic lake-front views, provides a tranquil environment to renew your vitality. Cozy up to fire pits, relax by the flagstone pool or bask at the soothing waterfall with tanning ledge. Each guest room at the inn is luxurious and unique; some have sitting areas and outside porches, all have feathered beds and fine linens. Recreational options abound on the scenic Lake Granbury, and downtown offers fine dining options and Broadway plays and musicals. With its spacious conference room and grounds, this is an idyllic setting for a corporate retreat, business meeting, family reunion or wedding.

HOTEL GRANDUCA

1080 UPTOWN PARK BOULEVARD, HOUSTON, TEXAS 77056
Tel: +1 713 418 1000 **Fax:** +1 713 418 1001 **U.S./Canada Toll Free:** 1 888 418 1000
Web: www.johansens.com/granduca **E-mail:** info@granducahouston.com

Our inspector loved: *The wonderful books about all things Italian, architecture, food, wine and history that are in every room of the hotel.*

Price Guide: (including breakfast)
rooms $295-$325
suites $350-$960

Attractions: Houston Galleria, 1 mile; Houston Ballet, 5 miles; Houston Rockets Basketball, 10 miles; Houston Astros - Minute Maid Park, 10 miles

Towns/Cities: Galveston, 50 miles; San Antonio, 200 miles

Airports: Houston Hobby Airport, 25 miles; George Bush Intercontinental Airport, 25 miles

Affiliations: The Leading Hotels of the World

Located just minutes from the shopping, dining, and nightlife opportunities of downtown Houston, this Italian-inspired hotel features spacious rooms with luxurious appointments. Rooms and suites come in a variety of sizes and feature modern luxuries such as wireless Internet and plasma High-Definition T.V.s yet a charm reminiscent of a Tuscan villa is maintained. Hotel Granduca ensures that you are well-fed thanks to fully-stocked kitchens in each of the rooms, an extensive 24-hour menu available in various locations within the hotel including the conservatory, the veranda and guest rooms, and Masraff restaurant with its Southern European-infused American cuisine. Inviting areas such as the billiards room and library lend a sense of intimacy generally found in smaller hotels.

U.S.A. - TEXAS (HOUSTON)

HOTEL ICON

220 MAIN, HOUSTON, TEXAS 77002
Tel: +1 713 224 4266 **Fax:** +1 713 223 3223 **U.S./Canada Toll Free:** 1 800 970 ICON (4266)
Web: www.johansens.com/hotelicon

Our inspector loved: The fine dining, exceptional service and location of BANK restaurant.

Price Guide:
rooms $159-$2,699

Attractions: Theater District, 0.5 miles; Aquarium and Minute Maid Park, 1 mile; Toyota Center, 2 miles; Museum District, Hermann Park, Houston and Rice Universities, 6 miles
Airports: Hobby Airport, 13 miles; Bush International Airport, 20 miles

Located in the heart of downtown Houston, Hotel ICON combines city sophistication with period style. Opulent yet unpretentious, its guest rooms are decorated in rich, colorful tones, with custom-designed period furniture and luxurious fabrics. Each includes many amenities designed with the business traveler in mind, such as a fax or printer on request, a workspace with an ergonomic chair and a safe big enough for laptops, making Hotel ICON ideal accommodations for those traveling for business as well as pleasure. Dining is a pleasure at BANK, the hotel's acclaimed restaurant that serves New American cuisine with Asian and French influences amidst 30-foot columns and under an intricate ceiling. More private dining is offered in the Wine Vault from the same menu.

American Falls

IDAHO

WYOMING

Lander

Preston

Logan

Kemmerer

Brigham City

NEVADA

Green
River

Ogden

Evanston

Farmington

Salt Lake City
Int. Airport

Manila

SALT LAKE CITY

Tooele

Heber City

243

Vernal

Provo

Duchesne

Ely

Nephi

Delta

Price

Manti

Fillmore

Castle Dale

Grand Junction

76

Richfield

Moab

Beaver

Loa

242

Delta

Panguitch

Cedar City

COLORADO

Monticello

15

St George
Municipal Airport

St. George

Blanding

Kanab

Colorado City

Cortez

Kayenta

ARIZONA

Aztec

NEW MEXICO

Tusayan

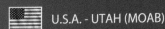
SORREL RIVER RANCH RESORT & SPA

MILE 17 SCENIC BYWAY 128, H.C. 64 BOX 4000, MOAB, UTAH 84532
Tel: +1 435 259 4642 **Fax:** +1 435 259 3016 **U.S./Canada Toll Free:** 1 877 359 2715
Web: www.johansens.com/sorrelriver **E-mail:** stay@sorrelriver.com

Our inspector loved: Watching the Colorado River flow by the porch.

Price Guide: (excluding 9% tax)
rooms $209-$349
suites $254-$529

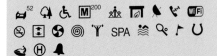

Awards/Ratings: Condé Nast Johansens Most Excellent Ranch, U.S.A. & Canada 2007

Attractions: Colorado River, on-site; Fisher Towers, 5 miles; Arches National Park, 19 miles; Canyonlands National Parks, 46 miles
Towns/Cities: Moab, 20 miles; Grand Junction, Colorado, 80 miles; Salt Lake City, 250 miles; Las Vegas, NV, 480 miles
Airports: Moab, 30 miles; Grand Junction Colorado, 80 miles; Salt Lake City, 250 miles

Affiliations: Small Luxury Hotels of the World

On a bend in the Colorado River, amid dramatic Red Rock cathedrals, Sorrel River Ranch Resort & Spa basks in peaceful seclusion beneath a flawless desert sky. Luxury accommodations, abundant outdoor activities, gourmet dining and full-service spa complete this impressive resort's resumé. Well-appointed guest rooms have kitchenettes, private decks and charming Western appeal. Some offer fireplaces and stunning river or mountain views. Those who yearn for adventure will enjoy mountain biking, hiking, 4x4 off-road driving and river rafting on the Colorado, followed by a riverside gourmet dining experience at the acclaimed Sorrel River Grill. For the perfect complement to your active vacation, the Health Spa's skilled therapists provide pampering and rejuvenation preparing you for more excitement tomorrow!

SUNDANCE RESORT

RR#3 BOX A-1, SUNDANCE, UTAH 84604

Tel: +1 801 225 4107 **Fax:** +1 801 226 1937 **U.S./Canada Toll Free:** 1 800 892 1600
Web: www.johansens.com/sundance **E-mail:** RESOP@sundance-utah.com

Our inspector loved: *The feeling of being so close to the mountains.*

Price Guide:
studios $250-$350
suites $275-$560
mountain homes $675-$1,700

SPA

Awards/Ratings: Wine Spectator Award of Excellence 2007; Condé Nast Traveler Gold List 2006

Attractions: Art Classes, 5-min walk; Musical Concerts, 5-min walk; Fly Fishing, 5-10-min drive; Sundance Film Festival, Park City, 45-min drive
Towns/Cities: Provo/Orem, 20-min drive; Park City, 45-min drive; Salt Lake City, 60-min drive
Airports: Salt Lake City International Airport, 60-min drive

Affiliations: Preferred Boutique

The brainchild of Robert Redford, Sundance Resort is a ski resort, arts center and nature reserve in one. The accommodations that dot the mountainside are spacious yet cozy with rough hewn wood, stone fireplaces, Western and Native American accents and warm tones that blend harmoniously with the alpine environment. The resort includes 2 highly-acclaimed restaurants, a Deli and the Owl Bar, which hosts live music on the weekend. Pamper yourself with a Native American-inspired treatment at the Spa at Sundance, or simply relax on your patio, taking in the magnificent views along with the fresh mountain air afforded by this place of pristine quietude. For a taste of culture, enjoy an art exhibition, film or concert, often available for your entertainment.

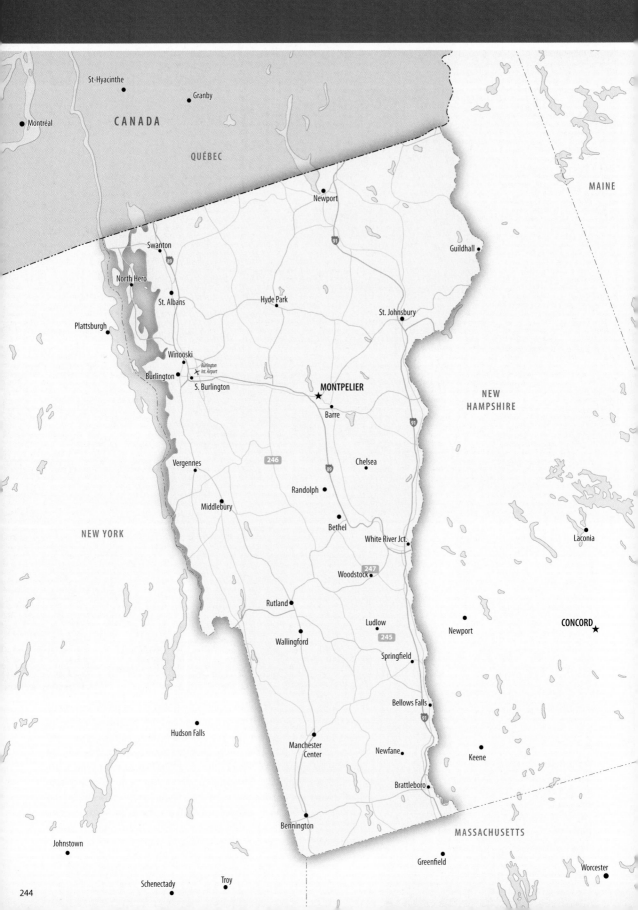

St-Hyacinthe

Granby

Montréal

CANADA

QUÉBEC

MAINE

Newport

91

Swanton

Guildhall

89

North Hero

St. Albans

Hyde Park

St. Johnsbury

Plattsburgh

Winooski

Burlington
Int. Airport

Burlington

S. Burlington

MONTPELIER

Barre

NEW
HAMPSHIRE

91

Vergennes

246

Chelsea

89

Randolph

Middlebury

Bethel

White River Jct.

NEW YORK

Laconia

Woodstock

247

Rutland

Ludlow

Newport

CONCORD

Wallingford

245

Springfield

Bellows Falls

91

Hudson Falls

Manchester
Center

Newfane

Keene

Brattleboro

Bennington

MASSACHUSETTS

Johnstown

Greenfield

Worcester

Schenectady

Troy

CASTLE HILL RESORT & SPA

JCT. ROUTES 103 AND 131, CAVENDISH, VERMONT 05142
Tel: +1 802 226 7361 **Fax:** +1 802 226 7301 **U.S./Canada Toll Free:** 1 888 764 6836
Web: www.johansens.com/castlehillvt **E-mail:** sales@thecastle-vt.com

Our inspector loved: *The spa, located in the circa 1860 carriage house, with heated walkways that melt snow.*

Price Guide:
deluxe rooms $245-$355
suites $295-$465
resort homes $295-$1,095

Attractions: Okemo Mountain Resort, 3 miles; President Coolidge Historic State Site, 12 miles; Marsh-Billings-Rockefeller National Historical Park, 21 miles; Manchester Village, 35 miles
Towns/Cities: Weston, 15 miles; Woodstock, 20 miles; Burlington, 122 miles; Montréal, QC, 220 miles
Airports: Hartford Bradley Intl., 126 miles; Boston Logan, 158 miles; New York City Airports, 248 miles

Affiliations: Small Luxury Hotels of the World

Set in Vermont's scenic Green Mountains, Castle Hill Resort & Spa offers intimate and elegant accommodations and serves as the perfect destination for a wedding, honeymoon or just for a relaxing getaway. Choose to stay in the mansion where rooms exude a sense of historic elegance updated with modern comforts, or in one of Castle Hill's Resort Homes, which provide plenty of privacy and room for friends and family. The Green Mountains offer an abundance of daytime activities, including snowboarding and snow shoeing in the winter. Hiking, biking and fly fishing are popular during the summer months. Castle Hill's classic dining room, with its wood-paneled walls and subtle antique flair, provides a cozy and historic atmosphere for you to enjoy French-inspired American cuisine made from fresh local produce and meats.

245

THE PITCHER INN

275 MAIN STREET, P.O. BOX 347, WARREN, VERMONT 05674
Tel: +1 802 496 6350 **Fax:** +1 802 496 6354
Web: www.johansens.com/pitcherinn **E-mail:** info@pitcherinn.com

Our inspector loved: The wonderfully appointed Mallard Room with the built-in nature sounds.

Price Guide: (Sunday - Thursday rates include a 3-course dinner)
rooms $350-$700

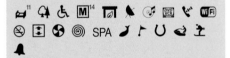

The Pitcher Inn is a delightful 11-room and suite inn located in the heart of Vermont's Green Mountains, at the foot of Sugarbush Resort. Welcoming guests since the early 1850s, each charming Vermont-themed room is located in the main house or in the adjacent barn brimming with original art, memorabilia and antiques. The Main Dining Room offers à la carte menus or for more casual fare there is Tracks. Chef Sue Schickler's seasonal menus highlight some of Vermont's freshest ingredients including lamb, quail, rabbit, organic vegetables, artisanal cheeses and seafood. The smell of freshly baked goods will wake you up each morning, and in the afternoon, enjoy tea and afternoon cocktails in the Library. Go ahead and treat yourself to some time at the Alta Day Spa where an array of spa and beauty treatments is available.

Attractions: Warren Country Store, 2-min walk; Sugarbush Golf Course, 5 miles; Skiing/ Snowboarding, 5 miles; Mad River Valley Soaring, 10 miles
Towns/Cities: Burlington, 45 miles; Montréal, QC, 140 miles; Boston, MA, 190 miles; New York City, NY, 325 miles
Airports: Burlington International Airport, 45 miles; Albany International Airport, 135 miles; Boston (Logan) International Airport, MA, 190 miles

Affiliations: Relais & Châteaux

THE JACKSON HOUSE INN

114-3 SENIOR LANE, WOODSTOCK, VERMONT 05091
Tel: +1 802 457 2065 **Fax:** +1 802 457 9290
Web: www.johansens.com/jacksonhouse **E-mail:** innkeeper@jacksonhouse.com

Our inspector loved: *The great location and wonderful restaurant.*

Price Guide: (including breakfast and Innkeepers' Reception each evening)
single/double rooms $220-$300
single/double suites $340-$440

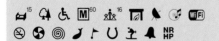

Awards/Ratings: Wine Spectator Award of Excellence 1998-2007

Attractions: Historic Town of Woodstock, 0.5 miles; Simon Pearce Glass, 5 miles; Dartmouth College, 10 miles; Killington Ski Area, 18 miles.
Towns/Cities: Woodstock, 0.5 miles; Hanover, NH, 10 miles
Airports: Lebanon Municipal Airport, 17 miles; Manchester Boston Regional Airport, 95 miles

This 15-room boutique-style New England inn, situated just outside the quaint Vermont town of Woodstock, is a great place from which to explore the countryside in all seasons. The rooms are all decorated in a different theme and are cozy and inviting. In summer hanging baskets of colorful flowers adorn the front porch and a stroll in the beautiful gardens is a must. The public rooms allow guests a place to meet and relax or to enjoy cheese and wine prior to dinner. The restaurant is renowned in the area, particularly for its seafood dishes prepared by Chef Jason Merrill who uses locally grown produce, beef, lamb, poultry, and pork from local and organic farms whenever possible and ingredients from his garden when in season.

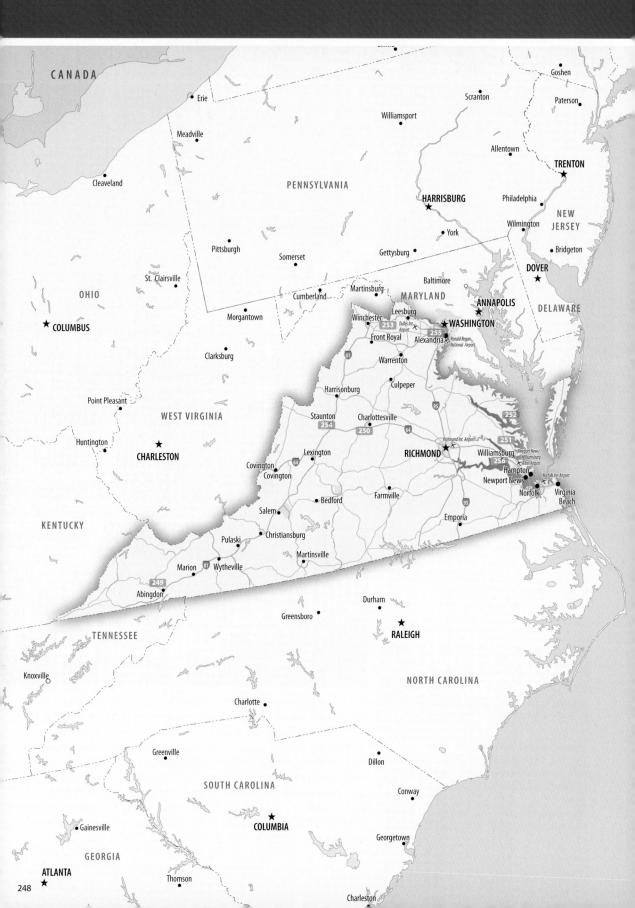

CANADA

Erie

Meadville

Cleaveland

PENNSYLVANIA

Williamsport

Scranton

Goshen

Paterson

Allentown

TRENTON

HARRISBURG

Philadelphia

York

Wilmington

NEW JERSEY

Bridgeton

Pittsburgh

Somerset

Gettysburg

DOVER

St. Clairsville

Cumberland

Baltimore

MARYLAND

ANNAPOLIS

DELAWARE

OHIO

Morgantown

Martinsburg

Winchester

Leesburg

WASHINGTON

COLUMBUS

Clarksburg

253 Dulles Int. Airport

Front Royal

Alexandria

Ronald Regan National Airport

81

Warrenton

Point Pleasant

WEST VIRGINIA

Harrisonburg

Culpeper

95

Staunton

Charlottesville

252

Huntington

254

250

Richmond Int. Airport

251

CHARLESTON

Lexington

64

RICHMOND

Williamsburg

Newport News/ Williamsburg Int. Airport

Covington

64

256

Hampton

Covington

Newport News

Norfolk Int. Airport

KENTUCKY

Bedford

Farmville

Norfolk

Virginia Beach

Salem

Emporia

Pulaski

Christiansburg

Marion

81

Wytheville

Martinsville

249

Abingdon

Durham

TENNESSEE

Greensboro

RALEIGH

Knoxville

NORTH CAROLINA

Charlotte

Greenville

Dillon

SOUTH CAROLINA

Conway

COLUMBIA

Georgetown

Gainesville

GEORGIA

ATLANTA

Thomson

Charleston

THE MARTHA WASHINGTON INN

150 WEST MAIN STREET, ABINGDON, VIRGINIA 24210
Tel: +1 276 628 3161 **Fax:** +1 276 628 8885 **U.S./Canada Toll Free:** 1 888 999 8078
Web: www.johansens.com/themartha **E-mail:** info@themartha.com

Our inspector loved: *The sense of history at the inn along with the outstanding service and amenities.*

Price Guide:
rooms $209-$359
suites $259-$450

 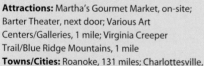

Attractions: Martha's Gourmet Market, on-site; Barter Theater, next door; Various Art Centers/Galleries, 1 mile; Virginia Creeper Trail/Blue Ridge Mountains, 1 mile
Towns/Cities: Roanoke, 131 miles; Charlottesville, 240 miles; Richmond, 300 miles
Airports: Tri-Cities Airport, 30 miles; Roanoke Airport, 131 miles

Originally built in 1832 as the private residence of a Virginian General, The Martha Washington Inn opened in 1935 and remains an elegant and majestic hotel. Set amongst 19th-century homes and brick walks, the inn has seen many notable guests including Eleanor Roosevelt, President Harry Truman, Lady Bird Johnson, Jimmy Carter and Elizabeth Taylor. The inn was also once a hospital during the Civil War and a finishing school for girls. Its 19th-century grand stairway and parlors have been retained and enhance the romance and serenity of this beautifully decorated property with beautiful period antiques alongside all the amenities expected from a modern hotel. In the summer months French doors and a retractable roof bring the outside in, and the pool's sundeck is a relaxing place to read a good book. The elegant Dining Room offers regional cuisine and serves a sumptuous Sunday brunch, while the private President's Club offers afternoon tea and cocktails.

BOAR'S HEAD INN

200 EDNAM DRIVE, CHARLOTTESVILLE, VIRGINIA 22903
Tel: +1 434 972 2232 **Fax:** +1 434 972 6021 **U.S./Canada Toll Free:** 1 800 476 1988
Web: www.johansens.com/boarsheadusa **E-mail:** reserve@boarsheadinn.com

Our inspector loved: *Enjoying a hot-air balloon ride over the heart of Virginia's historic countryside.*

Price Guide: (excluding taxes and resort fees)
rooms $160-$325
suites $325-$575

Built from the materials of an old gristmill dating back to 1834, the quintessentially Virginian Boar's Head Inn offers excellent fare, charming accommodations and authentic ambience throughout. The AAA Four-Diamond-rated Old Mill Room serves flavorful dishes that make use of the finest local ingredients while maintaining a casual, distinctly Charlottesville atmosphere. The inn's rooms and suites, with their high ceilings of hand-hewn beams and authentic wood cabinetry, feature four-poster beds covered with linens so comfortable that guests have asked to buy them. Carefully-concealed modern appliances ensure nothing will disturb the charming, antique ambience. A spa and full-service health club, complete with tennis courts, pools, and fitness equipment are just a few of the services that can be enjoyed at this esteemed Virginian property.

Awards/Ratings: Wine Spectator Award of Excellence 2005

Attractions: Monticello, 9.4 miles; King Family Vineyard, 12 miles; Ash Lawn-Highlands, 11.9 miles; Barboursville Vineyard, 22 miles
Towns/Cities: Charlottesville, 2 miles; Richmond, 70 miles; Washington D.C., 120 miles
Airports: Charlottesville/Albemarle Airport, 10 miles; Richmond Intl. Airport, 86 miles; Dulles International Airport, 95 miles

THE INN AT WARNER HALL

4750 WARNER HALL ROAD, GLOUCESTER, VIRGINIA 23061
Tel: +1 804 695 9565 **Fax:** +1 804 695 9566 **U.S./Canada Toll Free:** 1 800 331 2720
Web: www.johansens.com/warnerhall **E-mail:** info@warnerhall.com

Our inspector loved: *The large, elegant and immaculate rooms that reflect a fascinating history.*

Price Guide:
rooms $175-$245

Attractions: Yorktown 11 miles; Colonial Williamsburg, 25 miles; Jamestown Settlement, 32 miles
Towns/Cities: Norfolk, 40 miles; Richmond, 45 miles; Virginia Beach, 50 miles
Airports: Williamsburg Airport, 28 miles

Established as a plantation by George Washington's great-great grandfather in 1642, this Colonial-Revival waterfront manor house has been restored to its original grandeur and transformed into a modern country inn. Many famous historic figures have ties to the inn, including Meriwether Lewis, General Robert E. Lee and Queen Elizabeth II. Each of the rooms has period antiques and Schumacher fabrics as well as comfortable seating areas, private baths and Gilchrist Soames products. The 38 acres of grounds include the tranquil Severn River where complimentary kayaks, canoes, fishing equipment and bicycles are available, and native wildlife and natural wonders of tidewater Virginia can be enjoyed. Formal dining is available on weekends, while during the week, sumptuous supper baskets can be enjoyed at the location of your choice.

HOPE AND GLORY INN

65 TAVERN ROAD, IRVINGTON, VIRGINIA 22480
Tel: +1 804 438 6053 **Fax:** +1 804 438 5362 **U.S./Canada Toll Free:** 1 800 497 8228
Web: www.johansens.com/hopeandglory **E-mail:** inquiries@hopeandglory.com

Our inspector loved: *The fun and hopelessly romantic outdoor shower.*

Price Guide:
rooms $175-$275
cottages $240-$340
tents $385-$685

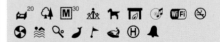

Set on the picturesque Chesapeake Bay Shore, Hope and Glory is a whimsical and elegantly restored schoolhouse with several guest cottages, each with their own private gardens. Children are welcome in the cottages only. The inn caters more to adult travelers looking for serenity. The surrounding English gardens are a gardener's delight, filled with old fashioned single hollyhocks, David Austin roses, artemesias and flowers rare to Virginia. A favorite area of the inn is the winding pathway that leads to a private outdoor shower, complete with a claw-foot tub and sink. In the evenings relax in the dreamy moon garden, and on a Friday night take part in the crab feast on the inn's 42-foot boat, The Faded Glory, and the prix-fixe wine paired "Dinner at our Chef's Table" on a Saturday. 7 additional cottages called "tents" are located within White Fences Vineyard & Winery.

Attractions: Downtown Irvington, 0.1 miles; White Fences Vineyard & Winery, 1 mile; Chesapeake Bay Shore, 2 miles; Colonial WIlliamsburg, 53 miles
Towns/Cities: Williamsburg, 53 miles; Richmond, 70 miles; Norfolk, 77 miles; Washington D.C., 145 miles
Airports: Richmond International Airport, 64 miles; Reagan National Airport, 143 miles

THE GOODSTONE INN & ESTATE

36205 SNAKE HILL ROAD, MIDDLEBURG, VIRGINIA 20117
Tel: +1 540 687 4645 **Fax:** +1 540 687 6115 **U.S./Canada Toll Free:** 1 877 219 4663
Web: www.johansens.com/goodstoneinn **E-mail:** information@goodstone.com

Our inspector loved: The gorgeous grounds and beauty surrounding this historic estate.

Price Guide: (including full country breakfast, afternoon tea and golf at Stoneleigh Golf Club)
rooms $250-$515
junior suites $285-$530
suites $300-$610

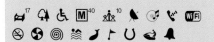

Attractions: Steeplechase Races, 2 miles; Downtown Middleburg, 3 miles; Shenandoah National Park, 50 miles; Washington D.C., 50 miles
Towns/Cities: Middleburg, 2 miles
Airports: Dulles International Airport, 25 miles

Affiliations: Small Luxury Hotels of the World

This superb inn is located in the heart of Virginia's famous hunt country and wine region. Situated on 265 acres of estate grounds with the Blue Ridge Mountains visible in the distance, each of the individually decorated guest rooms and suites is located in residences renovated in elegant English and French country styles. The heart of the inn is the Carriage House where afternoon tea is served daily and Hilltoppers Restaurant is located. Complimentary recreational activities include mountain biking, canoeing, a woodland nature trail and a round of golf at Stoneleigh Country Club. On-site massage and horse-trail rides in the foothills of the mountains can be arranged.

FREDERICK HOUSE

28 NORTH NEW STREET, STAUNTON, VIRGINIA 24401
Tel: +1 540 885 4220 **Fax:** +1 540 885 5180 **U.S./Canada Toll Free:** 1 800 334 5575
Web: www.johansens.com/frederickhouse **E-mail:** stay@frederickhouse.com

Our inspector loved: The hand-painted wall stencils in many of the rooms.

Price Guide: (including breakfast)
oversized guest rooms $139-$169
1-bedroom suites $159-$199
2-bedroom suites $209-$259

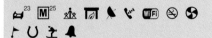

3 adjoining 19th-century town houses and 2 mid-1800 residences lie in the quiet downtown of historic Staunton, which in itself is a great starting point for a tour of Virginia's sites. Frederick's fine architecture welcomes you into its intimate ambience that reflects the conviviality of this small town where a wide variety of shopping and cultural activities are on offer. The earliest of the Frederick houses dates back to 1809 and is the epitome of period elegance with its Federal staircase. Each of the rooms has been painstakingly designed to incorporate period features and charm with modern facilities. Each is also uniquely decorated and displays original antiques, books and pictures. Making careful use of the building's hillside setting, the balconies, terraces and front porches are the perfect location to enjoy a glass of wine before attending the theater or enjoying the many restaurants all within walking distance.

Attractions: American Shakespeare Center, 0.1 miles; Woodrow Wilson Presidential Library, 0.1 miles; Frontier Cultural Museum, 2 miles; Skyline Drive/Blue Ridge Parkway, 15 miles
Towns/Cities: Charlottesville, 30 miles; Roanoke, 90 miles; Richmond, 120 miles; Washington D.C., 180 miles
Airports: Shenandoah Valley Regional Airport, 15 miles; Charlottesville Airport, 30 miles; Richmond Airport, 120 miles

MORRISON HOUSE

116 SOUTH ALFRED STREET, ALEXANDRIA, VIRGINIA 22314
Tel: +1 703 838 8000 **Fax:** +1 703 684 6283 **U.S./Canada Toll Free:** 1 866 834 6628
Web: www.johansens.com/morrisonhouse **E-mail:** concierge@morrisonhouse.com

Our inspector loved: *The in-room check-in, and the piano bar.*

Price Guide:
rooms $179-$399
suites $279-$499

Attractions: Old Town Alexandria, on-site; The White House, 7 miles
Towns/Cities: Old Town Alexandria, on-site; Washington, D.C., 5 miles
Airports: Ronald Reagan Washington National Airport, 5 miles; Dulles International Airport, 35 miles; Baltimore Washington International Airport, 40 miles

Nestled in historic Old Town Alexandria is a detailed work of art: Morrison House, a new member of the Kimpton Hotel & Restaurants Group. A striking reproduction of an 18th-century Federal manor house with period furnishings, the hotel features quiet sophistication without pretense. A beautiful brick courtyard and sculpture fountain beckon you into the marble foyer, where upon entering, you are escorted directly to an elegant guest room with mahogany poster bed, Italian marble bath and ultra-luxurious linens. From welcoming butlers to attentive concierges, every detail is handled with impeccable care. Acclaimed cuisine, flawless service and a comfortable atmosphere successfully combine for a memorable evening in the restaurant where an extensive wine list offers over 200 bottles and 16 wines by the glass. Gracious hospitality and attentive service provide the perfect combination for corporate and social events alike.

WEDMORE PLACE

5810 WESSEX HUNDRED, WILLIAMSBURG, VIRGINIA 23185

Tel: +1 757 941 0310 **Fax:** +1 757 941 0318 **U.S./Canada Toll Free:** 1 866 933 6673

Web: www.johansens.com/wedmore **E-mail:** info@wedmoreplace.com

Our inspector loved: *The European style and state-of-the-art amenities that enhance the wonderful guest experience.*

Price Guide: (including breakfast)
rooms $190-$325
suites $300-$650

A European-themed country hotel on the outskirts of Colonial Williamsburg, Wedmore Place is situated on 300 acres of farmland and is imbued in culture and history. Each of the elegant, luxuriously appointed rooms is individually styled in the theme of a different European province and period of history. The Corinthian Room, inspired by ancient Greece, features a large marble statue, white ceramic tiling, and Corinthian columns. The sumptuous Venetian Suite has an impressive 20-foot, frescoed ceiling. Each room offers wood-burning fireplaces, antique furnishings, king-size beds, wireless Internet, and reading material about the history the room is depicting. The hotel has an English club-inspired library, a pool set within woodland, and the Gabriel Archer Tavern at The Williamsburg Winery.

Attractions: Colonial Williamsburg, 3 miles; Jamestowne/Yorktown Settlements, 5 miles; Busch Gardens, 5 miles

Towns/Cities: Williamsburg, on-site; Richmond, 50 miles

Airports: Newport News/Williamsburg International Airport, 26 miles; Richmond International Airport, 50 miles; Norfolk/Virginia Beach International Airport, 55 miles

Affiliations: Small Luxury Hotels of the World

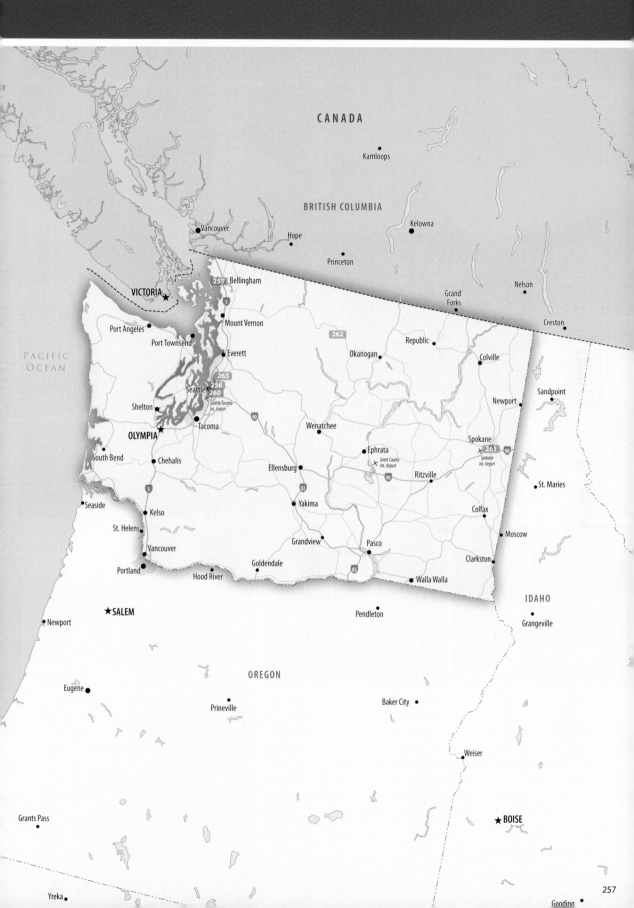

CANADA

Kamloops

BRITISH COLUMBIA

Kelowna

Vancouver

Hope

Princeton

Grand
Forks

Nelson

259 Bellingham

Creston

VICTORIA ★

Mount Vernon

Port Angeles

262

Republic

Port Townsend

Okanogan

Colville

Everett

Sandpoint

263

Seattle

258
260

Newport

Seattle/Tacoma
Int. Airport

Wenatchee

Shelton

90

Spokane

Tacoma

261

Spokane
Int. Airport

OLYMPIA ★

Ephrata

St. Maries

Grant County
Int. Airport

Chehalis

Ellensburg

90

Ritzville

South Bend

82

Colfax

Seaside

Yakima

Moscow

Kelso

St. Helens

Clarkston

Grandview

Pasco

Vancouver

Goldendale

82

Walla Walla

Portland

Hood River

IDAHO

★ SALEM

Pendleton

Newport

Grangeville

OREGON

Eugene

Prineville

Baker City

Weiser

Grants Pass

★ BOISE

PACIFIC
OCEAN

5

5

Yreka

Gooding

THE BELLEVUE CLUB HOTEL

11200 S.E. 6TH STREET, BELLEVUE, WASHINGTON 98004
Tel: +1 425 455 1616 **Fax:** +1 425 688 3197 **U.S./Canada Toll Free:** 1 800 579 1110
Web: www.johansens.com/bellevue **E-mail:** hotel@bellevueclub.com

Our inspector loved: The wonderful 180,000 sq. ft. athletic facility adjacent to the hotel.

Price Guide:
rooms $255-$335
suites $625-$1,500

Surrounded by lush green gardens, yet in close proximity to downtown Seattle, The Bellevue Club Hotel is an ideal oasis with a distinct air of seclusion and luxury. The hotel offers a truly all-inclusive experience where guests can enjoy the Club's extensive athletic and social resources, or simply unwind in the comfortable living room setting of The Terrace Room with coffee each morning and tea and cookies in the afternoon. There are no less than 4 restaurants ranging from Polaris's sophisticated and chic atmosphere to the Luna Express Café's menu of espresso drinks, sandwiches and salads. Set just 15 minutes from Seattle's waterfront, and in the heart of downtown Bellevue, those of you with some spare time have innumerable dining, galleries, and outdoor activities to choose from.

Attractions: Bellevue Square, 15-min walk; Newcastle Golf and Country Club, 7 miles; Downtown Seattle, 12 miles
Towns/Cities: Redmond, 8 miles; Seattle, 12 miles; Woodenville, 12 miles
Airports: Seattle/Tacoma International Aiport, 17 miles

Affiliations: Small Luxury Hotels of the World

THE CHRYSALIS INN AND SPA

804 10TH STREET, BELLINGHAM, WASHINGTON 98225
Tel: +1 360 756 1005 **Fax:** +1 360 647 0342 **U.S./Canada Toll Free:** 1 888 808 0005
Web: www.johansens.com/chrysalis **E-mail:** info@thechrysalisinn.com

Our inspector loved: *The large window seats in every room with the panoramic view of Bellingham Bay.*

Price Guide: (including breakfast)
rooms $179-$189
suites $200-$299

Attractions: Walking Trails; Kayaking, 5-min walk; Vineyards, 14 miles; Mount Baker, 50 miles
Towns/Cities: Bellingham, 20-min walk; Vancouver, BC, 45 miles; Seattle, 90 miles
Airports: Bellingham Airport, 7 miles

Set on the waterfront in the historic Fairhaven district, this peaceful inn captures the essence of the Northwest. The architectural style is modern and distinct and is ideal for a romantic weekend or undisturbed business meeting. The bedrooms are cleverly designed with corner fireplaces and deep window seats perfect for relaxing with a glass of wine. Modern cherrywood bathrooms feature 2-person tubs with marvelous views of the Northwest seascape. The Inn's restaurant, Fino Wine Bar, serves classic European food and wine and features a popular "exhibition" kitchen where the chef produces regional and international specialties. The Chrysalis Spa is a sensory delight with stone floors, glass art and soothing music.

U.S.A. - WASHINGTON (SEATTLE)

Hotel Ändra

2000 FOURTH AVENUE, SEATTLE, WASHINGTON 98121
Tel: +1 206 448 8600 **Fax:** +1 206 441 7140 **U.S./Canada Toll Free:** 1 877 448 8600
Web: www.johansens.com/hotelandra **E-mail:** hotelandra@hotelandra.com

Our inspector loved: *The unique fusion of Scandinavian style with Pacific Northwest hospitality.*

Price Guide:
ändra studios-ändra rooms $309-$329
ändra suites-ändra lux suites $339-$400

Awards/Ratings: Condé Nast Traveler Gold List 2005

Attractions: Pike Place Market, 5-min walk; Downtown Shopping, 5-min walk; Space Needle, 15-min walk; Waterfront, 15-min walk
Towns/Cities: Seattle, on-site; Bellevue, 11 miles
Airports: Seattle Airport, 15 miles

Affiliations: Small Luxury Hotels of the World

Close to the fashionable and thriving retail neighborhood of Belltown, which is renowned for its innovative art, music and dining scene, Hotel Ändra is a stylish retreat with a welcoming atmosphere. Following an extensive renovation in 2004, the new interior features strong Northwestern décor with Scandinavian design influences, rich wooden furnishings and ambient lighting. The impressive Lobby Living Room is filled with rich woods and wool hand-knotted rugs, and each bedroom and suite displays original artwork and has a plush bed fitted with goose-down comforters, an oversized walnut desk and modern features. Highly-acclaimed chef/author Tom Douglas oversees the Northwest ingredients served in the Greek-inspired Lola restaurant. Alternately, Assaggio Ristorante serves authentic Italian cuisine.

THE DAVENPORT HOTEL AND TOWER

10 SOUTH POST STREET, SPOKANE, WASHINGTON 99201
Tel: +1 509 455 8888 **Fax:** +1 509 624 4455 **U.S./Canada Toll Free:** 1 800 899 1482
Web: www.johansens.com/davenport **E-mail:** reservations@thedavenporthotel.com

Our inspector loved: *The custom-made Davenport beds wrapped in the finest linens, and the historical walking tour of the property.*

Price Guide:
rooms $299-$369
suites $419-$2,500

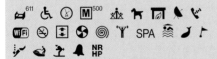

Awards/Ratings: Condé Nast Traveler Gold List 2007

Attractions: Bing Crosby Performing Arts Center, 1-min walk; River Park Square Shopping, 2-min walk; Big Easy Concert House, 2-min walk; Riverfront Park, 5-min walk
Towns/Cities: Spokane, on the doorstep; Coeur D' Alene, 26 miles; Idaho, 26 miles
Airports: Spokane Airport, 8 miles

This stately hotel was established in 1914 and retains its classical architecture and large formal rooms that create the perfect atmosphere for meetings, parties and weddings. Each guest room and suite is spacious and well-planned. The Penthouse floor houses the most spectacular collection of suites. The Venetian-inspired Hall of the Doges and the Grand Pennington Ballroom combine to accommodate 500 guests for banquets, and some smaller meeting rooms seat 150. The Palm Court Grill restaurant serves a selection of Northwest-inspired cuisine accompanied by a fine wine selection, and the Lobby fireside is great for breakfast, tea or cocktails. The Tower's Safari Room Fresh Grill and Bar Restaurant offers seasonally-inspired dishes. The 328-room Tower, located across the street, adds a contemporary flavor of world travel.

SUN MOUNTAIN LODGE

P.O. BOX 1,000, WINTHROP, WASHINGTON 98862
Tel: +1 509 996 2211 **Fax:** +1 509 996 3133 **U.S./Canada Toll Free:** 1 800 572 0493
Web: www.johansens.com/sunmountain **E-mail:** sunres@methow.com

Our inspector loved: The wonderful views of the North Cascade Mountains and the 124 miles of trails on the property.

Price Guide:
rooms $165-$370
suites $260-$430

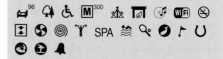

Awards/Ratings: DiRoNa; Previous Recipient of Wine Spectator Award of Excellence

Attractions: Miles of Hiking and Biking Trails, on-site; Wineries, 10 miles; North Cascade National Park, 25 miles; Lake Chelan, 60 miles
Towns/Cities: Winthrop, 10 miles
Airports: Winthrop Airport, 12 miles; Seattle Airport, 212 miles

Set against the magnificent North Cascade Mountain Range and surrounded by pristine countryside, Sun Mountain Lodge is an ideal getaway for nature-lovers, as well as those simply seeking a first-class resort experience in a beautiful setting. The Lodge, situated amidst the second largest cross-country ski trail system in the U.S., offers a myriad of outdoor activities, features large, spacious interiors framed with huge Douglas Fir beams and floors laden with Idaho Quartz. The rooms are filled with hand-made wood furniture and original artwork; many have fireplaces, and all offer breathtaking views. Enjoy innovative dishes using fresh, locally-grown Northwest ingredients in the award-winning Dining Room, and the extensive, 450-label wine list.

THE HERBFARM

14590 NORTH EAST 145TH STREET, WOODINVILLE, WASHINGTON 98072
Tel: +1 425 485 5300 **Fax:** +1 425 424 2925
Web: www.johansens.com/herbfarm **E-mail:** reservations@theherbfarm.com

Our inspector loved: *The 9-course dinner showcasing the foods and wines of the Pacific Northwest.*

Price Guide: (including breakfast)
rooms $300-$395

Awards/Ratings: Wine Spectator Award of Excellence 2006

Attractions: Sammamish River Trail, 1-min walk; Wineries, 5-min walk/drive; Redmond Town Center, 9 miles
Towns/Cities: Downtown Woodinville, 4-min drive; Redmond, 9 miles; Seattle, 20 miles
Airports: Seattle Airport, 28 miles

Bask in the warm and personalized hospitality of owners, husband and wife Ron Zimmerman and Carrie Van Dyck, and enjoy the exceptional cuisine, which is the centerpiece of this magnificent place. Themed dinner evenings run throughout the year with menus created just hours before service to utilize the best produce at the peak of its perfection. The majestic 9-course dinners are accompanied by a selection of 5 or 6 fine wines chosen by The Herbfarm's sommeliers. The Herbfarm offers 2 luxurious suites on the property in romantic Willows Lodge. The Orchard House Suite is decorated in rich hues of red and gold embellished with paintings and sculptures, while the Herb Garden Suite features serene shades of green and mauve complemented by delicate lighting.

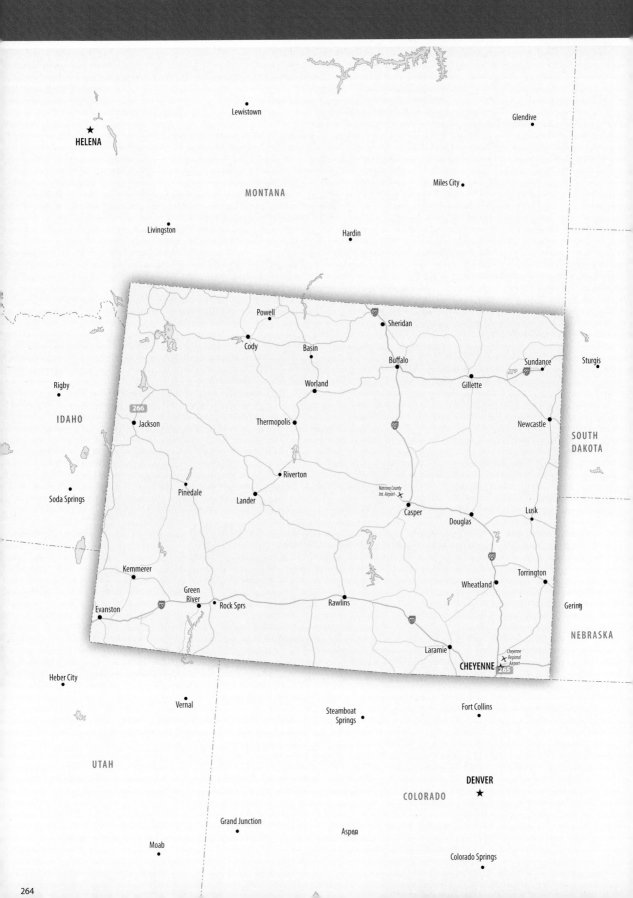

NAGLE WARREN MANSION

222 EAST 17TH STREET, CHEYENNE, WYOMING 82001
Tel: +1 307 637 3333 **Fax:** +1 307 638 6879 **U.S./Canada Toll Free:** 1 800 811 2610
Web: www.johansens.com/naglewarrenmansion **E-mail:** jim@nwmbb.com

Our inspector loved: *The attention to historical details that successfully recreates the Victorian era combined with the luxury and comfort of modern amenites.*

Price Guide: (including breakfast)
rooms $120-$290
suites $120-$290

Attractions: Transcontinental Railroad Museum, 5-min walk; Old West Museum, 5-min walk; Art Galleries, 5-min walk; Western Wear Shopping, 5-min walk
Towns/Cities: Denver, 70 miles
Airports: Cheyenne Airport, 1 mile; Denver Airport, 85 miles

On the edge of downtown Cheyenne, this stylish residence is steeped in a rich and interesting history. Built in 1888 by Erasmus Nagle, the inn became home to Francis E. Warren, Governor and Wyoming Senator. The elegant Victorian décor is complemented by the fine craftsmanship of a bygone era with vestiges of the past evident as you walk up the ornate wooden staircases where authentic period touches abound. The delicious breakfast includes freshly baked muffins, and special recipes by the cook are a daily treat. Why not spend the day hiking through the mountains followed by a soak in the outdoor hot tub set in an enclosed gazebo? Alternately, there is shopping and exploring historic Cheyenne to enjoy.

JENNY LAKE LODGE

INNER PARK LOOP ROAD, GRAND TETON NATIONAL PARK, WYOMING 83013
Tel: +1 307 543 3300 **Fax:** +1 307 543 3358 **U.S./Canada Toll Free:** 1 800 628 9988
Web: www.johansens.com/jennylake **E-mail:** reservations@GTLC.com

Our inspector loved: *The fascinating history of the property recounted weekly to guests by Jenny Lake's very own historian.*

Price Guide: (including breakfast, 5-course dinner, horseback riding and cycling)
rooms $525
suites $695-$750

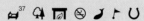

Attractions: Hiking and Mountain Vistas, 5-min walk; Boating, 10-min drive; Fly Fishing on Snake River, 15-min drive; Rodeos in Jackson, 45-min drive;
Towns/Cities: Jackson, 45-min drive
Airports: Jackson Airport, 45-min drive

Offering first-class hospitality since the 1920s, Jenny Lake Lodge stands in the heart of Grand Teton National Park. The 31 single room log cabins and 6 log cabin suites have a traditional Old West charm and entice many guests to return. The main lodge offers wonderful food, exceptional wine and attentive service. Box lunches are available as well as an à la carte lunch in the dining room. Hiking trails are steps away, boating and canoeing are enjoyed on nearby lakes and fly fishing takes place in the Snake River and numerous, nearby creeks. Alternately, attend a talk about the creation of Danny Ranch through to the present day, held by the Lodge's historian.

MEXICO

Chetumal

Corozal

Libertad

Sarteneja

Xcalak

Buena
Vista

Icaiché

San Roman

Orange Walk

Ambergris Cay

August Pine Ridge

Neustadt

San Felipe

Corozalito

268 San Pedro

Crooked Tree

Sond Hill

Gallon Jug

Burrell Boom

Rancho Dolores

Belize

Freetown Sibun

Tu-tu Camp

Turneffe
Islands

Tikal

BELMOPAN

San Ignacio

Gales Point

269

Melchor de Mencos

San Antonio

CARIBBEAN
SEA

BenqueViego
del Carmen

El Cruce

Dangriga

Cohune Ridge

Hopkins

GUATEMALA

Alabama

Riversdale

Dolores

Placentia Village

Monkey
River Town

San Antonio

San Luis

Punta Gorda

Crique Sarco

Barranco

GULF OF
HONDURAS

Modesto
Méndez

Chahal

Puerto Cortés

HONDURAS

BELIZE - AMBERGRIS CAYE (SAN PEDRO)

VICTORIA HOUSE

P.O. BOX 22, SAN PEDRO, AMBERGRIS CAYE
Tel: +501 226 2067 **Fax:** +501 226 2429 **U.S./Canada Toll Free:** 1 800 247 5159
Web: www.johansens.com/victoriahouse **E-mail:** info@victoria-house.com

Our inspector loved: Drinking a delicious caipirinha at the Palapa Beach Bar, while watching the spectacular sunset.

Price Guide:
casitas/plantation-style rooms U.S.$225-U.S.$345
suites/villas U.S.$500-U.S.$1,900

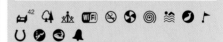

Situated along a pristine stretch of white sand beach, palm trees and clear turquoise water, this island resort offers the utmost in comfort and tranquility. The absence of radios and telephones ensures that nothing will disturb your relaxation and quiet enjoyment of the abundant natural beauty surrounding this plantation-style property. The varied accommodations include charming thatched-roof casitas with locally handcrafted mahogany beds, the Rainforest Suite, a spacious casita featuring frescoed walls and bamboo furniture, and elegant, fully-equipped infinity poolside private villas. Each accommodation is set in lush gardens with a private balcony or veranda offering sea views. The poolside Restaurant Palmilla serves fresh fish and a variety of Asian-inspired Caribbean dishes, and Admiral Nelson's Bar features live music under a palapa thatched roof.

Attractions: Hol Chan Marine Reserve, 20-min boat ride; Caye Chapel (18-Golf Course), 45-min boat ride; Great Blue Hole, 90-min boat ride; Caye Caulker, 25-min flight
Towns/Cities: San Pedro Town, 2 miles; Belize City, 17-min flight; Corozal Town, 20-min flight; Dangriga, 40-min flight
Airports: Belize International Airport, 17-min drive; Caye Caulker Airstrip, 25-min drive

THE LODGE AT CHAA CREEK

P.O. BOX 53, SAN IGNACIO, CAYO
Tel: +501 824 2037 **Fax:** +501 824 2501 **U.S./Canada Toll Free:** 1 877 709 8708
Web: www.johansens.com/chaacreek **E-mail:** reservations@chaacreek.com, frontdesk@chaacreek.com

Our inspector loved: The "Sunset Canoe Trip" on the beautiful Macal River.

Price Guide: (including breakfast)
cottages U.S.$135-U.S.$150 per person
suites/macal cottages U.S.$400-U.S.$450
spa villa U.S.$550-U.S.$575

Attractions: Guided Nature Tours, on-site; Maya Archaeological Tours, 7 miles; Chumpiate Cave at Chechem Ha, 14 miles; Actun Tunichil Muknal (an ancient Maya ceremonial cave), 40 miles
Towns/Cities: San Ignacio, 7 miles; Benque Viejo, 11 miles; Belmopan, 30 miles; Belize City, 77 miles
Airports: Belize Municipal Airport, 70 miles; Belize International Airport, 74 miles; Flores Airport, 84 miles

Perched on the edge of a grassy knoll overlooking the sleepy Macal River in the foothills of the Maya Mountains, The Lodge at Chaa Creek's individually designed thatched cottages reflect an atmosphere of elegance. Charmingly decorated villas and suites blend fine fabrics, elegant furnishings, and antiques to create a romantic ambience in a stunning rainforest setting. Recognized by Travel & Leisure Magazine in their Top 25 Best Hotels in Mexico, Central and South America and the recipient of notable environmental accreditations, Chaa Creek's 365-acre private reserve offers you a truly unforgettable rainforest experience. Miles of forested trails lead to a Natural History Center, Butterfly Farm, Rainforest Medicine Trail, an Organic Maya Farm and a full-service Spa. Country-wide tours offering easy access to Belize's richest Maya archaeological sites, national parks, and Reef and Rainforest Adventures are always available.

269

PACIFIC
OCEAN

CARIBBEAN
SEA

NICARAGUA

PANAMA

Masaya
Granada
Jinotepe
Rivas
Cárdenas
La Cruz
San Carlos
Santa Rosa
Upala
El Castillo
San Juan del Norte
Liberia
San Rafael
Barra del Colorado
Cañas
272
Quesada
Puerto Viejo
Parismina
Santa Cruz
274
Naranjo
271
Guápiles
Río Jiménez
Puerto Moreno
Puntarenas
Heredia
San Juanillo
Paquera
San Mateo
Alajuela
SAN JOSÉ
Puerto Limón
Sámara
273
Santiago
Cartago
Moravia
Cóbano
Santa María
Cahuita
Esterillos Oeste
Changuinola
Quepos
276
San Isidro
Bocas del Toro
Dominical
Juntas
Almirante
Buenos Aires
Palmar Norte
San Vito
Rincón
Ciudad Neily
PANAMA
Jiménez
275
David
Puerto Armurelles

El Silencio Lodge & Spa

BAJOS DEL TORO, ALAJUELA
Tel: +506 291 3044 **Fax:** +506 232 2183
Web: www.johansens.com/elsilencio **E-mail:** info@elsilenciolodge.com

Our inspector loved: *The beautiful lush location, and having a personal Eco-Concierge Guide.*

Price Guide: (including 3 daily meals, 2-night minimum stay, per person, double occupancy) suites U.S.$210-U.S.$280

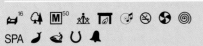

SPA

Attractions: Nature Hiking, Lake Kayaking, Horseback Riding and Canopy Zip-lining, 60-min drive; Sarapiqui River Rafting, 60-min drive; Arenal and Poas Volcanos, 60-min drive
Towns/Cities: Sarchi Arts and Crafts Town, 30-min drive; San José, 90-min drive; Arenal/La Fortuna, 90-min drive; Sarapiqui, 90-min drive
Airports: San José International Juan Santamaria Airport, 90-min drive; San José Tobias Bolanos Domestic Airport, 90-min drive

Situated within a 500-acre private tropical cloud forest reserve next to a gently flowing river, the appropriately named El Silencio Lodge & Spa is an ideal retreat for those seeking peace and quiet in a serene natural setting. Built with environmentally friendly materials, the lodge features 16 luxury suites offering views of either the river or the forest. Each includes a whirlpool tub, gas fireplace and complimentary mini-bar. Rejuvenation and relaxation is taken seriously at El Silencio, with a full-service spa providing a variety of treatments enhanced by the surrounding nature and a yoga platform set within the forest. The daily rate includes 3 meals composed of Costa Rican specialties with an innovative, international flare using fresh, organic ingredients.

TABACÓN GRAND SPA THERMAL RESORT

LA FORTUNA DE SAN CARLOS, ARENAL
Tel: +1 506 519 1900 **Fax:** +1 506 519 1940 **U.S./Canada Toll Free:** 1 877 277 8291
Web: www.johansens.com/tabacon **E-mail:** sales@tabacon.com

Our inspector loved: Enjoying a volcanic ash spa treatment in a secluded bungalow and then relaxing in a hot spring.

Price Guide:
rooms U.S.$250-U.S.$375
suites U.S.$350-U.S.$575

Set in the heart of the Costa Rican rainforest, this luxury resort serves as the perfect place to rejuvenate and explore stunning natural surroundings. Each of the 114 rooms features deep-soaking tubs and floor-to-ceiling windows allowing you to relax and enjoy the resort's environs from the comfort and privacy of your own room. In Tabacón's Grand Spa you can enjoy the unique experience of soaking in outdoor thermal mineral springs at the base of the Arenal Volcano, and daytime activities, including nature cruises and zip lines, are endless. A hike up the Arenal Volcano, Costa Rica's most active (and closely monitored) volcano is an unforgettable experience not to be missed. There are both casual and elegant dining options including a private dinner set in a romantic rainforest bungalow prepared for you by your own personal chef.

Attractions: Arenal Volcano National Park, 10-min drive; Hanging Bridges, 10-min drive; Canopy Tours, Sky Tram & Trek, 20-min drive; White-Water Rafting, 90-min drive
Towns/Cities: La Fortuna, 9 miles; Liberia, 75 miles; San José, 78 miles
Airports: La Fortuna Domestic Airport, 9 miles; San José International Airport - Juan Santamaira, 72 miles; Liberia International Airport - Daniel Oduber International, 81 miles

Affiliations: The Leading Hotels of the World

HOTEL PUNTA ISLITA

GUANACASTE

Tel: +506 231 6122 **Fax:** +506 231 0715
Web: www.johansens.com/hotelpuntaislita **E-mail:** reservas@hotelpuntaislita.com

Our inspector loved: *The tropical and ocean views from every location.*

Price Guide:
deluxe rooms U.S.$250-U.S.$350
suites U.S.$360-U.S.$495
villas U.S.$570-U.S.$760

SPA 〰 ♘ 🌀 ♪ 🕐 ∪ Ⓗ 🔔

Awards/Ratings: Condé Nast Johansens Most Excellent Eco Resort, Mexico & Central America 2007; Condé Nast Traveler Gold List 2007

Attractions: Contemporary Art Museum, 1 mile; Camaronal Wildlife Refuge, 3 miles; Playa Samara, 9 miles; Cabo Blanco Nature Reserve, 30 miles
Towns/Cities: Samara, 9 miles; Nosara, 15 miles; Tamarindo, 50 miles
Airports: Punta Islita Airport, 2 miles; Liberia Intl. Airport, 70 miles; San José Intl. Airport, 120 miles

Affiliations: Small Luxury Hotels

Hotel Punta Islita offers an authentic Costa Rican experience courtesy of its close ties with surrounding villages and internationally lauded responsible tourism model focusing on community, art and the environment. Spanning 35 acres, its tiered layout discreetly tucks away rooms, suites and family-friendly villas offering privacy and ocean views. Many have private outdoor whirlpools or plunge pools. The 1492 Restaurant, with its open layout and native-inspired 50-foot thatched palm ceiling, serves Costa Rican fusion cuisine, and the Borrancho Beach Club Restaurant provides casual poolside dining. You can participate in unique activities led by local guides such as zip-lining over the forest canopy, monkey safaris or surfing. The on-site Casa Spa offers a menu of stress-reducing treatments including the Punta Islita Ritual, a relaxing blend of Costa Rican healing traditions.

PARADISUS PLAYA CONCHAL

BAHÍA BRASILITO, PLAYA CONCHAL, SANTA CRUZ, GUANACASTE
Tel: +506 654 4123 **Fax:** +506 654 4181 **U.S./Canada Toll Free:** 1 888 956 3542
Web: www.johansens.com/paradisusplayaconchal **E-mail:** info@paradisusplayaconchal.com

Our inspector loved: The lovely beach location and the wide selection of water sports.

Price Guide: (all inclusive)
rooms U.S.$250-U.S.$550
suites U.S.$375-U.S.$1,800

Enchantment awaits you at Paradisus Playa Conchal, a luxurious seaside retreat amidst green forests in the North-Pacific Riviera. Surrounded by meandering walkways, bubbling fountains, shimmering lakes and lush tropical gardens, this is a top-of-the-line, all-inclusive beach and golf resort in Costa Rica. Luxurious guest rooms are spacious living areas with private terraces, and a personalized concierge and butler service is available for a truly indulgent experience. There are no less than 7 restaurants to choose from where fine Italian, Caribbean and Asian-fusion cuisine will surely delight the senses. Entertainment options include nightly musical reviews, 4 bars, a casino, kids' center, spa and water sports along the resort's 1½-mile white sand beach. A championship eco-golf course, Reserva Conchal Golf Club, incorporates majestic ocean vistas, while the truly adventurous can enjoy white-water rafting, deep-sea fishing and scuba diving nearby.

Attractions: Sailing and Snorkeling Tours, 15-min drive; Canopy Tours, 30-min drive; Rafting and River Tours, 45-min drive; Rincon De La Vieja Volcano, 44 miles
Towns/Cities: Brasilito, 10-min walk; Tamarindo, 20-min drive; Arenal, 78 miles
Airports: Tamarindo Domestic Airport, 6 miles; Liberia International Airport, 37 miles; San José International Airport, 124 miles

Affiliations: The Leading Hotels of the World

LAPA RIOS ECO LODGE

PUERTO JIMENEZ, OSA PENISULA
Tel: +506 735 5130 **Fax:** +506 735 5179
Web: www.johansens.com/laparios **E-mail:** info@laparios.com

Our inspector loved: Relaxing on the porch of my bungalow and watching 2 scarlet macaws playing in the tree above, and of course the morning wake up calls from the howler monkeys!

Price Guide: (per person, all inclusive, including transfer to and from Puerto Jimenez Airport) bungalows U.S.$330-U.S.$490

Attractions: Beach, Surfing and Kayaking, 15-min walk; Dolphin Tours, 45-min drive; Corcovado National Park, 37 miles
Towns/Cities: Puerto Jimenez, 45-min drive; Drake Bay, 28 miles; Quepos, 200km; San José, 230 miles
Airports: Puerto Jimenez Airport, 45-min drive

Set in a private nature reserve encompassing over 1,000 acres of untouched natural beauty, Lapa Rios Eco Lodge is the embodiment of paradise. John and Karen Lewis, the hotel's founders, envisioned this special place as a refuge for wildlife and guests alike, where travelers could come to relax and enjoy their pristine rainforest surroundings. Overlooking the Gulfo Dulce and the Pacific Ocean, the hotel's 16 private bungalows offer comfortable and luxurious accommodations that evoke the tranquility and natural beauty of their setting, each with its own private wooden deck. A variety of tours and activities are available to help you explore your unique surroundings, including bird watching, rainforest walks and surf lessons. Meals are prepared by local chefs who create gourmet dishes that draw upon Costa Rican flavors and culture.

GAIA HOTEL & RESERVE

KM 2.7 CARRETERA QUEPOS, MANUEL ANTONIO, PUNTARENAS
Tel: +506 777 9797 **Fax:** +506 777 9126 **U.S./Canada Toll Free:** 1 800 226 2515
Web: www.johansens.com/gaiahr **E-mail:** reservations@gaiahr.com

Our inspector loved: The spectacular setting and view from the infinity-edge pool.

Price Guide: (including breakfast)
studios U.S.$275-U.S.$360
suites U.S.$330-U.S.$545
villas U.S.$770-U.S.$970

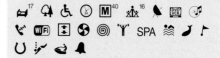

Nestled high on a hill above Costa Rica's Pacific coastline, Gaia offers the ultimate in luxury and personal service amidst pristine wilderness. The sleek Bauhaus design is fresh and modern, and each room has amazing views of the surrounding jungle and ocean. Your personal concierge will cater to your every need. Spend your afternoons at the spectacular 3-tiered, infinity-edge pool with its unique in-water table dining. La Luna restaurant offers exceptional cuisine featuring international and local dishes and special dietary requirements can be accommodated. Take time to tour Gaia's 12.1 acres of nature reserve with a certified nature guide. The reserve contains a wide range of rare flora, fauna and mammals such as the White Face and Squirrel monkeys, 3-toed sloths and red-eyed tree frogs.

Awards/Ratings: Condé Nast Johansens Most Excellent Hotel, Mexico & Central America 2007

Attractions: Nature Reserve, on-site; Manuel Antonio National Park, 2 miles; Quepos Marina Sport Fishing, 2 miles; Damas Island, 5 miles
Towns/Cities: Manuel Antonio, 2 miles; Quepos, 2 miles; Jaco, 40 miles; San José, 110 miles
Airports: Quepos Airport, 2 miles; San José-Juan Santamaria International Airport, 110 miles

Affiliations: Small Luxury Hotels of the World

Iahermosa

Orange Walk

Emiliano
Zapata

Tenosique

Carmelita

Belize

BELMOPAN

San Ignacio

Dangriga

San Cristóbal
de las Casas

Flores

Mundo Maya
Int. Airport

BELIZE

MEXICO

Sayaxché

San Antonio

Comitán de Domínguez

San Luis

Punta Corda

CARIBBEAN
SEA

Puerto Cortés

San Mateo
Ixtatán

Sebol

Modesto
Méndez

Puerto Barrios
Airport

San Pedro
Sula

Cobán

Puerto Barrios

Huixtla

Huehuetenango

Uspantán

Morales

Mariscos

Tapachula

San Marcos

Santa Cruz
del Quiché

Salama

Zacapa

HONDURAS

Totonicapán

El Progreso

Chiquimula

Coatepeque

Quezaltenango

Chimaltenango

GUATEMALA

Santa Rosa
de Copán

Retalhuleu

Mazatenango

Antigua

La Aurora
Int. Airport

Jalapa

Champerico

Pueblo Nuevo
Tiquisate

Sta Lucia
Cotzulmalguapa

Escuintla

Cuilapa

Jutiapa

San José
Airport

Santa Ana

Tecojate

San José

Las Lilas

EL SALVADOR

PACIFIC
OCEAN

SAN SALVADOR

FILADELFIA COFFEE RESORT & SPA

150 METERS NORTH OF THE SAN FELIPE CHAPEL, ANTIGUA GUATEMALA
Tel: +502 7728 0800 **U.S. Tel:** +1 646 257 4959
Web: www.johansens.com/filadelfia **E-mail:** hotel@filadelfiaresort.com

Our inspector loved: *The very informative and professional guided coffee tour that ends with a delicious coffee tasting.*

Price Guide: (including breakfast)
standard rooms U.S.$235
superior double rooms U.S.$280
master suites U.S.$500

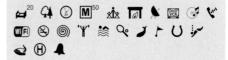

Sitting on a working coffee plantation for more than 130 years, Filadelfia Coffee Resort & Spa comprises 750-acres of coffee and ecological reserve, including a mountain of 7,000 to 8,000 feet high. Capturing Old World charm the resort also provides modern-day comfort with spacious rooms decorated in warm hues and creams evoking Guatemalan elegant simplicity and feature very comfortable beds prepared with Egyptian cotton sheets. Most offer a panoramic view of the Agua Volcano and the poolside garden. Contemporary lifestyle luxuries include iPods with sound bases, large televisions and WiFi connection. Pergaminos Restaurant serves international, beautifully presented gourmet dishes, and Cafetenango Restaurant offers delicious local dishes. The resort's specialty coffee-based drinks are prepared with beans harvested from their award-winning coffee plantation.

Attractions: Iximché Archeological Park, 37 miles; Monterrico Beach, 72 miles; Panajachel in Lake Atitlan, 75 miles; Chichicastenango, 75 miles
Towns/Cities: Jocotenango, 1 mile; Ciudad Vieja, 3 miles; Guatemala City, 26 miles; Puerto San José, 56 miles
Airports: Guatemala City Airport, 26 miles; Petén Airport, 342 miles

Affiliations: Small Luxury Hotels of the World

MEXICO

CARIBBEAN SEA

Belize

BELOMOPAN

BELIZE

San Antonio

Punta Corda

Roatan
Islas de la Bahía

Puerto Castilla

Puerto Cortés

Tela

La Ceiba

Trujillo

Puerto Barrios

GUATEMALA

San Pedro
Sula

El Progrese

280

San Esteban

Pueblo
Viejo

Nuevo
Arcadia

Santa Rita

Yoro

Dulce Nombre
de Culmí

Santa
Barbara

Puerto
Lempira

Siguatepeque

Salamá

Auasbila

Gracias

Comayagua

Juticalpa

Catacamas

Nuevo
Ocotepeque

La Esperanza

La Paz

TEGUCIGALPA

Danlí

Yuscaran

SAN SALVADOR

Nacaome

Ocotal

EL SALVADOR

San Miguel

Choluteca

Matagalpa

NICARAGUA

Chinandega

Juigalpa

MANAGUA

PACIFIC OCEAN

San Carlos

La Cruz

Los Chiles

COSTA RICA

THE LODGE AT PICO BONITO

A. P. 710, LA CEIBA, ATLÁNTIDA, C. P. 31101
Tel: +504 440 0388 **Fax:** +504 440 0468 **U.S./Canada Toll Free:** 1 888 428 0221
Web: www.johansens.com/picobonito **E-mail:** picobonito@caribe.hn

Our inspector loved: *Enjoying the view and a "marañon" juice from the restaurant's veranda.*

Price Guide: (including breakfast, airport transfer, welcome drink and visits to Butterfly Farm, Serpentarium and loop trail hike)
standard cabin U.S.$226-U.S.$296.10
standard plus cabin U.S.$277.20-U.S.$346.50
superior plus cabin U.S.$321.30-U.S.$396.90

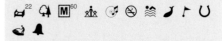

Awards/Ratings: C. N. Johansens Eco Resort 2006

Cradled between the Caribbean Sea and Pico Bonito Mountain, which soars 8,000 feet above the jungle floor, the lodge lies in the heart of the rainforest, surrounded by 200 acres bursting with exotic flora and fauna. Accommodation is provided in a series of enchanting secluded cabins. Each cabin has its own private veranda, which is a refreshing place to start the day and where a typical Honduran breakfast is served each morning. English speaking guides will escort you through the tropical jungle to see manatees, monkeys, parrots and toucans. The canoe trip into the wildlife reserve is an absolute must, and for the intrepid there are guided night hikes. The local chef prides himself on his delicate Meso-American recipes served in the beautifully appointed restaurant, or on one of the many outdoor decks.

Attractions: Butterfly Farm and Serpentarium, 5-min walk; Waterfalls of the Rio Zacate, 2 miles; Cuero y Salado Rivers Wildlife Refuge, 5 miles; White-Water Rafting on Cangrejal River, 11 miles
Towns/Cities: La Ceiba, 9 miles; Tela, 49 miles; San Pedro Sula, 124 miles; Tegucigalpa, 264 miles
Airports: La Ceiba, 9 miles; San Pedro Sula, 124 miles; Tegucigalpa, 264 miles

Affiliations: Small Luxury Hotels of the World

BOLIVIA

Villazón

Mariscal
Estigarribia

Dourados

Marilia

Calama

Orán

PARAGUAY

Pedro Juan
Caballero

Maringá

San Salvador
de Jujuy

San Pedro

Salta

ASUNCIÓN

Cascavel

San Miguel
de Tucumán

Presidencia Roque
Sáenz Peña

Formosa

Encarnación

Paranagua

El Salvador

Santiago
del Estero

Resistencia

Corrientes

Posadas

Chapecó

Florianópolis

BRAZIL

San Fernando
del Valle de
Catamarca

Goya

Uruguaiana

Santa
Maria

Porto Alegre

La Rioja

Coquimbo

Córdoba

Santa Fé

Concordia

Rivera

Rio Grande

San Juan

Paraná

Tacuarembó

Melo

PACIFIC

Mendoza

Río Cuarto

Rosario

Gualeguaychu

URUGUAY

OCEAN

San
Luis

San Nicolás
de los Arroyos

BUENOS
AIRES

MONTEVIDEO

Mercedes

Santiago

SANTIAGO

San Rafael

282 283
284 285

Curicó

CHILE

Santa Rosa

Olavarría

Concepción

Mar del Plata

Neuquén

Bahía
Blanca

Necochea

ATLANTIC

Puerto Montt

286
287
288

San Carlos
de Bariloche

Viedma

OCEAN

Coihaique

Rawson

Comodoro Rivadavia

Stanley

289 El Calafate

Río Gallegos

Punta Arenas

Ushuaia

1555 MALABIA HOUSE

MALABIA 1555, C1414DME BUENOS AIRES, CIUDAD DE BUENOS AIRES
Tel: +54 11 4832 3345 **Fax:** +54 11 4832 3345
Web: www.johansens.com/malabiahouse **E-mail:** info@malabiahouse.com.ar

Our inspector loved: The charming details of the décor, and the delicious breakfast.

Price Guide:
rooms U.S.$127-U.S.$170

Attractions: Palermo Soho Boutiques, 5-min walk; Historical Center, 20-min drive
Airports: Ezeiza International Airport, 45-min drive; Aeroparque Domestic Airport, 15-min drive

In the heart of the most exclusive neighborhood in Buenos Aires stands the first designer bed and breakfast in Argentina. A century ago, this historic house was donated by a French noblewoman to the Church of Santo Domingo as lodging for single women. Today, 1555 Malabia House welcomes those who seek an environment more relaxing than that offered by traditional hotels. Rather than windows, each room has tall doors that open out to fresh breezes. The stylish, warm décor conveys a sense of home and the staff provides 24-hour concierge and room service. The central patio, library and executive lounge, with fax and Internet access, afford guests space for conversation, reflection and productivity. Each morning, a delectable buffet breakfast is served in the dining room.

HOME BUENOS AIRES

HONDURAS 5860, CIUDAD DE BUENOS AIRES, BUENOS AIRES 1414
Tel: +54 11 4778 1008 **Fax:** +54 11 4779 1006
Web: www.johansens.com/homebuenosaires **E-mail:** info@homebuenosaires.com

Our inspector loved: *Enjoying a drink at the charming RestoBar after a walk in the cool Palermo Viejo.*

Price Guide: (including breakfast)
rooms U.S.$145-U.S.$405

SPA

Attractions: Palermo Soho Boutiques, 5-min walk; Historical Center, 20-min drive
Airports: Buenos Aires' Domestic Airport, 15-min drive; Ezeiza's International Airport, 45-min drive

Located in a trendy district of the city, Home Buenos Aires is hip and stylish, while maintaining a cozy, intimate atmosphere. Owned and realized by spouses Patricia O'Shea and London music producer Tom Rixton, the hotel combines O'Shea's Argentine heritage and Rixton's music savvy with superb results. The modern, glass-walled RestoBar serves up innovative and exciting cocktails as well as traditional Argentinian tapas by the pool and landscaped garden, and features a D.J. and dancing on Friday nights. The colorful rooms, decorated with French vintage wallpaper and hip, comfortable furniture, feature stereo-systems on which to play C.D.s from the hotel's extensive music library. A spa, outdoor heated pool, and weekly Argentinian barbecues round off this intimate boutique hotel's impressive résumé.

LoiSuites Recoleta Hotel

VICENTE LÓPEZ 1955 – C1128ACC, CIUDAD DE BUENOS AIRES, BUENOS AIRES
Tel: +54 11 5777 8950 **Fax:** +54 11 5777 8999 **U.S./Canada Toll Free:** 1 800 961 4643
Web: www.johansens.com/loisuites **E-mail:** recoleta@loisuites.com.ar

Our inspector loved: *The great location of this comfortable hotel.*

Price Guide:
rooms U.S.$250-U.S.$400

Attractions: Recoleta Cemetery, 5-min walk; Museo Nacional de Bellas Artes, 10-min walk; National Fine Arts Museum and National Museum of Decorative Art, 15-min walk; Puerto Madero, 15-min drive
Airports: Aeroparque Domestic Airport, 20-min drive; Ezeiza's International Airport, 45-min drive

LoiSuites is a contemporary hotel with 112 well-appointed studios and suites combining style, comfort and technology in the upscale district of Recoleta. A great choice for both business and leisure visitors, all rooms are spacious and furnished in modern style with luxury amenities such as mobile phones. Breakfast can be enjoyed on the delightful winter garden patio, and the restaurant menu offers an interesting variety of international cuisine. For those wishing to dine in, there is also a room service menu. An excellent concierge is available to help you navigate the many offerings of Recoleta with its historical parks, art galleries and restaurants reminiscent of a European city. There is also a meeting space and an efficient business center available.

MORENO HOTEL BUENOS AIRES

MORENO 376, CIUDAD DE BUENOS AIRES, SAN TELMO, BUENOS AIRES C1091AAH

Tel: +54 11 6091 2000 **Fax:** +54 11 6091 2001
Web: www.johansens.com/moreno **E-mail:** info@morenobuenosaires.com

Our inspector loved: The extra-large and trendy bedrooms.

Price Guide: (including Continental breakfast, Internet and gym access)
rooms U.S.$100-U.S.$200
lofts U.S.$250-U.S.$400

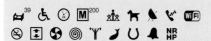

Attractions: Puerto Madero, 0.3 miles; San Telmo's Flea Market, 0.4 miles; La Boca, 1.9 miles; Recoleta, 2 miles
Airports: Jorge Newbery-Aeroparque Domestic Airport, 4 miles; Ministro Pistarini-Ezeiza International Airport, 19 miles

Moreno Hotel offers everything a discerning modern traveler's heart could desire from a boutique hotel - with style. Its 39 rooms are spacious and strikingly designed so as to epitomize modern elegance. The hotel, which occupies a 1920s art-deco building in the heart of Buenos Aires features, among other luxuries, a gym open 24 hours, an on-site 130-seat theater that regularly hosts a variety of live shows, and a rooftop terrace complete with Jacuzzi and river-views. Food-lovers will enjoy the Latin-American-inspired cuisine at the hotel's upscale restaurant, and wine-aficionados will delight in the bar's 300 labels of Argentinean wine. A traditional Argentinean barbecue is served on the rooftop terrace for an authentic taste of Buenos Aires.

CORRENTOSO LAKE & RIVER HOTEL

AV. SIETE LAGOS 4505, VILLA LA ANGOSTURA, PATAGONIA
Tel: +54 11 4803 0030 **Fax:** +54 11 4803 0030
Web: www.johansens.com/correntoso **E-mail:** info@correntoso.com

Our inspector loved: *Enjoying a superb dinner overlooking Nahuel Huapi Lake.*

Price Guide:
rooms U.S.$290-U.S.$400

Attractions: Parque Los Arrayanes, 10-min drive; Cerro Bayo, 15-min drive; Villa Traful, 90-min drive
Towns/Cities: Bariloche, 90-min drive
Airports: Bariloche's International Airport, 60-min drive

A traditional hotel, Correntoso is situated at the mouth of the Correntoso River where it enters Nahuel Huapi Lake at the foot of the Andes. Accommodations are beautifully decorated with fine woodwork and elegant furnishings, and the fine dining restaurant and wine bar specializes in Mediterranean cuisine fused with traditional Patagonian dishes and regionally produced wines. Correntoso serves more casual fare on a deck overlooking the lake, while at teatime, a variety of home-made pastries, chocolates and special tea blends are available. The hotel's Spirit & Adventures department can arrange custom-designed excursions, with gourmet picnics or asado (Argentine barbecue) lunches on most tours. For a relaxing day, enjoy a massage, the herbal hammam, heated pool or a good book in the Patagonian-themed library.

ARGENTINA - NEUQUÉN (VILLA LA ANGOSTURA)

HOTEL LAS BALSAS

BAHÍA LAS BALSAS S/N, VILLA LA ANGOSTURA, NEUQUÉN 8407
Tel: +54 2944 494308 **Fax:** +54 2944 494308
Web: www.johansens.com/lasbalsas **E-mail:** info@lasbalsas.com.ar

Our inspector loved: *Enjoying the gourmet food and first-class service after relaxing in the great Spa by the Lake.*

Price Guide: (including breakfast and access to spa)
single/double standard U.S.$375
single/double suite U.S.$600

Attractions: Wine Tastings, on-site; Cooking Classes, on-site
Towns/Cities: Villa La Angostura, 2 miles; Cardenal Samore, 28 miles; Villa Traful, 39 miles; Bariloche, 50 miles
Airports: San Carlos de Bariloche International Airport, 50 miles

Affiliations: Relais & Châteaux

In this most serene and romantic of locations stands the fantastic Hotel Las Balsas. Magnificently set within the Nahuel Huapi National Park of Argentine Patagonia, with a backdrop of snow-capped mountains and green forests, Las Balsas looks out to the tranquil Nahuel Huapi Lake. Exclusivity and comfort are hallmarks of this idyllic retreat where additional services such as babysitting, concierge advice and private use of the dock and beach are available. Each guest room and suite is individually styled and has a lake view, which is also enjoyed from the gourmet restaurant. A visit to the wine-tasting lounge and wine cellar, where over 150 samples are kept, is well worth your while, as is a day of indulgence at the relaxing spa. Outdoor activities abound in the spectacular surroundings, making Hotel Las Balsas an ideal destination for those looking both to unwind and explore.

Isla Victoria Lodge

ISLA VICTORIA, PARQUE NACIONAL NAHUEL HUAPI, C.C. 26 (R8401AKU)
Tel: +54 43 94 96 05 **Fax:** +54 11 43 94 95 99
Web: www.johansens.com/islavictoria **E-mail:** maresur@maresur.com

Our inspector loved: *The overwhelming natural beauty of the island, and the atmosphere of the lodge.*

Price Guide: (all inclusive, 2-night stay and all transfers included)
per person U.S.$570

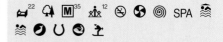

Awards/Ratings: Condé Nast Johansens Most Excellent Lodge South America 2007

Attractions: Circuito Chico, 30-min drive; Cerro Cathedral, Bariloche, 45-min drive
Towns/Cities: Bariloche, 30-min boat ride; Villa La Angostura, 2-hour drive
Airports: Bariloche's International Airport, 45-min drive

Situated on a cliff overlooking the lake and forests of cohiues and cypresses, Isla Victoria Lodge is part of the Nahuel Huapi National Park, one of the most unique areas of the Argentinean Patagonia. Bilingual guides are available to lead outdoor activities including deer sighting, photographic safari, kayaking and trekking. Every activity is carefully designed to make sure that you enjoy and learn all about the area, get closer to nature and find out the infinite world that Victoria Island offers. The Lodge itself has 3 living rooms, a cozy bar with fireplace, a spa-solarium and a wine cellar with some of the best wines the area has to offer, as well as an inviting library offering a relaxing environment. The restaurant looks out to a breathtaking view while serving delightful local cuisine.

LOS SAUCES CASA PATAGÓNICA

LOS GAUCHOS 1352/70, CP9405, EL CALAFATE, SANTA CRUZ
Tel: +54 2902 495854 **Fax:** +54 2902 495855
Web: www.johansens.com/lossauces **E-mail:** info@casalossauces.com

Our inspector loved: *The authentic Patagonian barbecue served in the resort's lovely garden.*

Price Guide: (all inclusive, 3-night minimum stay) rooms from U.S.$1,349

Attractions: Perito Moreno Glacier, 49 miles; Parque Nacional Los Glaciares, 49 miles; El Chalten, 137 miles; Estancia Cristina, 2-hour drive
Towns/Cities: Patagonia, on-site
Airports: Calafate's International Airport, 14 miles

Affiliations: Small Luxury Hotels of the World

Bordered by the Calafate River, within a natural landscape of willows and rosehips surrounded by majestic mountains and massive glaciers, Los Sauces Casa Patagónica is an elegant boutique hotel with an intimate atmosphere. Each room is individually and beautifully decorated using a different color as its theme, and features Argentinian art and details such as brass chandeliers, authentic leather, custom bed frames and engraved cabinets. Aside from the excellent gourmet Argentinian cuisine, unique features such as musical instruments for the use of guests, a library, a nightly photo contest in which the guest with the most impressive picture from that day's adventures wins a prize, occasional science lectures, and authentic Patagonian asados served in the garden, contribute to an unforgettable experience.

POUSADA DO TOQUE

RUA FELISBERTO DE ATAIDE, POVOADO DO TOQUE, SÃO MIGUEL DOS MILAGRES, 57940-000 ALAGOAS
Tel: +55 82 3295 1127 **Fax:** +55 82 3295 1127
Web: www.johansens.com/pousadadotoque **E-mail:** pousadadotoque@uol.com.br

Our inspector loved: *The coziness and comfort of all the guest rooms, in addition to the owner's attentive service.*

Price Guide: (including dinner)
rooms U.S.$160-U.S.$210
suites U.S.$290-U.S.$430

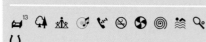

Attractions: Ocean Pools of Maragogi, 45-min drive
Towns/Cities: Porto de Galinhas, 90-min drive; Maceió, 90-min drive
Airports: Maceió's International Airport, 90-min drive

Located on the private and pristine beach of Praia do Toque, this pleasant pousada has quickly become a favorite beach retreat. Combining intimacy, rusticity and charm, owners Nilo Burgarelli and his wife Gilda Peixoto have created an inspiring retreat where its simplicity and comfort provides the ultimate escape. Blending in beautifully with the surrounding coconut grove plantation, there are 13 guest rooms called chalets, which include private pools, sundecks, Jacuzzis and verandas with hammocks. Nilo is a former restaurateur and uses his talents to create international cuisine featuring fresh local seafood and local dishes from fresh vegetables supplied by the pousada's garden. Spend the day at the beach-front pool, chill out at the rustic gazebos situated near the lawn, or have a relaxing massage in the small massage parlor.

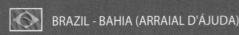

MAITEI HOTEL

ESTRADA DO MUCUGÊ, 475, ARRAIAL D'ÁJUDA, PORTO SEGURO, BAHIA 45816-000
Tel: +55 73 3575 3877 **Fax:** +55 73 3575 3799
Web: www.johansens.com/maitei **E-mail:** hotelmaitei@hotmail.com

Our inspector loved: The amazing view while sipping a drink by the pool, and taking an evening stroll to the lively village.

Price Guide: (including breakfast)
rooms U.S.$200-U.S.$250

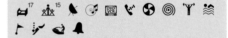

Attractions: Arraial Beach; Arraial's Boutiques, 2-min walk; Pitinga Beach, 20 meters
Towns/Cities: Trancoso, 15 miles
Airports: Porto Seguro's International Airport, 6 miles

Flanked by clear aquamarine waves on one side and forest dense with palm trees on the other, Maitei Hotel combines Brazilian flare with sophisticated design to create the perfect beach getaway for the discerning traveler. The interior design and architecture of this tile-roofed hotel is simple yet stylish, with interesting touches such as modern art, elegant pottery, lamps with paper shades and sponge-painted Stucco walls alongside luxury amenities such as Jacuzzis in all rooms. Outside, cushioned white lounge chairs are plentiful on the many decks and around the 2 pools, and each room offers a balcony with hammock overlooking the sea, encouraging you to lounge outside and enjoy the breathtaking view afforded by the hotel's location. Meals are served in the restaurant, which also offers a view, and the pool bar serve drinks and snacks.

FAZENDA SÃO FRANCISCO

PONTA DO CORUMBAU S/N, PRADO, BAHIA
Tel: +55 11 3078 4411 **Fax:** +55 73 3294 2250
Web: www.johansens.com/fazenda **E-mail:** reservas@corumbau.com.br

Our inspector loved: *The great feeling of staying at a farmhouse with its comfortable rooms located directly in front of the exclusive beach.*

Price Guide: (including breakfast, lunch, dinner and coconut water, excluding tax)
suites from U.S.$465
bungalows from U.S.$700

Attractions: A Variety of Schooner Trips; Canoe Trips; Visit to the Indian Reserve at Monte Pascoal National Park; Corumbau River, 15-min walk
Towns/Cities: Corumbau Village, 5-min walk; Caraiva, 60-min drive
Airports: Porto Seguro's International Airport, 124 miles

Set on a coconut palm farm surrounded by virgin mangrove swamps and a mile-long pristine golden beach, Fazenda São Francisco combines modern architecture with rustic simplicity to create a retreat offering unparalleled serenity. Interiors are characterized by bright colors and bold patterns tranquilized by dark Brazilian woods and clean whites, fusing innovative design and a natural elegance in perfect harmony with the resort's unspoiled location. The spacious and sophisticated suites and bungalows, situated on the beach and shaded by palm fronds, afford guests ultimate privacy and stunning views, which can be enjoyed over a glass of wine or gourmet meal served on large, private terraces. Those seeking adventure will appreciate the fantastic diving to be found on the farm's front doorstep.

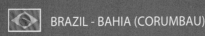

TAUANA

CORUMBAU, PRADO, BAHIA
Tel: +55 73 3668 5172 **Fax:** +55 73 3668 5172
Web: www.johansens.com/tauana **E-mail:** info@tauana.com

Our inspector loved: The impact of a perfectly designed, built and furnished property in the remote and beautiful beach of Corumbau.

Price Guide: (all inclusive)
bungalows U.S.$500-U.S.$900

Attractions: Corumbau River, 10-min drive; Barra do Cahy, 1-hour walk along the beach; Monte Pascola National Park, 2-hour drive
Towns/Cities: Corumbau Village, 6 miles; Trancoso, 112 miles
Airports: Porto Seguro International Airport, 124 miles and 15-min flight

The 9 villas of Tauana are set only steps away from an idyllic expanse of sandy beach and lapping waves on the Brazilian coast. The villas, each appointed with walls specially designed to let in the sea breeze, outdoor showers, and expansive terraces affording breathtaking views of the ocean, take full advantage of their stunning natural surroundings. The high-ceilinged, spacious interiors of simple yet elegant minimalist design, offer large, comfy canopy beds with sheer, airy curtains, polished wood floors and plenty of windows to capture the light. Tauana is an ideal retreat for the environmentally conscious traveler. The eco-friendly resort's restaurant with outdoor terrace serves 3 sumptuous meals a day made with produce from Tauana's own organic farm.

VILA NAIÁ - PARALELO 17°

PONTA DO CORUMBAU, BAHIA
Tel: +55 11 3061 1872 **Fax:** +55 11 3061 1872
Web: www.johansens.com/vilanaia **E-mail:** info@vilanaia.com.br

Our inspector loved: *The tropical influence and relaxed atmosphere.*

Price Guide: (all meals included)
rooms U.S.$450-U.S.$800

     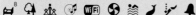 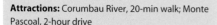

Attractions: Corumbau River, 20-min walk; Monte Pascoal, 2-hour drive
Towns/Cities: Corumbau Village, 10-min walk; Caraíva, 60-min drive
Airports: Porto Seguro's International Airport, 124 miles

Set on the 9 miles stretch of white sandy Corumbau Beach and surrounded by spit wood and palm trees, Vila Naiá combines the simplistic charm of a Brazilian fisherman's village with modern sophistication. Its bungalows and suites, connected by a web of tree-lined platforms, are of rustic design made with re-used timber and feature interiors laden with traditional, hand-made tiles with colorful accents such as sheer flowing curtains and modern furniture that complement the rich wood floor and walls. Dining is a special treat with sophisticated dishes including seafood caught by local fishermen and ingredients from Vila Naiá's own organic farm in the restaurant. Cool drinks are served by the beach and at the Quadrado, an open-air, hammock-adorned lounge area.

TXAI RESORT

ROD. ILHÉUS-ITACARÉ KM 48, ITACARÉ, BAHIA 45530-000
Tel: +55 73 2101 5000 **Fax:** +55 73 2101 5251
Web: www.johansens.com/txairesort **E-mail:** reserva@txairesort.com.br

Our inspector loved: *The excellent service provided by the staff, and the natural beauty of the area.*

Price Guide:
rooms U.S.$398-U.S.$1,000

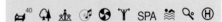

Awards/Ratings: Condé Nast Johansens Most Excellent Resort, South America 2007

Attractions: Surfing Lessons, on-site; Cycling routes, close by; Mansions and Historical Sites of Itacaré, 15-min drive
Towns/Cities: Itacaré Village, 15-min drive
Airports: Ilhéus International Airport, 37 miles

Located on a 100-hectare coconut plantation set along Itacarezinho beach and surrounded by unspoiled Atlantic rainforest, this sophisticated beach resort comprises 40 comfortable bungalows tucked amidst the coconut palms. Bungalows are built on stilts with wooden decks, palm-thatch detailing and look out to beautiful natural vistas. Each has been decorated in earth tones with king beds, open-air showers, whirlpool baths and massage and relaxation beds. The ocean-view restaurant, with its traditional Bahia architecture, serves both regional and international cuisine accompanied by a great choice of wines. After dinner rest in the Colonial-style lounge, filled with Brazilian art and furniture, surrounded by a reflecting pool, and enjoy the views. Txai's blue-tiled pool is just a few yards from the beach, and the Txai Health Spa offers a tempting variety of massages, treatments and classes.

KIAROA ECO-LUXURY RESORT

LOTEAMENTO DA COSTA, ÁREA SD6, DISTRITO DE BARRA GRANDE, MUNICIPIO DE MARAÚ, BAHIA, CEP 45 520-000
Tel: +55 71 3272 1320 **Fax:** +55 71 3272 1320
Web: www.johansens.com/kiaroa **E-mail:** kiaroa@kiaroa.com.br

Our inspector loved: *The sense of isolation at this beach-front place where top service and a wonderful mix of regional and international food is guaranteed.*

Price Guide: (including breakfast and dinner, excluding taxes)
Tropical luxury rooms U.S.$532
Moorea luxury bunglows U.S.$760
Bali luxury bungalows U.S.$1,090

 SPA

Attractions: Península de Maraú, on-site; Natural Swimming Pools and Reefs, on-site; Camamu Bay, 15-min drive; Land Excursions, 20/30-min drive
Towns/Cities: Barra Grande Village, 15-min drive; Ilheus, 106 miles; Salvador, 230 miles
Airports: Private Air Strip, on-site; Ilheus National Airport, 106 miles; Salvador International Airport, 230 miles

Situated in the Maraú Peninsula eco-sanctuary, Kiaroa Eco-Luxury Resort offers luxurious accommodations that blend seamlessly into their natural surroundings. With just 28 intimate rooms and bungalows, Kiaroa offers you seclusion along with comfort and sophistication. Experience Kiaroa's unique setting by taking a boat trip, snorkeling or great day's surf in the warm clear waters. Kiaroa's naturally-inspired, yet sophisticated atmosphere, is also reflected in its cuisine, which incorporates fresh local seafood and ingredients to create mouth-watering dishes. Overall, Kiaroa is a welcoming tropical oasis for those of you seeking to submerge yourself in nature while still enjoying the comforts of a luxury hotel.

PRAIA DO FORTE ECORESORT & THALASSO SPA

AVENIDA DO FAROL, PRAIA DO FORTE - MATA DE SÃO JOÃO, BAHIA
Tel: +55 71 36 76 40 00 **Fax:** +55 71 36 76 11 12
Web: www.johansens.com/praiadoforte **E-mail:** reservas@ecoresort.com.br

Our inspector loved: The beauty, and wide range of services and treatments offered at both the thalasso spa and resort.

Price Guide: (including breakfast and dinner)
rooms U.S.$300-U.S.$400

Awards/Ratings: Condé Nast Johansens Most Excellent Spa Hotel 2006

Attractions: Turtles Preservation Project, 10-min walk
Towns/Cities: Praia do Forte Village, 10-min walk
Airports: Salvador's International Airport, 34 miles

This is one of the most beautiful coastal regions in Brazil where ecological reserves adjoin semi-deserted white sand beaches surrounded by natural Atlantic forests, coral reefs, lagoons and lush tropical gardens, enormous coconut groves and quiet beaches. With intricate piaçava straw roofs thatched by local craftsmen, the resort's buildings are made from locally sourced natural materials that blend effortlessly into the environment. Thoughtful attention to detail is evident in the spacious and peaceful bedrooms, and friendly staff create a welcoming atmosphere. A feast of 115 different items on the breakfast buffet include exotic fruits, fresh breads and local specialties such as tapioca couscous and beiju. For dinner, there is a large selection of home-made, mouth-watering dishes. The prawn kiosk is popular and serves unique fish and fresh lobster as well as tropical drinks during the day.

ESTRELA D'AGUA

ESTRADA ARRAIAL D'AJUDA, TRANCOSO S/N, TRANCOSO PORTO SEGURO, BAHIA 45818-000
Tel: +55 73 3668 1030 **Fax:** +55 73 3668 1030
Web: www.johansens.com/estreladagua **E-mail:** reservas@estreladagua.com.br

Our inspector loved: *Enjoying the excellent regional food and wine in this unique location.*

Price Guide: (excluding 15% tax)
rooms U.S.$345-U.S.$865

Attractions: Quadrado, 10-min walk; Praia do Espelho, 16 miles; Praia de Caraíva, 25 miles
Towns/Cities: Porto Seguro, 62 miles
Airports: Porto Seguro Airport (B.P.S.), 1-hour drive

Affiliations: Relais & Châteaux

Estrela d'Agua is located in a charming village founded in 1516 that has become one of the places to vacation in north-eastern Brazil. The historic square, with its carefully preserved colorful houses, attracts people from all over the world and has become a meeting place where artists, architects and designers come together to develop styles and ideas that are fast becoming recognized throughout Brazil. Set on the beach amidst local scenery of rivers, cliffs, natural pools and virgin beaches, accommodations have been inspired by the natural beauty of the region, and are rustic yet comfortable. All of the suites have verandas with hammocks and the 8 master suites have private pools, Jacuzzis or beach-front locations. There are 2 bars and a restaurant: Costa Bar on the beach, with comfortable chairs and sofas, and the Veranda Bar, equally enjoyable day and night, while delicious traditional and international cuisine, as well as excellent wines, are available at the Restaurant.

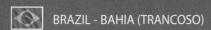

ETNIA POUSADA AND BOUTIQUE

TRANCOSO, BAHIA 45818-000
Tel: +55 73 3668 1137 **Fax:** + 55 73 3668 1780
Web: www.johansens.com/etnia **E-mail:** etniabrasil@etniabrasil.com.br

Our inspector loved: *The comfortable bedrooms and the relaxed atmosphere at this perfectly located pousada.*

Price Guide: (including breakfast)
rooms U.S.$200-U.S.$350

Attractions: Trancoso Square (Quadrado), 5-min walk; Trancoso Beach, 15-min walk
Towns/Cities: Arraial D'Ájuda, 45-min drive
Airports: Porto Seguro's International Airport, 1-hour drive

Located amidst natural rainforest vegetation in the small Bohemian-chic coastal town of Trancoso, Etnia is exotic and ethnic while maintaining a simple, barefoot elegance. The hotel, which consists of 8 bungalows scattered throughout the woodland, is an ideal spot for those of you seeking rest and relaxation, with massage, yoga, meditation and artistic therapy on-hand to enhance your well-being. The hotel features a pool, a wooded garden with hammocks and open-air bar-restaurant, which serves a sumptuous breakfast each morning and light fare later in the day. Each bungalow, designed to evoke a particular culture with theme-appropriate names such as Tribal, Kyoto, and Morocco, is stylishly appointed with ethnic touches including African-inspired art in the Tribal bungalow and Japanese prints in Kyoto.

Pousada dos Inconfidentes

RUA JOÃO RODRIGUES SOBRINHO 91, 36325-000, TIRADENTES, MINAS GERAIS
Tel: +55 32 3355 2135 **Fax:** +55 32 3355 2135
Web: www.johansens.com/inconfidentes **E-mail:** reservas@pousadadosinconfidentes.com.br

Our inspector loved: *Reading a book in the garden as the sun sets behind the beautiful mountains.*

Price Guide:
rooms U.S.$180-U.S.$275

Attractions: Historical Center, 5-min drive
Towns/Cities: São João Del Rei, 15-min drive
Airports: Rio de Janeiro's International Airport, 213 miles

Located in a quiet street, Pousada dos Inconfidentes is an elegant, new Colonial-style inn with 13 nicely outfitted suites decorated by a famous Brazilian interior designer. The inn itself is named after the "Inconfidentes," 18th-century Colonial rebels who stood against the Portuguese crown, and each suite bears the name of a different local rebellion hero. There is a lovely library where you can enjoy a good read with a cup of tea or coffee and cookies, and beautiful gardens that are equally pleasant on sunny days. In the evenings, savor a drink at the cozy piano bar or take advantage of the inn's home theater. There is also a semi-Olympic outdoor swimming pool and poolside bar serving drinks, sandwiches and fresh fruit. Serenity reigns throughout this adults-only refuge.

SOLAR DA PONTE

PRAÇA DAS MERCÊS S/N, TIRADENTES, MINAS GERAIS 36325-000
Tel: +55 32 33 55 12 55 **Fax:** +55 32 33 55 12 01
Web: www.johansens.com/solardaponte **E-mail:** reservas@solardaponte.com.br

Our inspector loved: *The comfort of the bedrooms, and enjoying the tasty breakfast while watching little monkeys playing in nearby trees.*

Price Guide:
rooms U.S.$160-U.S.$260

Attractions: Historic Center, close by; Historical Monuments, Shopping and Dining, 5-min walk; Steam Train, 15-min walk
Towns/Cities: São João del Rei, 15-min drive
Airports: São João del Rey Airport; 8 miles; Belo Horizonte (Confins) International Airport, 124 miles; Rio de Janeiro (Galeão) International Airport, 186 miles

This beautiful country mansion is set within peaceful shady gardens in the historical 18th-century mountain village of Tiradentes, with quaint winding streets and Baroque churches. The Colonial-style architecture creates a comfortable environment, and the spacious interiors feature light color schemes complemented by traditional décor and locally made furniture. Healthy, light meals are served in the bar and delicious breakfasts and afternoon teas are served in a spacious room with tree-top view. Take a stroll around the historic center of the town and admire the local, contemporary artworks on display and the variety of delightful handicrafts. The native tropical forests are breathtaking, and the imposing São José Mountain Range, now an ecological reserve, creates an awe-inspiring backdrop.

POUSADA MARAVILHA

RODOVIA BR-363, S/N, SUESTE, ILHA DE FERNANDO DE NORONHA, PERNAMBUCO 53990-000
Tel: +55 81 3619 0028 **Fax:** +55 81 3619 0162
Web: www.johansens.com/maravilha **E-mail:** reservas@pousadamaravilha.com.br

Our inspector loved: *The magnificent view of "Baía do Sueste" from all rooms, bungalows and the main building.*

Price Guide: (including breakfast and airport transfers)
rooms U.S.$615-U.S.$1,150
suites U.S.$720-U.S.$1,360

Attractions: Remédio's Village, 3 miles; Praia do Leão, 20-min walk
Towns/Cities: Natal, 224 miles; Recife, 336 miles
Airports: Local Airport, 0.6 miles

The sole tourist destination in a rugged, beautiful archipelago surrounded by dolphin-filled azure waters, Pousada Maravilha offers clean, minimalist luxury in harmony with its stunning natural setting. Rich Brazilian woods and comfortable, stylish furniture characterize the pousada's relaxed, but luxurious interior ambience. Bamboo hammocks, an elegant infinity pool, and an emphasis on large, open verandas create the perfect environment for outdoor contemplation and enjoyment of the breathtaking scenery. Candle-lit poolside meals are served at the restaurant, which specializes in inventive Brazilian and Italian-influenced cuisine. With a special emphasis on environmental preservation, no doubt inspired by its stunning surroundings, Pousada Maravilha is as eco-friendly as it is posh, making it an ideal location for the environmentally conscious traveler.

NANNAI BEACH RESORT

RODOVIA PE-09, ACESSO À MURO ALTO, KM 3, IPOJUCA, PERNAMBUCO 55590-000
Tel: +55 81 3552 0100 **Fax:** +55 81 3552 1474
Web: www.johansens.com/nannaibeach **E-mail:** reservas@nannai.com.br

Our inspector loved: *The charming premium bungalows with private swimming pools, located right in front of Muro Alto beach.*

Price Guide: (including breakfast and dinner)
rooms U.S.$370-U.S.$560
bungalows U.S.$650-U.S.$1,200

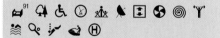

Attractions: Tide Pools and Offshore Reefs, close by
Towns/Cities: Porto de Galinhas Village, 6 miles
Airports: Recife's International Airport, 37 miles

This Bali-style beach resort is tucked along the Atlantic coast of Pernambuco with private bungalows and terraced apartments nestled among beautiful tropical gardens and pools. Beautiful hardwood, bright colors and light linens create a fresh, cheerful atmosphere, and the personalized service enhances this oasis of relaxation. Enjoy live music while dining on regional and international cuisine in the ocean-facing restaurant or opt for the more casual atmosphere of the lounge, cyber café or beach bar. The plethora of activities available include beach soccer, volleyball, water volleyball, hydro-gymnastics and dance classes, while complimentary water sports such as snorkeling, kayaking, laser and jangada (a Brazilian raft) and sailing can be organized; motorized water sports are available for an additional fee. A dedicated children's area, babysitting services and children's programs are also offered, and massages, beauty services and excursions can all be arranged.

SÍTIO DO LOBO

PONTA DO LOBO, ILHA GRANDE, ANGRA DOS REIS, RIO DE JANEIRO
Tel: +55 21 2227 4138 **Fax:** +55 21 2267 7841
Web: www.johansens.com/sitiodolobo **E-mail:** reservas@sitiodolobo.com.br

Our inspector loved: *The perfect integration of the rustic, beautiful décor with the amazing natural beauty surrounding the property.*

Price Guide: (contact the property for special packages, per couple, excluding 12% tax)
suites R$682-R$1,248
apartments R$556-R$729

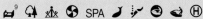

Awards/Ratings: Condé Nast Johansens Most Excellent Romantic Hideaway, South America 2007

Attractions: Hiking and Kayaking Trips, close by; Beaches, 5-min boat ride; Vila do Abraão, 10-min boat ride; Restaurants, 10-min boat ride
Towns/Cities: Angra dos Reis, 45-min boat ride; Rio de Janeiro, 90-min drive; Paraty, 2.5-hour drive; São Paulo, 5-hour drive
Airports: Angra dos Reis Airport, 50-min drive; Rio de Janeiro International Airport, 90-min drive; São Paulo Airport, 5-hour drive

Situated in an area of environmental protection on the island of Ilha Grande, Sítio do Lobo is a restful paradise of unspoiled beauty. Reached only by boat or helicopter, it offers isolation and intimacy where you can be as active or inactive as you wish. On the water's edge of a dense green forest, this quiet "enseada" was once a thriving coffee plantation and then the home of José Serrado and his interior decorator wife, Julinha. Julinha's personal touch and exquisite taste are evident in the rustic-styled guest rooms that range from small doubles to a lavish suite with ocean views. Facilities include a volleyball court and a sauna hut next to a freshwater spring.

CASAS BRANCAS BOUTIQUE-HOTEL & SPA

ALTO DO HUMAITÁ 10, ARMAÇÃO DOS BÚZIOS, RIO DE JANEIRO 28950-000
Tel: +55 22 2623 1458 **Fax:** +55 22 2623 2147
Web: www.johansens.com/casasbrancas **E-mail:** info@casasbrancas.com.br

Our inspector loved: *Eating the great food while admiring the view of the charming fishing village.*

Price Guide:
rooms U.S.$220-U.S.$380

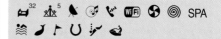

SPA

Attractions: Búzios Center, 5-min walk; Geriba's Beach, 10-min drive
Towns/Cities: Arraial do Cabo, 45-min drive
Airports: Rio de Janeiro International Airport, 112 miles

The unspoiled fishing village of Búzios became the place to visit and to be seen following a visit by Brigitte Bardot in 1964. Situated on a peninsula protruding into the Atlantic Ocean, and surrounded by no less than 25 beaches, the area soon became known as a tropical St. Tropez, and like its equivalent in the south of France, the village has grown over the years but retains a certain charm that is emphasized by seafront vistas and a cobbled main street. Built in a cool, Mediterranean style, the hotel has an appealing, elegant, laid back atmosphere with guest rooms looking out to the sea or garden. The restaurant is a dining experience to cherish thanks to the talented kitchen staff who produce excellent, imaginative international cuisine and Brazilian delights.

PÉROLA BÚZIOS DESIGN HOTEL

AV. JOSÉ BENTO RIBEIRO DANTAS, 222, ARMAÇÃO DOS BÚZIOS, RIO DE JANEIRO 28950-000
Tel: +55 22 2620 8507 **Fax:** +55 22 2623 9015
Web: www.johansens.com/perolabuzios **E-mail:** reservas@perolabuzios.com

Our inspector loved: *Walking in the charming village of Búzios before enjoying a relaxed dinner at Pérola's restaurant.*

Price Guide:
rooms U.S.$200-U.S.$775

Attractions: Búzios Main Street, 2-min walk; Geriba Beach, 10-min drive
Towns/Cities: Cabo Frio, 30-min drive; Arraial do Cabo, 45-min drive
Airports: Rio de Janeiro's International Airport, 112 miles

A design hotel, Pérola Búzios is a modern, artistic environment created with comfort in mind. The white, orange and dark wood décor creates a crisp, bright and cheerful ambience accented by over 700 unique pieces of contemporary art, special lighting and music. The 7 different categories of guest rooms and apartments offer a variety of accommodations for singles, couples and families and feature every modern amenity. Pérola's restaurant serves a constantly evolving menu created from fresh local products and seafood to showcase the flavors, scents and colors of Brazilian cuisine. Meals can also be enjoyed at the pool bar. Take advantage of the fitness center, massage service and dry and steam saunas.

PORTO BAY GLENZHAUS

RUA DOS COQUEIROS, 27, ARMAÇÃO DOS BÚZIOS, RIO DE JANEIRO 28950-000
Tel: +55 22 2623 2823 **Fax:** +55 22 2623 5293
Web: www.johansens.com/glenzhaus **E-mail:** glenzhaus@portobay.com.br

Our inspector loved: Eating a rich breakfast by the pool, and relaxing on the guest room's large veranda.

Price Guide:
rooms U.S.$155-U.S.$330

Attractions: Búzios Main Street, 3-min drive; Geriba Beach, 10-min drive
Towns/Cities: Cabo Frio, 30-min drive; Arraial do Cabo, 45-min drive
Airports: Rio de Janeiro's International Airport, 112 miles

This beautiful house sits on a hilltop surrounded by a tropical environment in a peaceful neighborhood, yet is only 500 meters from "Rua das Pedras," the famous lively street in Búzios, brimming with popular restaurants, shops and bars. This magnificent property has been decorated by former owner Cris Glenz with memorabilia from her 30 years of travel. All of the suites have private terraces overlooking the bay and exceptional crisp, cool décor; the spacious Royal Suite is ideal for the perfect romantic getaway or honeymoon. Before relaxing at the beach, enjoy breakfast alfresco by the magnificent pool surrounded by the property's lush gardens. Later, drift off in the decadent Gazebo or visit the Bali-style massage room.

PARADOR SANTARÉM MARINA

ESTRADA CORREIA DA VEIGA, 96, PETRÓPOLIS, RIO DE JANEIRO 25745-260
Tel: +55 24 2222 9933 **Fax:** +55 24 2222 9933
Web: www.johansens.com/paradorsantarem **E-mail:** reservas@paradorsantarem.com.br

Our inspector loved: The variety of places to relax and enjoy a good book or a glass of wine at this beautiful property.

Price Guide:
suites U.S.$175-U.S.$410

Attractions: Itaipava District and Shops, 15-min drive; Serra dos Órgãos National Park, 30-min drive
Towns/Cities: Itaipava, 15-min drive; Petrópolis, 40-min drive
Airports: Rio de Janeiro's International Airport, 90-min drive

This boutique resort is surrounded by beautiful green mountain scenery of forests and waterfalls. Suites are designed for privacy and equipped with modern amenities. In addition, Orquídeas Suites feature granite or marble bathrooms and private verandas or covered patios. Hortênsias Suites have garden views, and several of the Bromélias Suites include sofa beds ideal for small families. Facilities include a swimming pool and bar, dry and steam saunas, Jacuzzi, volleyball and basketball courts and beaten sand tennis courts. In summer, breakfast can be enjoyed by the swimming pool overlooking a small lake, and the renowned good weather lends itself to the full enjoyment of these outdoor on-site activities including the 9-hole golf course and nearby horse stables.

SOLAR DO IMPÉRIO

KOELER AVENUE, 376 - CENTRO, PETRÓPOLIS, RIO DE JANEIRO
Tel: +55 24 2103 3000 **Fax:** +55 24 2242 0034
Web: www.johansens.com/solardoimperio **E-mail:** atendimento@solardoimperio.com.br

Our inspector loved: *The careful restoration of this 1875 mansion that creates a feeling of absolute peace.*

Price Guide:
imperial U.S.$180-U.S.$220
real U.S.$206-U.S.$260
master U.S.$280-U.S.$260

Located on a beautiful street in Petrópolis, Solar do Império is a 16-room hotel that offers a comfortable retreat in Rio de Janeiro's mountain region. Built within a mansion, the hotel is decorated in a neoclassical style with modern amenities such a dry and wet sauna, spa and massage area. Leopoldina restaurant offers breakfast each morning, and lunch and dinner menus are created by Executive Chef Claudia Mascarenhas who serves contemporary, international and Brazilian dishes. The restored and modernized former stables can be turned into 3 adjoining large halls for events, business meetings and parties. For an unusual experience take a ride on Vitorias: horse-drawn wagons that will pick you up from the hotel's gardens for tours through the nearby historical center and Imperial Museum.

Attractions: Historical Center, 5-min walk; Imperial Museum, 10-min walk; Cathedral and Crystal Palace, 10-min walk
Towns/Cities: Teresópolis, 31 miles; Friburgo, 37 miles; Rio de Janeiro, 50 miles
Airports: Rio de Janeiro's International Airport, 60-min drive

TANKAMANA EcoResort

ESTRADA JÚLIO CÁPUA, S/N VALE DO CUIABÁ, ITAIPAVA - PETRÓPOLIS, RIO DE JANEIRO 25745-050
Tel: +55 24 2222 9181 **Fax:** +55 24 2222 9181
Web: www.johansens.com/tankamana **E-mail:** tankamana@tankamana.com.br

Our inspector loved: *The comfort of the cabins and the overwhelming beauty of the forest that surrounds the property.*

Price Guide:
cabins U.S.$250-U.S.$450

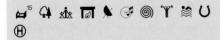

Attractions: Rainforest Reserve, 5-min walk; Itaipava District and Shops, 20-min drive; Serra dos Órgãos National Park, 30-min drive
Towns/Cities: Petrópolis, 40-min drive; Teresópolis, 60-min drive
Airports: Rio de Janeiro's International Airport, 90-min drive

The freshest, cleanest of air and the densest of greenery envelop this rustic mountain retreat. Surrounds are lush rainforests, almost impenetrable vegetation, sparkling waterfalls and the majestic heights of the Serra dos Órgãos Range. Sprawling over 880,000m^2 of parkland, the resort offers a unique vacation experience and the opportunity to shake off the stresses of busy, modern life. The 15 exclusive, well-spaced log cabins are the ultimate in relaxation and country-style luxury; built from eucalyptus trunks, each boasts 21st-century facilities and has delightful décor and furnishings. One cabin has a hydro-massage tub and direct access to a natural stone pool. Mouth-watering combinations of regional specialties and international cuisine are enjoyed in the transparent, glass-floored restaurant built over trout breeding tanks.

HOTEL MARINA ALL SUITES

AV. DELFIM MOREIRA, 696, PRAIA DO LEBLON, RIO DE JANEIRO 22441-000
Tel: +55 21 2172 1001 **Fax:** +55 21 2172 1110
Web: www.johansens.com/marinaallsuites **E-mail:** reservas@hotelmarina.com.br

Our inspector loved: *The comfort, the unique décor and beautiful ocean view from some of the designer suites.*

Price Guide: (including breakfast, excluding tax)
suites U.S.$399-U.S.$1,115

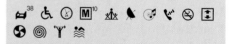

Awards/Ratings: Condé Nast Johansens Most Excellent Boutique Hotel 2006

Attractions: Ipanema Beach, 10-min walk; Botanical Garden, 5-min drive
Towns/Cities: Petrópolis - Imperial City, 90-min drive; Búzios, 150-min drive
Airports: Rio de Janeiro's Domestic Airport, 20-min drive; Rio de Janeiro's International Airport, 40-min drive

With its prime location directly on Leblon Beach, this fashionable and sophisticated hotel will truly make you feel at home. This is the only deluxe boutique hotel in the city, and everything here is immensely stylish and aesthetically pleasing. All of the 38 individually decorated suites have ocean views and include generous living areas, and some have mini-kitchens. For a very special experience, choose one of the 8 designer suites, which have been created by some of the most talented Brazilian architects and interior designers. Delicious modern French cuisine is served in the Bar d'Hôtel restaurant, which attracts great numbers of "the beautiful people" of Rio. Movie lovers will be delighted with the charming air-conditioned home theater, which allows total privacy for up to 8 guests.

TOCA DA CORUJA

AV. BAIA DOS GOLFINHOS, 464, PRAIA DA PIPA, TIBAU DO SUL, RIO GRANDE DO NORTE 59178-000
Tel: +55 84 3246 2226 **Fax:** +55 84 3246 2225
Web: www.johansens.com/rocadacoruja **E-mail:** tocadacoruja@tocadacoruja.com.br

Our inspector loved: *Relaxing in the charming and beautifully designed gardens, which surround all rooms and bungalows.*

Price Guide: (including breakfast, excluding tax)
rooms U.S.$160-U.S.$260
bungalows from U.S.$476

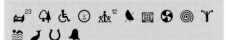

Attractions: Pipa's Main Street, 1-min walk; "Praia do Amor", 10-min drive; "Praia do Madeiro", 10-min drive; Ecological Sanctuary, 10-min drive
Towns/Cities: Natal, 53 miles; Goianinha, 16 miles
Airports: Natal Airport, 40 miles; Recife International Airport, 165 miles

Located 100 meters from the unspoiled Pipa Beach, within 25,000m² of lush gardens, Toca da Coruja is a tropical hideaway for nature lovers desiring a break from the pressures of every-day life. The hammock-adorned grounds include plenty of fruit trees, exotic birds and other fauna, a semi-Olympic size swimming pool, a sauna, hydro-massage and 23 colorful, well-appointed chalets and apartments, each with their own veranda. The hotel's interiors feature bright colors, bamboo furniture, ceramics by sculptor Francisco Brennard, and a distinctly Brazilian ambience. Brazilian-fusion and local dishes are served in the atmospheric restaurant and a poolside bar provides personalized service during the day. Hand-woven crafts can be purchased in the gift shop of this charming and stylish retreat.

ESTALAGEM ST. HUBERTUS

RUA CARRIERI, 974, GRAMADO, RIO GRANDE DO SUL 95670-000
Tel: +55 54 3286 1273 **Fax:** +55 54 3286 1273
Web: www.johansens.com/sthubertus **E-mail:** sthubertus@sthubertus.com

Our inspector loved: Having a delicious breakfast overlooking the beautiful "Black Lake".

Price Guide: (including breakfast)
rooms U.S.$150-U.S.$900

Attractions: Black Lake; Downtown Gramado, 1 mile
Towns/Cities: Canela, 5 miles
Airports: Porto Alegre's International Airport, 83 miles

Situated above peaceful Lake Negro, Estalagem St. Hubertus offers cozy charm in an idyllic setting. Each room is individually decorated with floral-print, wood furniture and a color-theme, and the romantic super luxury themed rooms come with names such as Tulip, Provence and Lake, and feature hand-painted furniture, floral wallpaper and luxurious marble bathrooms with hydro-massage tubs. The hotel also offers 16 deluxe 2-story apartments with beautiful valley views. The charming ambience extends beyond the guest rooms to the reading room with mini-library and antlers set above its cozy fireplace. Sunlit dining areas overlook the lake. Pamper yourself with a massage, de-stress in the steam sauna or take a dip in the heated swimming pool at this bucolic yet upscale hotel.

KUROTEL

RUA NAÇÕES UNIDAS 533, P.O. BOX 65, GRAMADO, RIO GRANDE DO SUL 95670-000
Tel: +55 54 3295 9393 **Fax:** +55 54 3286 1203
Web: www.johansens.com/kurotel **E-mail:** reservas@kurotel.com.br

Our inspector loved: *The first-class service at the spa and the restaurant.*

Price Guide: (all inclusive, including nutritional guidance, select number of treatments, exercise classes, medical, psychological and beauty assessments)
apartments and suites U.S.$1,793-U.S.$3,833

Awards/Ratings: Condé Nast Johansens Most Excellent Spa Hotel, South America 2007

Attractions: Waterfall Cable Car, 10-min drive; Rafting, 10-min drive; Canyons, 90-min drive; Vineyard, 90-min drive
Towns/Cities: Canela,10-min drive; Nova Petrópolis, 30-min drive; Caxias do Sul, 60-min drive; Porto Alegre, 100-min drive
Airports: Porto Alegre's International Airport, 100-min drive

With an international reputation for helping people achieve better health through predictive, preventive medicine, Kurotel Longevity Center and Spa offers over 25 years of family-guided experience. Kurotel's European-Colonial exterior is complemented by classic, richly appointed rooms and suites and is part pampering spa, part state-of-the-art medical center. There are many innovative programs including executive health, smoke cessation, stress control, weight control, and lifestyle focused on optimum health, as well as Kinder Kur, designed exclusively for mothers and their newborn babies. On the cutting-edge, the Cellular Revitalization Treatment assists in the organic functions and immunologic responses quality. With more than 2 staff members to attend to each client, the center provides truly personalized service by addressing all aspects of human behavior and makes each guest feel at home.

BRAZIL - RIO GRANDE DO SUL (SÃO FRANCISCO DE PAULA)

POUSADA DO ENGENHO

RUA ODON CAVALCANTE, 330, SÃO FRANCISCO DE PAULA 95400-000, RIO GRANDE DO SUL
Tel: +55 54 3244 1270 **Fax:** +55 54 3244 1270
Web: www.johansens.com/pousadadoengenho **E-mail:** pousadadoengenho@pousadadoengenho.com.br

Our inspector loved: The exuberance evoked by the comfortable cabanas.

Price Guide:
cabanas U.S.$120-U.S.$240

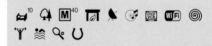

Attractions: São Bernardo Lake, 0.4 miles; Passeio a Cavalo (Horse Riding) and Passo Alegre Farm, 14 miles; Buddhist Temple, 15 miles; Canions, 56 miles
Towns/Cities: Gramado, 25 miles
Airports: Porto Alegre's International Airport, 2-hour drive

This small eco-friendly lodge is nestled in the forests of southern Brazil on the border between subtropical and temperate climate zones. The result is a beautiful and unique environment abundant with diverse flora and fauna. The Pousada consists of 10 individual cabanas tucked away in the forest for complete privacy whose rustic appearance blends into the surroundings and belies the modern comforts within such as Jacuzzis and wireless Internet access. Cabanas also feature skylights and verandas with hammocks. The cozy Casa de Babette restaurant, managed by the owners, offers a variety of fare from traditional Brazilian to Indian cuisine. Enjoy games in the lounge or venture out to try nearby trekking, rafting and horseback riding that can all be arranged for you.

PONTA DOS GANCHOS

RUA EUPÍDIO ALVES DO NASCIMENTO, 104, GOVERNADOR CELSO RAMOS, SANTA CATARINA 88190-000
Tel: +55 48 3262 5000 **Fax:** +55 48 3262 5046
Web: www.johansens.com/pontadosganchos **E-mail:** reservas@pontadosganchos.com.br

Our inspector loved: *The sophisticated service and the food after a day at the exclusive beach.*

Price Guide: (all inclusive)
bungalows U.S.$580-U.S.$1,075

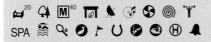
SPA

Awards/Ratings: Condé Nast Johansens Most Excellent Hotel, South America 2007

Attractions: Dolphins Bay, on the doorstep; Ilha do Arvoredo, 25-min boat ride
Towns/Cities: Florianópolis, 19 miles; Balneário Camboriú, 34 miles
Airports: Florianópolis' International Airport, 50-min drive

Affiliations: Relais & Châteaux

Clear blue water and lush green fauna surround this adults-only resort. All meals are included in the rates, and the restaurant closes after the last guest has retired for the evening. The gourmet kitchen serves regional Catarinese cuisine at lunch and international fare for dinner, while the well-stocked bars offer over 200 wines, fine liquors and various Cuban cigars. For a truly memorable evening, savor an evening meal on a private island served by your very own waiter. Scuba diving in the Marine Reserve and diving lessons with instructors, qualified by the P.A.D.I., can be arranged but for those who simply wish to kick back, there is a wide selection of D.V.D.s that can be viewed in the resort's cinema or in your very own bungalow. Alternately, spend some time in the Dior Spa.

ILHA DO PAPAGAIO

ILHA DO PAPAGAIO, PALHOÇA, SANTA CATARINA 88131-970
Tel: +55 48 3286 1242 **Fax:** +55 48 3286 1342
Web: www.johansens.com/ilhadopapagaio **E-mail:** papagaio@papagaio.com.br

Our inspector loved: The exclusivity of the comfortable ocean-front chalets.

Price Guide: (including breakfast)
rooms U.S.$189-U.S.$426

Attractions: Whale Watching; Marine Farm Raising Oysters and Mussels; State Park "Serra do Tabuleiro"
Towns/Cities: Florianópolis, 19 miles
Airports: Florianópolis International Airport, 24 miles

Surrounded by more than 100,000m² of naturally preserved vegetation, Ilha do Papagaio, or "Parrot Island," is perfect for nature lovers dreaming of a luxury eco-resort experience. This family-run resort is the only establishment on the island providing its guests with an escape from civilization that sacrifices none of its luxuries. The resort's 20 colorfully-decorated chalets, often featuring canopy beds, fireplaces, and balconies with exquisite views, are well-equipped with every modern amenity, and in the resort's grounds you will find a gym and games room. Relax by sitting under the thatched roof of the bar sipping a delicious island cocktail, or receive a complimentary massage. The restaurant, at which Chef Jarbas Meurer serves a wide variety of beautifully-presented and delicious dishes, comes highly recommended.

POUSADA SOLAR MIRADOR

ESTRADA GERAL DO ROSA S/N, PRAIA DO ROSA, IMBITUBA, SANTA CATARINA 88780-000
Tel: +55 48 3355 6144 **Fax:** +55 48 3355 6697
Web: www.johansens.com/solarmirador **E-mail:** reserva@solarmirador.com.br

Our inspector loved: *Eating the famous local seafood dish ("moqueca") while looking out to the wonderfull Praia do Rosa.*

Price Guide: (including breakfast)
rooms U.S.$145-U.S.$290

Attractions: Whale Watching, close by; Beach, 2-min walk; Surfing, Windsurfing and Horse Riding, 5-min walk; Praia Vermelha Trail, 40-min walk
Towns/Cities: Garopaba, 11 miles; Imbituba, 11 miles; Florianópolis, 40 miles
Airports: Florianópolis' International Airport, 44 miles

Perched high over Rosa Lake with privileged views of the beautiful Praia do Rosa, Pousada Solar Mirador is an intimate hotel immersed in natural beauty. Rooms are bright and airy and offer panoramic views of the beach, and public spaces decorated with stucco, stone and local art evoke a rustic elegance. The Pousada offers a lavish breakfast each morning, featuring home-made jams, quiches and cakes among other things, and Urucum restaurant serves Brazilian cuisine with an innovative fusion of native, African and Portuguese influences. During the day, lounge by the pool on the spacious deck that overlooks Rosa Bay or take a walk to the beautiful lake through the lush native vegetation.

Quinta do Bucanero

ESTRADA GERAL DO ROSA S/N, PRAIA DO ROSA, IMBITUBA, SANTA CATARINA 88780-000
Tel: +55 48 3355 6056 **Fax:** +55 48 3355 6056
Web: www.johansens.com/bucanero **E-mail:** bucanero@terra.com.br

Our inspector loved: *Enjoying the beautiful sunset while sitting in the outdoor Jacuzzi.*

Price Guide: (including breakfast)
rooms U.S.$182-U.S.$250

Attractions: Surfing and Windsurfing, 10-min walk; Whale Watching, from bedroom balconies
Towns/Cities: Garopaba, 9 miles; Imbituba 12 miles
Airports: Florianópolis International Airport, 44 miles

Situated in 17,000 meters of greenery, high above the stunning Praia do Rosa Beach, the 10-room Quinta do Bucanero is as dramatic as it is intimate. The hotel takes full advantage of its location by featuring floor-to-ceiling windows, an outdoor swimming pool and Jacuzzi, and balconies off each room that allow you to enjoy the breathtaking vistas of lush greenery, lagoons, sandy coastline, and ocean as often as possible. The interior is elegant yet relaxed with warm tones and wood-paneled walls. Each guest room is unique with a charming and homey ambience, while at the same time offering all the amenities of a large hotel. Though small, the hotel features a gym, sauna, bar, and restaurant specializing in fresh seafood dishes.

HOTEL FRONTENAC

AV. DR. PAULO RIBAS, 295 CAPIVARI, CAMPOS DO JORDÃO 12460-000
Tel: +55 12 3669 1000 **Fax:** +55 12 3669 1009
Web: www.johansens.com/frontenac **E-mail:** reservas@frontenac.com.br

Our inspector loved: *The atmosphere of the Brahm's Bar.*

Price Guide: (excluding tax)
rooms U.S.$178-U.S.$695

Attractions: Capivari's Touristic Center, 219 yards
Towns/Cities: Santo Antonio dos Pinhais, 15-min drive
Airports: São Paulo International Airport, 112 miles; Rio de Janeiro International Airport, 220 miles

This warm and inviting European-styled hotel has 41 guest rooms within the main building and 6 located in the private Frontenac Chalet. Superior rooms are comfortable and have Internet access and L.C.D. televisions, while others range from special deluxe rooms with private balconies or indoor terraces to the Presidential Suite. Choose from dining on the relaxed, informal terrace or in the elegant Charpentier Restaurant where an extensive worldwide wine list accompanies creative cuisine such as "shrimp in papaya" based on the tradition and knowledge of the French culinary revival. Brahm's Bar is an authentic British pub; the ideal place to meet friends and play songs on the jukebox. There is also a library, a home theater and a fitness center.

DPNY Beach Hotel Boutique

AV. JOSÉ PACHECO DO NASCIMENTO, 7668, PRAIA DO CURRAL , ILHABELA, SÃO PAULO 11630-000
Tel: +55 12 3894 2121 **Fax:** +55 12 3894 2060
Web: www.johansens.com/dpnybeach **E-mail:** reservas@dpnybeach.com.br

Our inspector loved: The hippie chic decór and mosaics.

Price Guide: (including breakfast)
rooms U.S.$120-U.S.$600

Attractions: 40 Beaches, nearby; Shipwrecks, Rivers and Streams, nearby; Cachoeira dos Três Tombos and Cachoeira do Gato Waterfalls, 30 and 45-min walk; Isolated Community of Surfing Bonete, 4-hour walk through rainforest
Airports: São Paulo International Airport, 124 miles; Rio de Janeiro International Airport, 218 miles

Located directly on the Ilhabela's north shore beach-front, this hotel is fashionable, luxurious, and undeniably Brazilian. Bright interiors decorated with hand-made clay figures and other local art, colorful tiled walls, animal-print furniture and an array of indoor vegetation, create a warm, tropical atmosphere. Rooms are sumptuous and well decorated, with touches such as shell detailing on the headboards of the king-sized canopied beds, muraled cabinets, bamboo furniture and native art creating an eclectic, stylish atmosphere. In addition to L.C.D. televisions, each room includes an iPod, Internet access and in some rooms a cordless phone reaching out to the beach. Enjoy Mediterranean-influenced Brazilian cuisine at Tróia, and spend the sunset and nights at the Hippie Chic Beach Club, where D.J.s spin fine Lounge and House music regularly.

HOTEL UNIQUE

AV. BRIGADEIRO LUIS ANTONIO, 4.700, SÃO PAULO, SÃO PAULO 01402-002
Tel: +55 11 3055 4710 **Fax:** +55 11 3889 8100
Web: www.johansens.com/hotelunique **E-mail:** reservas@hotelunique.com.br

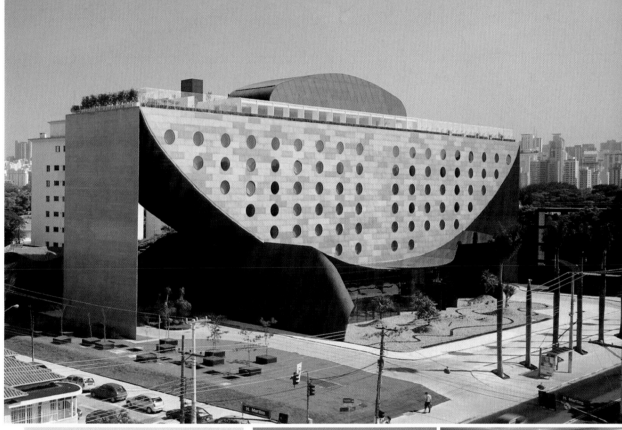

Our inspector loved: *Having a drink at the great lobby bar or at the hip rooftop restaurant with its unique view of São Paulo.*

Price Guide: (excluding taxes)
rooms U.S.$330-U.S.$5,500

Attractions: Iguatemi Shopping Mall, 10-min drive
Airports: São Paulo's Domestic Airport, 15-min drive; São Paulo's International Airport, 40-min drive

Living up to its name, this hotel boasts a bold and modern design with its curved copper façade and sleek, modern interior. Choose from a variety of rooms designed to stimulate your senses with their innovative use of geometric shapes and color. Or experience a blend of glamour and art in a lavishly-appointed suite, which offers spacious accommodations and every technological amenity. The Body & Soul Fitness Center, as well as surrounding São Paulo, provide guests with opportunities to relax and explore. The hotel's main attraction however, consists of its trendy rooftop pool and bar area, featuring Skye restaurant. This fashionable venue offers stunning views of the São Paulo skyline as well as an exciting social scene, to be enjoyed either on the open-air deck or from the restaurant's floor-to-ceiling glass windows.

HOTEL ANTUMALAL

CARRETERA PUCÓN - VILLARRICA HIGHWAY AT KM 2 FROM PUCÓN, PUCÓN, ARAUCANÍA

Tel: +56 45 441 011 **Fax:** +56 45 441 013

Web: www.johansens.com/antumalal **E-mail:** info@antumalal.com

Our inspector loved: *The magnificent location with spectacular views of the lake, and the amazing tours.*

Price Guide: (including breakfast)
rooms U.S.$180-U.S.$220
suites U.S.$250-U.S.$270

Attractions: Mountain Biking and White-Water Rafting, close by; Volcano Villarica Climb, 19 miles; Visit to an Indigenous Community, 31 miles; Express Tour to Patagonia, 186 miles

Towns/Cities: Pucón, 1 mile; Villarrica, 9 miles; Temuco, 59 miles

Airports: Temuco Airport, 59 miles

Perched high on the hillside overlooking Lake Villarrica within a 5-hectare park, this Frank Lloyd Wright-inspired building presents airy living areas with unusual furnishings and colorful goat skin rugs. Accommodations are simply furnished with stone floors and wooden walls that are complemented by natural colors and natural light from floor to ceiling windows that "bring the outside in." The Royal Suite comprises 2 bedrooms, a dining area and a huge sitting room with fabulous "picture" windows. Only the best local produce is used in the restaurant whose reputation for being one of the finest places to dine in the region is testament to its innovative international flare. Lunch may be taken on the roof terrace, and the cozy bar features a hearth fire and large terrace overlooking the lake. Enjoy the private beach with 2 docks, the sauna, hot tub and variety of massages at the spa.

VILLARRICA PARK LAKE HOTEL

CAMINO A VILLARRICA KM.13, ARAUCANÍA, VILLARRICA
Tel: +56 2 207 7070 **Fax:** +56 2 207 7020
Web: www.johansens.com/villarrica **E-mail:** reservas@villarricaparklakehotel.cl

Our inspector loved: *The luxurious Aquarius Spa.*

Price Guide: (including breakfast)
rooms U.S.$355-U.S.$385
suites U.S.$425-U.S.$2300

Attractions: Canopi Tour, 13 miles; Volcanic Cave Tour, 19 miles; Skiing, 19 miles
Towns/Cities: Pucon, 3 miles; Villarrica, 8 miles; Temuco, 56 miles
Airports: Temuco Airport, 56 miles

Set against the stunning backdrop of a magnificent snow-capped volcano, surrounded by beautiful gardens and perched at the edge of a vast, deep blue lake, Villarrica Park Lake Hotel combines sophisticated comfort with a location as dramatic as it is peaceful. Private guest room balconies, large floor-to-ceiling windows and terraces, found liberally throughout the main areas of the hotel, highlight the privileged views of the resort's unique location in the Villarrica region, creating a sense of serenity within the hotel. Treat yourself to a massage at the Aquarius Spa, enjoy a local specialty in the Aguas Verdes restaurant and taste Chilean wines in the fifth floor Vertigo Bar to round off a well-spent day of relaxation or exploration.

Hacienda Tres Lagos

CARRETERA AUSTRAL SUR KM 274, LOCALIDAD LAGO NEGRO, PUERTO GUADAL, PATAGONIA
Tel: +56 2 333 4122 **Fax:** +56 2 334 5294
Web: www.johansens.com/treslagos **E-mail:** ventas@haciendatreslagos.cl

Our inspector loved: *The incredible menu of outdoor activities: glacier trekking, fly fishing, fossil excursions, rafting...*

Price Guide: (including breakfast, per person) rooms U.S.$257-U.S.$352

Attractions: 1-hour tour of Marble Caves; Glacier Trekking, 8 miles; San Rafael Lagoon, 35-min helicopter ride; The Vallley of Explorers, 32 miles
Towns/Cities: Puerto Guadal, 7 miles; Puerto Tranquilo, 32 miles; Chile Chico, 68 miles; Coyhaique, 170 miles
Airports: Balmaceda Airport, 140 miles

This beautifully designed hotel consists of individual bungalows and suites looking out to the spectacular Negro Lake. Tres Lagos means Three Lakes and that is exactly what surrounds the property. Standing on the shoreline of Negro Lake, with its own private beach, General Carrera Lake, the second largest in South America, is located behind the Hacienda, while a few minutes' walk away is Lake Bertrand, also with its own private beach. The 2 restaurants, Parador Austral and Quincho Patagónico serve a wide variety of traditional Patagonian and international food including barbecue, and there is a bar in which to relax. This is a unique eco-tourism area where the adventurous can explore the enveloping nature but return to comfort at the end of each day. Activities arranged by the hotel include canopy lining, boat trips, 4x4 adventure tours, bird-watching, rafting, trekking and star-gazing with telescopes. There is also a games room, hot tubs, sauna and massages to enjoy.

TERMAS DE JAHUEL HOTEL & SPA

JAHUEL S/N, SAN FELIPE, VALPARAISO
Tel: +56 2 411 1720 Fax: +56 2 411 1701
Web: www.johansens.com/jahuel E-mail: reservas@jahuel.cl

Our inspector loved: *The incredible spa with its thermal water treatments.*

Price Guide: (including breakfast, lunch and dinner)
classic U.S.$356
superior U.S.$390
vip U.S.$410

Attractions: Horseback Riding and Trekking, close by; Vinyard Tours, 12 miles; Ski Centers, 31 miles
Towns/Cities: San Felipe, 9 miles; Santiago, 61 miles; Valparaiso, 75 miles
Airports: Santiago International Airport, 61 miles

Just 61 miles from Santiago, the capital of Chile, Termas de Jahuel Hotel & Spa is located in the Valley of Aconcagua, surrounded by an outstanding natural environment. Jahuel uses an ancient thermal spring to provide water for all the hotel's needs. The mineral composition of the water is ideal for relaxing and helping to repair many aspects of tired and stressed bodies and minds. The large swimming pools, both outside and inside, are filled with thermal spring water, and a selection of natural treatments is available for guests at Spa Termal. The 94 rooms are located in a 500-hectare park that offers many recreational activities not only for adults but for families as well. Local tours can be taken to Chilean vineyards and ski facilities. In the evening relax at the bar before taking dinner in one of the splendid restaurants.

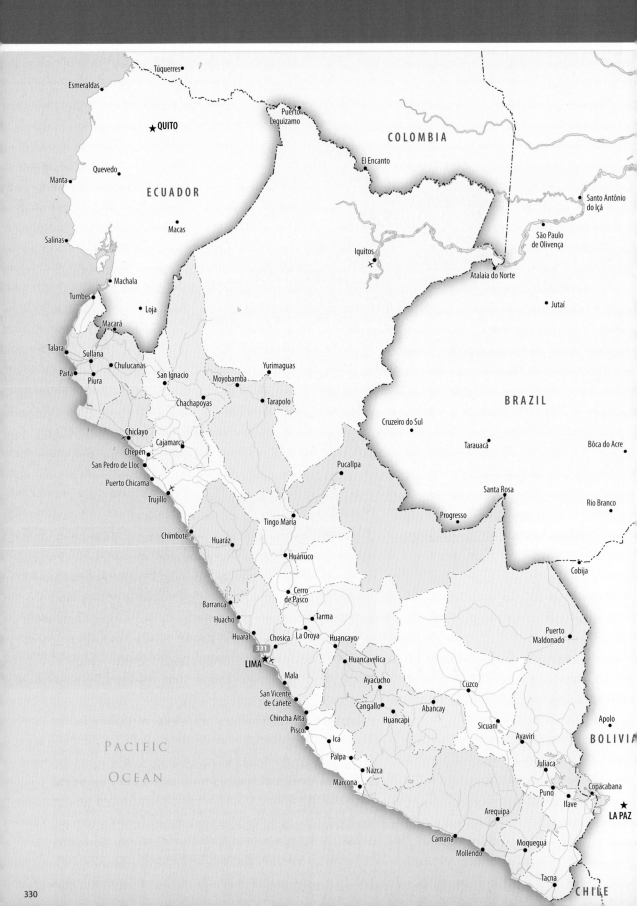

Túquerres

Esmeraldas

★ QUITO

Quevedo

Manta

ECUADOR

Salinas

Machala

Macas

Tumbes

Loja

Macará

Talara

Sullana

Chulucanàs

Paita

Piura

San Ignacio

Yurimaguas

Moyobamba

Chachapoyas

Tarapolo

Chiclayo

Cajamarca

Chepén

San Pedro de Lloc

Puerto Chicama

Trujillo

Chimbote

Huaráz

Tingo María

Huánuco

Barranca

Cerro de Pasco

Huacho

Tarma

Huaral

Chosica

La Oroya

331

LIMA ★

Mala

Huancayo

Huancavelica

San Vicente de Cañete

Ayacucho

Chincha Alta

Cangallo

Pisco

Huancapi

Ica

Palpa

Nazca

Marcona

PACIFIC

OCEAN

Puerto Leguizamo

COLOMBIA

El Encanto

Santo Antônio do Içá

São Paulo de Olivença

Iquitos

Atalaia do Norte

Jutaí

BRAZIL

Cruzeiro do Sul

Tarauacá

Bôca do Acre

Pucallpa

Santa Rosa

Rio Branco

Progresso

Cobija

Puerto Maldonado

Cuzco

Abancay

Sicuani

Apolo

Ayaviri

BOLIVIA

Juliaca

Copacabana

Puno

Arequipa

Ilave

★ LA PAZ

Camaná

Moquegua

Mollendo

Tacna

CHILE

REFUGIOS DEL PERU - VIÑAK REICHRAMING

SANTIAGO DE VIÑAK, YAUYOS, LIMA
Tel: +511 421 7777 **Fax:** +511 421 8476
Web: www.johansens.com/refugiosdelperu **E-mail:** info@refugiosdelperu.com

Our inspector loved: *The breathtaking scenery and vivid culture surrounding the lodge.*

Price Guide: (all inclusive, including unlimited mountain bike hire and hiking with guide) rooms U.S.$75-U.S.$99

    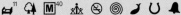

Attractions: Trekking, 50 miles; Canoeing, 50 miles; Inca Archeological Ruins of Inkawasi, 62 miles
Towns/Cities: Lunahuana, 50 miles; Lima, 124 miles
Airports: Lima International Airport, 124 miles

Refugios del Peru is a cozy, intimate hotel situated high in unforgettably beautiful scenery. With extremely comfortable accommodations, you will be spoilt by the personal service and quiet charm, perfect for unwinding and leaving the pressures of modern life behind. Warm wood and stone buildings bathe in sunlight and effortlessly blend into the surrounding rural landscapes. There are over 44 miles of walking paths and mountain bike trails in the area and many diverse outdoor activities to choose from. Rooms are spacious and light with natural wood furniture and subtle color schemes; all benefit from a breathtaking outlook as well as independent water and heating control. The stunning panoramic restaurant has views that stretch as far as the eye can see over rolling hillsides, and serves a delicious fusion of Andean and European cuisine.

UNITED
STATES

Fort Lauderdale

Miami

*Bimini
Islands*

West End

334

Freeport

Grand Bahama

Little Abaco

Marsh Harbour

Sandy Point

Great Abaco

Berry I.

STRAIT OF
FLORIDA

Morgan's
Bluff

Andros

Andros Town

333

Moxey Town

Red Shank Cay

Mars Bay

Spanish Wells

335 *Harbour Island*

NASSAU

*New
Providence*

Governors Harbour

Eleuthera

Arthurs Town

Cat Island

Devils
Point

ATLANTIC

OCEAN

San Salvador

Great Exuma

Seymour's

George
Town

Rum Cay

OLD BAHAMA CHANNEL

Long Island

Clarence Town

Ciego de Ávila

Colonel Hill

Florida

Spring Point

Mayaguana

Betsy
Bay

*Acklins
Islands*

CUBA

TURKS AND
CAICOS

Holguín

Little Inagua

Manzanillo

Great Inagua

Matthew Town

Guantánamo

CARIBBEAN SEA

Santiago
de Cuba

KAMALAME CAY

STANIARD CREEK, ANDROS

Tel: +1 242 368 6281 **Fax:** +1 242 368 6279 **U.S./Canada Toll Free:** 1 800 790 7971
Web: www.johansens.com/kamalame **E-mail:** info@kamalame.com

Our inspector loved: The bonefishing, and the over-the-water spa (150 feet into the ocean).

Price Guide: (all inclusive, excluding house staff gratuities and taxes)
rooms U.S.$840-U.S.$1,190
suites U.S.$1,100-U.S.$6,000

 SPA

Attractions: Nassau, 15-min flight; Paradise Island, 1-hour boat ride
Towns/Cities: Andros Town, 20-min drive; Nassau, 18-min flight
Airports: Andros Town Airport, 20-min drive

Nestled within silver palms on a 96-acre private island accessible only by the resort's private ferry or seaplane, Kamalame Cay exudes a laid-back, welcoming atmosphere at the same time as being romantic and exclusive. Open, airy accommodations blend Old World charm with barefoot elegance and stunning views of the turquoise Caribbean combined with soft down comforters and Roman soaking tubs, making them ideal havens for complete relaxation. The Great House is decorated with an array of art, antiques and Bahamian furniture and serves as a social space for guests, who gather for drinks and candle-lit Caribbean meals that utilize the best of local ingredients. For a more private dining experience, couples may arrange a romantic meal, specially-prepared on the beach.

OLD BAHAMA BAY AT GINN SUR MER

WEST END, GRAND BAHAMA ISLAND

Tel: +1 242 350 6500 **Fax:** +1 242 346 6546 **U.S./Canada Toll Free:** 1 800 444 9469
Web: www.johansens.com/oldbahamabay **E-mail:** info@oldbahamabay.com

Our inspector loved: The marina where one's yacht can be berthed.

Price Guide: (excluding 12% service charge per night)
junior suites U.S.$235-U.S.$620
2-bedroom suites U.S.$560-U.S.1,240

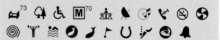

Attractions: Eight Mile Rock, 15 miles; Port Lucaya Marketplace, 35 miles
Towns/Cities: Freeport, 25 miles; Lucaya, 35 miles
Airports: Grand Bahama Island International Airport, 25 miles

Affiliations: Small Luxury Hotels of the World

Situated within 228 acres on the western-most tip of Grand Bahama Island, just 56 miles from the Florida coast, stands the tranquil and luxurious Old Bahama Bay. A family-friendly destination, it comprises 73 spacious ocean view and ocean-front junior suites and 2-bedroom suites, an ocean-front pool, restaurants, massage pavilion, a 72-slip port of entry marina and a waterfront residential community. Each of the junior suites and 1 and 2-bedroom suites include custom-designed furnishings, a fiber-optic cable for phone, ocean-front terraces and much more. The luxurious bathrooms feature Kohler fixtures, either 6-ft. soaking tubs or whirlpool tubs. Relax in the 4,000 sq. ft. heated pool with infinity-edge lounging area and massage jets, overlooking the ocean before adjourning to one of the 3 restaurants. The Bonefish Folley's Bar & Grille overlooks the marina, the Straw Bar is an ocean-side café and bar, and Aqua offers Bahamian fusion cuisine.

PINK SANDS

CHAPEL STREET, HARBOUR ISLAND

Tel: +1 242 333 2030 **Fax:** +1 242 333 2060 **U.S./Canada Toll Free:** 1 800 407 4776
Web: www.johansens.com/pinksands **E-mail:** info@pinksandsresort.com

Our inspector loved: *The beautiful Indian/Moroccan lounge.*

Price Guide: (excluding 20% service charge)
rooms U.S.$600-U.S.$850
cottages U.S.$975-U.S.$2,350

Attractions: Reef Deep Sea or Bone Fishing
Towns/Cities: Nassau, 50 miles
Airports: North Eleuthera International Airport, 10-min water taxi ride

Harbour Island is renowned for its shimmering pink sand beaches and Colonial charm, and Pink Sands prides itself on offering both. The 25 pastel-hued cottages dotted around lush tropical gardens are a celebrity-magnet. Breakfast and lunch are served in the beach-front Blue Bar and Caribbean dinners are served in the garden terrace restaurant. Depending on your mood, lounge by the freshwater pool, play tennis or billiards, visit the exercise studio or explore the grounds. Coconut palm, hibiscus, jasmine and ground orchids all grow around the cottages and the area is an official designated bird sanctuary.

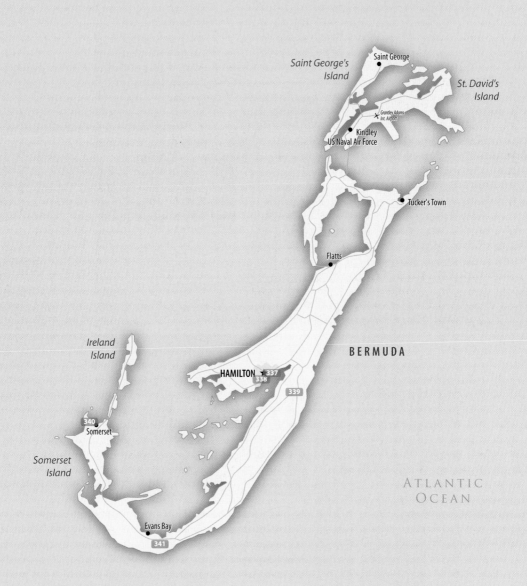

Saint George's
Island

Saint George

St. David's
Island

Grantley Adams
Int. Airport

Kindley
US Naval Air Force

Tucker's Town

Flatts

Ireland
Island

BERMUDA

HAMILTON   337
           338
              339

340
Somerset

Somerset
Island

ATLANTIC
OCEAN

Evans Bay

341

ROSEDON HOTEL

P.O. BOX HM 290, HAMILTON HMAX

Tel: +1 441 295 1640 **Fax:** +1 441 295 5904 **U.S./Canada Toll Free:** 1 800 742 5008
Web: www.johansens.com/rosedonhotel **E-mail:** info@rosedon.com

Our inspector loved: The new "honor larder" where you can help yourself to a snack.

Price Guide: (including breakfast)
rooms U.S.$240-U.S.$402

Attractions: Front Street Hamilton, 1 mile; Harbor, 1 mile; South Shore Beach, 2 miles
Airports: Bermuda Airport, 9 mile

Originally built in 1903 by an expatriate English family, this stunningly refurbished Colonial hotel provides a quiet, friendly and relaxed atmosphere in sensational surroundings. Enclosed by natural tropical gardens, this is a tranquil sanctuary only minutes from the bustling town of Hamilton. Suffused with the atmosphere of Colonial splendor, the main house is decorated in a traditional style and is festooned with antique furniture. The Bermudian-style rooms are all spacious and have balconies overlooking the swimming pool. Breakfast and lunch are served at the poolside patio and light dinners are available on request. Introductions to the island's championship golf courses can be organized, and transportation to a South Shore Beach and tennis club is available.

WATERLOO HOUSE

P.O. BOX H.M. 333, HAMILTON H.M. B.X.
Tel: +1 441 295 4480 **Fax:** +1 441 295 2585 **U.S./Canada Toll Free:** 1 800 468 4100
Web: www.johansens.com/waterloohouse **E-mail:** reservations@waterloohouse.bm

Our inspector loved: The unique harborside location of this beautiful small property.

Price Guide:
rooms U.S.$285-U.S.$480
suites U.S.$360-U.S.$780

Attractions: Scuba Diving, 15-min drive; Naval Dockyard, 20-min drive; Panorama Submarine, 20-min drive
Towns/Cities: Hamilton, 2-min walk
Airports: Bermuda International Airport, 20-min drive

This elegant manor house, with surrounding cottages that date back to 1815, stands amidst 4 acres of terraced gardens directly on Hamilton Harbor. The 20 rooms and 10 spacious suites overlook the harbor or gardens, have dressing areas and are appointed with original paintings, antiques, French and Italian fabrics and furnishings. Waterloo House is known around the world as one of Bermuda's best restaurants, and the executive chef has won numerous awards for cuisine both in North America and Europe. Enjoy his exquisite dishes at the Poinciana Terrace, on the water's edge, or in the elegant Wellington Room where popular Bermuda shorts are acceptable attire. Afternoon tea is served in the garden or flagpole terrace, and a delectable tapas menu is available in Long Room Bar.

HORIZONS AND COTTAGES

33 SOUTH SHORE ROAD, PAGET, P.G. 04
Tel: +1 441 236 0048 **Fax:** +1 441 236 1981 **U.S./Canada Toll Free:** 1 800 468 0022
Web: www.johansens.com/horizons **E-mail:** reservations@horizons.bm

Our inspector loved: *The "horizon" vistas from this hilltop property.*

Price Guide:
rooms U.S.$330-U.S.$440
suites U.S.$450-U.S.$800

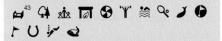

Attractions: Hamilton Front Street, 10-min drive; Scuba Diving, 15-min drive; Naval Dockyard, 20-min drive; Panorama Submarine, 20-min drive
Towns/Cities: Hamilton, 10-min drive
Airports: Bermuda International Airport, 20-min drive

Affiliations: Relais & Châteaux

Founded on an 18th-century plantation, Horizons and Cottages is Bermuda's oldest cottage colony set on a hilltop amongst 25 acres of exotic gardens. The 9-room main house and the 32 suites and cottages opened in 1922. Today, the cottages range from intimate 1-bedroom accommodations to large 5-bedroom retreats. You can enjoy breakfast each morning on the cottage veranda served by a personal maid or on your very own private room terrace overlooking the gardens and sea. Staff will prepare canapés and snacks to be enjoyed in your room and complimentary afternoon tea can be taken on the Pool Terrace. Dinner is served on the Ocean Terrace, Barbecue Terrace or in the Middleton Room, while barmen mix popular island cocktails and hand out Cuban cigars in the old-style English pub.

CAMBRIDGE BEACHES RESORT & SPA

KINGS POINT, SOMERSET
Tel: +1 441 234 0331 **Fax:** +1 441 234 3352 **U.S./Canada Toll Free:** 1 800 468 7300
Web: www.johansens.com/cambeaches **E-mail:** cambeach@ibl.bm

Our inspector loved: The Sothy of Paris facial at the Ocean Spa.

Price Guide:
rooms U.S.$270-U.S.$795
suites U.S.$475-U.S.$900
pool suites U.S.$795-U.S.$1,650

Awards/Ratings: Condé Nast Johansens Most Excellent Spa Hotel 2006

Attractions: Naval Dockyard & Dolphin Quest, 10-min drive; Hamilton Front Street, 30-min drive
Towns/Cities: Hamilton, 30-min drive; St. Georges, 40-min by ferry
Airports: Bermuda's L.F. Wade International Airport, 40-min drive

Set on a private 30-acre peninsula, Cambridge Beaches enjoys spectacular sea views, charming cottage accommodations, beautiful private beaches and award-winning cuisine. Incredible water-front pool suites (the only ones in Bermuda) offer complete privacy and panoramic views, and the gourmet cuisine at the international Tamarisk Room remains among Bermuda's best. Dinner may also be taken by torchlight around the infinity pool overlooking Mangrove Bay or on Long Bay Beach at the trendy beach-front bistro, Breezes. For the ultimate romantic experience couples can enjoy private beach dinners or exclusive evenings on a nearby private island. There are endless activities with extensive leisure facilities including a world-class spa and wellness center, a putting green and private marina. Enquire about year-round family and reunion packages.

THE REEFS

56 SOUTH SHORE ROAD, SOUTHAMPTON
Tel: +1 441 238 0222 **Fax:** +1 441 238 8372 **U.S./Canada Toll Free:** 1 800 742 2008
Web: www.johansens.com/thereefs **E-mail:** irr@worldnet.att.net

Our inspector loved: *The "dining on the beach" option - very romantic.*

Price Guide: (per person)
rooms U.S.$294-U.S.$544

 SPA

Attractions: Bermuda Aquarium, 35-min drive; Crystal Caves, 35-min drive; Bermuda Maritime Museum, 40-min drive
Towns/Cities: Hamilton, 20-min drive
Airports: Bermuda International Airport, 40-min drive

Nestled along high coral cliffs and overlooking its own private beach, this intimate 65-room resort provides a relaxing atmosphere where you will feel perfectly at ease. With great rooms, exquisite cuisine and impeccable service, every room and suite in the main resort commands sweeping ocean and sunset vistas. There are also 1, 2, and 3-bedroom Bermudian cottages popular with small groups of friends and families, and each has its own private Jacuzzi. There are 3 different dining options that open on a rotational basis. Ocean Echo is perched on the cliff-side and offers spectacular views of South Shore, while Grill 56 is where the talents of the Executive Chef are highlighted. Coconuts is an ocean-front restaurant where you can dine with your toes in the sand. For an after-diner drink head to the Lounge, a favorite rendezvous where traditional English Tea and live entertainment are enjoyed daily. For an indulgent break, stop by the highly-acclaimed day spa.

341

CURTAIN BLUFF

P.O. BOX 288, ST. JOHN'S
Tel: +1 268 462 8400 **Fax:** +1 268 462 8409 **U.S./Canada Toll Free:** 1 888 289 9898
Web: www.johansens.com/curtainbluff **E-mail:** curtainbluff@curtainbluff.com

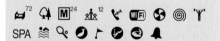

Our inspector loved: The new full-service spa with its beautiful ocean views.

Price Guide: (all inclusive)
rooms from U.S.$595

SPA

Awards/Ratings: Condé Nast Traveler Gold List 2006 and 2007

With a smooth, lagoon-fed beach on one side and windward surf on the other, Curtain Bluff is truly idyllic. Meticulous attention to detail is evident throughout, from the immaculate tropical gardens to the spacious rattan-styled bedrooms. Culinary excellence is in the capable hands of French-born Chef Christophe Blatz, and the impressive wine cellar consists of 25,000 bottles. Fine dining is available in the garden pavilion, while greater informality is found at the beach bar. For total privacy, dinner may be taken on your balcony. Facilities include a 5,000 sq. ft. spa, 5-star tennis facilities, squash and a putting green. With its private peninsula, the water-sport activities are unrivaled. There is even the opportunity to sail on Sentio, Curtain Bluff's 49-ft. Wellington ketch.

Attractions: Rainforest Canopy Tour, 2 miles; Sting Ray City, 4 miles; Nelson's Dockyard, 5 miles; Shirley Heights, 5 miles
Towns/Cities: St. John's, 8 miles
Airports: V.C. Bird International Airport, 10 miles

GALLEY BAY

FIVE ISLANDS, ST. JOHN'S

Tel: +1 954 481 8787 **Fax:** +1 954 481 1661 **U.S./Canada Toll Free:** 1 800 858 4618
Web: www.johansens.com/galleybay **E-mail:** res@eliteislandresorts.com

Our inspector loved: *The intimate ocean-front dining with nightly live entertainment.*

Price Guide: (including all meals, beverages, non-motorized water sports, taxes and service charges)
rooms U.S.$665-U.S.$990
suites U.S.$690-U.S.$1,350

Awards/Ratings: Condé Nast Traveler Gold List 2005

Attractions: St. John's, 10-min drive; Shirley Heights, 45-min drive; Devil's Bridge, 45-min drive; English Harbour, 50-min drive
Towns/Cities: St John's, 10-min drive
Airports: V.C. Bird International Airport, 25-min drive

This adults-only Tahitian-style resort is situated on a pristine ³/₄-mile stretch of white sandy beach. A romantic Caribbean hideaway, the endless sunshine and unspoiled beauty of Antigua makes this an ideal laid-back vacation destination. Located directly on the beach, thatch-roofed bungalows and ocean-front rooms are set amidst 40 acres of lush gardens filled with majestic coconut palms, a lagoon and bird sanctuary. The décor is simple yet stylish with rattan and bamboo furniture filling each of the spacious rooms. Creole and Euro-Caribbean dishes are available in the Sea Grape Restaurant, while traditional grilled fare is served at the beach-side Gauguin Restaurant where an idyllic evening can be spent sipping sundowners and watching the sunset. Cascading waterfalls are a feature of the freeform swimming pool, and the fitness center overlooks the lagoon.

347

THE VERANDAH

INDIAN TOWN ROAD, ST. JOHN'S
Tel: +1 268 460 5000 **U.S./Canada Toll Free:** 1 800 858 4618
Web: www.johansens.com/verandah **E-mail:** Reservations@eliteislandresorts.com

Our inspector loved: The family friendliness of this new all-inclusive resort.

Price Guide: (all inclusive)
villas U.S.$495-U.S.$685

Attractions: Devil's Bridge, 10-min walk; Green Island and Bird Island, 15-min boat ride; Shirley Heights, 40-min drive; Nelson's Dockyard, 40-min drive
Towns/Cities: St. John's, 30-min drive
Airports: V.C. Bird International Airport, 30-min drive

Located on 30 spectacular waterfront acres, The Verandah is a new luxury eco-friendly retreat hidden away on the beautiful north-east coast of Antigua. Lush landscapes and classic Caribbean décor make the resort feel like a tropical home-away-from-home, and the spacious verandahs are perfect for taking in views of the turquoise waters of this reef-protected bay. Spend the afternoon walking the nature trails at the adjacent national park or snorkeling off the white sand beach. In the evenings enjoy drinks at one of 5 bars with live entertainment. There are 3 restaurants: the gourmet Nicole's; Seabreeze, which serves Caribbean specialties and international favorites; and Bucaneers, a family-themed restaurant. Children will enjoy their own dedicated restaurant and activities.

CARLISLE BAY

OLD ROAD, ST. MARY'S
Tel: +1 268 484 0000 **Fax:** +1 268 484 0001
Web: www.johansens.com/carlislebay **E-mail:** info@carlisle-bay.com

Our inspector loved: *Taking a daily yoga or Pilates class in the Pavilion.*

Price Guide: (including breakfast)
suites U.S.$775-U.S.$3,550

Awards/Ratings: Condé Nast Traveler Gold List 2006 and 2007

Attractions: Fig Tree Drive, 0.5 mile; Antigua Rainforest Canopy Tour, 15-min drive; Nelson's Dockyard, 20-min drive; Betty Hope's Sugar Plantation, 45-min drive
Towns/Cities: English Harbour, 20-min drive; St. John's, 30-min drive
Airports: V.C. Bird International Airport, 30-min drive

Affiliations: The Leading Small Hotels of the World

This contemporary luxury resort is set against a dramatic backdrop of rolling hills and rainforest on the magnificent south coast of Antigua. Each spacious suite has cool, calm interiors and a private balcony or terrace from which to take in the breathtaking ocean views. Carlisle Bay's philosophy of well-being and feeling great is enhanced by the exceptional spa services, yoga and Pilates Pavilion, 9 tennis courts and an array of complimentary water sports. There are 2 excellent restaurants: East, with its pan-Asian menu in a contemporary setting and the more informal Indigo on the Beach offering delicious healthy grills, seafood and salads. The Cool Kids Club for children aged 6 months to 12 years, the library and a screening room ensure a good time is had by all.

THE BEACH HOUSE

PALMETTO POINT

Tel: +1 516 767 3057 **Fax:** +1 516 767 6529 **U.S./Canada Toll Free:** 1 888 776 0333
Web: www.johansens.com/beachbarbuda **E-mail:** info@thebeachhousebarbuda.com

Our inspector loved: The privacy of the resort with miles and miles of pink sand beach to explore.

Price Guide: (including breakfast and dinner)
suites U.S.$750-U.S.$1,275

Attractions: Locally Guided One-On-One Private Tours of Frigate Bird Sanctuary, Darby Caves, Codrington Lagoon, Spanish Point and Lobster Snorkeling
Airports: Barbuda Airport, 2 miles

The Beach House is the ultimate hideaway on the pristine and undeveloped island of Barbuda. Located on an unparalleled and expansive stretch of distinctive pink sand beach, with no-one in sight for miles, The Beach House makes you feel as though you've been invited into someone's private home. White-washed interiors, teak furniture and calming minimal décor enhance the natural setting. Friendly Service Ambassadors offer discreet yet attentive service allowing you to relax by the freshwater pool, take romantic walks on the beach or simply just be. Dining is a sublime experience: enjoy classic Caribbean cuisine under the twinkling stars at night. Try the sweet Barbuda lobster or the daily catch. You will feel miles away from civilization yet the island is easily accessible via Antigua.

ATLANTIC OCEAN

Greenidge
Hope
Cave Hill
Nesfield
Boscobel
Road Fustic
Rose Hill
Mont Brevitor
Belleplaine
Speightstown
355
Sion Hill
Mose Bottom
Bathsheba
353
354
Chimborazo
Holetown
Rock Hall
Pothouse
Holders Hill
Ashbury
Steward Hill
Eden Lodge
Robinsons
Black Rock
Turnpike
Six Cross Roads
The Crame
Belleville
Edey
St. Patrick
BRIDGETOWN
Bartletts
Gemswick
Newton Terrace
Charnocks
Grantley Adams Int. Airport
Hastings
Worthing
Oistins
352

CARIBBEAN SEA

LITTLE ARCHES

ENTERPRISE BEACH ROAD, CHRIST CHURCH

Tel: +1 246 420 4689 **Fax:** +1 246 418 0207 **U.S./Canada Toll Free:** 1 800 764 1000
Web: www.johansens.com/littlearches **E-mail:** paradise@littlearches.com

Our inspector loved: *The vivid blue of the Caribbean Sea from the magnificent Café Luna restaurant.*

Price Guide: (excluding 7.5% tax and 10% gratuity)
rooms U.S.$192-U.S.$399
suites U.S.$336-U.S.$552

This charming boutique hotel is situated in the parish of Christ Church on the southern edge of the island, steps from a pristine white sand beach. With only 10 rooms and suites, this privately owned hotel lends an ambience of informality and intimacy. Each of the rooms is carefully appointed with cool, crisp linens and terrazzo flooring, and 2 of the suites have private Jacuzzis, oversized beds and dramatic ocean views. The alfresco restaurant, Café Luna, is the perfect spot to watch the sun set while enjoying international cuisine. Little Arches' villa-charm continues with yachting fun aboard a 44-ft. luxury catamaran, available for private charters and memorable small weddings.

Attractions: Oistins' Fish Market, 5-min drive; Bridgetown, 20-min drive
Towns/Cities: Oistins, 5-min drive; Bridgetown, 20-min drive
Airports: Grantley Adams, 10-min drive

CORAL REEF CLUB

ST. JAMES

Tel: +1 246 422 2372 **Fax:** +1 246 422 1776 **U.S./Canada Toll Free:** 1 800 223 1108
Web: www.johansens.com/coralreefclub **E-mail:** coral@caribsurf.com

Our inspector loved: *The cocktail party for guests, hosted at the owners' family home on the property.*

Price Guide: (including breakfast)
rooms U.S.$245-U.S.$800
suites U.S.$440-U.S.$2,400

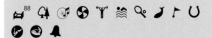

Attractions: Wildlife Reserve, 5 miles; Plantation Houses, 7 miles; Barbados Museum, 10 miles
Towns/Cities: Holetown, 1 mile; Bridgetown, 9 miles
Airports: Grantley Adams Airport, 18 miles

Affiliations: Small Luxury Hotels of the World

Quietly nestled in 12 acres of lush tropical gardens and white sand beach on Barbados's famed west coast, this is a wonderful family-owned and managed property. For the past 50 years, the O'Hara family has been dedicated to providing the most excellent and comfortable getaway possible. A quiet stroll along the coast is a great way to explore the surroundings before sampling fresh seafood at the elegant ocean-front restaurant. You will notice that each of the rooms is cleverly named after the flowers, fruit and trees found within the grounds. Choose to stay in a luxury cottage with your own private plunge pool or for the utmost luxury, unwind in one of the 5 Plantation Suites; the epitome of 21st-century style.

THE SANDPIPER

HOLETOWN, ST. JAMES

Tel: +1 246 422 2251 **Fax:** +1 246 422 0900 **U.S./Canada Toll Free:** 1 800 223 1108
Web: www.johansens.com/sandpiper **E-mail:** coral@caribsurf.com

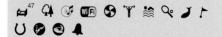

Our inspector loved: The "South Seas" atmosphere of the hotel at night, with the flaming torches subtly lighting up the waterfalls.

Price Guide: (including breakfast)
rooms U.S.$280-U.S.$765
suites U.S.$405-U.S.$2,400

This gem of a hotel is located on the desirable west coast of Barbados and has quickly become a favorite spot for discerning guests looking for intimacy, relaxation and privacy. Lush tropical gardens lead to the white sand beach in the middle of a large bay sloping down to the clear Caribbean Sea. Each of the bedrooms and suites has its own private terrace with spacious and airy décor and touches of the Caribbean. 2 premier Tree Top Suites benefit from beach-front locations and have private plunge pools, sun decks and chic furnishings, adding further luxury to this family-owned hotel. The restaurant, set in a blossoming garden and surrounded by tranquil koi ponds, offers an international menu with a Caribbean flair.

Attractions: Limestone Caves, 5 miles; Wildlife Reserve, 5 miles; Atlantis Submarine, 8 miles; Historic Houses, 8 miles
Towns/Cities: Holetown, 0.5 miles
Airports: Grantley Adams Airport, 18 miles

Affiliations: Small Luxury Hotels of the World

COBBLERS COVE

SPEIGHTSTOWN, ST. PETER

Tel: +1 246 422 2291 **Fax:** +1 246 422 1460 **U.S./Canada Toll Free:** 1 800 890 6060
Web: www.johansens.com/cobblerscove **E-mail:** reservations@cobblerscove.com

Our inspector loved: *The Friday evening fish lover's fantasy with a selection of locally caught fish and international caviar.*

Price Guide:
rooms U.S.$460-U.S.$2,450

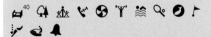

Attractions: Harrison's Cave, 25-min drive
Towns/Cities: Bridgetown, 25-min drive
Airports: Grantley Adams Airport, 45-min drive

Affiliations: Relais & Châteaux

Cobblers Cove is a classic English country house-style hotel located on the northwest coast of Barbados. Each spacious suite has a private balcony or patio, private bath with English-style toiletries and wet bar with stocked refrigerator. The beautifully landscaped gardens are filled with winding terracotta brick pathways lined by hibiscus and a wide variety of tropical palms and flowers. Pathways from the suites lead down to the lounge, bar and restaurant, near the pool. The open-air Terrace Restaurant is situated at the edge of the beach where Executive Chef Neil Hitchen's blends classical French, British and American cuisine from fresh local ingredients including fish caught by the resort's own fisherman. Complimentary high tea is served each day.

Condé Nast Johansens Preferred Partner for

HOSPITALITY
RECRUITMENT

CHH EXECUTIVE SEARCH
1 Morton Drive, Suite 504,
Charlottesville, Virginia 22903

Tel. 434 977 5029 Fax. 434 977 5431
www.chhsearch.com
info@chhsearch.com

British Virgin Islands

Anegada

The Settlement

CARIBBEAN SEA

Virgin Gorda

Spanish Town

Ginger Island

Cooper Island

Salt Island

Tortola

Road Town

Jost Van Dyke

Peter Island

Norman Island

St. John

PETER ISLAND RESORT

PETER ISLAND

Tel: +770 476 9988 **Fax:** +770 476 4979 **U.S./Canada Toll Free:** 1 800 346 4451
Web: www.johansens.com/peterislandresort **E-mail:** reservations@peterisland.com

Our inspector loved: *The privacy and exclusivity of Peter Island.*

Price Guide: (including breakfast, lunch and dinner, excluding 18% tax and service charges)
rooms U.S.$325-U.S.$1,170
junior suites U.S.$625-U.S.$1,835

Awards/Ratings: Condé Nast Traveler Gold List 2007

Attractions: Rhone Marine Park, 2 miles; Sunset at The Loop, 20-min drive; The Baths, Virgin Gorda, 30-min boat ride
Towns/Cities: Road Town, Tortola, 4 miles; Charlotte Amalie, St. Thomas, 90-min boat ride
Airports: Beef Island Airport, Tortola, 4 miles

Affiliations: Preferred Boutique

Located on its own pristine private island in the heart of the British Virgin Islands, Peter Island Resort offers unspoiled white sand beaches, turquoise waters, lush vegetation and an unforgettable Resort experience. Both the Ocean View Rooms and Beach Front Junior Suites offer stunning views of colorful gardens, palm-fringed Deadman's Bay and the shimmering sea from hammock-slung balconies. The Resort's grounds include tennis courts, a swimming pool, elegant beach-front Spa and fitness center, and delicious dining opportunities abound. The Tradewinds Restaurant serves international cuisine with a selection of local Caribbean flavors. Guests may reserve a spot in the Restaurant's Wine Room for a more intimate dining experience. Culinary events such as the weekly West Indian night and the magnificent Seafood Buffet ensure that you are well-fed, comfortable and happy at this Caribbean gem.

THE VILLAS AT PETER ISLAND

PETER ISLAND

Tel: +770 476 9988 **Fax:** +770 476 4979 **U.S./Canada Toll Free:** 1 800 346 4451
Web: www.johansens.com/villaspeterisland **E-mail:** reservations@peterisland.com

Our inspector loved: *These stunning villas in a fabulous location.*

Price Guide: (including breakfast, lunch, afternoon refreshments and dinner, excluding 18% tax and service charges)
3-6-bedroom villas U.S.$3,000-U.S.$15,000

Attractions: Rhone Marine Park, 2 miles; Sunset at The Loop, 20-min drive; The Baths, Virgin Gorda, 30-min boat ride
Towns/Cities: Road Town, Tortola, 4 miles; Charlotte Amalie, St. Thomas, 90-min boat ride
Airports: Beef Island Airport, Tortola, 4 miles

For those seeking the ultimate privacy a private island can offer, The Peter Island Resort offers The Villas at Peter Island: 3 elegantly furnished Villa Estates as luxurious as they are exclusive. Each Villa, nestled into the hillside overlooking the Caribbean Sea and surrounded by lush tropical vegetation, is customized according to guests' preferences so that when you arrive it is stocked with your preferred beverages, music and bedding, and ready to serve your favorite meals. Villas are individually designed although private plunge pools and wraparound sundecks are custom fittings, and a full private staff dedicated to most. Falcon's Nest, the most recent addition, offers 6 sumptuous master bedrooms and evokes an Old World Caribbean atmosphere with a modern perspective. It includes an infinity pool, cascading waterfall, swim-up pool bar, 2 kitchens and a custom couples Spa room.

BIRAS CREEK RESORT

NORTH SOUND, VIRGIN GORDA

Tel: +1 310 440 4225 **Fax:** +1 310 440 4220 **U.S./Canada Toll Free:** 1 800 223 1108
Web: www.johansens.com/birascreek **E-mail:** biras@biras.com

Our inspector loved: *Watching the sunset behind the North Sound Lagoon through the open walls of the hilltop restaurant.*

Price Guide: (including breakfast, lunch, afternoon tea, dinner and airport transfers with minimum 4-night stay, excluding tax)
rooms U.S.$675-U.S.$1,075
suites U.S.$1,200-U.S.$1,500

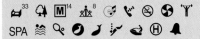

Awards/Ratings: Condé Nast Traveler Gold List 2006

Attractions: Snorkeling at Oil Nut Bay, 15-min boat ride; The Baths Day Trip, 40-min boat ride; Anegada Day Trip, 60-min boat ride
Airports: Beef Island Airport, Tortola, 30-min boat ride

Affiliations: Relais & Châteaux

This elegant and rustic hideaway, located on a 140-acre nature reserve, is accessible only by boat or helicopter. The 33 luxury suites are set amidst 3 distinct bodies of water: the North Sound; Atlantic Ocean; and Caribbean Bay. All feature a comfortable, stylish décor capitalizing on the outdoor beauty. Each suite has a lovely garden view or vista of Bercher's Bay on the Atlantic shore. Central to the property is a hilltop stone castle, which accommodates the reception, main dining room and a lovely terrace bar. The private white sand beach is a paradise for swimming, sailing, and snorkeling. Guests receive complimentary usage of Boston Whalers, Hobi sailboats, snorkel gear and windsurfing equipment. Sip afternoon tea in the Arawak Room overlooking the North Sound, enjoy the many hiking trails, or visit the Spa by the Sea, which uses signature Decléor aromatherapy treatments. The restaurant has an extensive wine menu and offers European and Caribbean dishes.

Westpunt

Lagún

Barber

Soto

CARIBBEAN SEA

San Willebrordus

Tera Kora

Grote Berg

Hato Airport

Sint Michiel

Buena Vista

Emmastad

Sinta Catharina

Santa Rosa

WILLEMSTAD

Salina

362

New Port

AVILA HOTEL ON THE BEACH

PENSTRAAT 130, WILLEMSTAD

Tel: +599 9 461 4377 **Fax:** +599 9 461 1493 **U.S./Canada Toll Free:** 1 800 747 8162
Web: www.johansens.com/avilabeach **E-mail:** info@avilahotel.com

Our inspector loved: *The spectacular ocean views.*

Price Guide: (excluding 12% service charge and 7% tax, breakfast $15)
rooms U.S.$200-U.S.$420
suites U.S.$290-U.S.$1,500

Attractions: Seaquarium, 3-min drive; Dive Center, 3-min drive
Towns/Cities: Willemstad, 10-min walk
Airports: Curaçao Hato Airport, 30-min drive

Originally the governor's residence, this hotel is a stunning testament to classic and contemporary Dutch-Caribbean-style architecture. The interiors are simply breathtaking: the "Blues Wing" consists of rooms on a pier, with vaulted ceilings in white and soft pastel colors and features Caribbean wicker and cane furniture. These rooms look out to a panoramic vista across the ocean and have a private balcony or terrace. The luxurious Octagon Wing has spacious rooms decorated in pastels with splashes of Caribbean colors, and there is also the amazing top-floor Bolivar Suite; an absolute indulgence! Renowned for its fine outdoor dining, you are truly spoiled for choice with the convivial Avila Café, the casual elegant Belle Terrace and the cool Blues Bar and Seafood Restaurant. Relax au Paradis spa offers a wide range of body and beauty treatments for men and women.

ATLANTIC OCEAN

San Felipe de
Puerto Plata

Gregorio Luperon
Int. Airport

San Fernando de
Monte Cristi

Cap-Haïtien

Mao

Dajabón

Santiago
de los Caballeros

Moca

Salcedo

Nagua

Santa Bárbara
de Samaná

Ouanaminthe

San Ignacio de
Sabaneta

San Francisco
de Macorís

HAITI

Concepcíon de
La Vega

Cotui

Hinche

Bonao

Monte Plata

Santa Cruz
del Seibo

Elías Piña

San Juan
de la Maguana

Hato Mayor
del Rey

Salvaléon de
Higüey

Belladère

Punta Cana
Int'l Airport

Compostela de
Azua

Neiba

PORT-AU-
PRINCE

Jimaní

San
Cristóbal

SANTO
DOMINGO

San Pedro
de Macorís

La Romana

Las Americas
Int. Airport

Bani

DOMINICAN REPUBLIC

Jacmel

Maria Montez
Int. Airport

Barahona

Anse-à-Pitre

Pedernales

CARIBBEAN
SEA

CASA COLONIAL BEACH & SPA

P.O. BOX 22, PUERTO PLATA
Tel: +1 809 320 3232 **Fax:** +1 809 320 3131
Web: www.johansens.com/casacolonial **E-mail:** reservascc@vhhr.com

Our inspector loved: *A relaxing treatment at Bagua Spa in an ocean-front gazebo.*

Price Guide:
suites U.S.$350-U.S.$1,400

Attractions: Playa Dorada Golf Course, 3-min walk; Playa Dorada Mall, 5-min walk; Ocean World, 20-min drive; Imbert Waterfall, 45-min drive
Towns/Cities: Puerto Plata, 5 miles; Sosua 16 miles; Cabarete, 25 miles; Santiago, 47 miles
Airports: Puerto Plata Airport, 15-min drive

Affiliations: Small Luxury Hotels of the World

Known for its stately Victorian houses and views of the Atlantic Ocean, Casa Colonial, with its style of a private estate nestled in the warmth of a Caribbean island, offers European elegance. Many of the suites reflect the style of great plantations, while others reveal a contemporary flair. All exceed expectations of comfort. The sands of Playa Dorada suggest a swim before breakfast, while the infinity pool and 4 temperature controlled Jacuzzi whirlpools on the rooftop, provide hours of relaxation. Vibrant sunsets can be viewed from the beach or from the bars offering panoramic "vistas." A gazebo on the beach is perfect for parties and unique wedding or anniversary celebrations. Lucia restaurant serves international gourmet food, and Bagua Spa uses natural resources to create treatments rooted in the ancient healing arts as well as classic therapies. Local activities include sport fishing and a round at Playa Dorada's golf course designed by Robert Trent Jones Sr.

Union Island

Ashton • Clifton

Petit St Vincent

Carriacou

Windward

Bogles

Hillsborough

Six Roads

Mt Pleasant

Petite
Martinique

Dumfries

CARIBBEAN
SEA

Ronde Island

Nonpareil

Sauteurs

Morne
Fendue

Victoria

Union

Mt Rose

Tivoli

Gouyave

Grand Roy • Concord

Paradise

Grenville

Grenada

Constantine

Marquis

Fontenoy

ATLANTIC
OCEAN

SAINT GEORGE'S 366

Providence

Belmont

Saint David's

Grand
Anse   Woburn   Calivigny

Bacolet

SPICE ISLAND BEACH RESORT

GRAND ANSE BEACH, ST. GEORGE'S

Tel: +1 473 444 4423/4258 **Fax:** +1 473 444 4807
Web: www.johansens.com/spiceisland **E-mail:** spiceisl@spiceisle.com

Our inspector loved: The new palatial 1-bedroom beach suites.

Price Guide: (all inclusive)
singles U.S.$535-U.S.$1,220
doubles U.S.$635-U.S.$1,625
suites U.S.$935-U.S.$2,475

Powdery white sands, the crystal clear waters of the Caribbean Sea and the shade of palm trees create the backdrop for this relaxing paradise. Courtyards and terraces are filled with tropical flora and fauna while bedrooms have breathtaking views of the sea or gardens. For the ultimate in luxury there are the 1,440 sq. ft. 1-bedroom Cinnamon and Saffron Suites set on the beach with wet bars, 6-person dining rooms, lounges and living rooms. The ocean-front restaurant serves an excellent table d'hôte menu, a Caribbean buffet on Friday nights and a barbecue lunch buffet on Sundays. In the evenings, international cuisine, with local and Creole infusions, can be enjoyed with local entertainment 3-6 times a week. Janissa's Spa boasts indoor and outdoor treatment rooms, a sauna and Jacuzzi.

Awards/Ratings: Condé Nast Johansens Most Excellent Business Partner, The Americas, Atlantic, Caribbean & Pacific Islands 2007

Attractions: Annadale Falls, 20-min drive; Grand Etang Rainforest and Lake, 35-min drive
Towns/Cities: St. George's, 15-min drive
Airports: Point Salines International Airport, 10-min drive

Jamaica

CARIBBEAN SEA

Lucea

Montego Bay 368

370 369

Falmouth

Rio Bueno

St. Ann's Bay

371

Ocho Rios

Port Maria

Montpelier

Negril

Savanna la Mar

Newmarket

Balaclava

Buff Bay

Ewarton

Port Antonio

Black River

Mandeville

Chapelton

May Pen

Spanish Town

KINGSTON

Bowden

Alligator Pond

Morant Bay

Portland Cave

CARIBBEAN SEA

CARIBBEAN - JAMAICA (MONTEGO BAY)

HALF MOON

ROSE HALL, MONTEGO BAY

Tel: +1 876 953 2211 **Fax:** +1 876 953 2731 **U.S./Canada Toll Free:** 1 866 648 6951
Web: www.johansens.com/halfmoon **E-mail:** reservations@halfmoon.com

Our inspector loved: The announcement that Fern Tree, The Spa at Half Moon, was opening in 2007.

Price Guide: (room only, excluding tax and service charge)
rooms U.S.$250-U.S.400
suites U.S.$380-U.S.$1,520

Attractions: Dunn's River Falls, 60 miles
Towns/Cities: Montego Bay, 6 miles
Airports: Sangster International Airport, 5 miles

Set in 400 acres of tropical gardens edged by a crescent-shaped bay and a 1.5 miles white sandy beach, this elegant, luxurious resort offers a wide variety of accommodations including 68 rooms and suites and 32 Royal Villas offering 5, 6 or 7 bedrooms, a private porch and pool, butler service, a maid and cook. For sheer indulgence stay in one of the 11 truly opulent Imperial Suites. Half Moon has no less than 6 restaurants ranging from the open-air Seagrape Terrace to the romantic Il Giardino and enchanting gourmet Sugar Mill. Enjoy your surroundings and swim with the dolphins, play on one of the 13 tennis courts, 4 squash courts or the 18-hole championship golf course, with pro-shop and the only David Leadbetter Golf Academy in The Caribbean.

ROUND HILL HOTEL AND VILLAS

P.O. BOX 64, MONTEGO BAY

Tel: +1 876 956 7050 **Fax:** +1 876 956 7505 **U.S./Canada Toll Free:** 1 800 972 2159
Web: www.johansens.com/roundhill **E-mail:** info@roundhilljamaica.com

Our inspector loved: The fabulous style and unique experience of this beautiful place.

Price Guide:
hotel rooms U.S.$370-U.S.$590
villa suites U.S.$410-U.S.$920
villa (exclusive use) U.S.$780-U.S.$4,100

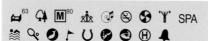 SPA

Attractions: Tryall Golf Course, 2 miles; Montego Bay Shopping, 6 miles
Towns/Cities: Montego Bay, 6 miles
Airports: Sangster International Airport, 8 miles

For over 50 years Round Hill has extended a special welcome and exemplary service to the most celebrated guests whose glamorous gatherings are captured in photographs adorning the famous Piano Bar. The 36 ocean-front rooms in the Pineapple House Hotel have been designed by Ralph Lauren with four-posters, 2 double beds or king-sized beds in mahogany-stained bamboo draped in white net and fitted with 300-count Egyptian cotton white sheets. Nestling in lusciously landscaped, subtropical hillside gardens are 27 cottages; most have a private pool and personal staff to ensure an unforgettable experience. The spa at Welcome Wharf offers a seductive choice of individualized treatments including yoga classes, Elemis pure aromatherapy skin care and professional therapy treatments.

TRYALL CLUB

P.O. BOX 1206, MONTEGO BAY
Tel: +1 876 956 5660 **Fax:** +1 876 956 5673 **U.S./Canada Toll Free:** 1 800 238 5290
Web: www.johansens.com/tryallclub **E-mail:** reservation@tryallclub.com

Our inspector loved: The stylish individuality of the villas, their privacy and stunning views.

Price Guide: (per week)
villas U.S.$2,750-U.S.$30,000

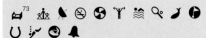

Attractions: Chukka Blue, 5-min drive; Mountain Valley Rafting, 40-min drive; Mayfield Falls, 45-min drive; Negril Beach, 45-min drive
Towns/Cities: Montego Bay, 12 miles; Lucea, 15 miles; Negril, 35 miles
Airports: Montego Bay Jamaica, Sangster International Airport, 12 miles; Norman Manley International Airport, Kingston, 220 miles

Along an avenue of tall, elegant coconut palms, is the imposing 18th-century "Georgian Great House" and Restaurant. A home-from-home on a grand estate of 2,200 acres, the individually designed and furnished, privately owned villas include the intriguingly named "No Problem" and "Satisfy my Soul". They offer from 1 to 7 bedrooms, private pools and full-time staff including a cook, maid, laundress and butler. The 18-hole, 72 par golf course, designed by Ralph Plummer, has hosted the Johnnie Walker World Championship, the Jamaica Classic and Mazda Championship. This challenging course enjoys a panorama of forest green hills, coconut palms, fruit trees, lily ponds and a full half-mile along the Caribbean shore. Facilities also include 9 "Nova-Cushion" night illuminated tennis courts.

ROYAL PLANTATION

MAIN STREET , P.O. BOX 2, OCHO RIOS, ST. ANN
Tel: +1 876 974 5601 **Fax:** +1 876 974 5912 **U.S./Canada Toll Free:** 1 888 48 ROYAL
Web: www.johansens.com/royalplantation **E-mail:** info@royalplantation.com

Our inspector loved: *Enjoying champagne and caviar in the C-Bar.*

Price Guide:
premium ocean-front junior suite U.S.$615
luxury ocean-front junior suite U.S.$650
honeymoon grande luxe ocean-front suite U.S.$750

Attractions: Glass Bottom Boat Tours, close by; Swimming with Dolphins, 15-min drive; Dunn's River Falls, 15-min drive
Towns/Cities: Ocho Rios, 10-min drive; Montego Bay, 90-min drive; Kinston, 2-hour drive
Airports: Montego Bay Airport, 90-min drive; Kinston Airport, 2-hour drive

Affiliations: The Leading Small Hotels of the World

Whether you are soaking up the sun sipping ice cold "mangosas" delivered by your beach butler, taking afternoon tea on the terrace, or indulging in a glass or two of champagne in the C-Bar, Royal Plantation knows exactly how to give you the perfect experience! Built in the glamorous 1950s, this serene sanctuary maintains a stellar reputation as one of Jamaica's most exquisite resort-inns. Royal Plantation sits on a bluff soaring 25ft. above the shimmering Caribbean, granting each of its 74 sumptuous suites heart-stopping views of the ocean. Bask on the spectacular twin beaches soaking in the sunshine or enjoy the complete privacy of Villa Plantana set in its own garden with 3 bedrooms, a private pool and butler. A superb choice of Italian or French cuisine, complemented by excellent wines, can be savored in the elegant surroundings of La Terrazza and Le Papillon restaurants. A visit to the Red Lane Spa is essential; try the "Lover's Lane" package, perfect pampering for two!

ATLANTIC
OCEAN

Puerto Rico

Isla desecheo

Isabela

Arecibo

Vega Baja

373

Aguadilla

Manatí

SAN JUAN

Rincon

San Sebastián

Bayamon

Carolina

Rio Grande

Luquillo

Isla de
Culebra

374

Añasco

Utuado

Comerio

Caguas

Fajardo

Mayagüez

Maricao

Baranquitas

Naguabo

Isabel Segunda

San Germán

Adjuntas

Cayey

Humacao

Esperanza

Isla de Mona

Yauco

Coamo

Yubucoa

Isla de Vieques

Boquerón

Ponce

Guayama

Guanica

Santa
Isabel

Salinas

Isla Caja
de Muertos

CARIBBEAN SEA

372

CHATEAU CERVANTES

RECINTO SUR 329, OLD SAN JUAN
Tel: +787 724 7722 **Fax:** +787 289 8909
Web: www.johansens.com/cervantes **E-mail:** reservations@cervantespr.com

Our inspector loved: The intimacy of this boutique hotel in the heart of Old San Juan.

Price Guide:
superior room U.S.$225-U.S.$300
presidential suite U.S.$1,500-U.S.$2,700

Attractions: El Morro Castle, San Cristobal Fortress, La Fortaleza, close by; Cathedral of San Juan, 5-min walk; Puerto Rico Art Museum, 10 miles; El Yunque Rainforest and Luquillo Beach, 25 miles
Towns/Cities: Old San Juan, on-site; Metropolitan San Juan/Condado, 3 miles; Isla Verde Beach, 10 miles
Airports: Luis Munoz Marin International Airport, 9 miles

Named for the author of Don Quixote, Chateau Cervantes is characterized by a combination of modern elegance, classic sophistication and a warm, personal ambience, brought to you in the heart of San Juan. The spacious accommodations inside this restored 16th-century building, with their tall, gracefully arched doorways and striking contemporary art by famous local artists, offer a custom-line of natural body care products in marble-tiled bathrooms and private balconies with views of the city. Larger suites offer a personalized butler service. Panza, the boutique hotel's aptly named restaurant, serves innovative, flavorful international cuisine presented with elegance in its high-ceilinged, mirrored dining room. Ask the knowledgeable wait staff for advice on choosing a vintage from the restaurant's extensive wine list.

CARIBBEAN - SAINT-BARTHÉLEMY (ANSE DE TOINY)

LE TOINY

ANSE DE TOINY
Tel: +590 590 27 88 88 **Fax:** +590 590 27 89 30
Web: www.johansens.com/letoiny **E-mail:** reservations@letoiny.com

Our inspector loved: *The privacy of each villa.*

Price Guide:
junior suite €495-€750
1-bedroom villa €675-€1,750
2/3-bedroom villa €1,250-€3,150

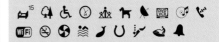

Awards/Ratings: Condé Nast Traveler Gold List 2006

Attractions: Shell Museum, 15-min drive
Towns/Cities: Gustavia, 15-min drive
Airports: Gustaf III Airport, 5 miles

Affiliations: Relais & Châteaux

Le Toiny is nestled on a hillside, overlooking the rugged Bay of Toiny, on the south-eastern tip of the idyllic island of St. Barths. The hues and architecture of its villas are reminiscent of traditional French plantation homes with interiors that feature mahogany furnishings and original four-poster beds handcrafted by native craftsmen. Each villa offers seclusion and comfort, and has its own heated private pool. The main house contains the Case Bar and renowned Le Gaiac restaurant, which offers French gourmet cuisine accented with a Creole undertone. Massages and beauty treatments are available from the Ligne St. Barth from the Caribbean's leading health advisors, and fitness and wellness machines can be delivered to your villa for that added special attention.

HOTEL GUANAHANI & SPA

GRAND CUL DE SAC

Tel: +590 590 27 66 60 **Fax:** +590 590 27 70 70 **U.S./Canada Toll Free:** 1 800 216 3774
Web: www.johansens.com/guanahani **E-mail:** guanahani@wanadoo.fr

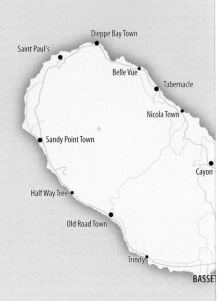

Our inspector loved: *The "Wellness Suite" where guests have private key access to the spa and pool after hours.*

Price Guide: (including Continental or American breakfast, non-motorized water sports and airport/port transfers)
rooms €350-€1,295
suites €705-€1,515
la villa €2,550-€5,670

Awards/Ratings: Condé Nast Traveler Gold List 2006

Attractions: Shops, 10-min drive; Beach, on-site
Towns/Cities: St. Jean, 10-min drive; Gustavia, 20-min drive
Airports: Gustaf III Airport, 15-min drive

Affiliations: The Leading Small Hotels of the World

This delightful luxury resort is set in a beautiful location overlooking 2 private bays on a private 16-acre peninsula. Its pastel interiors with bright furnishings, rich mahogany floors and tropical woods in each of the bungalow-styled suites creates an ideal romantic honeymoon getaway. Gourmet cuisine is central to Guanahani: Executive Chef Philippe Masseglia creates international cuisine with a French flair in Bartolomeo and Indigo is a casual poolside restaurant overlooking the beach. The exquisite menu at Bartolomeo is complemented by nightly music, while the Lounge Bart'ô bar is a pleasant setting for pre-dinner cocktails. The open-air Spa by Clarins offers 8 treatment rooms, hammam ritual bath, beauty salon, herbal tea room and Frederic Fekkai hairdressing salon. Private boat, plane and helicopter charters can be arranged, and complimentary children's programs are available.

CARIBBEAN SEA

LE SERENO

GRAND CUL DE SAC

Tel: +590 590 298 300 **Fax:** +590 590 277 547
Web: www.johansens.com/lesereno **E-mail:** info...

Sitting on 600 feet of pristine white sandy beach, Le S...
elegance with an exquisite natural location. The re...
offer every desirable technology, including WiFi, co...
plasma T.V.s and iPods with docking stations, as w...
exemplified by the custom-made bathrobes and to...
Voto Paris amenities, down comforters set on king-...
terraces overlooking private gardens. The resort fe...
center, a bar and lounge, a seaside fresh-water s...
Restaurant des Pêcheurs serves fresh seafood in...
setting. Designed by famed Parisian architect Chris...
are modern yet classical with whites and rich woo...
stylish design.

MONTPELIER PLANTATION INN

P.O. BOX 474, NEVIS

Tel: +1 869 469 3462 **Fax:** +1 869 469 2932
Web: www.johansens.com/montpelierplantation **E-mail:** info@montpeliernevis.com

Located 750 feet above the sea on the slopes of Mount Nevis, this completely refurbished inn was once a sugar estate and in 1787 the venue for Horatio Nelson and Fanny Nisbet's wedding. Today, the Hoffman family has created a "country house" hotel ambience with an informal style and unspoiled tranquility. Each of the rooms is designed to catch the breeze and has a private veranda offering stunning views of the sea, mountains and the lights of Nevis and St. Kitts at night. The Plantation rooms are recently refurbished and the new Villa Suite has a private pool and 2 bedrooms. A large freshwater pool is found in the tropical gardens and during the day a complimentary bus service travels to the inn's private 2-acre Caribbean beach. The inn's Nevisian and international chefs create classic cuisine with a Caribbean contemporary twist using fresh local produce, and after cocktails in The Great Room, dinner is served outside on The Terrace or inside The Mill.

Our inspector loved: *Intimate dining by candlelight in the inn's 18th-century sugar mill.*

Price Guide: (including English breakfast, afternoon tea, private beach access with transfers and book and D.V.D. rental)
premier U.S.$290-U.S.$490
plantation U.S.$325-U.S.$525
suite U.S.$365-U.S.$900

Attractions: The Botanical Gardens, 5-min walk; Horatio Nelson Museum, 3 miles; 18th-Century Thermal Baths, 3 miles
Towns/Cities: Charlestown, 4 miles
Airports: Nevis Airport, 25-min drive

Affiliations: Relais & Châteaux

ATLANTIC
OCEAN

Gros Islet

Marisule Estate

Grande Rivière

Marquis

★ CASTRIES

Grande Anse

Cicéron

Forestière

La Croix
Maingot

Dernière Rivière

Anse la Raye

Dennery

Canaries

Millet

Praslin

382
383
384

Soufrière

Fond St. Jacques

Micoud

Desruisseaux

La Pointe

Morne
Vert

Choiseul

Saint-Urbain

Laborie

CARIBBEAN
SEA

Vieux Fort

ANSE CHASTANET

SOUFRIÈRE

Tel: +1 758 459 7000 **Fax:** +1 758 459 7700 **U.S./Canada Toll Free:** 1 800 223 1108
Web: www.johansens.com/ansechastanet **E-mail:** ansechastanet@candw.lc

Our inspector loved: The beach-front location with pristine coral reefs right off shore, and the Piton Mountains views from open-air rooms.

Price Guide: (double occupancy, excluding tax, winter rates include breakfast and dinner)
standard U.S.$280-U.S.$575
superior U.S.$360-U.S.$850
beach/hillside U.S.$600-U.S.$965

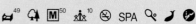

Awards/Ratings: Condé Nast Traveler Gold List 2006

This romantic hideaway is situated on a 600-acre estate with 2 stunning natural beaches and 2 natural valleys, capped off by spectacular mountains. Each of the bedrooms incorporates locally crafted furniture and features art from local and international artists. Scattered over the flower-decked hillside, many of the bedrooms benefit from views of the Piton Mountains and Caribbean Sea; 12 are found at beach level and are just a few steps from the water's edge. Piton Restaurant serves tropical world cuisine while the more informal beach-side restaurant offers Creole and traditional favorites. The resort operates its own P.A.D.I. 5-star Gold Palm/S.S.I. scuba center and there is also mountain biking, the resort's 42-ft. yacht, a library and art gallery to browse around. Kai Belte offers traditional and Ayurvedic treatments from professional therapists.

Attractions: Marine Park, close by; Botanical Gardens, 15-min drive; Volcano and Sulphur Springs, 25-min drive; Rainforest, 35-min drive
Towns/Cities: Soufrière, 1.5 miles; Castries, 27 miles
Airports: Hewanorra International Airport, 60-min drive

JADE MOUNTAIN AT ANSE CHASTANET

SOUFRIÈRE

Tel: +1 758 459 4000 **Fax:** +1 758 459 4002 **U.S./Canada Toll Free:** 1 800 223 1108
Web: www.johansens.com/jademountain **E-mail:** jademountain@ansechastanet.com

Our inspector loved: *Each sanctuary's private infinity pool, surfaced in glass tiles and illuminated at night with colored fiber-optic lights.*

Price Guide: (double occupancy, excluding tax, including breakfast and dinner)
star sanctuaries U.S.$1,150-U.S.$1,600
moon sanctuaries U.S.$1,300-U.S.$1,750
sun sanctuaries U.S.$1,600-U.S.$2,050

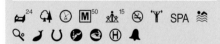

Attractions: Marine Park, close by; Botanical Gardens, 15-min drive; Volcano and Sulphur Springs, 25-min drive; Rainforest, 35-min drive
Towns/Cities: Soufrière, 1.5 miles; Castries, 27 miles
Airports: Hewanorra International Airport, 60-min drive

Jade Mountain is a beautifully designed "resort within a resort" that combines sophistication and style with its pristine setting. The star, moon and sun sanctuaries, individually designed by owner/architect Nick Troubetzkoy, have tropical hardwood floors, stunning private infinity pools and unparalleled views of the Pitons and Caribbean Sea. To create a living experience where you can become one with your surroundings, the fourth wall of each sanctuary is missing and beautiful one-of-a-kind glass tiles extend from the infinity pool to the bathroom. All furnishings are locally made and sanctuaries are deliberately "techno-free". Enjoy Anse Chastanet's 2 unspoiled beaches, magnificent coral reefs, scuba center and the Jungle Biking Center. The Jade Mountain Club serves drinks and light meals in a casual setting.

LADERA RESORT

SOUFRIÈRE

Tel: +1 758 459 7323 **Fax:** +1 758 459 5156 **U.S./Canada Toll Free:** 1 800 738 4752
Web: www.johansens.com/ladera **E-mail:** ladera@candw.lc

This hilltop resort is nestled in mango groves and takes full advantage of its natural surroundings. All of the secluded suites and villas are designed with an "open wall" that faces west, affording breathtaking views of the 2 volcanic Piton peaks and the ocean, and feature private plunge or swimming pools. Dasheene serves an eclectic, stylish interpretation of St. Lucian cuisine and offers a menu of fresh fish caught by the island's fishermen and fruits and vegetables that are grown locally. Cooking classes are available every Saturday morning. Enjoy cocktails at the Tcholit Bar or by the infinity pool, and a relaxing treatment at the Ti Kai Posé Spa. Staff will organize activities such as hiking and rainforest walks, sailing excursions and island tours.

Our inspector loved: *The feeling of "hiding away" in a luxurious treehouse, where the Piton Mountains seem only a touch away.*

Price Guide: (including breakfast, afternoon tea, resort facilities, beach shuttle and snorkeling equipment)
rooms U.S.$375-U.S.$660
suites U.S.$560-U.S.$810
villas U.S.$430-U.S.$705

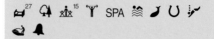

Awards/Ratings: Condé Nast Traveler Gold List 2007; Condé Nast Johansens Most Excellent Resort 2006

Attractions: Piton Mountains, 10-min drive; Diamond Waterfalls, 15-min drive; Botanical Gardens, 15-min drive; Rainforest Tours, 40-min drive
Towns/Cities: Soufrière, 2 miles
Airports: Hewanorra Intl. Airport, 40-min drive

CARIBBEAN
SEA

Grand Case

French
Cul de Sac

Saint-Martin

Orleans

MARIGOT

Terres
Basses

Mornes
Rouge

Columbier

386

South Reward

Lowlands

St. Peter

Cul de Sac

Almond Grove

Sucker
Garden

Billy Folly

PHILIPSBURG

Point
Blanche

Sint Maarten

LA SAMANNA

P.O. BOX 4077, 97064 CEDEX
Tel: +590 590 87 64 00 **Fax:** +590 590 87 87 86 **U.S./Canada Toll Free:** 1 800 854 2252
Web: www.johansens.com/lasamanna **E-mail:** reservations@lasamanna.com

Our inspector loved: *The new infinity-edge pool with views of the pristine Baie Long Beach where you can dine or have drinks at sunset.*

Price Guide:
rooms from U.S.$475
suites U.S.$1,750-U.S.$5,400

Awards/Ratings: Condé Nast Traveler Gold List 2007

Attractions: Cupecoy Beach, 1 mile; Marigot Market, 6 miles; Loterie Farm, 7 miles; Butterfly Farm, 10 miles
Towns/Cities: Marigot, 6 miles; Grand Case, 12 miles; Orient, 15 miles; Phillipsburg, 15 miles
Airports: Princess Juliana Airport, 4 miles

Affiliations: The Leading Hotels of the World

Cloaked in lush foliage with colorful splashes of flowers, this elegant resort appeals to discriminating, international travelers looking for seclusion, relaxation, fine dining and attentive personalized service. La Samanna evokes a French spirit with a Caribbean soul and offers 81 suites located on 55 acres of breathtaking beach-front. The comfortable suites range from 1 to 3 bedrooms with private terraces and rich amenities; there are 5 specialty suites. The Baie Longue Suite is an exclusive 3-bedroom Presidential Suite; often a celebrity hideaway. After a day at the beach, savor French-Caribbean cuisine at the Grill or in the elegant restaurant. Bar de Champagne and the Beach Bar are popular gathering spots. Wine enthusiasts will enjoy the award-winning wine cellar with over 10,000 bottles. Take a Pilates class at the only studio in the Caribbean or have a treatment at the world-class Elysées Spa.

Fancy

St. Vincent

Orange Hill

Chateaubelair

Georgetown

Barrouallie

Layou

Biabou

Mesopotamia

KINGSTOWN

Stubbs

CARIBBEAN
SEA

Bequia

Port Elizabeth

Little Nevis

Battowia

Isle-à-quatre

Baliceaux

The Pillories

Lovell Village
388 *Mustique*

Little Mustique

Savan Island

Little Canouan

Canouan

Charlestown

Sation Hill

Mayreau *Tobago cays*

Union Island

ATLANTIC
OCEAN

Ashton
Clifton **389** *Palm Island*

Frigate Island

Petit St. Vincent

Petit Martinique

GRENADA

Carriacou

FIREFLY

MUSTIQUE ISLAND

Tel: +1 784 488 8414 **Fax:** +1 784 488 8514
Web: www.johansens.com/firefly **E-mail:** stan@fireflymustique.com

Our inspector loved: *Firefly's bar lounge, a lively place during the evening, with its grand piano and impromptu perfomances by the occasional star guest!*

Price Guide: (including breakfast, lunch, afternoon tea and dinner, flight transfer from Barbados to Mustique and a motorized "mule")
rooms U.S.$850-U.S.$950

Attractions: Basil's Bar, close by; Firefly Bequia, 8 miles; Tobago Keys, 8 miles
Airports: Mustique Airport, 5-min drive

Exquisitely perched on a hillside with amazing views of the Caribbean Sea, this boutique hotel offers 5 light and airy individually designed bedrooms. All rooms feature fully loaded iPods, four-poster beds, and mesmerizing views of the sea; some come with "tropical plunge pools". Lush tropical gardens criss-crossed by paths, surround the hotel. A pagoda has comfortable lounge chairs looking out at the garden and sea and hammocks are idyllically placed by the pool and Jacuzzi. Dining on the covered terrace affords beautiful sunset views and the frequently changing menu features fresh seafood in a Caribbean style alongside an excellent choice of international wines. Each guest has the use of a "mule" (motorized vehicle) to explore this unspoiled island.

PALM ISLAND

PALM ISLAND

Tel: +1 954 481 8787 **Fax:** +1 954 481 1661 **U.S./Canada Toll Free:** 1 800 858 4618
Web: www.johansens.com/palmisland **E-mail:** reservations@eliteislandresorts.com

Our inspector loved: *Playing Robinson Crusoe in this luxurious paradise.*

Price Guide: (including all meals, beverages, non-motorized water sports, Internet access, tax, service charge and transfer from Union Island)
rooms U.S.$650-U.S.$1,090
island lofts U.S.$775-U.S.$1,315
suites U.S.$745-U.S.$1,485

Attractions: Tobago Cays, 30-min boat ride
Towns/Cities: Union Island, 5-min boat ride; St. Vincent, 15-min flight
Airports: Union Island, 10-min flight

This is a tranquil paradise of dazzling white sand beaches fringed with palms, breathtaking seascapes and tropical landscapes. There are 5 beaches, a swimming pool with cascading waterfalls, 2 bars, 2 restaurants, a vast range of activities and, at an additional charge, boat trips to the nearby Tobago Cays. Accommodation is simple but stylish; all guest rooms have air conditioning, rattan and bamboo furniture, original artwork and a balcony or patio. The Palm View and Beachfront bungalows are nestled among shady palm trees and colorful gardens, just a few yards from the sand and with views of distant islands, and the stilted Island Lofts - individual wooden cottages - have private terraces, deep-soaking tubs and a separate shower. Gourmet meals are enjoyed in the Royal Palm, while casual, grill-type fare is served in the Sunset Beach Restaurant.

West Caicos

Providenciales

Blue Hills

✈ Providenciales

395
396
394
393 **391**

Parrot Cay

392 ✈ Sandy Point

Whitby

Kew

North Caicos

Bottle Creek

A T L A N T I C
O C E A N

Conch Bar

Bambarra

C A I C O S   B A N K

Middle Caicos

Lorimers

Jacksonville   *East Caicos*

Cockburn Harbour ✈   *South Caicos*

Ambergris Cays

T U R K S   I S L A N D S   P A S S A G E

Grand Turk

Salt Cay   ✈ Cockburn Town

Balfour Town

GRACE BAY CLUB

P.O. BOX 128, PROVIDENCIALES

Tel: +1 649 946 5050 **Fax:** +1 649 946 5758 **U.S./Canada Toll Free:** 1 800 946 5757
Web: www.johansens.com/gracebayclub **E-mail:** info@gracebayclub.com

Our inspector loved: *The fresh grilled Mahi-Mahi in the new seaside, open-air Grill located near the outdoor fire.*

Price Guide: (including breakfast)
rooms U.S.$501-U.S.$3,482
suites U.S.$3,295-U.S.$8,470

Awards/Ratings: Condé Nast Johansens Most Excellent Resort, Atlantic, Caribbean & Pacific Islands 2007; Condé Nast Traveler Gold List 2006 and 2007

Attractions: Turtle Cove Marina, 3 miles; Provo Golf Club, 3 miles; Conch Farm, 4 miles
Towns/Cities: Leeward Marina, 3 miles
Airports: Providenciales Intl. Airport, 7 miles

Affiliations: The Leading Small Hotels of the World

Many high profile celebrities have stayed at this paradise with white sands, pristine waters and clear blue skies. Its magnificent suites feature eclectic furnishings, large terraces with ocean views, luxurious linens and have a spacious design that creates a harmonious balance blending into the natural surroundings. The original 21-suite hotel is restricted to adults but the recently built 38-suite villas, complete with Euro-Caribbean Anani Spa, are ideal for family vacations and offer organized water sports, hiking, cycling and eco-tourism activities. Alfresco dining is available at the Grill and Bar, and the beach-side award-winning Anacaona restaurant has a comprehensive fine wines list. Funky world music and modern décor set the scene in the ocean-front Lounge, where you may sip cocktails at sunset or try a delicious vintage rum.

PARROT CAY

P.O. BOX 164, PROVIDENCIALES
Tel: +1 649 946 7788 **Fax:** +1 649 946 7789 **U.S./Canada Toll Free:** 1 877 754 0726
Web: www.johansens.com/parrotcay **E-mail:** res@parrotcay.como.bz

Our inspector loved: The Dr. Perricone facial at the COMO Shambhala Retreat.

Price Guide: (incl. breakfast and transfer to/from airport, excl. service charge and 10% tax)
rooms U.S.$535-U.S.$950
suites U.S.$1,270-U.S.$1,580
villas US.$2,245-U.S.$10,000

Awards/Ratings: Condé Nast Johansens Most Excellent Spa Hotel 2007

Attractions: Iguana Island, 20-min boat ride; Bottom Reef Fishing; 20-min boat ride; Provo Golf & Country Club, 30-min boat ride; Sand Dollar Island, 30-min boat ride
Towns/Cities: Providenciales, 10 miles
Airports: Providenciales Intl. Airport, 10 miles

Affiliations: Leading Small Hotels of the World

Parrot Cay is a 1,000-acre private island surrounded by over 3 miles of unspoiled white sand and clear turquoise water. There is a combination of rooms, suites and villas from garden and ocean-facing rooms with four-poster beds to ocean-front beach houses, 30 meters from the beach. The larger villas, Parrot Cay Estates, come complete with a private butler. The interiors are sleek with white-washed walls accentuated by clean-lined teak furniture, expansive bathrooms and soft linens. In the main building of the hotel the Terrace Restaurant & Bar serves a Mediterranean influenced menu, while Lotus, the poolside restaurant, offers light meals at lunchtime and Asian and Caribbean cuisine at dinner. COMO Shambhala Retreat has extensive facilities including specialized therapists who administer Asian-inspired holistic treatments.

POINT GRACE

P.O. BOX 700, PROVIDENCIALES

Tel: +1 649 946 5096 **Fax:** +1 649 946 5097 **U.S./Canada Toll Free:** 1 866 924 7223
Web: www.johansens.com/pointgrace **E-mail:** reservations@pointgrace.com

Our inspector loved: *The in-suite private chef services.*

Price Guide:
suites U.S.$425-U.S.$2,500
penthouse U.S.$4,000-U.S.$7,500

Awards/Ratings: Condé Nast Traveler Gold List 2006

Attractions: Provo Golf Club, 2 miles; Conch Farm, 2 miles
Airports: Providenciales International Airport, 6 miles

This exceptional hideaway is beautifully designed and overlooks spectacular views of the pristine 12-mile beach of Grace Bay. The attention to detail is inspiring with its cool colors, stylish fabrics and tastefully decorated suites. Each suite is filled with exquisite Indonesian teak furniture and has an expansive living area and luxurious bathroom. Grace's Cottage, the elegant gourmet restaurant, is open for dinner, while breakfast and lunch are served at Hutchings. Bar service is available throughout the day and complimentary bottled water and mister service is available at the pool and beach. Outdoor pursuits include diving and sailing in the clear waters and coral reefs, and the marine parks and wildlife reserves in the area are exciting to explore.

THE SOMERSET ON GRACE BAY

PRINCESS DRIVE, PROVIDENCIALES
Tel: +1 649 946 5900 **Fax:** +1 649 946 5944
Web: www.johansens.com/somersetgracebay **E-mail:** reservations@thesomerset.com

Our inspector loved: *The romantic gourmet dining at O'Soleil restaurant and cocktails in the Pearl Lounge.*

Price Guide: (including Continental breakfast)
suites U.S.$570-U.S.$3,000
3-5-bedroom suites U.S.$1,080-U.S.$7,200

On the water's edge of Grace Bay Beach, this luxury resort comprises several accommodations: Estate Suites, Stirling House and English Cottages. The spectacular Estate Suites range from 1 to 5-bedroom suites with panoramic ocean views, marble baths, private outdoor Jacuzzis, gourmet kitchens, wired audio systems and spacious terraces. The Stirling House also offers ocean views, a master suite and many of the exquisite amenities of the Estate Suites. The charming English Cottages have lovely garden views. Central to the resort is the beautiful infinity pool with underwater surround stereo system and lap current for swimming. Enjoy a tropical drink or casual fare at the poolside bar before sampling gourmet cuisine at O'Soleil. Rejuvenate and pamper yourself with a spa treatment in the comfort of your very own suite, go diving, parasailing or take a tour of the local conch farm.

Attractions: Provo Golf Club, 2.5 miles; Smith's Reef, 3 miles; Conch Farm, 4 miles
Airports: Providenciales International Airport, 7 miles

Affiliations: Small Luxury Hotels of the World

TURKS & CAICOS CLUB

WEST GRACE BAY BEACH, P.O. BOX 687, PROVIDENCIALES
Tel: +1 649 946 5800 **Fax:** +1 649 946 5858
Web: www.johansens.com/turksandcaicos **E-mail:** info@turksandcaicosclub.com

Our inspector loved: *The intimate ocean-front setting where you can snorkel right off the hotel's sugary white sand beach.*

Price Guide: (including full American breakfast, closed September 1st-30th)
1-bedroom suite U.S.$315-U.S.$625
2-bedroom suite U.S.$525-U.S.$1,295

Attractions: Turtle Cove Marina, 1 mile; Bight Reef, 2-min walk; Provo Golf Club, 2 miles; Conch Farm, 4 miles
Airports: Providenciales International Airport, 3 miles

Located on a stunning stretch of the Grace Bay Beach's white sands, steps from the island's best snorkeling reef, this elegant Colonial-style mansion is the epitome of intimate island luxury. There are just 21 suites with 1 or 2 bedrooms featuring all the amenities of a private home-away-from-home. Ideal for romantic getaways or family vacations, each suite is beautifully designed with custom rattan furnishings, maple cabinetry, fully-fitted kitchens, four-poster beds and subtle safari prints. Large private balconies provide cool seclusion for a rejuvenating seaside massage. The discreet and friendly service ensures a relaxing stay. The popular Simba Restaurant & Bar offers Caribbean lobster and native conch. Simply relax on the beach with a tropical drink or go windsurfing, sea-kayaking, HobieCat sailing or snorkeling.

THE REGENT PALMS

P.O. BOX 681, GRACE BAY, PROVIDENCIALES
Tel: +649 946 8666 **Fax:** +649 946 5188 **U.S./Canada Toll Free:** 1 866 877 7756
Web: www.johansens.com/regentpalms **E-mail:** reservationstc@regentexperience.com

Our inspector loved: The signature spa treatment, "Mother of Pearl Body Exfoliation."

Price Guide: (including breakfast)
rooms U.S.$325-U.S.$1,400
suites U.S.$625-U.S.$4,700
3-bedroom penthouses U.S.$2,100-U.S.$6,500

Awards/Ratings: Condé Nast Traveler Gold List 2005

Attractions: Provo Golf Club, 5-min drive; Princess Alexandra Marine Park, 5-min drive; Turtle Cove Marina, 10-min drive; Conch Farm, 15-min drive
Airports: Providenciales International Airport, 15-min drive

Beautifully situated on 12 acres of landscaped gardens on the world-famous Grace Bay Beach, The Regent Palms is a stunning property with white-washed exteriors and the turquoise sea as its backdrop. Marble floors, impressive vaulted ceilings and custom-made mahogany furnishings offer you a residential feel. Luxury rooms and suites, some with ocean views, are elegantly appointed with cool Caribbean colors and feature hand-tufted king bedding. Daily butler service is available in the penthouses for those looking for a little extra pampering. Dine inside or alfresco by candlelight at Parallel23, which features wonderful Tropical Fusion cuisine with an impressive wine list of boutique wines from around the world. For more casual fare, the poolside Plunge restaurant is a nice option. World-class treatments at the 25,000 sq. ft. spa are sublime.

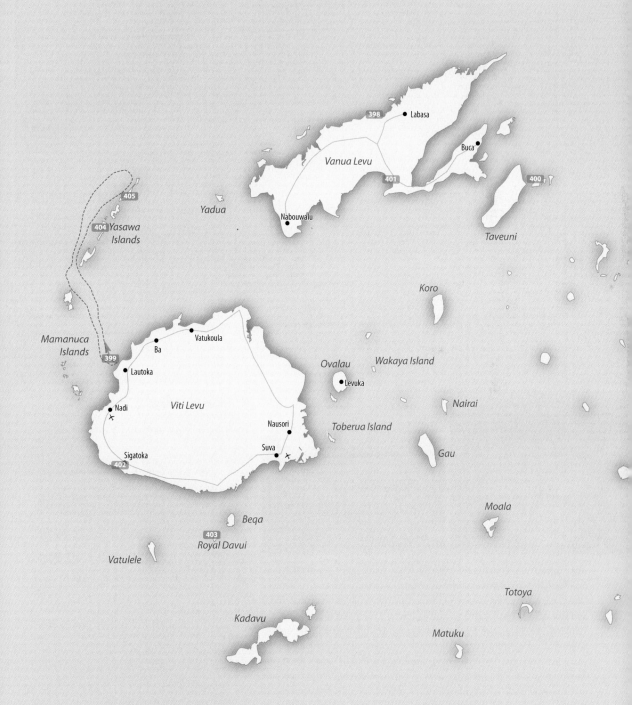

NUKUBATI ISLAND, GREAT SEA REEF, FIJI

P.O. BOX 1928, LABASA
Tel: +61 2 93888 196 **Fax:** +61 2 93888 204 **U.S./Canada Toll Free:** 1 800 224 0220
Web: www.johansens.com/nukubati **E-mail:** info@nukubati.com

Our inspector loved: *The intimacy of this exclusive 5-star island retreat with pristine reefs and pure white sand all to yourself.*

Price Guide: (including all meals, alcoholic and non-alcoholic beverages, non-motorized sporting activities, daily laundry service, return transfers and taxes, per couple)
beach-front bures U.S.$820.05
honeymoon bures U.S.$993.30

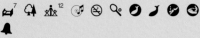

Upon arrival by sea plane step onto the white sands and instantly feel free from working-day stresses and the concept of time. Alternately, arrive via Labasa Airport and drive through lush farmland past sugar cane and rice crops, and stop to pick fresh guava and other seasonal fruit. The airy pavilion is a stunning place to relax and sip an evening cocktail while watching the sunset, although it is a hard choice to make between this and the intimate privacy of your own veranda. The open-plan layout is beautifully appointed with comfortable lounges and quiet writing tables, while the bathrooms are luxuriously large. The extremely fresh food is all taken from Chef's island garden or the local waters, and the fruit from the "Fijian Garden" is unrivaled.

Attractions: Day Trips to Savusavu and Labasa Villages; Pearl Farm, 4 miles; Great Sea Reef, 20-min boat ride
Towns/Cities: Labasa, 30 miles
Airports: Labasa Airport, 30 miles

BLUE LAGOON CRUISES

183 VITOGO PARADE, LAUTOKA

Tel: +679 6661 622 **Fax:** +679 6664 098 **U.S./Canada Toll Free:** 1 818 424 7550
Web: www.johansens.com/bluelagooncruises **E-mail:** reservations@blc.com.fj

Our inspector loved: The true Fijian experience - it is a MUST for your "to do" list! This is small luxury boat cruising at its best and the only way to access these pristine waters and reefs.

Price Guide: (all inclusive)
4-day cruise U.S.$1,000-U.S.$1,500
7-day cruise U.S.$1,350-U.S.$1,650

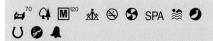

Attractions: Yasawa Islands
Towns/Cities: Lautoka, 2 miles; Nadi, 16 miles
Airports: Nadi International Airport, 12 miles

The magnificent Blue Lagoon Cruises provides a choice of 2 stunning vessels that will take you on a breathtaking 4 or 7-day cruise around the beautiful and untouched Yasawa Islands. The M.V. Fiji Princess is an awe-inspiring 60-meter catamaran. Its 34 deluxe air-conditioned cabins are spacious and luxuriously appointed with large panoramic windows and every modern convenience imaginable. Built with the utmost in comfort and extravagance in mind, the Mystique Princess is truly a millionaire's yacht for you to enjoy. The friendly crew create an atmosphere perfect for you to feel pampered and let any worries drift away. Take an early morning swim in warm azure waters followed by a stroll along white sandy beaches before sampling the delicious fresh local cuisine.

PACIFIC - FIJI ISLANDS (QAMEA ISLAND)

QAMEA RESORT & SPA

P.A. MATEI, TAVEUNI
Tel: +679 888 0220 **Fax:** +679 888 0092 **U.S./Canada Toll Free:** 1 866 867 2632
Web: www.johansens.com/qamea **E-mail:** reservations@qamea.com

Our inspector loved: *This award-winning resort is a true find: great location, great price, great service and easy to access.*

Price Guide: (including all meals and non-motorized activities, excluding tax)
rooms U.S.$600-U.S.$1,050

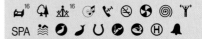

On a mile-long pristine white sandy beach, this intimate luxury property consists of 16 spacious ocean-front bures and villas nestled in 100 acres of landscaped gardens and bushland, with a stunning backdrop of jagged South Pacific mountains. Strategically positioned for maximum privacy and unobstructed views of the sunset, each thatched roof bure and villa has been designed in traditional Fijian style. A split-level honeymoon villa and 2 honeymoon bures have Jacuzzis and the 2 premium villas have private pools. 4 Fijian chefs and visiting chefs from Australia and New Zealand create gourmet Fijian and Continental Pacific Rim dining in the Bure Kalau. Some of the world's best diving and snorkeling sites can be found on the doorstep, while excursions to the neighboring islands can be arranged.

Attractions: World Renowned Scuba Diving, on the doorstep; Pearl Farm, 6 miles; Bouma Waterfall, 10 miles
Airports: Matei Airport, Taveuni Island, 10 miles

JEAN-MICHEL COUSTEAU FIJI ISLANDS RESORT

LESIACEVA POINT, SAVUSAVU

Tel: +1 415 788 5794 **Tel Australia:** +61 3 98 15 03 79 **U.S./Canada Toll Free:** 1 800 246 3454
Web: www.johansens.com/jean-michelcousteau **E-mail:** jmcfir@alphalink.com.au

Our inspector loved: *The complimentary welcome foot massage upon arrival.*

Price Guide: (all inclusive, per couple, excluding alcoholic and specialty beverages and tax)
bures U.S.$608-U.S.$1,071
villa U.S.$2,400

Awards/Ratings: Condé Nast Traveler Gold List 2006; Condé Nast Johansens Most Excellent Resort 2006

Attractions: Private Island Escapes, 10-min boat ride; Black Pearl Farm, 15-min drive; Fijian Village Visit, 30-min drive; Savusavu Farmers' Market, 15-min drive
Towns/Cities: Savusavu, 5 miles
Airports: Savusavu Airport, 8 miles

This multi-award winning luxury eco-friendly resort is situated on 17 acres of the unspoiled island of Vanua Levu overlooking the peaceful clear waters of Savusavu Bay. Reminiscent of an authentic Fijian village, it is surrounded by world-renowned pristine coral reefs, secluded coastline, tropical gardens and stunning sunset ocean views. The 24 spacious individual bures exude tropical elegance, and the magnificent villa features a four-poster bedroom suite, sunken bathroom with Jacuzzi, pool and daybed pavilion. Guests dine by lantern light on mouth-watering fusions of local and international cuisine. The resort is the perfect combination of relaxation and discovery for discerning travelers of all ages. The variety of complimentary activities is exceptional and includes yoga classes, world-class snorkeling with resident marine biologist, diving, sailing and much more.

MYOLA PLANTATION

P.O. BOX 638, SIGATOKA
Tel: +679 652 1084 **Fax:** +679 652 0899
Web: www.johansens.com/myola **E-mail:** myola@connect.com.fj

Our inspector loved: Escaping to this lovers' paradise where you are utterly pampered.

Price Guide: (all inclusive)
2-suite villas U.S.$2,100-U.S.$2,400

Awards/Ratings: AAA 5 Diamond

Atop a cliff on 10 acres of Viti Levu, just west of Sigatoka, this secluded private estate of landscaped tropical gardens and citrus groves offers unrivaled Pacific views across a pristine turquoise coral reef. Each of the 2 Master Suites has its own spa, outdoor shower and plunge pool. A large open-plan lounge, entertainment area, dining area, fully-equipped kitchen and office complete the facilities, and sweeping balconies, luxury amenities and objets d'art complete the ambience. Discover the exotic flavours of Fijian and Western cuisine, expertly prepared by the Plantation's personal chef with only the freshest of ingredients harvested from the nearby lush Sigatoka Valley and local seafood is plentiful. 10 personal staff, maid service and extras such as in-room massages make for a truly indulgent stay.

Attractions: Sigatoka Sand Dunes, 5-min drive; Sigatoka Shopping, 20-min train ride; Kula Eco Bird Park, 20-min drive; Natadola Beach, 25-min drive
Towns/Cities: Sigatoka, 10-min drive; Nadi, 45-min drive; Suva, 2-hour drive
Airports: Nadi International Airport, 45-min drive

ROYAL DAVUI ISLAND RESORT - FIJI

P.O. BOX 3171, LAMI
Tel: +679 336 1624 **Fax:** +679 336 1253
Web: www.johansens.com/royaldavui **E-mail:** res@royaldavui.com

Our inspector loved: *This ultimate getaway offering the 3 "r's": Rest, Relaxation and Rejuventaion.*

Price Guide: (all inclusive)
deluxe U.S.$1,180
premium U.S.$1,380
Davui Suite U.S.$1,545

Awards/Ratings: Condé Nast Johansens Most Romantic Hideaway, Atlantic, Caribbean & Pacific Islands 2007

Attractions: Diving, Snorkeling and Fishing, 2-min walk; Fiji Village Visit, Nacewa, 4 miles; Picnic on a Sand Island, 4 miles
Towns/Cities: Pacific Harbour, 16 miles; Suva, 50 miles
Airports: Nausori Airport, 50 miles; Suva Airport, 50 miles; Nadi International Airport, 180 miles

Idyllic, romantic and exclusive, Royal Davui offers true island seclusion in total luxury and style. This remote and lush green hideaway stands above a colorful barrier reef fringed by soft, pristine white sandy beaches and clear sapphire waters. 16 spacious vales (villas) nestle in the cliffs' tropical vegetation with dramatic views over Beqa Lagoon. Each is cool with mahogany floors, thatched roof, sea-grass ceiling and an open-plan layout featuring extensive glass areas and bi-folding doors that take full advantage of the stunning views. They also feature king-size beds, Jacuzzis, indoor and outdoor showers, 2 decks and plunge pools. Delicious à la carte breakfasts, lunches and dinners are beautifully presented in the sumptuous Banyan restaurant, and the menu is Pacific rim inspired with the emphasis on fruit, vegetables and seafood. Picnic hampers can be delivered to your room or to a special location.

NAVUTU STARS RESORT

P.O. BOX 1838, LAUTOKA

Tel: +679 664 0553 and +679 664 0554 **Fax:** +679 666 0807
Web: www.johansens.com/navutustars **E-mail:** reservations@navutustarsfiji.com

Our inspector loved: *The sophisticated and stylish blend of Italian and Fijian influences.*

Price Guide: (all inclusive, per couple)
grand bures U.S.$590-U.S.$850

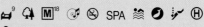

Attractions: Blue Lagoon, 1 mile; Traditional Fijian Village, 1 mile; Underwater Relic, 2 miles; Underwater Caves, 5 miles
Airports: Nadi International Airport, 60 miles

Tucked away on a peaceful turquoise bay, each of the 9 spacious, open-plan bures is decorated in a fusion of Asian-Mediterranean-Fijian styles, with Southeast Asian art pieces and fabrics. Bures also feature double stone vanities, open-plan living rooms, wet bars and an outdoor daybed. Cook up your catch in a local cuisine demonstration, take part in a yoga workshop - only available in season - or attend a Lovo night with local singing and a South Pacific Kava ceremony. Italian cuisine, with a tropical twist, featuring local seafood and produce, is served on the main veranda under the stars. You may choose to enjoy your meal at a table on the beach or on our very own private terrace. Relax in the spa with a menu of treatments based on local ingredients such as algae, coconut oil and clay.

YASAWA ISLAND RESORT & SPA

P.O. BOX 10128, NADI AIRPORT, NADI
Tel: +679 672 2266 **Fax:** +679 672 4456
Web: www.johansens.com/yasawaisland **E-mail:** reservations@yasawa.com.fj

Our inspector loved: *The new spa, the superb dining, great wine list and wonderful surroundings.*

Price Guide: (all inclusive)
rooms U.S.$900-U.S.$1,300
honeymoon suite U.S.$1,800

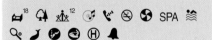

Awards/Ratings: Condé Nast Johansens Most Excellent Romantic Hideaway 2006

Attractions: Deep Sea Fishing, 4 meters; Fijian Village Visits, 20-min walk; Blue Lagoon Caves, 2 miles
Airports: Yasawa Island Airport, 4-min drive; Nadi International Airport, 50 miles

Secluded and exclusive, this exceptional resort nestles on 1km of white sandy beach with a backdrop of palm trees and grass hut villages. Combining beauty and tranquility with the modern and romantic, the ultimate in luxury and pampering is found here where each of the en-suite bures is beautifully decorated and includes a separate living area. The ultra-secluded Lomalagi is recognized as the most exclusive bure in Fiji and has a private infinity lap pool and beach. The beach-front Bavari Spa is housed beneath a thatched roof with a 180° view of the ocean and offers 4 different massages as well as many other treatments. Fresh seafood is caught and served daily, and some real treasures are found on the wine list, considered the best in the Pacific.

Hotels, Great Britain & Ireland

All the properties listed below can be found in our Recommended Hotels & Spas, Great Britain & Ireland 2008 Guide. More information on our portfolio of guides can be found on page 447.

Channel Islands

The Atlantic Hotel	Jersey	+44 (0)1534 744101
The Club Hotel & Spa	Jersey	+44 (0)1534 876500
Longueville Manor	Jersey	+44 (0)1534 725501

England

The Bath Priory Hotel and Restaurant	B&NE Somerset	+44 (0)1225 331922
The Bath Spa Hotel	B&NE Somerset	+44 (0)1225 444424
Dukes Hotel	B&NE Somerset	+44 (0)1225 787960
Homewood Park	B&NE Somerset	+44 (0)1225 723731
Hunstrete House	B&NE Somerset	+44 (0)1761 490490
The Park	B&NE Somerset	+44 (0)117 937 1800
The Royal Crescent Hotel	B&NE Somerset	+44 (0)1225 823333
Luton Hoo Hotel, Golf & Spa	Bedfordshire	+44 (0)1582 734437
Moore Place Hotel	Bedfordshire	+44 (0)1908 282000
The Bear Hotel	Berkshire	+44 (0)1488 682512
Cliveden	Berkshire	+44 (0)1628 668561
The Crab at Chieveley	Berkshire	+44 (0)1635 247550
Donnington Valley Hotel and Spa	Berkshire	+44 (0)1635 551199
Fredrick's – Hotel Restaurant Spa	Berkshire	+44 (0)1628 581000
The French Horn	Berkshire	+44 (0)1189 692204
The Great House	Berkshire	+44 (0)118 9692277
Oakley Court Hotel	Berkshire	+44 (0)1753 609988
The Vineyard At Stockcross	Berkshire	+44 (0)1635 528770
New Hall	Birmingham	+44 (0)121 378 2442
Danesfield House Hotel and Spa	Buckinghamshire	+44 (0)1628 891010
Hartwell House Hotel, Restaurant	Buckinghamshire	+44 (0)1296 747444
The Kings Hotel	Buckinghamshire	+44 (0)1494 609 090
Stoke Park Club	Buckinghamshire	+44 (0)1753 717171
Stoke Place	Buckinghamshire	+44 (0)1753 534 790
Cambridge Garden House	Cambridgeshire	+44 (0)1223 259988
Hotel Felix	Cambridgeshire	+44 (0)1223 277977
Green Bough Hotel	Cheshire	+44 (0)1244 326241
Mere Court Hotel	Cheshire	+44 (0)1565 831000
Nunsmere Hall	Cheshire	+44 (0)1606 889100
Rowton Hall Hotel, Health Club & Spa	Cheshire	+44 (0)1244 335262
Alverton Manor	Cornwall	+44 (0)1872 276633
Budock Vean - The Hotel on the River	Cornwall	+44 (0)1326 252100
Fowey Hall Hotel & Restaurant	Cornwall	+44 (0)1726 833866
The Garrack Hotel & Restaurant	Cornwall	+44 (0)1736 796199
Hell Bay	Cornwall	+44 (0)1720 422947
Meudon Hotel	Cornwall	+44 (0)1326 250541
The Nare Hotel	Cornwall	+44 (0)1872 501111
The Polurrian Hotel	Cornwall	+44 (0)1326 240421
The Rosevine Hotel	Cornwall	+44 (0)1872 580206
St Michael's Hotel & Spa	Cornwall	+44 (0)1326 312707
Talland Bay Hotel	Cornwall	+44 (0)1503 272667
Armathwaite Hall Hotel	Cumbria	+44 (0)17687 76551
Farlam Hall Hotel	Cumbria	+44 (0)16977 46234
Gilpin Lodge	Cumbria	+44 (0)15394 88818
Holbeck Ghyll Country House Hotel	Cumbria	+44 (0)15394 32375
The Inn on the Lake	Cumbria	+44 (0)17684 82444
Lakeside Hotel on Lake Windermere	Cumbria	+44 (0)15395 30001
Linthwaite House Hotel	Cumbria	+44 (0)15394 88600
The Lodore Falls Hotel	Cumbria	+44 (0)17687 77285
Lovelady Shield Country House Hotel	Cumbria	+44 (0)1434 381203
Netherwood Hotel	Cumbria	+44 (0)15395 32552
Rampsbeck Country House Hotel	Cumbria	+44 (0)17684 86442
Rothay Manor	Cumbria	+44 (0)15394 33605
Sharrow Bay Country House Hotel	Cumbria	+44 (0)17684 86301
Tufton Arms Hotel	Cumbria	+44 (0)17683 51593
Callow Hall	Derbyshire	+44 (0)1335 300900

East Lodge Country House Hotel	Derbyshire	+44 (0)1629 734474
The Izaak Walton Hotel	Derbyshire	+44 (0)1335 350555
The Arundell Arms	Devon	+44 (0)1566 784666
Buckland-Tout-Saints	Devon	+44 (0)1548 853055
Gidleigh Park	Devon	+44 (0)1647 432367
The Horn of Plenty Country House	Devon	+44 (0)1822 832528
Hotel Riviera	Devon	+44 (0)1395 515201
Langdon Court Hotel & Restaurant	Devon	+44 (0)1752 862358
Lewtrenchard Manor	Devon	+44 (0)1566 783222
Northcote Manor Country House Hotel	Devon	+44 (0)1769 560501
Orestone Manor	Devon	+44 (0)1803 328098
Soar Mill Cove Hotel	Devon	+44 (0)1548 561566
The Tides Reach Hotel	Devon	+44 (0)1548 843466
Watersmeet Hotel	Devon	+44 (0)1271 870333
Woolacombe Bay Hotel	Devon	+44 (0)1271 870388
Moonfleet Manor	Dorset	+44 (0)1305 786948
Plumber Manor	Dorset	+44 (0)1258 472507
The Priory Hotel	Dorset	+44 (0)1929 551666
Stock Hill Country House Hotel	Dorset	+44 (0)1747 823626
Summer Lodge Country House Hotel	Dorset	+44 (0)1935 482000
Headlam Hall	Durham	+44 (0)1325 730238
Burleigh Court	Gloucestershire	+44 (0)1453 883804
Calcot Manor Hotel & Spa	Gloucestershire	+44 (0)1666 890391
Charingworth Manor	Gloucestershire	+44 (0)1386 593555
Corse Lawn House Hotel	Gloucestershire	+44 (0)1452 780479
Cotswold House Hotel	Gloucestershire	+44 (0)1386 840330
Cowley Manor	Gloucestershire	+44 (0)1242 870900
The Dial House	Gloucestershire	+44 (0)1451 822244
The Grapevine Hotel	Gloucestershire	+44 (0)1451 830344
The Greenway	Gloucestershire	+44 (0)1242 862352
The Hare and Hounds Hotel	Gloucestershire	+44 (0)1666 880233
Hotel On The Park	Gloucestershire	+44 (0)1242 518898
Lords of the Manor Hotel	Gloucestershire	+44 (0)1451 820243
Lower Slaughter Manor	Gloucestershire	+44 (0)1451 820456
The Noel Arms Hotel	Gloucestershire	+44 (0)1386 840317
Stonehouse Court Hotel	Gloucestershire	+44 (0)1453 794950

The Swan Hotel At Bibury	**Gloucestershire**	**+44 (0)1285 740695**
Washbourne	Gloucestershire	+44 (0)1451 822143
Thornbury Castle	S Gloucestershire	+44 (0)1454 281182
Audleys Wood	Hampshire	+44 (0)1256 817555
Chewton Glen	Hampshire	+44 (0)1425 275341
Chilworth Manor	Hampshire	+44 (0)23 8076 7333
Esseborne Manor	Hampshire	+44 (0)1264 736444
Hotel TerraVina	Hampshire	+44 (0)23 8029 3784
The Montagu Arms Hotel	Hampshire	+44 (0)1590 612324
New Park Manor & Bath House Spa	Hampshire	+44 (0)1590 623467
Passford House Hotel	Hampshire	+44 (0)1590 682398
Tylney Hall	Hampshire	+44 (0)1256 764881
Westover Hall	Hampshire	+44 (0)1590 643044
Castle House	Herefordshire	+44 (0)1432 356321

Hotels, Great Britain & Ireland

All the properties listed below can be found in our Recommended Hotels & Spas, Great Britain & Ireland 2008 Guide. More information on our portfolio of guides can be found on page 447.

Shendish Manor Hotel & Golf Club	Hertfordshire	+44 (0)1442232220
St Michael's Manor	Hertfordshire	+44 (0)1727 864444
West Lodge Park Country House Hotel	Hertfordshire	+44 (0)20 8216 3900
Eastwell Manor	Kent	+44 (0)1233 213000
The Spa Hotel	Kent	+44 (0)1892 520331
Eaves Hall	Lancashire	+44 (0)1200 425 271
The Farington Lodge Hotel	Lancashire	+44 (0)1772 421321
The Gibbon Bridge Hotel	Lancashire	+44 (0)1995 61456
Stapleford Park Country House Hotel	Leicestershire	+44 (0)1572 787 000
The George Of Stamford	Lincolnshire	+44 (0)1780 750750
41	London	+44 (0)20 7300 0041
51 Buckingham Gate Luxury Suites and Apartments	London	+44 (0)20 7769 7766
Beaufort House	London	+44 (0)20 7584 2600
Cannizaro House	London	+44 (0)208 879 1464
The Capital Hotel & Restaurant	London	+44 (0)20 7589 5171
The Egerton House Hotel	London	+44 (0)20 7589 2412
Hendon Hall Hotel	London	+44 (0)20 8203 3341
Jumeirah Carlton Tower	London	+44 (0)20 7235 1234
Jumeirah Lowndes Hotel	London	+44 (0)20 7823 1234
Kensington House Hotel	London	+44 (0)20 7937 2345
The Mandeville Hotel	London	+44 (0)20 7935 5599
The Mayflower Hotel	London	+44 (0)20 7370 0991
The Milestone Hotel & Apartments	London	+44 (0)20 7917 1000
The Richmond Gate Hotel	London	+44 (0)20 8940 0061
Sofitel St James	London	+44 (0)20 7747 2200
The Sumner	London	+44 (0)20 7723 2244
Twenty Nevern Square	London	+44 (0)20 7565 9555
Congham Hall	Norfolk	+44 (0)1485 600250
Fawsley Hall	Northamptonshire	+44 (0)1327 892000
Rushton Hall	Northamptonshire	+44 (0)1536 713001
Whittlebury Hall	Northamptonshire	+44 (0)1327 857857
Matfen Hall	Northumberland	+44 (0)1661 886500
Lace Market Hotel	Nottinghamshire	+44 (0)115 852 3232
Langar Hall	Nottinghamshire	+44 (0)1949 860559
Ye Olde Bell	Nottinghamshire	+44 (0)1777 705121
Le Manoir Aux Quat' Saisons	Oxfordshire	+44 (0)1844 278881
Phyllis Court Club	Oxfordshire	+44 (0)1491 570500
The Springs Hotel & Golf Club	Oxfordshire	+44 (0)1491 836687
Hambleton Hall	Rutland	+44 (0)1572 756991
Dinham Hall	Shropshire	+44 (0)1584 876464
Avon Gorge Hotel	Somerset	+44 (0)117 973 8955
The Castle at Taunton	Somerset	+44 (0)1823 272671
Charlton House	Somerset	+44 (0)1749 342008
Combe House Hotel	Somerset	+44 (0)1278 741382
Mount Somerset Country House Hotel	Somerset	+44 (0)1823 442500
Ston Easton Park	Somerset	+44 (0)1761 241631
Hoar Cross Hall Spa Resort	Staffordshire	+44 (0)1283 575671
Brudenell Hotel	Suffolk	+44 (0)1728 452071
Hintlesham Hall	Suffolk	+44 (0)1473 652334
The Ickworth Hotel and Apartments	Suffolk	+44 (0)1284 735350
Ravenwood Hall Country Hotel	Suffolk	+44 (0)1359 270345
Seckford Hall	Suffolk	+44 (0)1394 385678
The Swan Hotel	Suffolk	+44 (0)1787 247477
The Westleton Crown	Suffolk	+44 (0)1728 648777
Foxhills	Surrey	+44 (0)1932 872050
Grayshott Spa	Surrey	+44 (0)1428 602020
Lythe Hill Hotel & Spa	Surrey	+44 (0)1428 651251
Ashdown Park Hotel and Country Club	East Sussex	+44 (0)1342 824988
Dale Hill	East Sussex	+44 (0)1580 200112
Deans Place Hotel	East Sussex	+44 (0)1323 870248
The Grand Hotel	East Sussex	+44 (0)1323 412345
Horsted Place Country House Hotel	East Sussex	+44 (0)1825 750581
Lansdowne Place, Boutique Hotel	East Sussex	+44 (0)1273 736266
Newick Park	East Sussex	+44 (0)1825 723633

The PowderMills	East Sussex	+44 (0)1424 775511
Rye Lodge	East Sussex	+44 (0)1797 223838
Amberley Castle	West Sussex	+44 (0)1798 831992
Bailiffscourt Hotel & Spa	West Sussex	+44 (0)1903 723511
Millstream Hotel	West Sussex	+44 (0)1243 573234
Ockenden Manor	West Sussex	+44 (0)1444 416111
The Spread Eagle Hotel & Health Spa	West Sussex	+44 (0)1730 816911
The Vermont Hotel	Tyne & Wear	+44 (0)191 233 1010
Ardencote Manor Hotel, Country Club	Warwickshire	+44 (0)1926 843111
Billesley Manor	Warwickshire	+44 (0)1789 279955
Ettington Park	Warwickshire	+44 (0)1789 450123
Mallory Court	Warwickshire	+44 (0)1926 330214
Nailcote Hall	Warwickshire	+44 (0)2476 466174
Wroxall Abbey Estate	Warwickshire	+44 (0)1926 484470
Bishopstrow House & Spa	Wiltshire	+44 (0)1985 212312
Howard's House	Wiltshire	+44 (0)1722 716392
Lucknam Park, Bath	Wiltshire	+44 (0)1225 742777
The Pear Tree At Purton	Wiltshire	+44 (0)1793 772100
Whatley Manor	Wiltshire	+44 (0)1666 822888
Woolley Grange	Wiltshire	+44 (0)1225 864705
Brockencote Hall	Worcestershire	+44 (0)1562 777876
Buckland Manor	Worcestershire	+44 (0)1386 852626
The Cottage in the Wood	Worcestershire	+44 (0)1684 575859
Dormy House	Worcestershire	+44 (0)1386 852711
The Elms	Worcestershire	+44 (0)1299 896666
The Evesham Hotel	Worcestershire	+44 (0)1386 765566
The Lygon Arms	Worcestershire	+44 (0)1386 852255
The Devonshire Arms Hotel	North Yorkshire	+44 (0)1756 718111
The Grange Hotel	North Yorkshire	+44 (0)1904 644744
Grants Hotel	North Yorkshire	+44 (0)1423 560666
Grinkle Park Hotel	North Yorkshire	+44 (0)1287 640515
Hob Green Hotel, Restaurant	North Yorkshire	+44 (0)1423 770031
Judges Country House Hotel	North Yorkshire	+44 (0)1642 789000
Middlethorpe Hall Hotel, Restaurant	North Yorkshire	+44 (0)1904 641241
Monk Fryston Hall Hotel	North Yorkshire	+44 (0)1977 682369
The Pheasant	North Yorkshire	+44 (0)1439 771241
Simonstone Hall	North Yorkshire	+44 (0)1969 667255
The Worsley Arms Hotel	North Yorkshire	+44 (0)1653 628234
Whitley Hall Hotel	South Yorkshire	+44 (0)114 245 4444
42 The Calls	West Yorkshire	+44 (0)113 244 0099

Ireland

Cabra Castle	Cavan	+353 42 9667030
Longueville House	Cork	+353 22 47156
Harvey's Point	Donegal	+353 74 972 2208
Brooks Hotel	Dublin	+353 1 670 4000
Abbeyglen Castle	Galway	+353 952 1201
Cashel House	Galway	+353 95 31001
Renvyle House Hotel	Galway	+353 95 43511
St. Clerans Manor House	Galway	+353 91 846555
Ballygarry House	Kerry	+353 66 7123322
The Brehon	Kerry	+353 64 30700
Cahernane House Hotel	Kerry	+353 64 31895
Hotel Dunloe Castle	Kerry	+353 64 44111
Park Hotel Kenmare & Sámas	Kerry	+353 64 41200
Sheen Falls Lodge	Kerry	+353 64 41600
Killashee House Hotel & Villa Spa	Kildare	+353 45 879277
Mount Juliet Conrad	Kilkenny	+353 56 777 3000
Ashford Castle	Mayo	+353 94 95 46003
Knockranny House Hotel & Spa	Mayo	+353 98 28600
The Hunting Lodge	Monaghan	+353 4788100
Nuremore Hotel and Country Club	Monaghan	+353 42 9661438
Dunbrody Country House	Wexford	+353 51 389 600

Hotels / Small Hotels, Great Britain & Ireland

All the properties listed below can be found in our Recommended Small Hotels, Inns and Restaurants, Great Britain & Ireland 2008 Guide. More information on our portfolio of guides can be found on page 447.

Kelly's Resort Hotel & Spa..............................Wexford ....+353 53 32114
Marlfield House ....Wexford ....+353 53 94 21124

Scotland

Darroch Learg ....Aberdeenshire ....+44 (0)13397 55443
Ardanaiseig ....Argyll & Bute ....+44 (0)1866 833333
Loch Melfort Hotel & Restaurant..............Argyll & Bute ....+44 (0)1852 200233
Cally Palace Hotel ....Dumfries & Galloway..+44 (0)1557 814341
Kirroughtree House ....Dumfries & Galloway..+44 (0)1671 402141
Channings...Edinburgh ....+44 (0)131 274 7401
Mar Hall Hotel & Spa...............................Glasgow ....+44 (0)141 812 9999
Bunchrew House Hotel ....Highland ....+44 (0)1463 234917
Cuillin Hills Hotel ....Highland ....+44 (0)1478 612003
Drumossie Hotel ....Highland ....+44 (0)1463 236451
Inverlochy Castle ....Highland ....+44 (0)1397 702177
Rocpool Reserve ....Highland ....+44 (0)1463 240089
The Torridon ....Highland ....+44 (0)1445 791242
Dalhousie Castle and Spa.........................Midlothian ....+44 (0)1875 820153
Ballathie House Hotel ....Perth & Kinross ......+44 (0)1250 883268
The Royal Hotel ....Perth & Kinross ......+44 (0)1764 679200
Glenapp Castle ....South Ayrshire.........+44 (0)1465 831212

Wales

Miskin Manor Country House Hotel ....Cardiff ....+44 (0)1443 224204
Falcondale Mansion Hotel.......................Ceredigion ....+44 (0)1570 422910
Ynyshir Hall...Ceredigion ....+44 (0)1654 781209
Bodysgallen Hall & Spa ....Conwy....................+44 (0)1492 584466
St Tudno Hotel & Restaurant ....Conwy....................+44 (0)1492 874411
Hotel Maes-Y-Neuadd ....Gwynedd ....+44 (0)1766 780200
Palé Hall ....Gwynedd ....+44 (0)1678 530285
Penmaenuchaf Hall ....Gwynedd ....+44 (0)1341 422129
Tre-Ysgawen Hall Country House Hotel..Isle of Anglesey........+44 (0)1248 750750
The Trearddur Bay Hotel ....Isle of Anglesey........+44 (0)1407 860301
Llansantffraed Court Hotel ....Monmouthshire ......+44 (0)1873 840678
Celtic Manor Resort ....Newport....................+44 (0)1633 413000
Warpool Court Hotel ....Pembrokeshire ....+44 (0)1437 720300
The Lake Country House and Spa ....Powys.......................+44 (0)1591 620202
Lake Vyrnwy Hotel ....Powys.......................+44 (0)1691 870 692
Llangoed Hall ....Powys.......................+44 (0)1874 754525
Holm House ....Vale of Glamorgan..+44 (0)2920 701572

Properties from our Recommended Small Hotels, Inns and Restaurants, Great Britain & Ireland 2008 Guide

Channel Islands

La Sablonnerie ....Guernsey ....+44 (0)1481 832061
The White House ....Guernsey ....+44 (0)1481 722159
Château La Chaire ....Jersey ....+44 (0)1534 863354

England

Cornfields Restaurant & Hotel ....Bedfordshire ....+44 (0)1234 378990
Cantley House Hotel ....Berkshire ....+44 (0)118 978 9912
The Cottage Inn ....Berkshire ....+44 (0)1344 882242
The Inn on the Green, Restaurant ....Berkshire ....+44 (0)1628 482638
L'ortolan Restaurant................................Berkshire ....+44 (0)1189 888 500

The Leatherne Bottel
  Riverside Restaurant ....Berkshire ....+44 (0)1491 872667
The Royal Oak Restaurant ....Berkshire ....+44 (0)1628 620541
Stirrups Country House Hotel ....Berkshire ....+44 (0)1344 882284
The Dinton Hermit ....Buckinghamshire.....+44 (0)1296 747473
The Crown and Punchbowl ....Cambridgeshire ......+44 (0)1223 860 643
The Tickell Arms, Restaurant....................Cambridgeshire ......+44 (0)1223 833128
Broxton Hall ....Cheshire ....+44 (0)1829 782321
The Beeches Hotel & Elemis Day Spa ......Cornwall ....+44 (0)1726 73106
Cormorant Hotel & Riverside Restaurant..Cornwall ....+44 (0)1726 833426
Highland Court Lodge..............................Cornwall ....+44 (0)1726 813320
The Old Coastguard Hotel ....Cornwall ....+44 (0)1736 731222
Rose-In-Vale Country House Hotel ....Cornwall ....+44 (0)1872 552202
Tredethy House ....Cornwall ....+44 (0)1208 841262
Trevalsa Court Country House Hotel ....Cornwall ....+44 (0)1726 842468
Crosby Lodge Country House Hotel ....Cumbria ....+44 (0)1228 573618
Dale Head Hall Lakeside Hotel ....Cumbria ....+44 (0)17687 72478
Fayrer Garden House Hotel ....Cumbria ....+44 (0)15394 88195
Hipping Hall ....Cumbria ....+44 (0)15242 71187
Linthwaite House Hotel ....Cumbria ....+44 (0)15394 88600
Nent Hall Country House Hotel ....Cumbria ....+44 (0)1434 381584
The Pheasant ....Cumbria ....+44 (0)17687 76234
Temple Sowerby House Hotel ....Cumbria ....+44 (0)17683 61578
West Vale Country House & Restaurant..Cumbria ....+44 (0)1539 442 817
The Wheatsheaf @ Brigsteer ....Cumbria ....+44 (0)15395 68254
The Crown Inn..Derbyshire ....+44 (0)1889 590 541
Dannah Farm Country House ....Derbyshire ....+44 (0)1773 550273
The Wind in the Willows ....Derbyshire ....+44 (0)1457 868001
Combe House ....Devon ....+44 (0)1404 540400
Heddon's Gate Hotel ....Devon ....+44 (0)1598 763481
Home Farm Hotel ....Devon ....+44 (0)1404 831278
Kingston House ....Devon ....+44 (0)1803 762 235
Mill End ....Devon ....+44 (0)1647 432282
The New Inn ....Devon ....+44 (0)1363 84242
Penhaven Country House Hotel ....Devon ....+44 (0)1237 451 711
Yeoldon House Hotel...............................Devon ....+44 (0)1237 474400
The Bridge House Hotel ....Dorset ....+44 (0)1308 862200
The Grange at Oborne..............................Dorset ....+44 (0)1935 813463
The Crown House ....Essex ....+44 (0)1799 530515
The Swan Inn ....Essex ....+44 (0)1371 870359
Bibury Court ....Gloucestershire.......+44 (0)1285 740337
Charlton Kings Hotel ....Gloucestershire.......+44 (0)1242 231061
The Fleece Hotel ....Gloucestershire.......+44 (0)1285 658507
Lower Brook House ....Gloucestershire.......+44 (0)1386 700286
Lypiatt House ....Gloucestershire.......+44 (0)1242 224994
New Inn At Coln ....Gloucestershire.......+44 (0)1285 750651
Langrish House..Hampshire ....+44 (0)1730 266941
The Mill At Gordleton...............................Hampshire ....+44 (0)1590 682219
The Nurse's Cottage
  Restaurant with Rooms ....Hampshire ....+44 (0)1590 683402
Aylestone Court ....Herefordshire.........+44 (0)1432 341891
The Chase Hotel ....Herefordshire.........+44 (0)1989 763161
Glewstone Court ....Herefordshire.........+44 (0)1989 770367
Moccas Court..Herefordshire.........+44 (0)1981 500 019
Wilton Court Hotel ....Herefordshire.........+44 (0)1989 562569
Redcoats Farmhouse Hotel ....Hertfordshire ....+44 (0)1438 729500
The White House and Lion & Lamb
  Bar & Restaurant...................................Hertfordshire ....+44 (0)1279 870257
The Hambrough..Isle of Wight ....+44 (0)1983 856333
The Priory Bay Hotel ....Isle of Wight ....+44 (0)1983 613146
Rylstone Manor ....Isle of Wight ....+44 (0)1983 862806
Winterbourne Country House ....Isle of Wight ....+44 (0)1983 852 535
Little Silver Country Hotel ....Kent ....+44 (0)1233 850321
Romney Bay House Hotel ....Kent ....+44 (0)1797 364747
The Royal Harbour Hotel ....Kent ....+44 (0)1843 591514

Small Hotels, Great Britain & Ireland

All the properties listed below can be found in our Recommended Small Hotels, Inns and Restaurants, Great Britain & Ireland 2008 Guide.
More information on our portfolio of guides can be found on page 447.

Wallett's Court Hotel & Spa ....Kent ....+44 (0)1304 852424
Ferrari's Restaurant & Hotel.................Lancashire ....+44 (0)1772 783148
The Inn at Whitewell ....Lancashire ....+44 (0)1200 448222
Horse & Trumpet ....Leicestershire ....+44 (0)1858 565000
Sysonby Knoll Hotel ....Leicestershire ....+44 (0)1664 563563
Bailhouse Hotel ....Lincolnshire ....+44 (0)1522 520883
The Crown Hotel ....Lincolnshire ....+44 (0)1780 763136
Washingborough Hall ....Lincolnshire ....+44 (0)1522 790340
Bingham ....London ....+44 (0)208 940 0902
The King's Arms Hotel ....London ....+44 (0)208 977 1729
Tree Tops Country House
    Restaurant & Hotel ....Merseyside ....+44 (0)1704 572430
Beechwood Hotel ....Norfolk ....+44 (0)1692 403231
Broad House ....Norfolk ....+44 (0)1603 783567
Felbrigg Lodge ....Norfolk ....+44 (0)1263 837588
The Kings Head Hotel ....Norfolk ....+44 (0)1485 578 265
The Neptune Inn & Restaurant ....Norfolk ....+44 (0)1485 532122
The Old Rectory ....Norfolk ....+44 (0)1603 700772
The Stower Grange ....Norfolk ....+44 (0)1603 860210
Titchwell Manor Hotel ....Norfolk ....+44 (0)1485 210221
The Orchard House..............................Northumberland....+44 (0)1669 620 684
The Otterburn Tower ....Northumberland ....+44 (0)1830 520620
Waren House Hotel.............................Northumberland ...+44 (0)1668 214581
Cockliffe Country House Hotel ....Nottinghamshire....+44 (0)115 968 0179
Greenwood Lodge ....Nottinghamshire....+44 (0)115 962 1206
Langar Hall ....Nottinghamshire ...+44 (0)1949 860559
Burford Lodge Hotel & Restaurant.........Oxfordshire ....+44 (0)1993 823354
Duke Of Marlborough Country Inn ....Oxfordshire ....+44 (0)1993 811460
Fallowfields......................................Oxfordshire ....+44 (0)1865 820416
The Feathers ....Oxfordshire ....+44 (0)1993 812291
The Jersey Arms ....Oxfordshire ....+44 (0)1869 343234
The Kings Head Inn & Restaurant ....Oxfordshire ....+44 (0)1608 658365
The Lamb Inn ....Oxfordshire ....+44 (0)1993 823155
The Nut Tree Inn ....Oxfordshire ....+44 (0)1865 331253
The Spread Eagle Hotel......................Oxfordshire ....+44 (0)1844 213661
Weston Manor ....Oxfordshire ....+44 (0)1869 350621
Barnsdale Lodge ....Rutland ....+44 (0)1572 724678
The Lake Isle Hotel & Restaurant.............Rutland ....+44 (0)1572 822951
Pen-Y-Dyffryn Country Hotel ....Shropshire ....+44 (0)1691 653700
Soulton Hall ....Shropshire ....+44 (0)1939 232786
Bellplot House Hotel ....Somerset ....+44 (0)1460 62600
Beryl ....Somerset ....+44 (0)1749 678738
Compton House..................................Somerset ....+44 (0)1934 733944
Farthings Country House Hotel.............Somerset ....+44 (0)1823 480664
Glencot House ....Somerset ....+44 (0)1749 677160
Karslake Country House ....Somerset ....+44 (0)1643 851242
Three Acres Country House ....Somerset ....+44 (0)1398 323730
Woodlands Country House Hotel ....Somerset ....+44 (0)1278 760232
The Bildeston Crown ....Suffolk ....+44 (0)1449 740 510
Clarice House.....................................Suffolk ....+44 (0)1284 705550
The Swan Inn.....................................Surrey ....+44 (0)1428 682073
The Hope Anchor Hotel ....East Sussex ....+44 (0)1797 222216
Burpham Country House ....West Sussex ....+44 (0)1903 882160
The Mill House Hotel ....West Sussex ....+44 (0)1903 892426
Beechfield House................................Wiltshire ....+44 (0)1225 703700
The Bell at Ramsbury ....Wiltshire ....+44 (0)1672 520230
The Castle Inn ....Wiltshire ....+44 (0)1249 783030
The Lamb at Hindon ....Wiltshire ....+44 (0)1747 820 573
The Old Manor Hotel ....Wiltshire ....+44 (0)1225 777393
Stanton Manor Hotel ....Wiltshire ....+44 (0)1666 837552
Widbrook Grange ....Wiltshire ....+44 (0)1225 864750
Colwall Park ....Worcestershire ....+44 (0)1684 540000
The Old Rectory ....Worcestershire ....+44 (0)1527 523000
The Peacock Inn ....Worcestershire ....+44 (0)1584 810506
Royal Forester Country Inn ....Worcestershire ....+44 (0)1299 266286

The White Lion Hotel ....Worcestershire ....+44 (0)1684 592551
The Austwick Traddock........................North Yorkshire.......+44 (0)15242 51224
The Devonshire Fell ....North Yorkshire.......+44 (0)1756 718111
Dunsley Hall ....North Yorkshire.......+44 (0)1947 893437
Hob Green Hotel, Restaurant ....North Yorkshire.......+44 (0)1423 770031
Marmadukes Hotel ....North Yorkshire.......+44 (0)1904 640099
Ox Pasture Hall Country Hotel ....North Yorkshire.......+44 (0)1723 365295
The Red Lion ....North Yorkshire.......+44 (0)1756 720204
Stow House ....North Yorkshire.......+44 (0)1969 663635
Hey Green Country House Hotel ....West Yorkshire ....+44 (0)1484 848000

Ireland

Ard Na Sidhe ....Kerry....................+353 66 976 9105

Ballyseede Castle ....Kerry ....**+353 66 712 5799**
Temple Country Retreat & Spa ....Westmeath ....+353 57 933 5118

Scotland

Norwood Hall ....Aberdeenshire ....+44 (0)1224 868951
Highland Cottage ....Argyll and Bute.......+44 (0)1688 302030
Balcary Bay Hotel...............................Dumfries and Galloway ..+44 (0)1556 640217
Corsewall Lighthouse Hotel ....Dumfries and Galloway ..+44 (0)1776 853220
Trigony House Hotel ....Dumfries and Galloway ..+44 (0)1848 331211
The Peat Inn ....Fife ....+44 (0)1334 840206
Forss House Hotel ....Highland ....+44 (0)1847 861201
Greshornish House Hotel ....Highland ....+44 (0)1470 582266
Ruddyglow Park.................................Highland ....+44 (0)1571 822216
The Steadings
    at The Grouse & Trout...................Highland ....+44 (0)1808 521314
Toravaig House..................................Highland ....+44 (0)1471 833231
Knockomie Hotel ....Moray ....+44 (0)1309 673146
Castle Venlaw ....Scottish Borders .....+44 (0)1721 720384
Cringletie House ....Scottish Borders .....+44 (0)1721 725750
Culzean Castle –
    The Eisenhower Apartment............South Ayrshire.........+44 (0)1655 884455

Wales

Jabajak Vineyard
    (Restaurant with Rooms)...............Carmarthenshire ....+44 (0)1994 448786
Sychnant Pass House..........................Conwy ....+44 (0)1492 596868
Tan-Y-Foel Country House ....Conwy ....+44 (0)1690 710507
Bae Abermaw ....Gwynedd...............+44 (0)1341 280550
Llwyndu Farmhouse ....Gwynedd...............+44 (0)1341 280144
Porth Tocyn Country House Hotel ....Gwynedd...............+44 (0)1758 713303
The Bell At Skenfrith ....Monmouthshire ......+44 (0)1600 750235
Penally Abbey ....Pembrokeshire ....+44 (0)1834 843033
Wolfscastle Country Hotel & Restaurant ..Pembrokeshire ....+44 (0)1437 741225
Glangrwyney Court ....Powys ....+44 (0)1873 811288
Egerton Grey ....Vale of Glamorgan..+44 (0)1446 711666

Historic Houses, Castles & Gardens

We are pleased to feature over 140 places to visit during your stay at a Condé Nast Johansens Recommendation. More information about these attractions, including opening times and entry fees, can be found on www.johansens.com

England

Cothay Manor and Gardens	Bath & NE Somerset	+44 (0)1823 672283
Great House Farm	Bath & NE Somerset	+44 (0)1934 713133
Orchard Wyndham	Bath & NE Somerset	+44 (0)1984 632309
Woburn Abbey	Bedfordshire	+44 (0)1525 290666
Moggerhanger Park	Bedfordshire	+44 (0)1767 641007
Doddershall Park	Buckinghamshire	+44 (0)1296 655238
Nether Winchendon House	Buckinghamshire	+44 (0)1844 290199
Stowe Landscape Gardens	Buckinghamshire	+44 (0)1280 822850
Waddesdon Manor	Buckinghamshire	+44 (0)1296 653211
The Manor	Cambridgeshire	+44 (0)1480 463134
Cholmondeley Castle Gardens	Cheshire	+44 (0)1829 720383
Dorfold Hall	Cheshire	+44 (0)1270 625245
Rode Hall and Gardens	Cheshire	+44 (0)1270 882961

The Bowes Museum	**Co Durham**	**+44 (0)1833 690606**
Holker Hall and Gardens	Cumbria	+44 (0)15395 58328
Isel Hall	Cumbria	+44 (0)1900 821778
Muncaster Castle, Gardens & Owl Centre	Cumbria	+44 (0)1229 717 614
Haddon Hall	Derbyshire	+44 (0)1629 812855
Melbourne Hall & Gardens	Derbyshire	+44 (0)1332 862502
Renishaw Hall Gardens	Derbyshire	+44 (0)1246 432310
Anderton House	Devon	+44 (0)1628 825920
Bowringsleigh	Devon	+44 (0)1548 852014
Downes	Devon	+44 (0)1392 439046
Lulworth Castle & Park	Dorset	+44 (0)1929 400352
Mapperton Gardens	Dorset	+44 (0)1308 862645
Minterne Gardens	Dorset	+44 (0)1300 341370
Moignes Court	Dorset	+44 (0)1305 853300
Auckland Castle	Durham	+44 (0)1388 601627
Burton Agnes Hall & Gardens	East Yorkshire	+44 (0)1262 490324
The Gardens of Easton Lodge	Essex	+44 (0)1371 876979
Ingatestone	Essex	+44 (0)1277 353010
Cheltenham Art Gallery & Museum	Gloucestershire	+44 (0)1242 237431
Frampton Court	Gloucestershire	+44 (0)1452 740267
Hardwicke court	Gloucestershire	+44 (0)1452 720212
Old Campden House	Gloucestershire	+44 (0)1628 825920
Sezincote House & Garden	Gloucestershire	+44 (0)1386 700444

Sudeley Castle Gardens and Exhibitions	Gloucestershire	+44 (0)1242 602308
Avington Park	Hampshire	+44 (0)1962 779260
Beaulieu	Hampshire	+44 (0)1590 612345
Broadlands	Hampshire	+44 (0)1794 505055
Buckler's Hard	Hampshire	+44 (0)1590 614641
Gilbert White's House & The Oates Museum	Hampshire	+44 (0)1420 511275
Greywell Hill House	Hampshire	
Pylewell Park Gardens	Hampshire	+44 (0)1725 513004
Kentchurch Court	Herefordshire	+44 (0)1981 240228
Ashridge	Hertfordshire	+44 (0)1442 841027
Hatfield House	Hertfordshire	+44 (0)1707 287010
Deacons Nursery (H.H)	Isle of Wight	+44 (0)1983 840750
Cobham Hall	Kent	+44 (0)1474 823371
The Grange	Kent	+44 (0)1628 825925
Groombridge Place Gardens & Enchanted Forest	Kent	+44 (0)1892 863999
Hever Castle and Gardens	Kent	+44 (0)1732 865224
Marle Place Gardens	Kent	+44 (0)1892 722304
The New College of Cobham	Kent	+44 (0)1474 812503
Penshurst Place and Gardens	Kent	+44 (0)1892 870307
Stonyhurst College	Lancashire	+44 (0)1254 826345
Townhead House	Lancashire	+44 (0)1772 421566
Handel House Museum	London	+44 (0)20 7495 1685
Pitzhanger Manor House	London	+44 (0)20 8567 1227
St Paul's Cathedral	London	+44 (0)20 7246 8350
Sir John Soane's Museum	London	+44 (0)20 7405 2107
Syon House	London	+44 (0)20 8560 0881
Fairhaven Woodland and Water Garden	Norfolk	+44 (0)1603 270449
Walsingham Abbey Grounds	Norfolk	+44 (0)1328 820259
Cottesbrooke Hall and Gardens	Northamptonshire	+44 (0)1604 505808
Haddonstone Show Gardens	Northamptonshire	+44 (0)1604 770711
Chipchase Castle & Gardens	Northumberland	+44 (0)1434 230203
Kingston Bagpuize House	Oxfordshire	+44 (0)1865 820259
Mapledurham House	Oxfordshire	+44 (0)1189 723350
Stonor Park	Oxfordshire	+44 (0)1491 638587
Sulgrave Manor	Oxfordshire	+44 (0)1295 760205
Wallingford Castle Gardens	Oxfordshire	+44 (0)1491 835373
Weston Park	Shropshire	+44 (0)1952 852100
Hestercombe Gardens	Somerset	+44 (0)1823 413923
Number One Royal Crescent	Somerset	+44 (0)1225 428126
Robin Hood's Hut	Somerset	+44 (0)1628 825925
Ancient High House	Staffordshire	+44 (0)1785 619131
Izaak Walton's Cottage	Staffordshire	+44 (0)1785 760278
Stafford Castle & Visitor Centre	Staffordshire	+44 (0)1785 257698
Whitmore Hall	Staffordshire	+44 (0)1782 680478
Ancient House	Suffolk	+44 (0)1628 825920
Freston Tower	Suffolk	+44 (0)1628 825920
Kentwell Hall	Suffolk	+44 (0)1787 310207
Newbourne Hall	Suffolk	+44 (0)1473 736764
Claremont House	Surrey	+44 (0)1372 473623
Goddards	Surrey	+44 (0)1628 825920
Guildford House Gallery	Surrey	+44 (0)1483 444740
Loseley Park	Surrey	+44 (0)1483 304 440

Historic Houses, Castles & Gardens

We are pleased to feature over 140 places to visit during your stay at a Condé Nast Johansens Recommendation.
More information about these attractions, including opening times and entry fees, can be found on www.johansens.com

Anne of Cleves House	East Sussex	+44 (0)1273 474610
Bentley Wildfowl & Motor Museum	East Sussex	+44 (0)1825 840573
Charleston	East Sussex	+44 (0)1323 811626
Gardens and Grounds of Herstmonceux Castle	East Sussex	+44 (0)1323 833816
Michelham Priory	East Sussex	+44 (0)1323 844224
Wilmington Priory	East Sussex	+44 (0)1628 825920
Denmans Garden	West Sussex	+44 (0)1243 542808
Firle Place	West Sussex	+44 (0)1273 858307
Fishbourne Roman Palace	West Sussex	+44 (0)1243 785859
Goodwood House	West Sussex	+44 (0)1243 538449
High Beeches Gardens	West Sussex	+44 (0)1444 400589
Leonardslee Lakes and Gardens	West Sussex	+44 (0)1403 891212
Lewes Castle	West Sussex	+44 (0)1273 486290
Marlipins Museum	West Sussex	+44 (0)1273 462994
Parham House & Gardens	West Sussex	+44 (0)1903 742021
The Priest House	West Sussex	+44 (0)1342 810479
West Dean Gardens	West Sussex	+44 (0)1243 818210
Worthing Museum & Art Gallery	West Sussex	+44 (0)1903 239999
Arbury Hall	Warwickshire	+44 (0)2476 382804
Kenilworth Castle	Warwickshire	+44 (0)1926 852078
Shakespeare Houses	Warwickshire	+44 (0)1789 204016
The Barber Institute of Fine Arts	West Midlands	+44 (0)121 414 7333
The Birmingham Botanical Gardens & Glasshouses	West Midlands	+44 (0)121 454 1860
Harvington Hall	Worcestershire	+44 (0)1562 777846
Little Malvern Court	Worcestershire	+44 (0)1684 892988
Witley Court and Gardens	Worcestershire	+44 (0)1299 896636
Castle Howard	North Yorkshire	+44 (0)1653 648333
Duncombe Park	North Yorkshire	+44 (0)1439 770213
Forbidden Corner	North Yorkshire	+44 (0)1969 640638
Fountains Abbey and Studley Royal Water Garden	North Yorkshire	+44 (0)1765 608888
Ripley Castle	North Yorkshire	+44 (0)1423 770152
Skipton Castle	North Yorkshire	+44 (0)1756 792442
Bramham Park	West Yorkshire	+44 (0)1937 846000
Bronte Parsonage Museum	West Yorkshire	+44 (0)1535 642323

N. Ireland

North Down Museum	Down	+44 (0)2891 271200
Seaforde Gardens	Down	+44 (0)2844 811225

Ireland

Dunloe Castle Hotel Gardens	Kerry	+353 64 44111
Blarney Castle, House and Gardens	Cork	+353 21 385252
Bantry House & Gardens	Cork	+353 27 50047
Lismore Castle Gardens & Art Gallery	Waterford	+353 (0)5854424
Kilmokea Country Manor and Gardens	Wexford	+353 51 388109

Scotland

Kelburn Castle and Country Centre	Ayrshire	+44 (0)1475 568685
Floors Castle	Borders	+44 (0)1573 223333
Ardwell Gardens	Dumfries & Galloway	+44 (0)1776 860227
Castle Kennedy Gardens	Dumfries & Galloway	+44 (0)1776 702024
Drumlanrig Castle, Gardens & Country Park	Dumfries & Galloway	+44 (0)1848 331555
Callendar House	Falkirk	+44 (0)1324 503770
Golden Grove	Flintshire	+44 (0)1745 854452
Inveraray Castle	Highland	+44 (0)1499 302 203
Auchinleck House	North Ayrshire	+44 (0)1628 825920
Balfour Castle	Orkney	+44 (0)1856 711282
Bowhill House & Country Park	Scottish Borders	+44 (0)1750 22204
Manderston	Scottish Borders	+44 (0)1361 883 450
Paxton House & Country Park	Scottish Borders	+44 (0)1289 386291
Traquair House	Scottish Borders	+44 (0)1896 830 323
Newliston	West Lothian	+44 (0)131 333 3231

Wales

Bodnant Garden	Conwy	+44 (0)1492 650460
Dolbelydr	Denbighshire	+44 (0)1628 825920
Plas Brondanw Gardens	Gwynedd	+44 (0)1743 241181
Llanvihangel Court	Monmouthshire	+44 (0)1873 890 217
Usk Castle	Monmouthshire	+44 (0)1291 672563
S. Davids Cathedral	Pembrokeshire	+44 (0)1437 720 199

France

Château de Chenonceau	Chenonceaux	+33 2 47 23 90 07

The Netherlands

Het Loo Palace National Museum	Apeldoorn	+31 55 577 2400

Hotels - Europe & The Mediterranean

Properties listed below can be found in our Recommended Hotels & Spas - Europe & The Mediterranean 2008 Guide. More information on our portfolio of guides can be found on page 447.

ANDORRA (SOLDEU)

Sport Hotel Hermitage & Spa

Ctra de Soldeu s/n, AD 100 Soldeu, Andorra

Tel: +376 870 670
www.johansens.com/sportwellness

AUSTRIA (VIENNA)

Palais Coburg Residenz

Coburgbastei 4, 1010 Vienna, Austria

Tel: +43 1 518 180
www.johansens.com/palaiscoburg

BELGIUM (ANTWERP)

Firean Hotel

Karel Oomsstraat 6, 2018 Antwerp, Belgium

Tel: +32 3 237 02 60
www.johansens.com/firean

BELGIUM (BRUGES)

Hotel Die Swaene

1 Steenhouwersdijk (Groene Rei), 8000 Bruges, Belgium

Tel: +32 50 34 27 98
www.johansens.com/swaene

BELGIUM (KNOKKE~HEIST)

Romantik Hotel Manoir du Dragon

Albertlaan 73, 8300 Knokke~Heist, Belgium

Tel: +32 50 63 05 80
www.johansens.com/dudragon

BELGIUM (KORTRIJK)

Grand Hotel Damier

Grote Markt 41, 8500 Kortrijk, Belgium

Tel: +32 56 22 15 47
www.johansens.com/damier

BELGIUM (TURNHOUT)

Hostellerie Ter Driezen

18 Herentalsstraat, 2300 Turnhout, Belgium

Tel: +32 14 41 87 57
www.johansens.com/terdriezen

CROATIA (BALE)

Stancija Meneghetti

52211 Bale (Istria), Croatia

Tel: +385 52 528 816
www.johansens.com/meneghetti

CROATIA (DUBROVNIK)

Grand Villa Argentina

Frana Supila 14, 20000 Dubrovnik, Croatia

Tel: +385 20 44 0555
www.johansens.com/grandvillaargentina

CZECH REPUBLIC (PRAGUE)

Alchymist Grand Hotel and Spa

Trziste 19, Malá Strana, 11800 Prague, Czech Republic

Tel: +420 257 286 011/016
www.johansens.com/alchymist

CZECH REPUBLIC (PRAGUE)

Aria Hotel Prague

Trziste 9, 118 00 Prague 1, Czech Republic

Tel: +420 225 334 111
www.johansens.com/aria

CZECH REPUBLIC (PRAGUE)

Bellagio Hotel Prague

U Milosrdnych 2, 110 00 Prague 1, Czech Republic

Tel: +420 221 778 999
www.johansens.com/bellagio

CZECH REPUBLIC (PRAGUE)

Golden Well Hotel

U Zlaté studne 166/4, 118 00 Prague 1, Czech Republic

Tel: +420 257 011 213
www.johansens.com/zlatestudna

CZECH REPUBLIC (PRAGUE)

The Iron Gate Hotel & Suites

Michalska 19, 110 00 Prague, Czech Republic

Tel: +420 225 777 777
www.johansens.com/irongate

CZECH REPUBLIC (PRAGUE)

Nosticova Residence

Nosticova 1, Malá Strana, 11800 Prague, Czech Republic

Tel: +420 257 312 513/516
www.johansens.com/nosticova

CZECH REPUBLIC (TÁBOR)

Hotel Nautilus

Žižkovo námestí 20, 39002 Tábor, Czech Republic

Tel: +420 380 900 900
www.johansens.com/nautilus

Hotels - Europe & The Mediterranean

Properties listed below can be found in our Recommended Hotels & Spas - Europe & The Mediterranean 2008 Guide. More information on our portfolio of guides can be found on page 447.

ESTONIA (PÄRNU)

Ammende Villa

Mere Pst 7, 80010 Pärnu, Estonia

Tel: +372 44 73 888
www.johansens.com/villaammende

ESTONIA (TALLINN)

The Three Sisters Hotel

Pikk 71/Tolli 2, 10133 Tallinn, Estonia

Tel: +372 630 6300
www.johansens.com/threesisters

FRANCE / ALSACE~LORRAINE (COLMAR)

Hôtel Les Têtes

19 Rue des Têtes, BP 69, 68000 Colmar, France

Tel: +33 3 89 24 43 43
www.johansens.com/lestetes

FRANCE / ALSACE~LORRAINE (COLMAR)

Romantik Hôtel le Maréchal

4 Place Six Montagnes Noires, Petite Venise, 68000 Colmar, France

Tel: +33 3 89 41 60 32
www.johansens.com/marechal

FRANCE / ALSACE~LORRAINE (CONDÉ NORTHEN)

Domaine de la Grange de Condé

41 rue des Deux Nied, 57220 Condé Northen, France

Tel: +33 3 87 79 30 50
www.johansens.com/grangedeconde

FRANCE / ALSACE~LORRAINE (GERARDMER)

Hostellerie les Bas Rupts Le Chalet Fleuri

181 Route de la Bresse, 88400 Gérardmer, Vosges, France

Tel: +33 3 29 63 09 25
www.johansens.com/lesbasrupts

FRANCE / ALSACE~LORRAINE (OBERNAI)

Hôtel à la Cour d'Alsace

3 Rue de Gail, 67210 Obernai, France

Tel: +33 3 88 95 07 00
www.johansens.com/couralsace

FRANCE / ALSACE~LORRAINE (ROUFFACH)

Château d'Isenbourg

68250 Rouffach, France

Tel: +33 3 89 78 58 50
www.johansens.com/isenbourg

FRANCE / ALSACE~LORRAINE (STRASBOURG)

Château de L'Ile

4 Quai Heydt, 67540 Strasbourg - Ostwald, France

Tel: +33 3 88 66 85 00
www.johansens.com/chateaudelile

FRANCE / BRITTANY (BILLIERS)

Domaine de Rochevilaine

Pointe de Pen Lan, BP 69, 56190 Billiers, France

Tel: +33 2 97 41 61 61
www.johansens.com/domainerochevilaine

FRANCE / BRITTANY (LA ROCHE BERNARD)

Domaine de Bodeuc

Route de Saint~Dolay, 56130 Nivillac, La Roche Bernard, France

Tel: +33 2 99 90 89 63
www.johansens.com/hotelbodeuc

FRANCE / BRITTANY (MISSILLAC)

Hôtel et Spa de La Bretesche

Domaine de la Bretesche, 44780 Missillac, France

Tel: +33 2 51 76 86 96
www.johansens.com/bretesche

FRANCE / BRITTANY (MOËLAN~SUR~MER)

Manoir de Kertalg

Route de Riec~Sur~Belon, 29350 Moëlan~sur~Mer, France

Tel: +33 2 98 39 77 77
www.johansens.com/manoirdekertalg

FRANCE / BRITTANY (PERROS~GUIREC)

Hôtel l'Agapa & Spa

12, Rue des Bons Enfants, 22700 Perros~Guirec, France

Tel: +33 2 96 49 01 10
www.johansens.com/lagapa

FRANCE / BRITTANY (ST~MALO - LA GOUESNIÈRE)

Château de Bonaban

35350 La Gouesnière, France

Tel: +33 2 99 58 24 50
www.johansens.com/chateaudebonaban

FRANCE / BRITTANY (TREBEURDEN)

Ti al Lannec

14 Allée de Mezo~Guen, 22560 Trebeurden, France

Tel: +33 2 96 15 01 01
www.johansens.com/tiallannec

Hotels - Europe & The Mediterranean

Properties listed below can be found in our Recommended Hotels & Spas - Europe & The Mediterranean 2008 Guide.
More information on our portfolio of guides can be found on page 447.

FRANCE / BURGUNDY - FRANCHE~COMTÉ
(CHAMBOLLE - MUSIGNY)

Château Hôtel André Ziltener

Rue de la Fontaine, 21220 Chambolle - Musigny,
France

Tel: +33 3 80 62 41 62
www.johansens.com/ziltener

FRANCE / BURGUNDY - FRANCHE~COMTÉ
(LA BUSSIÈRE~SUR~OUCHE)

Abbaye de la Bussière

21360 La Bussière~sur~Ouche, Côte d'Or, France

Tel: +33 3 80 49 02 29
www.johansens.com/abbayedelabussiere

FRANCE / BURGUNDY - FRANCHE~COMTÉ
(MONT~ST~JEAN)

Château les Roches

Rue de Glanot, 21320 Mont~Saint-Jean, France

Tel: +33 3 80 84 32 71
www.johansens.com/lesroches

FRANCE / BURGUNDY - FRANCHE~COMTÉ (POLIGNY)

Hostellerie des Monts de Vaux

Les Monts de Vaux, 39800 Poligny, France

Tel: +33 3 84 37 12 50
www.johansens.com/montsdevaux

FRANCE / BURGUNDY - FRANCHE~COMTÉ
(VAULT DE LUGNY)

Château de Vault de Lugny

11 Rue du Château, 89200 Vault de Lugny, France

Tel: +33 3 86 34 07 86
www.johansens.com/vaultdelugny

FRANCE / BURGUNDY - FRANCHE~COMTÉ (VOUGEOT)

Château de Gilly

Gilly~lès~Cîteaux, 21640 Vougeot, France

Tel: +33 3 80 62 89 98
www.johansens.com/gilly

FRANCE / CHAMPAGNE~ARDENNES (DOLANCOURT)

Le Moulin du Landion

5 rue Saint~Léger, 10200 Dolancourt, France

Tel: +33 3 25 27 92 17
www.johansens.com/moulindulandion

FRANCE / CHAMPAGNE~ARDENNES
(ETOGES~EN~CHAMPAGNE)

Château d'Etoges

51270 Etoges~en~Champagne, France

Tel: +33 3 26 59 30 08
www.johansens.com/etoges

FRANCE / CHAMPAGNE~ARDENNES
(FÈRE~EN~TARDENOIS)

Château de Fère

02130 Fère~en~Tardenois, France

Tel: +33 3 23 82 21 13
www.johansens.com/chateaufere

FRANCE / CHAMPAGNE~ARDENNES
(STE~PREUVE - LAON)

Domaine du Château de Barive

02350 Sainte~Preuve, France

Tel: +33 3 23 22 15 15
www.johansens.com/barive

FRANCE / CÔTE D'AZUR (ÈZE VILLAGE)

Château Eza

Rue de la Pise, 06360 Èze Village, France

Tel: +33 4 93 41 12 24
www.johansens.com/eza

FRANCE / CÔTE D'AZUR
(LE RAYOL - CANADEL~SUR~MER)

Le Bailli de Suffren

Avenue des Américains, Golfe de Saint~Tropez,
83820 Le Rayol – Canadel~Sur~Mer, France

Tel: +33 4 98 04 47 00
www.johansens.com/lebaillidesuffren

FRANCE / CÔTE D'AZUR (MOUGINS)

Alain Llorca - Le Moulin de Mougins

Quartier Notre~Dame~de~Vie, 06250 Mougins,
France

Tel: +33 4 93 75 78 24
www.johansens.com/moulindemougins

FRANCE / CÔTE D'AZUR (RAMATUELLE - ST~TROPEZ)

La Ferme d'Augustin

Plage de Tahiti, 83350 Ramatuelle, Near
Saint~Tropez, France

Tel: +33 4 94 55 97 00
www.johansens.com/fermeaugustin

FRANCE / CÔTE D'AZUR (ST~PAUL~DE~VENCE)

Le Mas d'Artigny & Spa

Route de la Colle, 06570 Saint~Paul~de~Vence,
France

Tel: +33 4 93 32 84 54
www.johansens.com/masdartigny

FRANCE / CÔTE D'AZUR (ST~RAPHAËL)

La Villa Mauresque

1792 route de la Corniche, 83700 Saint~Raphaël,
France

Tel: +33 494 83 02 42
www.johansens.com/mauresque

Hotels - Europe & The Mediterranean

Properties listed below can be found in our Recommended Hotels & Spas - Europe & The Mediterranean 2008 Guide. More information on our portfolio of guides can be found on page 447.

FRANCE / LOIRE VALLEY (AMBOISE)

Château de Pray

Route de Chargé, 37400 Amboise, France

Tel: +33 247 57 23 67

www.johansens.com/chateaudepray

FRANCE / LOIRE VALLEY (AMBOISE)

Le Choiseul

36 Quai Charles Guinot, 37400 Amboise, France

Tel: +33 2 47 30 45 45

www.johansens.com/lechoiseul

FRANCE / LOIRE VALLEY (AMBOISE)

Le Manoir les Minimes

34 Quai Charles Guinot, 37400 Amboise, France

Tel: +33 2 47 30 40 40

www.johansens.com/lemanoirlesminimes

FRANCE / LOIRE VALLEY (LUYNES)

Domaine de Beauvois

Le Pont Clouet, Route de Cléré~les~Pins, 37230 Luynes, France

Tel: +33 2 47 55 50 11

www.johansens.com/domainedebeauvois

FRANCE / LOIRE VALLEY (MONTBAZON)

Château d'Artigny

37250 Montbazon, France

Tel: +33 2 47 34 30 30

www.johansens.com/dartigny

FRANCE / LOIRE VALLEY (MONTBAZON)

Domaine de la Tortinière

Route de Ballan~Miré, 37250 Montbazon, France

Tel: +33 2 47 34 35 00

www.johansens.com/domainetortiniere

FRANCE / LOIRE VALLEY (SAUMUR)

Le Prieuré

49350 Chênehutte~les~Tuffeaux, France

Tel: +33 2 41 67 90 14

www.johansens.com/leprieure

FRANCE / LOIRE VALLEY (ST~CALAIS)

Château de la Barre

72120 Conflans~sur~Anille, France

Tel: +33 2 43 35 00 17

www.johansens.com/delabarre

FRANCE / LOIRE VALLEY (STE~MAURE~DE~TOURAINE)

Hostellerie des Hauts de Sainte~Maure

2-4 avenue du Général~de~Gaulle, 37800 Sainte~Maure~de~Touraine, France

Tel: +33 2 47 65 50 65

www.johansens.com/saintemaure

FRANCE / MIDI~PYRÉNÉES (CARCASSONNE - FLOURE)

Château de Floure

1, Allée Gaston Bonheur, 11800 Floure, France

Tel: +33 4 68 79 11 29

www.johansens.com/floure

FRANCE / MIDI~PYRÉNÉES (CARCASSONNE - MIREPOIX)

Relais Royal

8, Rue Maréchal Clauzel, 09500 Mirepoix, Carcassonne, France

Tel: +33 5 61 60 19 19

www.johansens.com/relaisroyal

FRANCE / MIDI~PYRÉNÉES (MARSOLAN - GERS)

Hôtel Lous Grits

Le Village, 32700 Marsolan - Gers, France

Tel: +33 562 283 710

www.johansens.com/lousgrits

FRANCE / NORMANDY (ARROMANCHES)

Manoir de Mathan

14480 Crépon, France

Tel: +33 2 31 22 21 73

www.johansens.com/mathan

FRANCE / NORMANDY (DEAUVILLE - CAMBREMER)

Château les Bruyères

Route du Cadran, 14340 Cambremer, France

Tel: +33 2 31 32 22 45

www.johansens.com/lesbruyeres

FRANCE / NORMANDY (ETRETAT)

Domaine Saint~Clair, Le Donjon

Chemin de Saint~Clair, 76790 Etretat, France

Tel: +33 2 35 27 08 23

www.johansens.com/donjon

FRANCE / NORMANDY (HONFLEUR - CRICQUEBOEUF)

Manoir de la Poterie, Spa "Les Thermes"

Chemin Paul Ruel, 14113 Cricqueboeuf, France

Tel: +33 2 31 88 10 40

www.johansens.com/manoirdelapoterie

Hotels - Europe & The Mediterranean

Properties listed below can be found in our Recommended Hotels & Spas - Europe & The Mediterranean 2008 Guide.
More information on our portfolio of guides can be found on page 447.

FRANCE / NORMANDY (MONTPICHON - ST~LÔ)

Le Castel

50210 Montpinchon, France

Tel: +33 2 33 17 00 45
www.johansens.com/lecastelnormandy

FRANCE / NORMANDY (PORT~EN~BESSIN)

Château la Chenevière

Escures-Commes, 14520 Port~en~Bessin, France

Tel: +33 2 31 51 25 25
www.johansens.com/cheneviere

FRANCE / NORTH - PICARDY (EMMERIN)

La Howarderie

1, Rue des Fusillés, 59320 Emmerin, France

Tel: +33 3 20 10 31 00
www.johansens.com/howarderie

FRANCE / NORTH - PICARDY (GOSNAY - BÉTHUNE)

La Chartreuse du Val Saint~Esprit

62199 Gosnay, France

Tel: +33 3 21 62 80 00
www.johansens.com/lachartreuse

FRANCE / NORTH - PICARDY (LILLE)

Carlton Hôtel

3 Rue de Paris, 59000 Lille, France

Tel: +33 3 20 13 33 13
www.johansens.com/carltonlille

FRANCE / NORTH - PICARDY (RECQUES~SUR~HEM - CALAIS)

Château de Cocove

62890 Recques~sur~Hem, France

Tel: +33 3 21 82 68 29
www.johansens.com/chateaudecocove

FRANCE / PARIS (CHAMPS~ELYSÉES)

Hospes Lancaster

7, Rue de Berri, 75008 Paris, France

Tel: +33 1 40 76 40 76
www.johansens.com/hospeslancaster

FRANCE / PARIS (CHAMPS~ELYSÉES)

Hôtel Balzac

6, Rue Balzac, 75008 Paris, France

Tel: +33 1 44 35 18 00
www.johansens.com/balzac

FRANCE / PARIS (CHAMPS~ELYSÉES)

Hôtel de Sers

41, Avenue Pierre 1er de Serbie, 75008 Paris, France

Tel: +33 1 53 23 75 75
www.johansens.com/hoteldesers

FRANCE / PARIS (CHAMPS~ELYSÉES)

Hôtel San Régis

12 Rue Jean Goujon, 75008 Paris, France

Tel: +33 1 44 95 16 16
www.johansens.com/sanregis

FRANCE / PARIS (CHAMPS~ELYSÉES)

La Trémoille

14 Rue de la Trémoille, 75008 Paris, France

Tel: +33 1 56 52 14 00
www.johansens.com/tremoille

FRANCE / PARIS (ETOILE - PORTE MAILLOT)

Hôtel Duret

30 rue Duret, 75116 Paris, France

Tel: +33 1 45 00 42 60
www.johansens.com/duret

FRANCE / PARIS (ETOILE - PORTE MAILLOT)

La Villa Maillot

143 Avenue de Malakoff, 75116 Paris, France

Tel: +33 1 53 64 52 52
www.johansens.com/lavillamaillot

FRANCE / PARIS (INVALIDES)

Hôtel le Tourville

16 Avenue de Tourville, 75007 Paris, France

Tel: +33 1 47 05 62 62
www.johansens.com/tourville

FRANCE / PARIS (JARDIN DU LUXEMBOURG)

Le Sainte~Beuve

9 Rue Sainte~Beuve, 75006 Paris, France

Tel: +33 1 45 48 20 07
www.johansens.com/saintebeuve

FRANCE / PARIS (MADELEINE)

Hôtel Opéra Richepanse

14 Rue du Chevalier de Saint~George, 75001 Paris, France

Tel: +33 1 42 60 36 00
www.johansens.com/richepanse

Hotels - Europe & The Mediterranean

Properties listed below can be found in our Recommended Hotels & Spas - Europe & The Mediterranean 2008 Guide.
More information on our portfolio of guides can be found on page 447.

FRANCE / PARIS (MARAIS)

Hôtel du Petit Moulin

29-31 Rue de Poitou, 75003 Paris, France

Tel: +33 1 42 74 10 10
www.johansens.com/petitmoulin

FRANCE / PARIS (ST~GERMAIN~DES~PRÉS)

Hôtel Duc de Saint~Simon

14 rue de Saint~Simon, 75007 Paris, France

Tel: +33 1 44 39 20 20
www.johansens.com/saintsimon

FRANCE / PARIS REGION (BARBIZON)

Hostellerie du Bas-Breau

22 Rue Grande, 77630 Barbizon, France

Tel: +33 1 60 66 40 05
www.johansens.com/basbreau

FRANCE / PARIS REGION
(CHARTRES - ST~SYMPHORIEN~LE~CHÂTEAU)

Château d'Esclimont

28700 Saint~Symphorien~Le~Château, France

Tel: +33 2 37 31 15 15
www.johansens.com/esclimont

FRANCE / PARIS REGION (GRESSY)

Le Manoir de Gressy

77410 Gressy~en~France, Paris, France

Tel: +33 1 60 26 68 00
www.johansens.com/manoirdegressy

FRANCE / PARIS REGION (ST~GERMAIN~EN~LAYE)

Cazaudehore "La Forestière"

1 Avenue du Président Kennedy, 78100
Saint~Germain~en~Laye, France

Tel: +33 1 30 61 64 64
www.johansens.com/cazaudehore

FRANCE / POITOU~CHARENTES
(CHÂTEAUBERNARD - COGNAC)

Château de l'Yeuse

65 Rue de Bellevue, Quartier de L'Echassier, 16100
Châteaubernard, France

Tel: +33 5 45 36 82 60
www.johansens.com/chateaudelyeuse

FRANCE / POITOU~CHARENTES (LA ROCHELLE)

Hôtel "Résidence de France"

43 Rue Minage, 17000 La Rochelle, France

Tel: +33 5 46 28 06 00
www.johansens.com/residencedefrance

FRANCE / POITOU~CHARENTES (ST~MARTIN~DE~RÉ)

Hôtel de Toiras

1 Quai Job-Foran, 17410 Saint~Martin~de~Ré,
France

Tel: +33 546 35 40 32
www.johansens.com/toiras

FRANCE / POITOU~CHARENTES (ST~PREUIL - COGNAC)

Relais de Saint~Preuil

Lieu-dit Chez Riviere, 16130 Saint~Preuil, France

Tel: +33 5 45 80 80 08
www.johansens.com/saintpreuil

FRANCE / PROVENCE (AUPS)

Bastide du Calalou

Village de Moissac-Bellevue, 83630 Aups, France

Tel: +33 4 94 70 17 91
www.johansens.com/calalou

FRANCE / PROVENCE (GORDES - JOUCAS)

Les Mas des Herbes Blanches

Joucas, 84220 Gordes, France

Tel: +33 4 90 05 79 79
www.johansens.com/herbesblanches

FRANCE / PROVENCE (GRIGNAN)

Manoir de la Roseraie

Route de Valréas, 26230 Grignan, France

Tel: +33 4 75 46 58 15
www.johansens.com/manoirdelaroseraie

FRANCE / PROVENCE
(LE PARADOU - LES BAUX~DE~PROVENCE)

Domaine le Hameau des Baux

Chemin de Bourgeac, 13520 Le Paradou, France

Tel: +33 4 90 54 10 30
www.johansens.com/hameaudesbaux

FRANCE / PROVENCE (LES STES~MARIES~DE~LA~MER)

L'Estelle en Camargue

Route du Petit Rhône, 13460 Les
Saintes~Maries~de~la~Mer, France

Tel: +33 4 90 97 89 01
www.johansens.com/lestelle

FRANCE / PROVENCE (ORGON - EYGALIÈRES)

Le Mas de la Rose

Route d'Eygalières, 13660 Orgon, France

Tel: +33 4 90 73 08 91
www.johansens.com/masdelarose

Hotels - Europe & The Mediterranean

Properties listed below can be found in our Recommended Hotels & Spas - Europe & The Mediterranean 2008 Guide. More information on our portfolio of guides can be found on page 447.

FRANCE / PROVENCE (PORT CAMARGUE)

Le Spinaker

Pointe de la Presqu'île, Port Camargue, 30240 Le Grau~du~Roi, France

Tel: +33 4 66 53 36 37
www.johansens.com/spinaker

FRANCE / PROVENCE (SABRAN - BAGNOLS~SUR~CÈZE)

Château de Montcaud

Combe, Bagnols~sur~Cèze, 30200 Sabran, Near Avignon, France

Tel: +33 4 66 89 60 60
www.johansens.com/montcaud

FRANCE / PROVENCE (ST~RÉMY~DE~PROVENCE)

Château des Alpilles

Route Départementale 31, Ancienne Route du Grès, 13210 Saint~Rémy~de~Provence, France

Tel: +33 4 90 92 03 33
www.johansens.com/chateaudesalpilles

FRANCE / PROVENCE (UCHAUX)

Château de Massillan

Chemin Hauteville, 84100 Uchaux, France

Tel: +33 4 90 40 64 51
www.johansens.com/massillan

FRANCE / RHÔNE~ALPES (BAGNOLS~EN~BEAUJOLAIS)

Château de Bagnols

69620 Bagnols, France

Tel: +33 4 74 71 40 00
www.johansens.com/bagnols

FRANCE / RHÔNE~ALPES (CONDRIEU)

Le Beau Rivage

2 rue du Beau-Rivage, 69420 Condrieu, France

Tel: +33 4 74 56 82 82
www.johansens.com/beaurivage

FRANCE / RHÔNE~ALPES (DIVONNE~LES~BAINS)

Château de Divonne

01220 Divonne~les~Bains, France

Tel: +33 4 50 20 00 32
www.johansens.com/chateaudedivonne

FRANCE / RHÔNE~ALPES (DIVONNE~LES~BAINS)

Domaine de Divonne

Avenue des Thermes, 01220 Divonne~les~Bains, France

Tel: +33 4 50 40 34 34
www.johansens.com/domainededivonne

FRANCE / RHÔNE~ALPES (LES GÊTS)

Chalet Hôtel La Marmotte

61 Rue du Chêne, 74260 Les Gêts, France

Tel: +33 4 50 75 80 33
www.johansens.com/chaletlamarmotte

FRANCE / RHÔNE~ALPES (MEGÈVE)

Le Fer à Cheval

36 route du Crêt d'Arbois, 74120 Megève, France

Tel: +33 4 50 21 30 39
www.johansens.com/cheval

FRANCE / RHÔNE~ALPES (SCIEZ~SUR~LÉMAN)

Château de Coudrée

Domaine de Coudrée, Bonnatrait, 74140 Sciez~sur~Léman, France

Tel: +33 4 50 72 62 33
www.johansens.com/decoudree

FRANCE / SOUTH WEST (BIARRITZ)

Hôtel du Palais

1 Avenue de L'Impératrice, 64200 Biarritz, France

Tel: +33 5 59 41 64 00
www.johansens.com/palais

FRANCE / SOUTH WEST (RIBÉRAC - DORDOGNE)

Château Le Mas de Montet

Petit-Bersac, 24600 Ribérac, Dordogne, France

Tel: +33 5 53 90 08 71
www.johansens.com/lemasdemontet

FRANCE / SOUTH WEST (ST~EMILION)

Le Relais du Château Franc Mayne

Château Franc Mayne, ROUTE Départementale 243, 33330 Saint~Emilion, France

Tel: +33 5 57 24 62 61
www.johansens.com/francmayne

FRANCE / SOUTH WEST (STE~RADEGONDE)

Château de Sanse

33350 Sainte~Radegonde, France

Tel: +33 5 57 56 41 10
www.johansens.com/chateaudesanse

FRANCE / WESTERN LOIRE (CHAMPIGNÉ)

Château des Briottières

49330 Champigné, France

Tel: +33 2 41 42 00 02
www.johansens.com/chateaudesbriottieres

Hotels - Europe & The Mediterranean

Properties listed below can be found in our Recommended Hotels & Spas - Europe & The Mediterranean 2008 Guide.
More information on our portfolio of guides can be found on page 447.

GREAT BRITAIN / ENGLAND (BEDFORDSHIRE)

Luton Hoo Hotel, Golf & Spa

The Mansion House, Luton Hoo, Luton,
Bedfordshire, LU1 3TQ, England

Tel: +44 1582 734437
www.johansens.com/lutonhoo

GREAT BRITAIN / ENGLAND (BERKSHIRE)

The French Horn

Sonning~on~Thames, Berkshire, RG4 6TN,
England

Tel: +44 1189 692 204
www.johansens.com/frenchhorneuro

GREAT BRITAIN / ENGLAND (DEVON)

Soar Mill Cove Hotel

Soar Mill Cove, Salcombe, South Devon, TQ7 3DS,
England

Tel: +44 1548 561 566
www.johansens.com/soarmillcoveeuro

GREAT BRITAIN / ENGLAND (HAMPSHIRE)

Tylney Hall

Rotherwick, Hook, Hampshire, RG27 9AZ, England

Tel: +44 1256 764881
www.johansens.com/tylneyhalleuro

GREAT BRITAIN / ENGLAND (LONDON)

Jumeirah Carlton Tower

On Cadogan Place, London, SW1X 9PY, England

Tel: +44 20 7235 1234
www.johansens.com/carltontowereuro

GREAT BRITAIN / ENGLAND (LONDON)

Jumeirah Lowndes Hotel

21 Lowndes Street, Knightsbridge, London, SW1X
9ES, England

Tel: +44 20 7823 1234
www.johansens.com/lowndeseuro

GREAT BRITAIN / ENGLAND (LONDON)

The Mayflower Hotel

26-28 Trebovir Road, London, SW5 9NJ, England

Tel: +44 20 7370 0991
www.johansens.com/mayflowereuro

GREAT BRITAIN / ENGLAND (LONDON)

Twenty Nevern Square

20 Nevern Square, London, SW5 9PD, England

Tel: +44 20 7565 9555
www.johansens.com/twentynevernsquareeuro

GREAT BRITAIN / ENGLAND (STAFFORDSHIRE)

Hoar Cross Hall Spa Resort

Hoar Cross, Near Yoxall, Staffordshire, DE13 8QS,
England

Tel: +44 1283 575671
www.johansens.com/hoarcrosshalleuro

GREAT BRITAIN / ENGLAND (EAST SUSSEX)

Ashdown Park Hotel

Wych Cross, Forest Row, East Sussex, RH18 5JR,
England

Tel: +44 1342 824 988
www.johansens.com/ashdownparkeuro

GREAT BRITAIN / ENGLAND (EAST SUSSEX)

The Grand Hotel

King Edward's Parade, Eastbourne, East Sussex,
BN21 4EQ, England

Tel: +44 1323 412345
www.johansens.com/grandeastbourneeuro

GREAT BRITAIN / ENGLAND (EAST SUSSEX)

Rye Lodge

Hilder's Cliff, Rye, East Sussex, TN31 7LD, England

Tel: +44 1797 223838
www.johansens.com/ryelodgeeuro

GREAT BRITAIN / ENGLAND (WARWICKSHIRE)

Nailcote Hall

Nailcote Lane, Berkswell, Near Solihull,
Warwickshire, CV7 7DE, England

Tel: +44 2476 466 174
www.johansens.com/nailcote

GREECE (ATHENS)

Hotel Pentelikon

66 Diligianni Street, 14562 Athens, Greece

Tel: +30 2 10 62 30 650
www.johansens.com/pentelikon

GREECE (CHIOS)

Argentikon Luxury Suites

Kambos, 82100 Chios, Greece

Tel: +30 227 10 33 111
www.johansens.com/argentikon

GREECE (CORFU)

Villa de Loulia

Peroulades, Corfu, Greece

Tel: +30 266 30 95 394
www.johansens.com/villadeloulia

Hotels - Europe & The Mediterranean

Properties listed below can be found in our Recommended Hotels & Spas - Europe & The Mediterranean 2008 Guide. More information on our portfolio of guides can be found on page 447.

GREECE (CRETE)

Elounda Peninsula All Suite Hotel

72053 Elounda, Crete, Greece

Tel: +30 28410 68250
www.johansens.com/peninsulacrete

GREECE (CRETE)

Elounda Gulf Villas & Suites

Elounda, 72053 Crete, Greece

Tel: +30 28410 90300
www.johansens.com/eloundagulf

GREECE (CRETE)

Paradise Island Villas

Aristophani Street, Anissaras Hersonissos, 70014 Crete, Greece

Tel: +30 289 702 2893
www.johansens.com/paradiseisland

GREECE (CRETE)

Pleiades Luxurious Villas

Plakes, 72100 Aghios Nikolaos, Crete, Greece

Tel: +30 28410 90450
www.johansens.com/pleiades

GREECE (CRETE)

St Nicolas Bay Resort Hotel & Villas

PO Box 47, 72100 Aghios Nikolaos, Crete, Greece

Tel: +30 2841 025041
www.johansens.com/stnicolasbay

GREECE (KAVALA)

Imaret

30-32 Poulidou Street, 65110 Kavala, Greece

Tel: +30 2510 620 151-55
www.johansens.com/imaret

GREECE (LEFKADA)

Pavezzo Country Retreat

Katouna, Lefkada, Greece

Tel: +30 26450 71782
www.johansens.com/pavezzo

GREECE (MYKONOS)

Apanema

Tagoo, Mykonos, Greece

Tel: +30 22890 28590
www.johansens.com/apanema

GREECE (MYKONOS)

Tharroe of Mykonos

Mykonos Town, Angelica, 84600 Mykonos, Greece

Tel: +30 22890 27370
www.johansens.com/tharroe

GREECE (RHODES)

Nikos Takis Fashion Hotel

Panetiou 26, Medieval Town, TK 85100, Rhodes, Greece

Tel: +30 22410 70773
www.johansens.com/fashionhotel

GREECE (SANTORINI)

Alexander's Boutique Hotel

84702 Oia, Santorini, Greece

Tel: +30 22860 71818
www.johansens.com/alexanders

GREECE (SANTORINI)

Canaves Oia

Oia, 87402 Santorini, Greece

Tel: +30 22860 71453/71128
www.johansens.com/canavesoia

GREECE (SPETSES)

Xenon Estate

Kokkinaria, 18050 Spetses, Greece

Tel: +30 22980 74120
www.johansens.com/xenon

HUNGARY (TIHANY - LAKE BALATON)

Allegro Hotel - Tihany Centrum

H-8237 Tihany, Batthyány u. 6, Hungary

Tel: +36 87 448456
www.johansens.com/hoteltihany

ITALY / CAMPANIA (FURORE)

Furore Inn Resort & Spa

Via Dell'Amore, 84010 Furore, Amalfi Coast, Italy

Tel: +39 089 830 4711
www.johansens.com/furoreinn

ITALY / CAMPANIA (ISCHIA)

Manzi Terme Hotel & Spa

Piazza Bagni, Casamicciola Terme, 80075 Ischia (NA), Italy

Tel: +39 081 994722
www.johansens.com/manziterme

Hotels - Europe & The Mediterranean

Properties listed below can be found in our Recommended Hotels & Spas - Europe & The Mediterranean 2008 Guide.
More information on our portfolio of guides can be found on page 447.

ITALY / CAMPANIA (RAVELLO)

Hotel Villa Maria

Via S. Chiara 2, 84010 Ravello (SA), Italy

Tel: +39 089 857255

www.johansens.com/villamaria

ITALY / CAMPANIA (SORRENTO)

Maison La Minervetta

Via Capo 25, Sorrento, 80067 Campania, Italy

Tel: +39 081 877 4455

www.johansens.com/minervettamaison

ITALY / EMILIA ROMAGNA (PARMA)

Palazzo Dalla Rosa Prati

Strada al Duomo 7, 43100 Parma, Italy

Tel: +39 0521 386 429

www.johansens.com/palazzodallarosaprati

ITALY / EMILIA ROMAGNA (PIACENZA - BORGO DI RIVALTA)

Torre di San Martino - Historical Residence

Loc. Borgo di Rivalta, 29010 Gazzola, Piacenza, Italy

Tel: +39 0523 972002

www.johansens.com/torredisanmartino

ITALY / EMILIA ROMAGNA (RAVENNA - RUSSI)

Hotel Villa Roncuzzi

Via M. Silvestroni, 6/10, 48026 San Pancrazio di Russi - Ravenna, Italy

Tel: +39 0544 534776

www.johansens.com/villaroncuzzi

ITALY / EMILIA ROMAGNA (REGGIO EMILIA)

Hotel Posta (Historical Residence)

Piazza del Monte, 2, 42100 Reggio Emilia, Italy

Tel: +39 05 22 43 29 44

www.johansens.com/posta

ITALY / EMILIA ROMAGNA (RICCIONE - ADRIATIC COAST)

Hotel des Nations

Lungomare Costituzione 2, 47838 Riccione (RN), Italy

Tel: +39 0541 647 878

www.johansens.com/hoteldesnations

ITALY / FRIULI VENEZIA (TRIESTE)

Urban Hotel Design

Androna Chiusa 4, 34121 Trieste, Italy

Tel: +39 040 302065

www.johansens.com/urbantrieste

ITALY / LAZIO (CIVITA CASTELLANA)

Relais Falisco

Via Don Minzoni 19, 01033 Civita Castellana (VT), Italy

Tel: +39 0761 54 98

www.johansens.com/falisco

ITALY / LAZIO (ORTE)

La Locanda della Chiocciola

Loc. Seripola SNC, 01028 Orte, Italy

Tel: +39 0761 402 734

www.johansens.com/lachiocciola

ITALY / LAZIO (PALO LAZIALE)

La Posta Vecchia Hotel Spa

Palo Laziale, 00055 Ladispoli, Rome, Italy

Tel: +39 0699 49501

www.johansens.com/postavecchia

ITALY / LAZIO (ROME)

Buonanotte Garibaldi

Via Garibaldi 83, 00153 Rome, Italy

Tel: +390 658 330 733

www.johansens.com/garibaldi

ITALY / LAZIO (ROME)

Hotel dei Borgognoni

Via del Bufalo 126 (Piazza di Spagna), 00187 Rome, Italy

Tel: +39 06 6994 1505

www.johansens.com/borgognoni

ITALY / LAZIO (ROME)

Hotel dei Consoli

Via Varrone 2/d, 00193 Rome, Italy

Tel: +39 0668 892 972

www.johansens.com/deiconsoli

ITALY / LAZIO (ROME)

Hotel Fenix

Viale Gorizia 5/7, 00198 Rome, Italy

Tel: +39 06 8540 741

www.johansens.com/fenix

ITALY / LAZIO (ROME)

Villa Spalletti Trivelli

via Piacenza 4, 00184 Rome, Italy

Tel: +39 06 48907934

www.johansens.com/villaspallettitrivelli

Hotels - Europe & The Mediterranean

Properties listed below can be found in our Recommended Hotels & Spas - Europe & The Mediterranean 2008 Guide. More information on our portfolio of guides can be found on page 447.

ITALY / LAZIO (ROME - BRACCIANO)

Hotel Villa Clementina

Via Traversa Quarto del Lago, 12/14, 00062 Bracciano (RM), Italy

Tel: +39 06 9986268

www.johansens.com/clementina

ITALY / LAZIO (SAN LORENZO NUOVO - LAKE BOLSENA)

Relais Le Torrette

Via Cassia km 120, 01020 San Lorenzo Nuovo (VT), Italy

Tel: +39 0763 726009

www.johansens.com/letorrette

ITALY / LIGURIA (FINALE LIGURE)

Hotel Punta Est

Via Aurelia 1, 17024 Finale Ligure (SV), Italy

Tel: +39 019 600611

www.johansens.com/puntaest

ITALY / LIGURIA (MONEGLIA)

Abbadia San Giorgio - Historical Residence

Piazzale San Giorgio, 16030 Moneglia (GE), Italy

Tel: +39 0185 491119

www.johansens.com/abbadiasangiorgio

ITALY / LIGURIA (PORTOFINO)

Hotel San Giorgio - Portofino House

Via del Fondaco, 11, 16034 Portofino (Genova), Italy

Tel: +39 0185 26991

www.johansens.com/portofinohouse

ITALY / LIGURIA (SANREMO COAST - DIANO MARINA)

Grand Hotel Diana Majestic

Via Oleandri 15, 18013 Diano Marina (IM), Italy

Tel: +39 0183 402 727

www.johansens.com/dianamajestic

ITALY / LIGURIA (SANTA MARGHERITA - PORTOFINO COAST)

Grand Hotel Miramare

Via Milite Ignoto, 30, 16038 Santa Margherita Ligure - Genova, Liguria, Italy

Tel: +39 0185 287013

www.johansens.com/grandmiramare

ITALY / LIGURIA (SESTRI LEVANTE)

Hotel Vis à Vis

Via della Chiusa 28, 16039 Sestri Levante (GE), Italy

Tel: +39 0185 42661

www.johansens.com/visavis

ITALY / LOMBARDY (BORMIO - BAGNI NUOVI - VALTELLINA)

Bagni di Bormio Spa Resort

Località Bagni Nuovi, 23038 Valdidentro (Sondrio), Italy

Tel: +39 0342 910131

www.johansens.com/bagnidibormio

ITALY / LOMBARDY (ERBUSCO)

L'Albereta

Via Vittorio Emanuele II, no 23, 25030 Erbusco (Bs), Italy

Tel: +39 030 7760 550

www.johansens.com/albereta

ITALY / LOMBARDY (ISEO HILLS - LAKE ISEO)

I Due Roccoli Relais

Via Silvio Bonomelli, Strada per Polaveno, 25049 Iseo (Brescia), Italy

Tel: +39 030 9822 977/8

www.johansens.com/idueroccoli

ITALY / LOMBARDY (LAKE COMO - BELLAGIO)

Grand Hotel Villa Serbelloni

Via Roma 1, 22021 Bellagio, Lake Como, Italy

Tel: +39 031 950 216

www.johansens.com/serbelloni

ITALY / LOMBARDY (LAKE GARDA - GARDONE RIVIERA)

Grand Hotel Gardone Riviera

Via Zanardelli 84, 25083 Gardone Riviera (BS), Lake Garda, Italy

Tel: +39 0365 20261

www.johansens.com/gardoneriviera

ITALY / LOMBARDY (LAKE GARDA - SALÒ)

Hotel Bellerive

Via Pietro da Salò 11, 25087 Salò (BS), Italy

Tel: +39 0365 520 410

www.johansens.com/bellerive

ITALY / LOMBARDY (MILAN)

Petit Palais maison de charme

Via Molino delle Armi 1, 20123 Milan, Italy

Tel: +39 02 584 891

www.johansens.com/petitpalais

ITALY / LOMBARDY (MILAN)

THE PLACE - Luxury serviced apartments

Via Romagnosi 4, 20121 Milan, Italy

Tel: +39 02 76026633

www.johansens.com/theplace

Hotels - Europe & The Mediterranean

Properties listed below can be found in our Recommended Hotels & Spas - Europe & The Mediterranean 2008 Guide.
More information on our portfolio of guides can be found on page 447.

ITALY / LOMBARDY (MILAN - MONZA)

Hotel de la Ville

Viale Regina Margherita di Savoia 15, 20052
Monza (MI), Italy

Tel: +39 039 3942 1
www.johansens.com/hoteldelaville

ITALY / PIEMONTE (ALAGNA - MONTE ROSA)

Hotel Cristallo

Piazza degli Alberghi, 13021 Alagna (VC), Italy

Tel: +39 0163 922 822/23
www.johansens.com/cristallo

ITALY / PIEMONTE (DOGLIANI - BAROLO DISTRICT)

Foresteria dei Poderi Einaudi

Borgata Gombe, 31, 12063 Dogliani (CN), Italy

Tel: +39 0173 70414
www.johansens.com/poderieinaudi

ITALY / PIEMONTE (GAVI)

Albergo L'Ostelliere

Frazione Monterotondo 56, 15065 Gavi (AL),
Piemonte, Italy

Tel: +39 0143 607 801
www.johansens.com/ostelliere

ITALY / PIEMONTE (LAKE MAGGIORE - BELGIRATE)

Villa dal Pozzo d'Annone

Strada Statale del Sempione 5, 28832 Belgirate
(VB), Lake Maggiore, Italy

Tel: +39 0322 7255
www.johansens.com/dalpozzodannone

ITALY / PIEMONTE (LAKE MAGGIORE - CANNOBIO)

Hotel Pironi

Via Marconi 35, 28822 Cannobio, Lake Maggiore
(VB), Italy

Tel: +39 0323 70624
www.johansens.com/hotelpironi

ITALY / PIEMONTE (LAKE MAGGIORE - STRESA)

Hotel Villa Aminta

Via Sempione Nord 123, 28838 Stresa (VB), Italy

Tel: +39 0323 933 818
www.johansens.com/aminta

ITALY / PIEMONTE (PENANGO - ASTI - MONFERRATO)

Relais Il Borgo

Via Biletta 60, 14030 Penango (AT), Italy

Tel: +39 0141 921272
www.johansens.com/relaisilborgo

ITALY / PIEMONTE (TORINO)

Hotel Principi di Piemonte

Via Gobetti, 15, 10123 Torino, Italy

Tel: +39 011 55151
www.johansens.com/principidipiemonte

ITALY / PUGLIA (CANOSA)

Country House Cefalicchio

Contrada Cefalicchio, Canosa di Puglia (Bari), Italy

Tel: +39 0883 662 736
www.johansens.com/cefalicchio

ITALY / SAN MARINO REPUBLIC (SAN MARINO)

Hotel Titano

Contrada del Collegio 31, 47890 San Marino
(RSM), San Marino Republic

Tel: +378 991007
www.johansens.com/hoteltitano

ITALY / SARDINIA (ALGHERO)

Villa Las Tronas

Lungomare Valencia 1, 07041 Alghero (SS), Italy

Tel: +39 079 981 818
www.johansens.com/lastronas

ITALY / SARDINIA (GUSPINI)

Tartheshotel

Via Parigi, 1, 09036 Guspini, Cagliari, Italy

Tel: +39 070 97 29000
www.johansens.com/thatheshotel

ITALY / SARDINIA (PORTO CERVO - COSTA SMERALDA)

Grand Hotel in Porto Cervo

Località Cala Granu, 07020 Porto Cervo (SS), Italy

Tel: +39 0789 91533
www.johansens.com/portocervo

ITALY / SARDINIA
(SANTA MARGHERITA DI PULA - CAGLIARI)

Villa del Parco and Spa, Forte Village

SS 195, Km 39.600, Santa Margherita di Pula,
09010 Cagliari, Italy

Tel: +39 070 92171
www.johansens.com/villadelparco

ITALY / SICILY (AEOLIAN ISLANDS - ISOLA DI VULCANO)

Therasia Resort

Loc. Vulcanello , Comune di Lipari, 98050 Aeolian
Islands - Isola di Vulcano, Italy

Tel: +39 090 9852555
www.johansens.com/therasia

Hotels - Europe & The Mediterranean

Properties listed below can be found in our Recommended Hotels & Spas - Europe & The Mediterranean 2008 Guide. More information on our portfolio of guides can be found on page 447.

ITALY / SICILY (AEOLIAN ISLANDS - LIMPARI)

Grand Hotel Arciduca

Via G Franza, 98055 Lipari (ME), Isole Eolie, Italy

Tel: +39 090 9812136
www.johansens.com/arciduca

ITALY / SICILY (AEOLIAN ISLANDS - SALINA)

Hotel Signum

Via Scalo 15, 98050 Salina~Malfa, Italy

Tel: +39 090 9844222
www.johansens.com/signum

ITALY / SICILY (MODICA)

Palazzo Failla Hotel

Via Blandini 5, 97010 Modica (RG), Italy

Tel: +39 0932 941059
www.johansens.com/plalazzopfailla

ITALY / SICILY (RAGUSA)

Locanda Don Serafino

Via XI Febbraio, 15 Ragusa Ibla, Italy

Tel: +39 0932 220065
www.johansens.com/serafino

ITALY / SICILY (RAGUSA)

Poggio del Sole Resort

S.P. Ragusa/Marina di Ragusa, km 57, 97100 Ragusa, Sicily, Italy

Tel: +39 0932 666 452
www.johansens.com/poggiodelsole

ITALY / SICILY (TAORMINA RIVIERA)

Baia Taormina Grand Palace Hotels & Spa

Via Nazionale, km 39, 98030 Marina d'Agro, Taormina Riviera (ME), Italy

Tel: +39 0942 756292
www.johansens.com/baiataormina

ITALY / SICILY (TAORMINA RIVIERA - GIARDINI NAXOS)

Grand Hotel Atlantis Bay

Via Nazionale 161, Taormina Mare (ME), Italy

Tel: +39 0942 618011
www.johansens.com/atlantis

ITALY / SICILY (TAORMINA RIVIERA - GIARDINI NAXOS)

Grand Hotel Mazzarò Sea Palace

Via Nazionale 147, 98030 Taormina (ME), Sicily, Italy

Tel: +39 0942 612111
www.johansens.com/mazzaroseapalace

ITALY / TRENTINO - ALTO ADIGE / DOLOMITES (COLFOSCO - CORVARA)

Romantik Hotel Art Hotel Cappella

Str. Pecei 17, Alta Badia - Dolomites, 39030 Colfosco - Corvara (BZ), Italy

Tel: +39 0471 836183
www.johansens.com/cappella

ITALY / TRENTINO - ALTO ADIGE / DOLOMITES (MERANO - BOLZANO)

Castel Fragsburg

Via Fragsburg 3, 39012 Merano, Italy

Tel: +39 0473 244071
www.johansens.com/fragsburg

ITALY / TRENTINO - ALTO ADIGE / DOLOMITES (NOVA LEVANTE)

Posthotel Cavallino Bianco

Via Carezza 30, 39056 Nova Levante (Bz), Dolomites, Italy

Tel: +39 0471 613113
www.johansens.com/weissesrossl

ITALY / TRENTINO - ALTO ADIGE / DOLOMITES (ORTISEI - VAL GARDENA)

Hotel Gardena Grödnerhof

Str. Vidalong 3, 39046 Ortisei, Italy

Tel: +39 0471 796 315
www.johansens.com/gardena

ITALY / TRENTINO - ALTO ADIGE / DOLOMITES (RIVA DEL GARDA)

Du Lac et du Parc Grand Resort

Viale Rovereto 44, 38066 Riva del Garda (TN), Italy

Tel: +39 0464 566600
www.johansens.com/dulacetduparc

ITALY / TUSCANY (AREZZO - LORO CIUFFENNA)

Relais Villa Belpoggio (Historical House)

Via Setteponti Ponente 40, 52024 Loro Ciuffenna, Arezzo, Italy

Tel: +39 055 9694411
www.johansens.com/villabelpoggio

ITALY / TUSCANY (CASTAGNETO CARDUCCI - MARINA)

Tombolo Talasso Resort

Via del Corallo 3, 57022 Marina di Castagneto Carducci (LI), Italy

Tel: +39 0565 74530
www.johansens.com/tombolo

ITALY / TUSCANY (CASTIGLIONE DELLA PESCAIA - MAREMMA)

L'Andana

Tenuta La Badiola, Localitá Badiola, 58043 Castiglione della Pescaia (Grosseto), Italy

Tel: +39 0564 944 800
www.johansens.com/andana

Hotels - Europe & The Mediterranean

Properties listed below can be found in our Recommended Hotels & Spas - Europe & The Mediterranean 2008 Guide.
More information on our portfolio of guides can be found on page 447.

ITALY / TUSCANY (CORTONA - AREZZO)

Villa Marsili

Viale Cesare Battisti 13, 52044 Cortona (Arezzo),
Italy

Tel: +39 0575 605 252
www.johansens.com/villamarsili

ITALY / TUSCANY (FORTE DEI MARMI)

Hotel Byron

Viale A Morin 46, 55042 Forte dei Marmi (LU), Italy

Tel: +39 0584 787 052
www.johansens.com/byron

ITALY / TUSCANY (ELBA ISLAND - PORTOFERRAIO)

Hotel Villa Ottone

Loc. Ottone, 57037 Portoferraio (LI), Isola d'Elba,
Italy

Tel: +39 0565 933 042
www.johansens.com/ottone

ITALY / TUSCANY (GREVE IN CHIANTI)

Villa Bordoni

Via San Cresci 31/32, Loc. Mezzuola, 50022 Greve
in Chianti (FI), Italy

Tel: +39 055 884 0004
www.johansens.com/villabordoni

ITALY / TUSCANY (FLORENCE)

**Casa Howard Guest Houses - Rome and
Florence**

18 via della Scala, Piazza Santa Maria Novella,
Florence, Italy

Tel: +39 066 992 4555
www.johansens.com/casahoward

ITALY / TUSCANY (LUCCA - PIETRASANTA)

**Albergo Pietrasanta - Palazzo Barsanti
Bonetti**

Via Garibaldi 35, 55045 Pietrasanta (Lucca), Italy

Tel: +39 0584 793 727
www.johansens.com/pietrasanta

ITALY / TUSCANY (FLORENCE)

Marignolle Relais & Charme

Via di S Quirichino a Marignolle 16, 50124
Florence, Italy

Tel: +39 055 228 6910
www.johansens.com/marignolle

ITALY / TUSCANY (LUCCA - SAN LORENZO A VACCOLI)

Albergo Villa Marta

Via del Ponte Guasperini 873, San Lorenzo a
Vaccoli, 55100 Lucca, Italy

Tel: +39 0583 37 01 01
www.johansens.com/villamarta

ITALY / TUSCANY (FLORENCE)

Relais Piazza Signoria

Via Vacchereccia 3, 50122 Florence, Italy

Tel: +39 055 3987239
www.johansens.com/piazzasignoria

ITALY / TUSCANY (LUCIGNANO D'ASSO - SIENA)

Lucignanello Bandini

Loc. Lucignano d'Asso, 53020 San Giovanni
d'Asso (SI), Italy

Tel: +39 0577 803 068
www.johansens.com/lucignanello

ITALY / TUSCANY (FLORENCE)

Residenza del Moro

Via del Moro 15, 50123 Florence, Italy

Tel: +39 055 290884
www.johansens.com/delmoro

ITALY / TUSCANY (MONTALCINO)

Castello Banfi - Il Borgo

Castello di Poggio alle Mura, 53024 Montalcino
(SI), Italy

Tel: +39 0577 877 700
www.johansens.com/castellobanfi

ITALY / TUSCANY (FLORENCE)

Villa le Piazzole

Via Suor Maria Celeste, 28, 50125 Florence, Italy

Tel: +39 055 223520
www.johansens.com/villalepiazzole

ITALY / TUSCANY (MONTEBENICHI - CHIANTI AREA)

Country House Casa Cornacchi

Loc. Montebenichi, 52021 Arezzo, Tuscany, Italy

Tel: +39 055 998229
www.johansens.com/cornacchi

ITALY / TUSCANY (FLORENCE - BORGO SAN LORENZO)

Monsignor Della Casa Country Resort

Via di Mucciano 16, 50032 Borgo San Lorenzo,
Florence, Italy

Tel: +39 055 840 821
www.johansens.com/monsignor

ITALY / TUSCANY (MONTEPULCIANO - SIENA)

Villa Poggiano

Via di Poggiano 7, 53045 Montepulciano (Siena),
Tuscany, Italy

Tel: +39 0578 758292
www.johansens.com/villapoggiano

Hotels - Europe & The Mediterranean

Properties listed below can be found in our Recommended Hotels & Spas - Europe & The Mediterranean 2008 Guide. More information on our portfolio of guides can be found on page 447.

ITALY / TUSCANY (PORTO ERCOLE - ARGENTARIO)

Il Pellicano Hotel & Spa

Loc. Sbarcatello, 58018 Porto Ercole (Gr), Tuscany, Italy

Tel: +39 0564 858111
www.johansens.com/ilpellicano

ITALY / TUSCANY (ROCCATEDERIGHI - GROSSETO)

Pieve di Caminino (Historical Residence)

Via Prov. di Peruzzo, 58028 Roccatederighi - Grosseto, Italy

Tel: +39 0564 569 736/7 or +39 3933 356 605
www.johansens.com/caminino

ITALY / TUSCANY (SIENA - BAGNAIA)

Borgo La Bagnaia Resort, Spa and Events Venue

Strada Statale 223, Km 56, 53016 Localita Bagnaia - Siena, Italy

Tel: +39 0577 813000
www.johansens.com/labagnaia

ITALY / TUSCANY (SIENA - PIEVESCOLA)

Relais la Suvera (Dimora Storica)

53030 Pievescola – Siena, Italy

Tel: +39 0577 960 300
www.johansens.com/relaislasuvera

ITALY / TUSCANY (VIAREGGIO)

Hotel Plaza e de Russie

Piazza d'Azeglio 1, 55049 Viareggio (LU), Italy

Tel: +39 0584 44449
www.johansens.com/russie

ITALY / UMBRIA (ASSISI - ARMENZANO)

Romantik Hotel le Silve di Armenzano

06081 Loc. Armenzano, Assisi (PG), Italy

Tel: +39 075 801 9000
www.johansens.com/silvediarmenzano

ITALY / UMBRIA (GUBBIO)

Castello di Petroia

Località Scritto di Gubbio, Petroia, 06020 Gubbio (Pg), Italy

Tel: +39 075 92 02 87
www.johansens.com/castellodipetroia

ITALY / UMBRIA (ORVIETO - ALLERONA)

I Casali di Monticchio

Vocabolo Monticchio 34, 05011 Allerona, Orvieto (TR), Italy

Tel: +39 0763 62 83 65
www.johansens.com/monticchio

ITALY / UMBRIA (PERUGIA - DERUTA)

L'Antico Forziere

Via della Rocca 2, 06051 Casalina Deruta (PG), Italy

Tel: +39 075 972 4314
www.johansens.com/anticoforziere

ITALY / UMBRIA (PERUGIA - PIEVE SAN QUIRICO)

Le Torri di Bagnara (Medieval Historical Residences)

Strada della Bruna 8, 06134 Pieve San Quirico, Perugia, Italy

Tel: +39 075 579 2001 and +39 335 6408 549
www.johansens.com/bagnara

ITALY / UMBRIA (PETRIGNANO - CORTONA)

Relais Alla Corte del Sole

Loc. I Giorgi, 06061 Petrignano del Lago (PG), Italy

Tel: +39 075 9689 008
www.johansens.com/cortedelsole

ITALY / UMBRIA (TODI)

Relais Todini

Frazione Collevalenza, 06059 Todi (PG), Italy

Tel: +39 075 887521
www.johansens.com/relaistodini

ITALY / UMBRIA (TORDANDREA DI ASSISI)

San Crispino Resort & Spa

Assisi, Tordandrea (PG), Italy

Tel: +39 075 804 3257
www.johansens.com/sancrispinoresortspa

ITALY / UMBRIA (UMBERTIDE - CAZOLARO)

La Preghiera

Via del Refari, 06018 (PG), Calzolaro, Umbertide, Italy

Tel: +39 075 9302 428
www.johansens.com/lapreghiera

ITALY / UMBRIA (UMBERTIDE - SAN FAUSTINO)

Abbazia San Faustino - Luxury Country House

Località San Faustino di Bagnolo, 06026 Pietralunga (PG), Italy

Tel: +39 339 720 1717
www.johansens.com/sanfaustino

ITALY / VALLE D'AOSTA (COURMAYEUR - MONT BLANC)

Mont Blanc Hotel Village

Localita La Croisette 36, 11015 La Salle (AO), Valle d'Aosta, Italy

Tel: +39 0165 864 111
www.johansens.com/montblanc

Hotels - Europe & The Mediterranean

Properties listed below can be found in our Recommended Hotels & Spas - Europe & The Mediterranean 2008 Guide.
More information on our portfolio of guides can be found on page 447.

ITALY / VALLE D'AOSTA (GRESSONEY~LA~TRINITÉ)

Hotel Jolanda Sport

Loc. Edelboden 31, Gressoney~La~Trinité, 11020
Gressoney~La~Trinité (Aosta), Italy

Tel: +39 0125 366 140

www.johansens.com/jolandasport

ITALY / VENETO (BARDOLINO - VERONA)

Color Hotel

Via Santa Cristina 5, 37011 Bardolino (VR), Italy

Tel: +39 045 621 0857

www.johansens.com/color

ITALY / VENETO (BASSANO DEL GRAPPA)

Hotel Villa Ca' Sette

Via Cunizza da Romano 4, 36061 Bassano del
Grappa, Italy

Tel: +39 0424 383 350

www.johansens.com/casette

ITALY / VENETO (COSTERMANO)

Locanda San Verolo

Località San Verolo, 37010 Costermano (VR), Italy

Tel: +39 045 720 09 30

www.johansens.com/sanverolo

ITALY / VENETO (GARDA)

Locanda San Vigilio

Località San Vigilio, 37016 Garda (VR), Italy

Tel: +39 045 725 66 88

www.johansens.com/sanvigilio

ITALY / VENETO (LIDO DI JESOLO)

Park Hotel Brasilia

Via Levantina, 30016 Lido di Jesolo, Italy

Tel: +39 0421 380851

www.johansens.com/parkhotelbrasilia

ITALY / VENETO (NEGRAR - VERONA)

Relais la Magioca

Via Moron 3, 37024 Negrar - Valpolicella (VR), Italy

Tel: +39 045 600 0167

www.johansens.com/lamagioca

ITALY / VENETO (PADOVA)

Methis Hotel

Riviera Paleocapa 70, 35141 Padova, Italy

Tel: +39 049 872 5555

www.johansens.com/methis

ITALY / VENETO (PESCHIERA DEL GARDA)

Ai Capitani Hotel

Via Castelletto 2/4, Peschiera del Garda (VR), Italy

Tel: +39 045 6400782 or 7553071

www.johansens.com/aicapitani

ITALY / VENETO (ROLLE DI CISON DI VALMARINO)

Relais Duca di Dolle

Via Piai Orientale 5, 31030 Rolle di Cison di
Valmarino (TV), Italy

Tel: +39 0438 975 809

www.johansens.com/foresteriabisol

ITALY / VENETO (VENICE)

Ca Maria Adele

Dorsoduro 111, 30123 Venice, Italy

Tel: +39 041 52 03 078

www.johansens.com/camariaadele

ITALY / VENETO (VENICE)

Ca' Nigra Lagoon Resort

Santa Croce 927, Venice, Italy

Tel: +39 041 2750047

www.johansens.com/canigra

ITALY / VENETO (VENICE)

Ca' Sagredo Hotel

Campo Santa Sofia 4198/99, 30121 Venice, Italy

Tel: +39 041 2413111

www.johansens.com/casagredo

ITALY / VENETO (VENICE)

Charming House DD724

Dorsoduro 724, 30123 Venice, Italy

Tel: +39 041 277 0262

www.johansens.com/charming

ITALY / VENETO (VENICE)

Hotel Flora

San Marco 2283/A, 30124 Venice, Italy

Tel: +39 041 52 05 844

www.johansens.com/hotelflora

ITALY / VENETO (VENICE)

Hotel Giorgione

SS Apostoli 4587, 30131 Venice, Italy

Tel: +39 041 522 5810

www.johansens.com/giorgione

Hotels - Europe & The Mediterranean

Properties listed below can be found in our Recommended Hotels & Spas - Europe & The Mediterranean 2008 Guide. More information on our portfolio of guides can be found on page 447.

ITALY / VENETO (VENICE)

Hotel Sant' Elena Venezia

Calle Buccari 10, Sant' Elena, 30132 Venice, Italy

Tel: +39 041 27 17 811

www.johansens.com/santelena

ITALY / VENETO (VENICE)

Londra Palace

Riva degli Schiavoni, 4171, 30122 Venice, Italy

Tel: +39 041 5200533

www.johansens.com/londra

ITALY / VENETO (VENICE)

Novecento Boutique Hotel

San Marco 2684, 30124 Venice, Italy

Tel: +39 041 24 13 765

www.johansens.com/novecento

ITALY / VENETO (VENICE - LIDO)

Albergo Quattro Fontane - Residenza d'Epoca

Via Quattro Fontane 16, 30126 Lido di Venezia, Venice, Italy

Tel: +39 041 526 0227

www.johansens.com/albergoquattrofontane

ITALY / VENETO (VERONA)

Hotel Gabbia d'Oro (Historical Residence)

Corso Porta Borsari 4A, 37121 Verona, Italy

Tel: +39 045 8003060

www.johansens.com/gabbiadoro

LATVIA (JÜRMALA)

TB Palace Hotel & Spa

Pilsonu Street 8, Jürmala, LV-2015, Latvia

Tel: +371 714 7094

www.johansens.com/tbpalace

LATVIA (RIGA)

Hotel Bergs

Bergs Bazaar, Elizabetes Street 83/85, LV-1050, Riga, Latvia

Tel: +371 6777 0900

www.johansens.com/bergs

LITHUANIA (VILNIUS)

Grotthuss Hotel

Ligoninès 7, 01134 Vilnius, Lithuania

Tel: +370 5 266 0322

www.johansens.com/grotthusshotel

LITHUANIA (VILNIUS)

The Narutis Hotel

24 Pilies Street, 01123 Vilnius, Lithuania

Tel: +370 5 2122 894

www.johansens.com/narutis

LUXEMBOURG (REMICH)

Hotel Saint~Nicolas

31 Esplanade, 5533 Remich, Luxembourg

Tel: +35 226 663

www.johansens.com/saintnicolas

THE NETHERLANDS (AMSTERDAM)

Ambassade Hotel

Herengracht 341, 1016 Amsterdam, The Netherlands

Tel: +31 20 5550 222

www.johansens.com/ambassade

THE NETHERLANDS (SANTPOORT)

Duin & Kruidberg Country Estate

Duin en Kruidbergerweg 60, 2071 Santpoort, Amsterdam, The Netherlands

Tel: +31 23 512 1800

www.johansens.com/duinkruidberg

THE NETHERLANDS (VEERE)

Auberge de Campveerse Toren

Kaai 2, 4351 AA Veere, The Netherlands

Tel: +31 0118 501 291

www.johansens.com/campveersetoren

PORTUGAL / ALENTEJO (BORBA)

Casa do Terreiro do Poço

Largo dos Combatentes da Grande Guerra 12, 7150-152 Borba, Portugal

Tel: +351 917 256077

www.johansens.com/casadoterreiro

PORTUGAL / ALENTEJO (EVORA)

Convento do Espinheiro Heritage Hotel & Spa

Canaviais, 7005-839 Évora, Portugal

Tel: +351 266 788 200

www.johansens.com/espinheiro

PORTUGAL / ALENTEJO (REDONDO)

Convento de São Paulo

Aldeia da Serra, 7170-120 Redondo, Portugal

Tel: +351 266 989 160

www.johansens.com/conventodesaopaulo

Hotels - Europe & The Mediterranean

Properties listed below can be found in our Recommended Hotels & Spas - Europe & The Mediterranean 2008 Guide. More information on our portfolio of guides can be found on page 447.

PORTUGAL / ALGARVE (ALMANCIL)

Quinta Jacintina - my secret garden hotel

Garrâo de Cima, 8135 - 025 Almancil, Portugal

Tel: +351 289 350 090

www.johansens.com/jacintina

PORTUGAL / ALGARVE (ALMANCIL)

Ria Park Hotel & Spa

Vale do Lobo, 8135-951 Almancil, Algarve, Portugal

Tel: +351 289 359 800

www.johansens.com/riapark

PORTUGAL / ALGARVE (QUINTA DO LAGO - ALMANCIL)

Hotel Quinta do Lago

8135-024 Almancil, Algarve, Portugal

Tel: +351 289 350 350

www.johansens.com/quintadolago

PORTUGAL / BEIRAS (MARIALVA - MÊDA)

Casas do Côro

Marialvamed Turismo Histórico e Lazer Lda, Largo do Côro, 6430-081 Marialva, Mêda, Portugal

Tel: +351 91 755 2020

www.johansens.com/casasdocoro

PORTUGAL / LISBON & TAGUS VALLEY (CASCAIS)

Albatroz Palace, Luxury Suites

Rua Frederico Arouca 100, 2750-353 Cascais, Lisbon, Portugal

Tel: +351 21 484 73 80

www.johansens.com/albatroz

PORTUGAL / LISBON & TAGUS VALLEY (CASCAIS)

Hotel Cascais Mirage

Av. Marginal, No 8554, 2754-536 Cascais, Portugal

Tel: +351 210 060 600

www.johansens.com/cascaismirage

PORTUGAL / LISBON & TAGUS VALLEY (ESTORIL)

Palacio Estoril, Hotel & Golf

Rua Particular, 2769-504 Estoril, Portugal

Tel: +351 21 468 0400 or +351 21 464 80 00

www.johansens.com/estoril

PORTUGAL / LISBON & TAGUS VALLEY (GOLEGÃ)

Hotel Lusitano

Rua Gil Vicente, 4, 2150-193 Golegã, Portugal

Tel: +351 249 979 170

www.johansens.com/lusitano

PORTUGAL / LISBON & TAGUS VALLEY (LISBON)

As Janelas Verdes

Rua das Janelas Verdes 47, 1200-690 Lisbon, Portugal

Tel: +351 21 39 68 143

www.johansens.com/janelasverdes

PORTUGAL / LISBON & TAGUS VALLEY (LISBON)

Heritage Av Liberdade

Avenida da Liberdade 28, 1250-145 Lisbon, Portugal

Tel: +351 213 404 040

www.johansens.com/liberdade

PORTUGAL / LISBON & TAGUS VALLEY (LISBON)

Hotel Aviz

Rua Duque de Palmela, 32, 1250-098 Lisbon, Portugal

Tel: +351 210 402 000

www.johansens.com/aviz

PORTUGAL / LISBON & TAGUS VALLEY (LISBON)

Hotel Britania

Rua Rodrigues Sampaio 17, 1150-278 Lisbon, Portugal

Tel: +351 21 31 55 016

www.johansens.com/britania

PORTUGAL / MADEIRA (FUNCHAL)

Quinta da Bela Vista

Caminho do Avista Navios 4, 9000 Funchal, Madeira, Portugal

Tel: +351 291 706 400

www.johansens.com/quintadabelavista

PORTUGAL / MADEIRA (FUNCHAL)

Quinta das Vistas Palace Gardens

Caminho de Santo Antonio 52, 9000-187 Funchal, Madeira, Portugal

Tel: +351 291 750 000

www.johansens.com/quintadasvistas

PORTUGAL / MADEIRA (PONTA DO SOL)

Estalagem da Ponta do Sol

Quinta da Rochinha, 9360 Ponta do Sol, Madeira, Portugal

Tel: +351 291 970 200

www.johansens.com/pontadosol

PORTUGAL / OPORTO & NORTHERN PORTUGAL (ERVEDOSA DO DOURO)

Quinta de San José

5130-123 Ervedosa do Douro, Portugal

Tel: +351 254 420000

www.johansens.com/quintasanjose

Hotels - Europe & The Mediterranean

Properties listed below can be found in our Recommended Hotels & Spas - Europe & The Mediterranean 2008 Guide. More information on our portfolio of guides can be found on page 447.

Vintage House

Lugar da Ponte, 5085-034 Pinhão, Portugal

Tel: +351 254 730 230
www.johansens.com/vintagehouse

SLOVENIA (BLED)

Hotel Golf Bled

Cankarjeva 4, 4260 Bled, Slovenia

Tel: +386 4579 1700
www.johansens.com/hotelgolfsi

SPAIN / ANDALUCÍA (AGUA AMARGA - ALMERÍA)

Mikasa Suites Resort

Ctra. de Carboneras, s/n,, 04149 Agua Amarga - Almería, Spain

Tel: +34 950 138 073
www.johansens.com/mikasa

SPAIN / ANDALUCÍA (ALCALÁ DE GUADAIRA - SEVILLA)

Hacienda La Boticaria

Ctra Alcalá - Utrera Km 12, 41500 Alcalá de Guadaira (Sevilla), Spain

Tel: +34 955 69 88 20
www.johansens.com/haciendalaboticaria

SPAIN / ANDALUCÍA (ARCOS DE LA FRONTERA)

Hotel Cortijo Faín

Carretera de Algar Km 3, 11630 Arcos de la Frontera, Cádiz, Spain

Tel: +34 956 704 131
www.johansens.com/cortijofain

SPAIN / ANDALUCÍA (BENALUP~CASAS VIEJAS)

Fairplay Golf Hotel & Spa

C/ La Torre s/n , 11190 Benalup~Casas Viejas (Cádiz), Spain

Tel: +34 956 429100
www.johansens.com/fairplaygolf

SPAIN / ANDALUCÍA (CARTAJIMA - MÁLAGA)

Los Castaños

Calle Iglesia 40, 29452 Cartajima (Málaga), Spain

Tel: +34 952 180 778
www.johansens.com/loscastanos

SPAIN / ANDALUCÍA (CAZALLA DE LA SIERRA - SEVILLA)

Palacio de San Benito

c/San Benito S/N, 41370 Cazalla de La Sierra, Sevilla, Spain

Tel: +34 954 88 33 36
www.johansens.com/palaciodesanbenito

SPAIN / ANDALUCÍA (CÓRDOBA)

Hospes Palacio del Bailío

Ramirez de las Casas Deza 10-12, 14001 Cordoba, Spain

Tel: +34 957 498 993
www.johansens.com/hospesbailio

SPAIN / ANDALUCÍA (ÉCIJA - SEVILLA)

Hotel Palacio de Los Granados

Emilio Castelar 42, 41400 Écija, Sevilla, Spain

Tel: +34 955 905 344
www.johansens.com/granados

SPAIN / ANDALUCÍA (ESTEPONA)

Gran Hotel Elba Estepona & Thalasso Spa

Urb. Arena Beach, Ctra. Estepona-Cádiz 151, 29680 Estepona, Spain

Tel: +34 952 809 200
www.johansens.com/elbaestepona

SPAIN / ANDALUCÍA (GRANADA)

El Ladrón de Agua

Carrera del Darro 13, 18010 Granada, Spain

Tel: +34 958 21 50 40
www.johansens.com/ladrondeagua

SPAIN / ANDALUCÍA (GRANADA)

Hospes Palacio de los Patos

C/ Solarillo de Gracia 1, 18002 Granada, Andalucía, Spain

Tel: +34 958 535 790
www.johansens.com/lospatos

SPAIN / ANDALUCÍA (GRANADA)

Hotel Casa Morisca

Cuesta de la Victoria 9, 18010 Granada, Spain

Tel: +34 958 221 100
www.johansens.com/morisca

SPAIN / ANDALUCÍA (GRANADA)

Hotel Palacio de Santa Inés

Cuesta de Santa Inés 9, 18010 Granada, Spain

Tel: +34 958 22 23 62
www.johansens.com/sanaines

SPAIN / ANDALUCÍA (GRANADA)

Palacio de los Navas

Calle Navas 1, 18009 Granada, Spain

Tel: +34 958 21 57 60
www.johansens.com/palaciodelosnavas

Hotels - Europe & The Mediterranean

Properties listed below can be found in our Recommended Hotels & Spas - Europe & The Mediterranean 2008 Guide.
More information on our portfolio of guides can be found on page 447.

SPAIN / ANDALUCÍA (GRANADA)

Santa Isabel la Real

C/Santa Isabel La Real 19, 18010 Granada, Spain

Tel: +34 958 294 658
www.johansens.com/santaisabel

SPAIN / ANDALUCÍA (GRANADA - LOJA)

Barceló la Bobadilla

Finca La Bobadilla, Apdo. 144, 18300 Loja, Granada, Spain

Tel: +34 958 32 18 61
www.johansens.com/bobadilla

SPAIN / ANDALUCÍA (JEREZ DE LA FRONTERA)

Casa Viña de Alcantara

Ctra. de Arcos Km 7.8, Jerez (Cádiz), Spain

Tel: +34 956 393 010
www.johansens.com/vinadealcantara

SPAIN / ANDALUCÍA (LA JOYA - ANTEQUERA)

Hotel La Fuente del Sol

Paraje Rosas Bajas, 29260 La Joya, Antequera, Spain

Tel: +34 95 12 39 823
www.johansens.com/fuentedelsol

SPAIN / ANDALUCÍA (LA VIÑUELA - MÁLAGA)

Hotel La Viñuela

Ctra. Vélez-Alhama S/n, 29712 La Viñuela (Málaga), Spain

Tel: +34 952 519 193
www.johansens.com/vinuela

SPAIN / ANDALUCÍA (LAS CABEZAS - SEVILLA)

Cortijo Soto Real

Ctra. Las Cabezas Villamartin Km 13, 41730 - Las Cabezas (Sevilla), Spain

Tel: +34 955 869 200
www.johansens.com/sotoreal

SPAIN / ANDALUCÍA (MÁLAGA)

Hotel Molina Lario

Molina Lario 22, 29015 Málaga, Spain

Tel: +34 952 06 002
www.johansens.com/hotelmolina

SPAIN / ANDALUCÍA (MOTRIL - GRANADA)

Casa de los Bates

Carretera Nacional 340 Málaga - Almeria, Km 329, 5 Salobreña - Motril, Provincia de Granada, Spain

Tel: +34 958 349 495
www.johansens.com/casadelosbates

SPAIN / ANDALUCÍA (RINCON DE LA VICTORIA - MÁLAGA)

El Molino de Santillán

Ctra. de Macharaviaya, Km 3, 29730 Rincón de la Victoria, Málaga, Spain

Tel: +34 952 40 09 49
www.johansens.com/molinodesantillan

SPAIN / ANDALUCÍA (SANLÚCAR DE BARRAMEDA - CÁDIZ)

Posada de Palacio

C/ Caballeros, 11, Sanlúcar de Barameda (Cádiz), Spain

Tel: +34 956 36 4840
www.johansens.com/posadadepalacio

SPAIN / ANDALUCÍA (SANLÚCAR LA MAYOR - SEVILLA)

Hacienda Benazuza el Bulli Hotel

C/Virgen de las Nieves S/N, 41800 Sanlúcar La Mayor, Seville, Spain

Tel: +34 955 70 33 44
www.johansens.com/haciendabenazuza

SPAIN / ANDALUCÍA (SEVILLA)

Casa No 7

Calle Virgenes No 7, 41004 Sevilla, Spain

Tel: +34 954 221 581
www.johansens.com/casanumero7

SPAIN / ANDALUCÍA (SEVILLA)

Casa Romana Hotel Boutique

Calle Trajano 15, 41002 Sevilla, Spain

Tel: +34 954 915 170
www.johansens.com/casaromana

SPAIN / ANDALUCÍA (SEVILLA)

Hospes las Casas del Rey de Baeza

C/Santiago, Plaza Jesús de la Redención 2, 41003 Sevilla, Spain

Tel: +34 954 561 496
www.johansens.com/casasdelrey

SPAIN / ANDALUCÍA (SOTOGRANDE - SAN ROQUE)

Hotel Almenara

A-7 (National Road), 11310 Sotogrande, Spain

Tel: +34 956 58 20 00
www.johansens.com/almenara

SPAIN / ANDALUCÍA (VILLANUEVA DE LA CONCEPCIÓN)

La Posada del Torcal

29230 Villanueva de la Concepción, Málaga, Spain

Tel: +34 952 03 11 77
www.johansens.com/posadadeltorcal

Hotels - Europe & The Mediterranean

Properties listed below can be found in our Recommended Hotels & Spas - Europe & The Mediterranean 2008 Guide.
More information on our portfolio of guides can be found on page 447.

SPAIN / ARAGÓN (TRAMACASTILLA DE TENA)

Hotel el Privilegio de Tena

Plaza Mayor, 22663 Tramacastilla de Tena, Aragón, Spain

Tel: +34 974 487 206
www.johansens.com/elprivilegiodetena

SPAIN / ASTURIAS (CANGAS DE ONIS)

Hotel La Cepada

Avenida Contranquil s/n, 33550 Cangas de Onís, Spain

Tel: +34 985 84 94 45
www.johansens.com/cepada

SPAIN / ASTURIAS (VILLAMAYOR)

Palacio de Cutre

La Goleta S/N, Villamayor, 33583 Infiesto, Asturias, Spain

Tel: +34 985 70 80 72
www.johansens.com/palaciodecutre

SPAIN / BALEARIC ISLANDS (IBIZA)

Atzaró Agroturismo

Ctra. San Juan, Km 15, 07840 Santa Eulalia, Ibiza, Balearic Islands

Tel: +34 971 33 88 38
www.johansens.com/atzaroagroturismo

SPAIN / BALEARIC ISLANDS (IBIZA)

Can Lluc

Crta. Santa Inés, km 2, 07816 San Rafael, Ibiza, Balearic Islands

Tel: +34 971 198 673
www.johansens.com/canlluc

SPAIN / BALEARIC ISLANDS (IBIZA)

Cas Gasi

Camino Viejo de Sant Mateu s/n, PO Box 117, 07814 Santa Gertrudis, Ibiza, Balearic Islands

Tel: +34 971 197 700
www.johansens.com/casgasi

SPAIN / BALEARIC ISLANDS (IBIZA)

Hotel Hacienda Na Xamena

San Miguel, 07815 Ibiza, Spain

Tel: +34 971 334 500
www.johansens.com/xamena

SPAIN / BALEARIC ISLANDS (MALLORCA)

Blau Porto Petro Beach Resort & Spa

Avenida des Far 12, 07691 Porto Petro (Santanyí), Mallorca, Balearic Islands

Tel: +34 971 648 282
www.johansens.com/blaupivilege

SPAIN / BALEARIC ISLANDS (MALLORCA)

Can Simoneta

Ctra. de Artá a Canyamel km 8, Finca Torre de Canyamel, 07580 Capdepera, Mallorca, Balearic Islands

Tel: +34 971 816 110
www.johansens.com/simoneta

SPAIN / BALEARIC ISLANDS (MALLORCA)

Hospes Maricel

Carretera d'Andratx 11, 07181 Cas Català, (Calvià) Mallorca, Balearic Islands

Tel: +34 971 707 744
www.johansens.com/maricel

SPAIN / BALEARIC ISLANDS (MALLORCA)

Hotel Aimia

Santa Maria del Camí, 1 07108 Port de Sóller, Mallorca, Balearic Islands, Spain

Tel: +34 971 631 200
www.johansens.com/aimia

SPAIN / BALEARIC ISLANDS (MALLORCA)

Hotel Cala Sant Vicenç

c/Maressers 2, Cala Sant Vicenç, 07469 Pollença, Mallorca, Balearic Islands, Spain

Tel: +34 971 53 02 50
www.johansens.com/hotelcala

SPAIN / BALEARIC ISLANDS (MALLORCA)

Hotel Dalt Murada

C/ Almudaina 6-A, 07001 Palma de Mallorca, Mallorca, Balearic Islands

Tel: +34 971 425 300
www.johansens.com/daltmurada

SPAIN / BALEARIC ISLANDS (MALLORCA)

Hotel La Moraleja

Urbanización Los Encinares s/n, 07469 Cala San Vicenç, Mallorca, Balearic Islands

Tel: +34 971 534 010
www.johansens.com/lamoraleja

SPAIN / BALEARIC ISLANDS (MALLORCA)

Hotel Migjorn

Poligono 18, Parcela 477, 07630 Campos, Mallorca, Balearic Islands

Tel: +34 971 650 668
www.johansens.com/hotelmigjorn

SPAIN / BALEARIC ISLANDS (MALLORCA)

Hotel Tres

C/ Apuntadores 3, 07012 Palma de Mallorca, Balearic Islands, Spain

Tel: +34 971 717 333
www.johansens.com/hoteltres

Hotels - Europe & The Mediterranean

Properties listed below can be found in our Recommended Hotels & Spas - Europe & The Mediterranean 2008 Guide.
More information on our portfolio of guides can be found on page 447.

SPAIN / BALEARIC ISLANDS (MALLORCA)

Palacio Ca Sa Galesa

Carrer de Miramar 8, 07001 Palma de Mallorca,
Balearic Islands

Tel: +34 971 715 400
www.johansens.com/casagalesa

SPAIN / BALEARIC ISLANDS (MALLORCA)

Read's Hotel & Vespasian Spa

Carretera Viejo de Alaro S/n, Santa María 07320,
Mallorca, Balearic Islands

Tel: +34 971 14 02 61
www.johansens.com/reads

SPAIN / BALEARIC ISLANDS (MALLORCA)

Son Brull Hotel & Spa

Ctra. Palma - Pollença, MA 2200 - Km 49.8, 07460
Pollença, Mallorca, Spain

Tel: +34 971 53 53 53
www.johansens.com/sonbrull

SPAIN / BALEARIC ISLANDS (MALLORCA)

Valldemossa Hotel & Restaurant

Ctra. Vieja de Valldemossa s/n, 07170
Valldemossa, Mallorca, Balearic Islands

Tel: +34 971 61 26 26
www.johansens.com/valldemossa

SPAIN / CANARY ISLANDS (FUERTEVENTURA)

Hotel Elba Palace Golf

Urb. Fuerteventura Golf Club, Ctra. de Jandia,
km11, 35610 Antigua, Fuerteventura, Canary
Islands

Tel: +34 928 16 39 22
www.johansens.com/elbapalacegolfhotel

SPAIN / CANARY ISLANDS (FUERTEVENTURA)

Kempinski Atlantis Bahía Real

Avenida Grandes Playas s/n, 35660 Corralejo,
Fuerteventura, Canary Islands

Tel: +34 928 53 64 44
www.johansens.com/atlantisbahiareal

SPAIN / CANARY ISLANDS (LANZAROTE)

Princesa Yaiza Suite Hotel Resort

Avenida Papagayo 6, 35580 Playa Blanca, Yaiza,
Lanzarote, Canary Islands

Tel: +34 928 519 222
www.johansens.com/yaiza

SPAIN / CANARY ISLANDS (TENERIFE)

Abama

Carretera General TF-47, Km 9, 38687 Guía de
Isora, Tenerife, Canary Islands

Tel: +34 902 105 600
www.johansens.com/abama

SPAIN / CANARY ISLANDS (TENERIFE)

Hotel Jardín Tropical

Calle Gran Bretaña, 38660 Costa Adeje, Tenerife,
Canary Islands

Tel: +34 922 74 60 00
www.johansens.com/jardintropical

SPAIN / CANARY ISLANDS (TENERIFE)

Hotel las Madrigueras

Golf Las Américas, 38660 Playa de Las Américas,
Tenerife, Canary Islands

Tel: +34 922 77 78 18
www.johansens.com/madrigueras

SPAIN / CANARY ISLANDS (TENERIFE)

Jardín de la Paz

Calle de Acentejo 48-52, 38370 La Matanza,
Tenerife, Canary Islands

Tel: +34 922 578 818
www.johansens.com/jardindelapaz

SPAIN / CANTABRIA (BARCENILLA)

Posada Los Nogales

Barrio la Partilla 7, Piélagos, 39477 Barcenilla,
Spain

Tel: +34 942 589 222
www.johansens.com/losnogales

SPAIN / CASTILLA~LA MANCHA
(BELVÍS DE LA JARA - TOLEDO)

Finca Canturias

Ctra. Alcaudete - Calera, Km 12, 45660 Belvís de la
Jara, Toledo, Spain

Tel: +34 925 59 41 08
www.johansens.com/canturias

SPAIN / CASTILLA~LA MANCHA (CIUDAD REAL)

Hotel Palacio de la Serna

C/ Cervantes, 18, Ballesteros de Calatrava, 13432
Ciudad Real, Castilla~La Mancha, Spain

Tel: +34 926 84 2413/2208
www.johansens.com/palaciodelaserna

SPAIN / CASTILLA Y LEÓN (AMPUDIA - PALENCIA)

Posada de la Casa del Abad de Ampudia

Plaza Francisco Martín Gromaz 12, 34160
Ampudia (Palencia), Spain

Tel: +34 979 768 008
www.johansens.com/abaddeampudia

SPAIN / CASTILLA Y LEÓN (SALAMANCA)

Hotel Rector

c/Rector Esperabé 10-Apartado 399, 37008
Salamanca, Spain

Tel: +34 923 21 84 82
www.johansens.com/rector

Hotels - Europe & The Mediterranean

Properties listed below can be found in our Recommended Hotels & Spas - Europe & The Mediterranean 2008 Guide. More information on our portfolio of guides can be found on page 447.

SPAIN / CASTILLA Y LEÓN (TOPAS - SALAMANCA)

Castillo de Buen Amor

Carretera National 630 Km 317.6, 37799 Topas, Salamanca, Spain

Tel: +34 923 355 002
www.johansens.com/buenamor

SPAIN / CASTILLA Y LEÓN (VALVERDÓN - SALAMANCA)

Hacienda Zorita

Carretera Salamanca-Ledesma, Km 8.7, 37115 Valverdón, Salamanca, Spain

Tel: +34 923 129 400
www.johansens.com/haciendazorita

SPAIN / CATALUÑA (BARCELONA)

Gallery Hotel

C/ Rosselló 249, 08008 Barcelona, Spain

Tel: +34 934 15 99 11
www.johansens.com/gallery

SPAIN / CATALUÑA (BARCELONA)

Grand Hotel Central

Via Laietana 30, 08003 Barcelona, Spain

Tel: +34 93 295 79 00
www.johansens.com/grandhotelcentral

SPAIN / CATALUÑA (BARCELONA)

Hotel Casa Fuster

Passeig de Gràcia 132, 08008 Barcelona, Spain

Tel: +34 93 255 30 00
www.johansens.com/fuster

SPAIN / CATALUÑA (BARCELONA)

Hotel Claris

Pau Claris 150, 08009 Barcelona, Spain

Tel: +34 93 487 62 62
www.johansens.com/claris

SPAIN / CATALUÑA (BARCELONA)

Hotel Cram

C/ Aribau 54, 8011 Barcelona, Spain

Tel: +34 93 216 77 00
www.johansens.com/hotelcram

SPAIN / CATALUÑA (BARCELONA)

Hotel Duquesa de Cardona

Paseo Colon 12, 08002 Barcelona, Spain

Tel: +34 93 268 90 90
www.johansens.com/duquesadecardona

SPAIN / CATALUÑA (BARCELONA)

Hotel Gran Derby

Calle Loreto 28, 08029 Barcelona, Spain

Tel: +34 93 445 2544
www.johansens.com/granderby

SPAIN / CATALUÑA (BARCELONA)

Hotel Granados 83

c/ Enric Granados 83, 08008 Barcelona, Spain

Tel: +34 93 492 96 70
www.johansens.com/granados83

SPAIN / CATALUÑA (BARCELONA)

Hotel Omm

Rosselló 265, 08008 Barcelona, Spain

Tel: +34 93 445 40 00
www.johansens.com/hotelomm

SPAIN / CATALUÑA (BEGUR)

El Convent Begur

c/del Racó 2, sa Riera, 17255 Begur, Spain

Tel: +34 972 62 30 91
www.johansens.com/conventbegur

SPAIN / CATALUÑA (COSTA BRAVA)

Hotel Rigat Park & Spa Beach Hotel

Av. America 1, Playa de Fenals, 17310 Lloret de Mar, Costa Brava, Gerona, Spain

Tel: +34 972 36 52 00
www.johansens.com/rigatpark

SPAIN / CATALUÑA (COSTA BRAVA)

Hotel Santa Marta

Playa de Santa Cristina, 17310 Lloret de Mar, Spain

Tel: +34 972 364 904
www.johansens.com/santamarta

SPAIN / CATALUÑA (EL VENDRELL)

Le Meridien Ra Beach Hotel & Spa

Avinguda Sanatori 1, 43880 El Vendrell, Spain

Tel: +34 977 694 200
www.johansens.com/hotelra

SPAIN / CATALUÑA (LA SELVA DEL CAMP)

Mas Passamaner

Camí de la Serra 52, 43470 La Selva del Camp (Tarragona), Spain

Tel: +34 977 766 333
www.johansens.com/passamaner

Hotels - Europe & The Mediterranean

Properties listed below can be found in our Recommended Hotels & Spas - Europe & The Mediterranean 2008 Guide.
More information on our portfolio of guides can be found on page 447.

SPAIN / CATALUÑA (MASQUEFA)

Can Bonastre Wine Resort

Ctra. B224 km 13.5, 08783 Masquefa, Spain

Tel: +34 91 772 87 67

www.johansens.com/canbonastre

SPAIN / CATALUÑA (PUIGCERDÀ)

Hospes Villa Paulita

Av. Pons i Gash, 15, 17520 Puigcerdà (Girona), Spain

Tel: +34 972 884 662

www.johansens.com/villapaulita

SPAIN / CATALUÑA (ROSES)

Romantic Villa - Hotel Vistabella

Cala Canyelles Petites, PO Box 3, 17480 Roses (Gerona), Spain

Tel: +34 972 25 62 00

www.johansens.com/vistabella

SPAIN / CATALUÑA (SITGES)

Dolce Sitges Hotel

Av. Cami de Miralpeix 12, Sitges 08870, Spain

Tel: +34 938 109 000

www.johansens.com/dolcesitges

SPAIN / CATALUÑA (SITGES)

San Sebastian Playa Hotel

Calle Port Alegre 53, 08870 Sitges (Barcelona), Spain

Tel: +34 93 894 86 76

www.johansens.com/sebastian

SPAIN / EXTREMADURA (ZAFRA)

Casa Palacio Conde de la Corte

Plaza Pilar Redondo 2, 06300 Zafra (Badajoz), Spain

Tel: +34 924 563 311

www.johansens.com/condedelacorte

SPAIN / MADRID (MADRID)

Gran Meliá Fénix

Hermosilla 2, 28001 Madrid, Spain

Tel: +34 91 431 67 00

www.johansens.com/granmeliafenix

SPAIN / MADRID (MADRID)

Hospes Madrid

Plaza de la Independencia, 3, 28001 Madrid, Spain

Tel: +34 914 322 911

www.johansens.com/hospesmadrid

SPAIN / MADRID (MADRID)

Hotel Orfila

C/Orfila, No 6, 28010 Madrid, Spain

Tel: +34 91 702 77 70

www.johansens.com/orfila

SPAIN / MADRID (MADRID)

Hotel Quinta de los Cedros

C/Allendesalazar 4, 28043 Madrid, Spain

Tel: +34 91 515 2200

www.johansens.com/loscedros

SPAIN / MADRID (MADRID)

Hotel Urban

Carrera de San Jerónimo 34, 28014 Madrid, Spain

Tel: +34 91 787 77 70

www.johansens.com/urban

SPAIN / MADRID (MADRID)

Hotel Villa Real

Plaza de las Cortes 10, 28014 Madrid, Spain

Tel: +34 914 20 37 67

www.johansens.com/villareal

SPAIN / MADRID (MADRID - BOADILLA DEL MONTE)

Antiguo Convento

C/ de Las Monjas, s/n Boadilla del Monte, 28660 Madrid, Spain

Tel: +34 91 632 22 20

www.johansens.com/elconvento

SPAIN / PAÍS VASCO (ZEANURI)

Hotel Etxegana

Ipiñaburu 38, Zeánuri, 48144 Bizkaia, Spain

Tel: +34 946 338 448

www.johansens.com/etxegana

SPAIN / VALENCIA (ALICANTE)

Hospes Amérigo

C/ Rafael Altamira 7, 03002 Alicante, Spain

Tel: +34 965 14 65 70

www.johansens.com/amerigo

SPAIN / VALENCIA (ALICANTE)

Hotel Sidi San Juan & Spa

C/ La Doblada, 8 - Playa de San Juan, 03540 Alicante, Spain

Tel: +34 96 516 13 00

www.johansens.com/sanjuan

Hotels - Europe & The Mediterranean

Properties listed below can be found in our Recommended Hotels & Spas - Europe & The Mediterranean 2008 Guide. More information on our portfolio of guides can be found on page 447.

SPAIN / VALENCIA (ALQUERIAS)

Torre la Mina

C/ La Regenta 1, 12539 Alquerias - Castellón, Spain

Tel: +34 964 57 1746/0180
www.johansens.com/torrelamina

SPAIN / VALENCIA (BENICÀSSIM)

Hotel Termas Marinas el Palasiet

Partida Cantallops s/n, 12560 Benicàssim, Castellón, Costa del Azahar, Spain

Tel: +34 964 300 250
www.johansens.com/termasmarinas

SPAIN / VALENCIA (CALPE - ALICANTE)

Hotel Marisol Park

Urbanización , Marisol Park. 1A, Apartado de correos 692, 03710 Calpe - Alicante, Spain

Tel: +34 965 875 700
www.johansens.com/marisol

SPAIN / VALENCIA (JÁTIVA - XÀTIVA)

Hotel Mont Sant

Subida Al Castillo, s/n Játiva - Xàtiva, 46800 Valencia, Spain

Tel: +34 962 27 50 81
www.johansens.com/montsant

SPAIN / VALENCIA (MUSEROS)

Ibb Masia de Lacy

Ctra Náquera - Massamagrell, CV 32, Km 8, 46136 Museros, Spain

Tel: +34 96 144 0567
www.johansens.com/masiadelacy

SPAIN / VALENCIA (TÁRBENA)

Casa Lehmi

El Buscarró 1-3, E-03518 Tárbena, Alicante, Spain

Tel: +34 96 588 4018
www.johansens.com/casalehmi

SPAIN / VALENCIA (VALENCIA)

Hospes Palau de la Mar

Navarro Reverter 14, 46004 Valencia, Spain

Tel: +34 96 316 2884
www.johansens.com/palaudelamar

SPAIN / VALENCIA (VALENCIA)

Hotel Neptuno

Paseo de Neptuno, 2, 46011 Valencia, Spain

Tel: +34 963 567 777
www.johansens.com/neptuno

SPAIN / VALENCIA (VALENCIA)

Hotel Sidi Saler & Spa

C/ Gola del Puchol, s/n - Playa El Saler, 46012 Valencia, Spain

Tel: +34 961 61 04 11
www.johansens.com/saler

SPAIN / VALENCIA (VILAMARXANT)

Mas de Canicattí

Ctra. de Pedralba, Km 2.9, 46191 Vilamarxant, Valencia, Spain

Tel: +34 96 165 05 34
www.johansens.com/canicatti

SWITZERLAND (WEGGIS)

Park Hotel Weggis

Hertensteinstrasse 34, 6353 Weggis, Switzerland

Tel: +41 41 392 05 05
www.johansens.com/weggis

SWITZERLAND (ZURICH)

Alden Hotel Splügenschloss

Splügenstrasse 2, Genferstrasse, 8002 Zürich, Switzerland

Tel: +41 44 289 99 99
www.johansens.com/aldenhotel

TURKEY (ANTALYA)

The Marmara Antalya

Eski Lara Yolu No 136, Sirinyali, Antalya, Turkey

Tel: +90 242 249 36 00
www.johansens.com/marmaraantalya

TURKEY (ANTALYA)

Tuvana Residence

Tuzcular Mahallesi, Karanlik Sokak 7, 07100 Kaleiçi - Antalya, Turkey

Tel: +90 242 247 60 15
www.johansens.com/tuvanaresidence

TURKEY (ANTALYA - KEMER)

Sungate Port Royal Deluxe Resort Hotel

Ciftecesmeler Mevkii 1, 1 Beldibi - Kemer, Antalya, Turkey

Tel: +90 242 824 9750
www.johansens.com/sungateport

TURKEY (ANTALYA - KEMER)

Turkiz Hotel Thalasso Centre & Marina

Yali Caddesi No 3, 07980 Antalya - Kemer, Turkey

Tel: +90 242 8144100
www.johansens.com/turkizhotel

Hotels - Europe & The Mediterranean

Properties listed below can be found in our Recommended Hotels & Spas - Europe & The Mediterranean 2008 Guide.
More information on our portfolio of guides can be found on page 447.

TURKEY (BODRUM)

Divan Bodrum Palmira

Kelesharim Caddesi 6, Göltürkbükü, Mugla, 48483
Bodrum, Turkey

Tel: +90 252 377 5601

www.johansens.com/divanpalmira

TURKEY (ISTANBUL)

The Marmara Istanbul

Taksim Meydani, Taksim, 34437 Istanbul, Turkey

Tel: +90 212 251 4696

www.johansens.com/maramaraistanbul

TURKEY (BODRUM)

The Marmara Bodrum

Suluhasan Caddesi, Yokusbasi, Mahallesi No 18,
PO Box 199, 48400 Bodrum, Turkey

Tel: +90 252 313 8130

www.johansens.com/marmarabodrum

TURKEY (ISTANBUL)

The Marmara Pera

Mesrutiyet Caddesi, Tepebasi, 34430 Istanbul,
Turkey

Tel: +90 212 251 4646

www.johansens.com/marmarapera

TURKEY (FETHIYE - ÖLÜDENIZ)

Oyster Residence

Belcekız Mevkii, 1.Sokak Ölüdeniz, Fethiye, Turkey

Tel: +90 252 617 0765

www.johansens.com/oyster

TURKEY (ISTANBUL)

Sumahan On The Water

Kuleli Caddesi No 51, Çengelköy, 34684 Istanbul,
Turkey

Tel: +90 216 422 8000

www.johansens.com/sumahan

TURKEY (GÖREME - CAPPADOCIA)

Cappadocia Cave Suites

Gafferli Mahallesi, unlü Sokak, 50180 Göreme -
Nevsehir, Turkey

Tel: +90 384 271 2800

www.johansens.com/cappadociacaves

TURKEY (KALKAN)

Villa Mahal

PO Box 4 Kalkan, 07960 Antalya, Turkey

Tel: +90 242 844 32 68

www.johansens.com/villamahal

TURKEY (ISTANBUL)

A'jia Hotel

Ahmet Rasim Pasa Yalisi, Çubuklu Caddesi, No 27,
Kanlica, Istanbul, Turkey

Tel: +90 216 413 9300

www.johansens.com/ajiahotel

TURKEY (SAPANCA - ADAPAZARI)

Richmond Nua Wellness - Spa

Sahilyolu, 54600 Sapanca, Adapazari, Turkey

Tel: +90 264 582 2100

www.johansens.com/richmondnua

For a great source of inspiration...
johansens.com

With over 1,300 Recommendations across The Americas, the UK and Europe, our website is a great reference point to source a property that fits the experience you're after, be it a luxury hotel, a coastal hideaway, a traditional inn, country house or resort. Each one is annually inspected and you can feel confident that we have taken care in helping you to select a place to stay.

You can search for a place by location, see what special breaks are on offer and send an enquiry. The on-line Bookshop offers great gift ideas – Guides and gift certificates to use in any of our worldwide destinations. You can also register on-line to receive our monthly Newsletter.

The Perfect Gift...

Condé Nast Johansens Gift Certificates

Condé Nast Johansens Gift Certificates make a unique and much valued gift for birthdays, weddings, anniversaries, special occasions or as a corporate incentive.

Certificates are available in denominations of $150, $75, £100, £50, €140, €70 and may be used as payment or part payment for your stay or a meal at any Condé Nast Johansens 2008 Recommended property.

Index by Property

Index by Property

Index by Property

Index by Property

Index by Location

The United States of America

Index by Location

Index by Location

Central America

South America

Index by Location

Atlantic

The Caribbean

Pacific